A Veteran Pea...
Subversion of...

Doug Traubel

THIRD EDITION

Published August 6, 2023

CHAPTER ONE _____ 36

Social Justice versus Criminal Justice

CHAPTER TWO _____ 65

The Reality of Marxism: A Sinister and Depraved Heart of Darkness

CHAPTER THREE _____ 110

The Purpose of (American) Government and the Role of Sheriff

CHAPTER FOUR _____ 128

The Cost of Free "Training"

CHAPTER FIVE _____ 135

The Thin Blue Line and Media Spin

CHAPTER SIX _____ 157

Policing the New Majority

CHAPTER SEVEN _____ 202

Securing the Border is Hateful?

CHAPTER EIGHT _____ 215

The Truth You Are Programmed to Dismiss as Crazy Talk

CHAPTER NINE _____ 241

Dispelling the Mythology behind Tailor-Made Laws, Race & Crime, and Multiculturalism

CHAPTER TEN _____ 331

Reclaiming Liberty

CHAPTER ELEVEN _____ 359

A View from the Past to See the Future

CONCLUSION _____ 388

Copyright Disclaimer

While researching and gathering information for this book over the course of 20 years, great pains were taken to recognize and credit other respected authors and columnists and to properly attribute original sources. Due to being an independent citizen-author with no sponsorship or financial backing, I am without the luxury of staff to assist me with editing and copyright verification. Therefore, I have made a good faith effort to perform those functions to the best of my ability. Please note that my "Required Reading for Patriots" and "Recommended Reading" lists at the back of the book also served as a bibliography.

This book may contain copyrighted material which was not placed in quotation marks, attributed to the original source or that the copyright owner did not specifically authorize. If this is the case, it is an unintentional error and oversight on my part. Such use is legally permitted however, under the "Fair Use" provisions of the Copyright Act of 1976, 17 U.S.C., Section 107, which states "the fair use of a copyrighted work...for purposes such as criticism, comment, news reporting, teaching, scholarship, or research, is not an infringement of copyright." This book is commentary and critique, as well as a teaching and educational product.

DEDICATION
TO MY SONS:

The torch of liberty will pass from me to you and from you to your children. Root your sons and daughters in our heritage. Know who you are. Do not compromise your values for fashionable thought. Do not stand idle when the shadow of darkness encroaches. Be vigilant guardians of the truth. Be men of your word.

Love,

Dad

    Also, to the victims of totalitarianism and to the human spirit's passion for freedom...

RED BADGE
ACKNOWLEDGMENT

Throughout this project I have had the steadfast support of my dear friend and colleague, John Hartmann. John spent time inside the Soviet Empire, witnessed some of the horrors presented in this book and feels fortunate to have made it out alive. John personally experienced the dreadful prison camp atmosphere and unconscionable evil of the communist system. John laments that words alone cannot describe the sinister reality that is the Marxist "Heart of Darkness" — that it must be endured to truly grasp the depths of its depravity and cruelty.

Several of the topics in this book are honed or inspired by my discussions with John surrounding our love of country, "the enemy inside the gates," and how to combat the great deception. You are a kindred spirit, an intellectual marvel and a patriot of the first order John. Thank you.

"The true value of a man is not determined by his possession, supposed or real, of Truth, but rather by his sincere exertion to get to the Truth. It is not possession of the Truth, but rather the pursuit of Truth by which he extends his powers and in which his ever-growing perfectibility is to be found. Possession makes one passive, indolent, and proud. If God were to hold all Truth concealed in his right hand, and in his left only the steady and diligent drive for Truth, albeit with the proviso that I would always and forever err in the process, and to offer me the choice, I would with all humility take the left hand and say: Father, I will take this — the pure Truth is for You alone."

Gotthold Ephraim Lessing

Eine Duplik (1778)

RED BADGE
A Veteran Peace Officer's Commentary on the Marxist Subversion of American Law Enforcement & Culture

ABOUT THE AUTHOR

Doug Traubel is a thirty-two-year veteran peace officer. In 1984 Doug's career began in Chula Vista, California, seven miles from the U.S. – Mexico border. His assignments included patrol officer, field training officer, SWAT team, and Street Team (a proactive patrol unit that targeted gangs and series related crimes i.e. robbery and other special enforcement projects).

Doug graduated from The San Diego County Sheriff's Academy in 1986. On the first day of instruction he attended a lecture from Sheriff John Duffy on the history, role and unique authority held by the Constitutional Office of Sheriff. It was then that he developed a reverence for the Office and an understanding of the necessary and substantive differences between Sheriffs, Chiefs of Police and Federal "law enforcement."

Doug graduated from San Diego State University with a BA in political science (emphasis on constitutional law) and a minor in the Spanish language.

In 1993, Doug was awarded the medal of valor for his response to three hostile, armed men he and his partner confronted while on plain-clothes foot patrol in the alley of a high-crime apartment complex.

Disgusted with the infiltration of Marxist philosophy in the California criminal justice system and its near paralyzing effect on police work, Doug moved to Idaho in 1994. The seed planted by Sheriff John Duffy determined his course: Doug became a Deputy Sheriff. His assignments included patrol, juvenile crimes detective (High School Resource Officer), and gang detective. In 1998, he was awarded the Field Services Director's Award for his work with troubled youth. In 2003 Doug transferred to the Ada County Prosecuting Attorney's Office as an investigator. Doug continues to serve as a trainer and private investigator.

Doug has been an instructor on the topic of gangs at the Idaho State Police Academy and an adjunct faculty member at Boise State University where he taught an upper-division class titled, "Gangs, Drugs and Violence."

In June of 2021 Doug received the most votes from the Ada County, (Idaho) Republican Central Committee of the three finalists selected to replace Sheriff Bartlett who abruptly left office under a cloud. When the three names were submitted to the Ada County Board of County Commissioners it was their prerogative to vote/appoint out of order. They passed over the #1 ranked Doug for the #3 ranked establishment candidate, Matt Clifford.

All three finalists were given separate and public job interviews before the three commissioners. Doug's interview was less an interview and more of a Grand Inquisition over the content of this book and his many writings from various publications. Doug was the only candidate to receive a standing ovation from the public at the conclusion.

The tie-breaking vote rested with Commissioner Rod Beck. Leading up to the public interview Beck had the establishment in one ear, fearful of Doug for his oath-centered passion and in the other ear, Constitutional-minded patriots including precinct committee members, state senators and state representatives.

The Idaho Statesman newspaper, Boise State University Public Radio, and TV News Channel 7 branded Doug an antisemite and racist due to content of this book taken out of context during his commissioner interview.

To the shock and surprise of his critics Doug doubled down. The following year, on May 17, 2022 he challenged the appointed sheriff in the primary.

Leading up to the election the Chairman of the Ada County Republican Central Committee, Victor Miller, would not facilitate a debate between the two candidates when asked to do so by Doug. He also did not publish a one-on-one video interview he did with Doug at a candidate forum claiming the audio was bad. This was quite odd considering the professional cameraman had a backup digital recorder running simultaneously.

Doug was unable to overcome the negative press and establishment high jinks. His energetic and educational meet & greets, speeches and alternative media interviews, combined with door knocking, radio spots and Web presence ended in a loss with 34.4% of the vote. Clifford won with low energy, no message and comparatively little campaigning. He was carried and insulated by the Marxist media and GOP establishment. Doug will run again in 2024 for the Constitution Party.

*** (Visit **Doug for Ada County** on **Facebook** to watch some of his substantive speeches) ***

The publishing of this book pokes the First Amendment. Is it alive and well? Are we free to speak the truth? Are we free to address taboo topics? Are we free to dissent from the state's narrative?

The level and origin of persecution that this book invokes against the author will prove whether or not the "freedom", "tolerance" and "civil rights" touted by the U.S.A. to its people and the world are lies.

Demonstrating courage with the bold printing of this provocative book, Doug Traubel hopes to inspire courage in YOU to wield the sword of truth and the shield of the First Amendment in defense of America and liberty.

Disclaimer:

The opinions of the author do not reflect or represent those of his employer(s) present or past. This book represents the author's research, personal opinions and thoughts as a private individual and American citizen. And so...

"Agree with me if I seem to you to speak the truth; or, if not, withstand me might and main that I may not deceive you as well as myself in my desire, and like the bee leave my sting in you before I die. And now let us proceed."   Socrates

CAUTION HAZARDOUS MATERIAL

WARNING!

You are about to read a politically incorrect book; one that will make you feel uncomfortable — as the truth it reveals shatters your paradigm. Sacred cows and taboo topics like race and crime are on the table, not immune here from question or thoughtful scrutiny.

RED BADGE
INTRODUCTION

"A nation can survive its fools, and even the ambitious. But it cannot survive treason from within. An enemy at the gates is less formidable, for he is known and carries his banner openly. But the traitor moves amongst those within the gate freely, his sly whispers rustling through all the alleys, heard in the very halls of government itself. For the traitor appears not a traitor; he speaks in accents familiar to his victims, and he wears their face and their arguments, he appeals to the baseness that lies deep in the hearts of all men. He rots the soul of a nation, he works secretly and unknown in the night to undermine the pillars of the city, he infects the body politic so that it can no longer resist. A murderer is less to be feared. The traitor is the plague." – Marcus Tullius Cicero

"Treason doth never prosper, what's the reason? For if it prosper, none dare call it treason."

Sir John Harrington, 1561-1612

"The individual is handicapped by coming face to face with a conspiracy so monstrous he cannot believe it exists. The American mind simply has not come to a realization of the evil which has been introduced into our midst."

J. Edgar Hoover, Elks magazine, 1956

DOJ-BOI Director, 1924-1935

FBI Director: 1935-1972

Upon walking out the doors at the completion of the U.S. Constitutional Convention Elizabeth Willing Powell asked Benjamin Franklin, "What have we got a republic or a monarchy?" He replied, "A republic, if you can keep it."

The life of our Republic depends on an informed, educated and moral people. It is "We the People" that are to keep our government accountable to the duties and limits placed on it by the U.S. Constitution and its Amendments. But the average American today is ignorant about our government and history; Why? In large part, it is due to the intentional dumbing-down of the population through government controlled public education.

"Give us the child for eight years and it will be a communist forever." Vladimir Lenin
(Founder of the Soviet Communist Party)

Oil Magnate and trans-national corporate thug John D. Rockefeller was instrumental in setting up the "General Education Board," forerunner to the U.S. Department of Education. Outwardly presented to the public as an effort to improve education for America's children, its actual long-range strategic goals were three-fold: Orwellian-style thought control, social engineering and the gradual dumbing-down of the nation's youth.

Consider this quote from the General Education Board's Occasional Letter No. 1, issued in 1904: **"In our dreams we have limitless resources and the people yield themselves with perfect docility to our molding hands... We have not to raise up from them authors, poets or men of letters...The task we set before ourselves is...to train these people as we find them to a perfectly ideal life just where they are."**

Translation: arrest their mental development; form, regiment and control their thoughts, ideas, opinions and expressions; and keep them perpetually placid, as mindless, submissive, obedient servants. Or, as Alexis de Tocqueville forewarned, "...a tyranny of mediocrity, a standardization of mind and spirit and condition."

RED BADGE

The corrupting influence of the tax-exempt Rockefeller, Ford and Carnegie Foundations on American education and their overall subversion of American society was so alarming that in 1953 a Congressional Committee headed by Representative Brazilla Carroll Reece of Tennessee attempted to hold a full investigation. Powerful interests in the Nation's Capital ultimately thwarted its efforts (the actual hearings before Congress abruptly ended after only two weeks!).

Rene Wormser was the Reece Committee's general counsel. After the disbandment of the committee, Wormser wrote an expose´ titled, ***Foundations: Their Power and Influence.***

Wormser stated that based on the facts the Reece Committee discovered, **"…leads one to the conclusion that there was, indeed, something in the nature of an actual conspiracy among certain leading educators in the United States to bring about Socialism through the use of our school systems..."**

In a revealing episode that took place in Autumn of 1953 at the headquarters of the Ford Foundation (after the disbandment of the congressional investigation), Rowan Gaither, who at the time was President of the Ford Foundation, stated to the Reece Committee's Director of Research Norman Dodd:

"Mr. Dodd, all of us here at the policy-making level have had experience, either in OSS[1] or the European Economic Administration, with directives from the White House. We operate under those directives here. Would you like to know what those directives are?"

When Dodd replied in the affirmative, Gaither continued, "The substance of them is that we shall use our grant-making

---

[1] OSS (Office of Strategic Services) was the WWII era predecessor of the CIA just as the NVKD was the WWII predecessor to the KGB.

power to so alter life in the United States that we can be comfortably merged with the Soviet Union."

When Dodd asked Gaither if he would testify to that in front of the Congressional Committee for the record Gaither replied, "This we would not think of doing." (Sources: Alan Stang, *Foundations Pay the Way*, American Opinion, January 1977 and *The Shadows of Power* by James Perloff, October 1988).

When one examines the fundamental "altering of American life" and the radical change in the citizen-government relationship financed, crafted and in many ways engineered by tax-exempt foundations over the past 60 years (from something uniquely "American" to something more resembling Eastern European socialism) and then places it in the context of the well-financed Trotskyite "One World Socialist Revolution", the "comfortable merger" begins to crystallize.

Recall that the first communist country in history was an Eastern European dictatorship named the "Union of Soviet SOCIALIST Republics" (U.S.S.R.), more commonly known as the Soviet Union. After seizing power in a bloodthirsty coup, the socialist rulers of the former Russia then went on to mass murder over 60 million of their own citizens and ran the largest network of slave labor camps in history, known as the Gulag, where political prisoners were tortured, starved and worked literally to death. Now, does this sound like the "worker's paradise" that socialists throughout the world proclaimed it was or does it sound more like hell on earth? Is this a system with which you would want to be "comfortably merged" with?

After inflicting its socialist ideology on four generations of Americans, — "Common Core" — is the continuation of this diabolical effort to *transform* (destroy) America through public "education." Dr. Terrence Moore of Hillsdale College made a compelling argument to that point. He said that through

Common Core we are creating, "cultural orphans." In a speech that can be found on You Tube called ***Story Killers***, Moore describes with example after example how Common Core's so-called "rigorous standards aimed at college and career readiness" is rhetoric and not reality.

The 45 states that signed on to Common Core will turn out uneducated worker drones. These drones will have a misunderstanding and negative view of our roots. Students are being raised without knowledge of the depth and context of our rich history. This severs the generational bonds of affection for America. Without affection for America one does not react *normally* — with jealousy and alarm — when our foundations are attacked. One is merely a spectator on the widget line.

"The greatest evil...is conceived and ordered...in clean, carpeted, warmed and well-lighted offices, by quiet men with white collars and cut fingernails and smooth-shaven cheeks who do not need to raise their voice."
C.S. Lewis, The Screwtape Letters, (Quoted by President Ronald Reagan before the National Association of Evangelicals, 1983)

In 2008 and again in 2012 America had a choice between two liberal candidates for president and chose Obama, the most far Left. Notwithstanding voter fraud putting him over the top, these elections were the result of generations of "purification" of thought through public education and the media.

"The danger to America is not Barack Obama but a citizenry capable of entrusting a man like him with the Presidency. It will be far easier to limit and undo the follies of an Obama presidency than to restore the necessary common sense and good judgment to a depraved electorate willing to have such a man for their president. The problem is much deeper and far more serious than Mr. Obama, who is a mere symptom of what ails

America. Blaming the prince of the fools should not blind anyone to the vast confederacy of fools that made him their prince. The Republic can survive a Barack Obama, who is, after all, merely a fool. It is less likely to survive a multitude of fools such as those who made him their president."

– Anonymous citizen of the Czech Republic

The above quote was sent to me in June of 2009. Within six months of Obama's first term a foreigner saw with great clarity what most here could not. Imagine what the Czech author believes now after the 2012 election. Granted, Obama's second win was more suspect than his first. In the first election Obama did not win in a single state that has voter ID laws. One-third (16/50) of the states' attorneys general conducted voter fraud investigations and sent them to the U.S. Attorney General, Eric Holder, who did nothing. Prior to Obama, no president had ever won a second term with unemployment over 8%, let alone 15%. Voter fraud continued in 2020, resulting in Biden as "president."

"It is enough that the people know there was an election. The people who cast the votes decide nothing. The people who count the votes decide everything." Josef Stalin

Legitimate or not, Obama sat in the Oval Office insulated by the media and supported by large segments of a rapidly changing population made hostile toward our traditions and culture.

Government-controlled "public schools", mainstream media, Hollywood and the courts have indoctrinated and intimidated the majority into processing events through the filter of a false reality developed and financed by powerful and largely "invisible" social engineers. This substitute for truth has impaired our ability to reason and think critically thereby eliminating any effective resistance to the advancement of the Marxist agenda.

Over the last 50 + years — just two generations — Americans have been subjected to the most sophisticated and highly polished propaganda campaign in history; one that would be the envy of North Korea, Red China, or the Soviet Union.

Today, voters truly believe they have two opposing ideologies from which to choose at the polls in national elections. What they really have in the two establishment political parties are nothing more than what Judge Andrew Napolitano has correctly described as "two wings of the same bird of prey", that 'bird' being a predatory government lurching over the American people, devouring our rights and our property piece by piece.

It is always the so-called "Right" that compromises. The Left never gives up ground. This is how over two generations we moved incrementally toward socialism. The GOP is merely the controlled (false) opposition.

Former presidential candidate and Reagan Administration official Alan Keyes has described the sham that is our national "elections" as the equivalent of playing in a rigged casino — "The House" always wins — to your great detriment!

(Note: For elaboration on the mechanisms of propaganda and the false choice of candidates and political parties, see the Chapter Eleven of this book).

At no other time in U.S. history could the nebulous slogan "change" have moved the *majority* (ostensibly) to vote for a candidate. Burdened with guilt spun by Marxists over what they describe as America's original sin (slavery) and its vestiges, white voters treated their ballots like antidepressants. What should have been a footnote in history — Obama's race —

became the obsession of his supporters, the focus of the media and a shield from criticism and accountability.

By voting for symbolism (race) over substance, voters did something more profound than electing America's first "black" (mulatto) president: they unwittingly elected a vehemently anti-American president.

Packaged by a complicit media as the savior, buyer's remorse set in as Obama defined "change" for the country one disastrous decision at a time — intentionally destroying the economy, our stature in the world, our institutions, and our culture.

Over the last 20 years, there has been an unrelenting effort by Marxists to soften the minds of American voters to embrace "change." Change from what? **Change from a fictitious** crisis of oppression, hate and intolerance perpetrated by white males and Christians.

An anti-American, psychological rip current is pulling our culture and institutions to the Left. Born of disinformation, revisionist history, ignorance, intimidation and moral relativism — as many as half of Americans citizens are increasingly becoming either indifferent about defending tradition or hostile toward it.

Marxists masquerade as champions of factions they deem "victims." They pit the victims against the vilified majority and rally them to attack our institutions and traditions as instruments of oppression. Arguing against the narrative paints one a hater. Consequently, the majority's timidity and silence encourage and embolden its enemies rendering the anchor points of America's culture and institutions defenseless.

America's two dominant political parties have become indistinguishable; they offer no hope for a restoration of America's traditions, unique culture and greatness. Each is trying to promote itself as the party of inclusion: they want to be all things to all people — except of course to the vilified, traditional White Christian majority.

Neither the Republicans nor the Democrats speak as though they want to really lead the country and promote the betterment of our peoples' standard of living — they seek only to manage and oversee its squabbling factions while maintaining their privileged, regal lifestyle. They have no desire to be our saviors or the saviors of our country — they want to remain our "Overlords."

These parties are not motivated by the paramount objective of preserving the constitutional and cultural integrity of our nation. Maintaining and solidifying power is their only objective.

The Reform Party, Libertarian Party, Constitution Party, Populist Party, and others were excluded from the 2000, 2004, 2008, 2012, 2016 and 2020 presidential debates. The mainstream media give little coverage to these increasingly popular parties, making obvious its complicit role in insulating and protecting the "two-party oligarchy."

(For those who insist a two-party "system" is adequate and acceptable, remember that a two-party system is only one more than dictatorship. And think about how much easier it is for two parties to collude and collaborate against the interests of the American people than it would be for four, five or more parties to do so in a truly "open field" of candidates and choices).

Most Republican congressmen have been intimidated or indoctrinated by the same thought control as the public. In addition, professional lobbyists and pressure groups buy, intimidate or blackmail our representatives.

This is why we see compromise after compromise by so-called conservatives. This is why we see only political theater and no accountability for scandal after scandal.

In reality, until the unforeseen arrival of President Trump we were living under a one-party system. At the national level, the Republican Party has merely been the "controlled opposition" — a sham opposition — a political charade. Its inaction is surrender. Under Obama both houses of Congress had Republican majorities (247 in the House and 54 in the Senate). There has not been this many Republicans in Congress since the Civil War and yet with that majority they did not hold Obama accountable or even put him in check. An example of this is the House and Senate on 12/18/15 passing a $1.1 Trillion omnibus spending bill. The 1,582-page bill funded Obama's Syrian-Muslim refugee plan, Climate Control agenda, Obama Care and Planned Parenthood. The GOP's disdain for Donald Trump was driven by fear that this outsider would expose the truth, strip power from the establishment and work to restore the Republic, returning power to The People.

Hillary Clinton was to be Obama's third term. Prior to the Trump phenomena America was in the final two years of complete transformation into an authoritarian, Soviet-style police state. With the increasing *takeovers* of local police departments by the federal government (through Department of Justice "monitors" and "consent decrees"), the passage of Obamacare, and the National Defense Authorization Act of 2012 (NDAA) — which guts your constitutional rights and essentially nullifies the U.S. Bill of Rights — there was no end in sight to the Obama Administration's usurpation and unconstitutional power grabs. Whether President Trump will be merely a speed bump to the Left or a pivot point to the restoration of the Republic is yet to be seen. Can one man undo over 85 years of Marxist social engineering, public indoctrination, judicial activism, socialism, and dilution of our culture through colonization, welfare dependence and a web of lurching unconstitutional bureaucracy? He interrupted the Left's momentum, but it is not defeated. The Deep State and most of the media conspire to discredit and stop him.

RED BADGE

International communists are backing what the American media casually call "protesters." These are highly organized, planned events. Thousands of people, many from out of the area, do not appear spontaneously and even at the same locations in different cities. Not only are these violent people not protesters, but neither are they rioters. They are worse. They are agents of communist revolution funded by foreign powers. President Trump's oath is to defend the USA from *all* enemies — foreign and domestic. Follow the money. Antifa and Black Lives Matter are supported by our enemies. President Trump must use all of his presidential power and resources to defend the USA from these domestic communist revolutionaries. This is of course made extremely difficult when "news" networks confuse the people by making the revolutionary look righteous. Roger Stone was correct when he said of CNN, it "...is not a news organization. It is a radical propaganda arm of the Soros Corporation."

Zbigniew Brzezinski, former National Security Advisor to President Jimmy Carter, Executive Director of the Trilateral Commission, member of the Board of Directors of the Council on Foreign Relations, Columbia University professor, Director of the Research Institute on International Change, avowed Marxist and one of the primary behind-the-scenes puppet masters of Barack Hussein Obama, wrote the following in his revealing, but little –known 1976 book, *Between Two Ages*:

"The nation-state is gradually yielding its sovereignty... Further progress will require greater American sacrifices. More intensive efforts to shape a new world monetary structure will have to be undertaken, with some consequent risk to the present relatively favorable American position."

(Think of our government's unwillingness to defend our borders, the move toward a borderless "North American Union", our military forces increasingly fighting under United Nations command and control, the destruction of the American dollar, the massive reduction in our standard of living coupled with the simultaneous increased costs, and the world-wide monetary chaos and calls for a "one world currency.")

Brzezinski continues:

"The (coming) era involves the gradual appearance of a more controlled society. Such a society would be dominated by an elite, unrestrained by traditional values. Soon it will be possible to assert almost continuous surveillance over every citizen and maintain up-to-date complete files containing even the most personal information about the citizen. These files will be subject to instantaneous retrieval by the authorities."

Think of our corrupt, out-of-control, no accountability federal government and the recent scandals and revelations regarding the truly Orwellian surveillance, spying and eavesdropping capabilities of the U.S. National Security Agency. Parts of our government spied on presidential candidate Donald Trump. Once elected a fabricated dossier – paid for by the Clinton Foundation and the DNC – was sworn to be true before a FISA court judge (multiple times) to authorize an investigation of our duly elected President. It does not matter if you like or dislike Donald Trump. Due Process and Rule of Law are nonpartisan pillars of the Republic and must be defended. Acts of treason and sedition must be brought to account – through military courts if necessary.

Brzezinski, the proud Marxist and high-level government advisor: **"Marxism represents a further vital and creative stage in the maturing of man's universal vision ... Marxism is simultaneously a victory of the external, active man over the inner, passive man and a victory of reason over belief ... Marxism, disseminated on the popular level in the form of communism, represents a major advance in man's ability to conceptualize his relationship to the world."**

And this man was influencing President Obama and shaping government policies that dramatically affect your future, your country, your individual freedoms, and your American way of life!

The Marxist Strategy

Socialism and communism come from the same seed — Marxism. The differences are only a matter of the degree of authoritarian or totalitarian centralized governmental control over the means of production, the population and the distribution of goods and services.

By using what the "Frankfurt School"[2] Marxists dubbed "critical theory", 21st Century Neo-Marxists get a foothold in societies first by finding fault, then identifying injured parties, and finally by organizing them in opposition to the institutions and establishment they seek to overthrow. The simplicity of this is that one can find fault in literally anything. And so it is with Marxists when they look at America.

The United States of America is the greatest country in world history. Yet Marxists always find fault and say, "There is much more work to do..." as if great flaws still exist and "change" is the aim of their struggle. Their protests are never based on righteousness or principle, only power and control. They do not truly care about those whose grievances they claim to champion. They appeal to their power base with emotion. The architects know it is a fraud, but the dupes, knaves and followers swallow the clichés and propaganda time and again, and regurgitate it ad nauseam. Marxist leaders posture to do the impossible. They promise to perfect society as envisioned in their populist, naive ideology.

---

[2] See page 216 of this book

The true goal is the seizure of power through subversion for the benefit of an elite ruling class. To accomplish this America must be discredited in the eyes of the majority. To that end, the Diversity Movement promotes the myth that even with a "black" president in the White House put there by white votes — the U.S. is a racist, bigoted country with no moral authority that oppresses victim classes made of non-white minorities, women and homosexual/transgender people. This hate and intolerance is said to come from generations of political and cultural dominance by white male conservatives and Christians.

None of these supposed victim groups of "white oppression" truly improve their circumstance under democrat-Marxist policies, but rather they become dependent on government programs translating to votes for democrat politicians. Ben Shapiro hit the mark when he said, for a Marxist "...everyone is either a tool or an obstacle." Marxists care only about the revolution, not the person and not the issue. In contrast, under Trump's free market and US sovereignty policies we have the lowest unemployment ever for blacks and Hispanics and the lowest unemployment in 18 years for women. The booming economy is not the result of Obama's Marxist policies. That is a baseless claim of the Left desperate to be seen as credible. Kanye West has seen through the deception of the Left and boldly educates other black Americans to leave the government plantation.

Marxists disparage traditionalists. In order to discredit their adversaries, they dismiss with laughter being pinned with the labels, "Marxist" and "Socialist" as though it is crazy talk coming from backward thinking people. Obama said of his critics, "They get bitter, they cling to guns or religion or antipathy to people who aren't like them or anti-immigrant sentiment or anti-trade sentiment as a way to explain their frustration." Regardless of the refusal of Marxist ideologues like

Obama to wear their brand openly, their transparent agenda and template convicts them just the same.

Marxism is the absolute consolidation of power and the expansion of regulation and control over individuals, capital, private property and businesses. Public dependence on government services reduces resistance to its unconstitutional overreach. What it cannot seduce it **forces** to conform. Marxism's enormous infrastructure is led by self-serving, self-righteous, secular and self-anointed elite.

Marxism is a philosophy that uses the worst of human nature to enslave the best of human nature. It is a lie and a threat to man's God-given, unalienable rights.

Winston Churchill put it best: *"Socialism is a philosophy of failure, the creed of ignorance, and gospel of envy; its inherent virtue is the equal sharing of misery."*

In order to see the modern face of Marxism in the United States, the reader must look through two lenses: ***The Diversity Movement and Political Correctness.***

The Diversity Movement is Marxism repackaged with a benevolent mask. It is a highly coordinated and well-financed effort among self-validating and overlapping forces; each promoting varying radical forms of "social justice" as the remedy for the ***BIG LIE*** about the character and history of the United States.

The premise of the BIG LIE is that our history (and most of world history) is nothing more than a series of injustices by whites resulting in oppression and the inequitable distribution of wealth, power, access, privilege and capital.

The Diversity Movement controls most of America's Academia Class. Its ranks comprise the overwhelming majority of instructors in public schools and universities. The Academia

Class in concert with most of the media, Hollywood and activist judges promote the Big Lie.

There is just enough truth woven in their lie (much of it out of context) to sound credible to a publicly "educated" population; one with shallow knowledge, short memories, shorter attention spans and weak in critical thinking. The Left amplify and validate each other. For over four generations they have worked successfully to shape public opinion.

Classic Marxism pits the labor class against those who control the means of production (proletariat vs. the bourgeoisie). Today's Marxism pits balkanized camps, deemed disenfranchised "victims," against what they are taught is their common oppressor — the Old Guard culture (made up mostly of Christians and conservative whites).

The Diversity Movement's aim is the forced realignment of society. Right out of Orwell's *1984*, the Diversity Movement uses the thought-limiting language of "Newspeak" to champion unobjectionable-sounding causes like *diversity, inclusion, tolerance, equality and justice.* How can anyone be opposed to these ideals?

Marxist social engineers are wordsmiths. These terms have been inverted. They have radical, culturally suicidal definitions for America. They contradict our history, ethos, and Judeo-Christian cultural roots.

We need to relearn how to think critically in order to see the deception. Walk with me through this mental exercise: Ask yourself, "How do contradictions hold up in the natural world?" A molecule of H_2O can be liquid, solid or gas. Each has its own name because each has distinct qualities. If something called by a name does not reflect the unique characteristics expected of it there is a deception, a contradiction, a lie.

Calling steam "water" does not transfer the defining properties of water and allow me to pour steam into a bucket.

Water is water. Steam is steam. Ice is ice. Marriage is marriage. Words mean things.

The danger in bending, contorting and misusing words and obfuscating their meaning was recognized over 2,500 years ago when the famous Chinese philosopher and teacher Confucius admonished his fellow Chinamen by telling them to "call a spade a spade" (Confucius meant that literally).

Just as two objects in the material world cannot occupy the same space at the same time, we cannot permit contradictions to occupy the same space in our mind. Doing otherwise creates confusion; it arrests the reasoning ability needed to recognize deception and defend truth.

The Diversity Movement's premise is a deception. Its architects seek to vilify, discredit, debase and dispossess the culture that built this great nation. They preach tolerance, but are intolerant of our nation's heritage and the race and religion of those who built it (White Christians). Their aim is to sever any remaining ties that this generation has with our roots. Their objective is a forced redistribution of power and wealth. To accomplish this, they must subvert and transform our culture and institutions. This is done by intimidating and shunning tradition while ushering in a rapidly forming *new majority* made of a permanent, unassimilated underclass to support them.

Political Correctness is the hammer of the Diversity Movement. It is found on campus — where grades suffer when you are treated as a heretic for challenging the state narrative; at work — when you are snared by a double standard hostile workplace complaint; on the street — when you are selectively charged with a hate crime; in civil court — when your business settles a bogus discrimination suit by hateful anti-White, anti-Christian, shake-down artists; and in the media — convicting and shunning you as a "racist" or bigot in the court of public opinion for speaking outside of the "correct" parameters.

Most of all it is in you. Political Correctness is a self-policing force of intellectual paralysis brought about by the *conditioning* (purifying or washing) of our minds to dodge the consequences of dissent by either being silent or parroting the false narrative. This conditioning of passivity to the Big Lie is the product of the complicit media, Marxist "educators", liberal human resource administrators, corrupt court officials, so-called civil rights activists, and leftist Hollywood — all promoting and legitimizing the false narrative and casting the roles of victims and suspect.

Political Correctness disarms tradition. It creates an environment of diluted discourse, censorship and self-censorship. Through intimidation, it enforces conformity of thought and expression that subvert our heroes and founding ethos.

A clear example of how political correctness is advanced is a new word: **Micro-aggression**. This is a Marxist construct that means: **"Social exchanges in which a member of a dominant culture says or does something, often accidentally, and without intended malice, that belittles and alienates a member of a marginalized group."** There are seminars based on Columbia University Psychology Professor Derald Wing Sue's book, *Microaggressions in Everyday Life: Race, Gender and Sexual Orientation*. This is an effort to cultivate hypersensitivity of "victim" groups and intimidate the legitimate and traditional American society to silence.

The First Amendment was given to us by the anti-federalists precisely to protect (unpopular) political speech, but for many whom think outside the confines of the state narrative they are too intimidated to use it. They see reputations destroyed by the media for defending traditional values and violent attacks for simply wearing a MAGA ball cap. Tradition loses ground without a voice and a fight.

For more evidence of the indoctrination by political correctness in education read *48 Liberal Lies about American History (That you Probably Learned in School)* by Professor Larry Schweikart. You will see the marginalization of our Founding Fathers and missing facts that mislead students about the history and character of America.

Have you scrolled through a calendar lately? We no longer celebrate George Washington's birthday, the victorious military leader of the War of Independence and our Nation's first president. As a poor substitute we have "Presidents' Day" which fails to honor Washington's actual birthday and minimizes him from the national memory.

Martin Luther King Jr. has his own day. Rather than consolidate civil rights leaders and call it "Civil Rights Day" MLK gets his own day, but not the father of our country, George Washington. **Why?**

MLK's face and name are used as propaganda to market social justice. This is a man that said and did some admirable things no doubt, and whose FBI file remains sealed because what is in there likely proves rumors that would discredit his lionization and be unproductive to the Left. Specifically, there have long been rumors of MLK committing brutal "date rapes" of white women in his hotel rooms and cavorting with communists. Up until the release of JFK files[3] that corroborate MLK's rumored abnormal sexual behavior and communist ties, the closest we got to the texture of the content in the file is a recorded interview of Jackie Kennedy where she calls MLK "terrible," "a phony" and "tricky." This is someone who would have heard regular and candid conversations about the FBI's surveillance of MLK spoken between the president and his brother the U.S. Attorney General. It has been fifty years and the

---

[3] *Explosive Martin Luther King document amid JFK files* November 4, 2017, BBC. https://www.bbc.com/news/world-us-canada-41871956

MLK file remains closed. This is Soviet-style suppression of information.

Then there are Earth Day, Cinco de Mayo, Native American Day, United Nations Day, Ramadan and Kwanzaa. Each of these squares on the calendar is a launch pad for Marxists to bash America and build momentum year after year. Black people have an **entire month** to prop up their victim status (albeit the shortest month of the year — clearly a racist conspiracy). The end of the calendar closes with public schools inviting families to a "winter festival" concert. Saying, "Merry Christmas" is presumptuous and offensive (a "micro-aggression").

Conspicuously absent of mention in the U.S. Press, is a story run in the United Kingdom's *Daily Mail* on December 16, 2015 about Riverheads High School in Virginia where in a 9th grade "calligraphy lesson" students were required to write the opening of the *shahada*, the Muslim conversion prayer: "There is no god but Allah, and Muhammad is the messenger of Allah." Meanwhile, in Johnson County, Kentucky the Board of Education forced the production of Charlie Brown's Christmas to remove Biblical reference to the Gospel of Luke.

Marxists want to remove Christmas as a national holiday. It is part of its agenda to secularize the population. Already, they have created an environment where it takes some courage to utter the words, "Merry Christmas" and doing so instantly creates tension in any room. "Happy Holidays" is a safe alternative that we are sold as inclusive. In fact it is exclusive. It excludes the name of our national holiday.

Marxists divide. They are desperate to find and create opportunities to defend counter cultures and express selective outrage over tradition. They advance the Cultural Revolution by making issues out of non-issues like the names and mascots of long-standing sports teams and landmarks. They pounce on any opportunity to stoke emotion, fear and division.

In the wake of the sensationalized reporting of a lone, Confederate-flag-wearing nut's murderous attack on parishioners at the Emanuel African Methodist Episcopal Church in Charleston, South Carolina (June 18, 2015) — where nine people were killed, New Orleans Mayor Mitch Landrieu swayed the City Council to vote to remove Civil War monuments including that of General Robert E. Lee (erected in 1884) from prominent places. He described the move as a "courageous decision to turn a page on our divisive past and chart the course for a more inclusive future."

Not to be outdone, on July 7, 2015 the Memphis City Council voted unanimously to exhume the body of Confederate General Nathan Bedford Forrest and move it as if the soil is contaminated. This is political fanaticism.

The Confederate flag is coming down from government buildings throughout the south as if it is a symbol of hate not heritage. These self-righteous, irrational and fanatical acts by state and local governments are out of proportion to current events, void of historical perspective and fuel the Big Lie. Riding the wave of emotion and spin the PC police kick American tradition and heritage to the curb. There is no room at the table for America. Americans are in retreat from their own government.

I will have none of that! I refuse to suspend reality! I will not abandon our history, heroes and heritage! I did not take an oath to defend a lie! It is time to wield the sword of truth and go on the offense to fight for what is left of America! That is what Red Badge does and prepares you to do.

The U.S. is the greatest country in the history of humankind. No country — but America — has had as large and broad a spectrum of its citizens (regardless of race or sex) enjoy such a high average standard of living with almost limitless social mobility. It is the free market and limits placed on government that unleashed the competition of ideas and rewards that rivaled or surpassed the world in every field. Americans walked on the moon; our flag is there! We lead the way. We are the most philanthropic nation in the world. America is exceptional!

Sit back for a moment and think of the countless masses of downtrodden and oppressed from the Third World who have risked their lives by boarding small boats and homemade rafts, braved 100-foot crushing waves and shark-filled oceans on the chance that they'll make it to our shores and have a shot at the "American Dream!"

The American experience has proven that a free market economy and a constitutional republic is the most moral and productive framework for man. The free market most closely mirrors man in his natural state where he created, competed, bartered, overcame adversity, and improved his skill sets. The Rule of Law protected the individual from mob rule.

Our example of limited government and freedom became a beacon to the world. It caused a brain drain on other countries as the best and brightest immigrated, assimilated and created. Our history is proof that the human spirit thrives best with freedom, private property rights, individual responsibility, small government and self-reliance. Today, Marxism has Lady Liberty in a headlock and its hand in her purse.

Political Correctness has rendered us nearly defenseless to our dispossession. With the American mind intimidated — the Diversity Movement vilifies tradition and promotes cultural anarchy virtually unopposed. Our roots to liberty and moral absolutes have grown shallow in the shadow of intimidation and in the soil of ignorance.

America's Old Guard culture and heritage are being demonized, debased and rejected. Hating our roots, heritage, language and history is the new patriotism. A cultural vacuum is being formed.

Society persecutes anyone who refutes the purported ethos of the Diversity Movement (tolerance, acceptance, diversity). If you are a realist you are a racist.

Fear of persecution results in a passive majority. At the same time architects of the Marxist revolution raise their volume, promoting the Big Lie and quickening their cadence daily, marching unopposed toward the goal of a highly regulated society to bring order and fill the vacuum they create.

The promotion of (radical) diversity as the remedy for the false crisis of hate and bigotry has divided America and turned us against our heritage. Our identity is unraveling. No longer are there moral or cultural absolutes. Marxists have smashed our compass with the heel of their jackboot.

So-called tolerance is the state religion. It has become the opiate of the masses. Judgment and condemnation have been suspended; except for America's Puritan, Anglo-Saxon, Christian roots. Tradition falls outside of the state's protection. With that deliberate exception, Marxists make all cultures and lifestyles feel welcome and equal — for now. In the end, there will be a culling. The least productive segments of society together with the most threatening to the regime (its most ardent, organized supporters) will be eliminated.

Marxists need the police to embrace their agenda in order to complete and secure the transfer of power. **Police must be depended on for crushing counter-revolutionary and post-revolutionary rebellion**. Just as successive generations of children were programmed to accept, parrot and obey the Big Lie, so too have generations of peace officers. They feel noble in their ignorance.

RED BADGE

RED BADGE will spur discussion on the importance of an officer's oath, local police control, and a citizen's role in a criminal justice system under intense federal pressure to conform to its rapidly expanding Marxist agenda.

CHAPTER ONE

Social Justice vs. Criminal Justice

Societies have always sought ways to regulate and control human behavior in a fair and just manner. Two methods of enforcing the mores and morals of society have evolved that are contrasted here: social justice and criminal justice.

Social Justice

Social justice is based on emotions and feelings; it is highly subjective. Hearsay and rumor are accepted as evidence. Fear and superstition are essential elements, and generally there are few or no fixed standards. In exclusive societies, such as tribes and religious groups, social justice will suffice.

Most commonly one finds social justice in the form of shunning to enforce an ideology or superstition. A formal example of shunning is excommunication used to enforce religious beliefs. Shunning is widespread during societal collapse and in extreme forms results in mob violence and vigilante action.

Criminal Justice

In more advanced, complex and larger societies with diverse cultures, religions, and behaviors social justice is inadequate. More quantitative and inflexible laws evolve. Effective enforcement of laws depends on well-defined, fixed, objective standards with incarceration, execution, or compensatory financial penalties.

Ideally, under the rule of law the code is simple, readily understood, and unchanging. Unfortunately, self-serving politicians are never content to let well enough alone. So the corpus of laws grows beyond comprehension and changes with the winds of politics.

Power and Control

The objective of both social and criminal justice has always been order and control.

In the United States, the more primitive social justice is being used by Marxists as a strategy to influence and undermine our criminal justice system.

For the Marxist there is neither "justice" nor "injustice" in their lexicon, only emotions and feelings of what is "right" and what is "wrong" in the situational ethics of the moment used to amass power.

The objective of Marxism is to seize and redistribute power and wealth. To that end Marxists use social justice to discredit and challenge society's fixed standards and values. The strategy is the ageless, "divide and conquer." But for them division must cut many ways in order to form multiple camps of people with grievances to be pinned against the singular villain: tradition and its principal trustees.

The most visible examples of social justice corrupting criminal justice are the passing of domestic violence and hate crime laws. These tailor-made laws are unnecessary and biased in their application. They move beyond providing equal protection; they provide extra protection — for select segments of society deemed victims. These laws are promoted by a false narrative that stokes the fires of division. Cast in the role of oppressor: men, (white men in particular) and Christians.

The anti-American influences of Hollywood, universities and public schools have predisposed our minds to accept the premise underscoring the need for social justice. The premise is that the U.S. is the product of immorality and oppression. This premise is woven into news reports, textbooks and commentaries. Daily, we hear of imagined and exaggerated faults in America. Social justice promises to rectify these supposed faults and sins. Americans are being indoctrinated to embrace a reckoning for the damage caused by our malignant footprint at home and around the world.

Using social justice to advance Marxism nurtures the victim mindset of entitlement among select segments of the population deemed to be injured. Simultaneously, it fosters the yielding force of guilt in the segment deemed the offender. Guilt makes people passive and even complicit to being *dispossessed* — a primary goal of Marxist revolutionaries.

When social justice is implemented through national law or policy, its costs are diffused among all taxpayers and consumers thereby reducing resistance. Examples of this include Affirmative Action, Obamacare and over regulation on manufactures to combat the fraud[4] of man-made Global Warming.

But what of those who see through the fog? What of those with the audacity to dissent from the narrative advocating social justice? Dissenters must be intimidated, silenced and discredited. We are living in the era of the New Inquisition. Dissenters (heretics) run from the Grand Inquisitors, who sling such labels as "racist," or "bigot" to defame and persecute the opposition.

The Marxists' patent on the use of these labels is brilliant. When you control the language you control the debate and suppress truth. The terms **racist** and **racism** are used as a sword and a shield. Criticize President Obama: You are a racist. Advocate deportation of illegal aliens: You are a racist. Use the accurate and legal descriptor *"illegal alien"* instead of the Marxist's substitute, *"undocumented immigrant"*: You are a racist. Support voter ID laws: You are a racist. Support English as the official language: You are a racist. Oppose Affirmative Action: You are a racist. Support equal rights for men: You are a

---

[4] Tony Olson, *SPIN GAME*, Chapter Two, *Climate Change*, Red Stag Publishing, 2014.

misogynist, a *"wife beater"* and woman hater. Oppose homosexual marriage: You are a *"bigot."* And the list goes on. Seldom is there a cogent argument. Always there are high emotions, intimidation and defamation. The followers of the deception do not think; they feel and react as programmed. They are husks of human beings; intellectually dead, empty of original thoughts. They are as close to a real zombie as possible.

Believers in the Big Lie scratch their heads at black members of the much-maligned TEA Party. They wonder what these presumably downtrodden victims can possibly have in common with the majority-white, *"Tea Baggers."* Supporters of Marxist-inspired social justice do not comprehend the attraction to reason, rational thought, and traditional values that are so inviting to black conservatives.

Nonetheless, clarity and truth transcend the Marxists' obsession with racial division. The architects of the Big Lie cannot permit black conservatives to gain traction. They make every effort to exclude them from public dialog because their message of truth could cause an uprising on what author Star Parker calls Uncle Sam's Plantation. This is why Marxist ideologues dodge debating them.

It is safer for the advancement of their agenda to keep to the talking points and use ad hominem attacks to shun independent (black) thinkers like Star Parker, Larry Elder, Jesse Lee Peterson, Candice Owens, Stacey Dash, Mia Love, Allen West, Walter Williams, Jason L. Riley, Angela McGlowan, Crystal Wright, Alan Keyes, Dr. Benjamin Carson, Dr. Thomas Sowell, Erik Rush, David Webb, Ward Connerly, and many others. Add to these voices entertainer Kanye West whose scales fell from his eyes in a red pill moment. He boldly wears the red MAGA ball cap and faces off with his lock-step demographic that twice voted for Marxist Obama in the 90+ percentile. Many blacks are turning away from the party of The Big Lie. In an effort to discredit Kanye for courageously breaking ranks and supporting

Trump, his mental health has been questioned by media commentators in Stalinist fashion.

The Rule of Law is being subverted by politically-driven social justice. Media propaganda and political correctness are powerful and effective ways to influence jurors and the electorate to accept social justice as right and necessary. One of the mechanisms used to make our minds fertile to embrace social justice is revisionist history taught in public schools.

Revisionist History

The re-writing of history has historically been a major signpost on the road to totalitarianism. All students — but White children especially — are taught to be ashamed of America's Founding Fathers, who are characterized as bickering "wealthy aristocrats" and "slave owners." American history in general is characterized as one plagued by racism, genocide, imperialism, and oppression at the hands of white men. American history is being systematically revised, rewritten and taught devoid of any and all nationalistic pride — and more often than not — as one worthy of scorn.

The ONLY exception is in regards to the European Theater of World War Two, where we are taught — and it is fashionable — to celebrate the fratricidal warfare of Whites killing Whites en masse. American history books, academia, the mass media, liberals, the Establishment, and most of the so-called "anti-war Left" is in complete lockstep in calling the war against Germany "The Good War" (the ONLY war to be characterized as such) and in condemning for time eternal the "evil, racist" German Nation. Jewish-American author Studs Terkel even wrote a book to this effect, titled *The Good War*, which was consecrated by the Establishment with a Pulitzer Prize. Incidentally, Terkel's book actually sympathizes with the mass-murdering, mass-raping savages of the Soviet Red Army, while ignoring their unconscionable war crimes and crimes against humanity!

(Visit the website http://www.hellstormdocumentary.com/

Buy or watch the DVD and read the book *Hellstorm* by Thomas Goodrich with an open mind. This eye-opening documentary has been banned in countless countries and scrubbed off of YouTube around the world. This aggressive suppression of The Truth clearly exposes the Orwellian tactics used by the "victors" of World War Two who do not want their false narrative questioned or revealed. Almost everything you know about World War Two and the German enemy are lies to misdirect you away from the greater evil of the Soviet Union.)

The American education establishment always describes the Nazi regime inaccurately as "fascist" in order to make the ignorant think of it as "right-wing" when in fact fascism and Nazism are left-wing ideologies, and Hitler's own ruling party was called a "socialist workers' party" ala Karl Marx. It is interesting to note that throughout the 1930's Marxists around the world — including the Communist Party USA and president Franklin D. Roosevelt — spoke openly of their admiration of Adolf Hitler's domestic policies and accomplishments. Time magazine even named Adolf Hitler "Man of the Year" in 1938! This attitude did an abrupt about-face once the German Army preemptively attacked the Soviet Army on June 22, 1941. From that point on and forever more, according to the Left and the Establishment, Hitler and Nazi Germany became the greatest evil the world had ever seen.

(For an excellent analysis of how closely Nazism {German National Socialism} parallels the modern U.S. Democrat Party, read the book *Liberal Fascism* by Jonah Goldberg.)

It is interesting that the Pacific Theater of World War Two is taught and portrayed vastly different. The Left accuses our military of "racism" in their brilliantly executed campaign that rid the various occupied Pacific Islands of fanatical Japanese armed resistance enroute to the Japanese mainland. Liberals further impugn the United States' dropping of atomic bombs on Japan as a racist act, though it saved the lives of hundreds of thousands of Americans and Japanese by avoiding an invasion of mainland Japan and a prolonged and destructive ground war.

However, liberals ignore or are completely ignorant of the blatantly racist attitudes held by the Japanese Imperial High Command and the racism articulated in Japanese Army training manuals, where the American fighting man (almost exclusively white males at the time) was described as "a simpleton", "lazy", "spoiled", "afraid to charge the enemy", "afraid of night fighting", "afraid of hand-to-hand combat", "not strongly motivated" and who has "little idea of dying for one's country." I'd bet that the courageous marines and soldiers who fought and died at Guadalcanal, Tarawa, Peleliu, Okinawa, Corregidor, and Iwo Jima, "where uncommon valor was a common virtue", would beg to differ.

Compare and contrast the racist Japanese view of American troops with the thoughtful, factual and objective German view.

In a German Army intelligence report generated during the "Battle of the Bulge" dated January 20, 1945, the Germans wrote that the American soldier was a "first rate, well-trained, and often physically superior opponent." When fighting in defense, American troops were stubborn and effective, and "often had to be wiped out in hand-to-hand fighting." And when attacking, American soldiers showed themselves to be "tough fighters in close quarters."

Further exposing their racial bias, the Left never directs any criticism toward the Japanese for their genocidal atrocities, their savage acts of barbarity committed against civilian women, children and babies, their vast and cruel germ warfare experiments conducted on unsuspecting civilian populations, and their extensive torture, cannibalism, mutilation and murder of captured American servicemen and civilian prisoners of war.

RED BADGE

The following is but one example among many of the psychopathic behavior and unconscionable war crimes committed by the Japanese Imperial Army: Upon entering the city of Nanking, China in 1937 Japanese troops under the command of General Matsui went on an orgy of rape, arson, looting and mass murder. They used pregnant women for bayonet practice, threw infants in the air and caught them on the ends of their bayonets, chopped the heads off of old men and boys with samurai swords for sport, and massacred over 350,000 people in six weeks!

As best-selling author Iris Chang points out, "the deaths at Nanking far exceeded the deaths from the American (firebombing) raids on Tokyo, and even the combined death toll of the two atomic blasts at Hiroshima and Nagasaki."

Robert Leckie, whose 1,024-page history of World War Two titled *Delivered from Evil: The Saga of World War II* wrote, "Nothing the Nazis under Hitler would do to disgrace their own victories could rival the atrocities of Japanese soldiers under General Iwane Matsui" in Nanking, China.

To this day Japan has never specifically apologized for this holocaust, and refers to it officially and in their school textbooks as "The Nanking Incident", as if their soldiers committed a few misdemeanors. Amazingly, numerous high government officials in Japan have actually outright denied that the genocidal rampage occurred at all, calling it a "fabrication." But where is the outrage from liberals and the Left?

Read the books *The Rape of Nanking: The Forgotten Holocaust of World War II* by Iris Chang, *A Plague Upon Humanity: The Secret Genocide of Axis Japan's Germ Warfare Operation* by Daniel Barenblatt, and *Hidden Horrors: Japanese War Crimes in World War II* by Yuki Tanaka for a detailed view into Japanese savagery that is all but ignored in public discourse and by academia, the Left, and the media. Then ask yourself why this is.

"History" books are also scrubbed of any mention of the mass internment of American citizens of German, Italian, and Hungarian descent in the United States during WWII. Without fail, they contain and focus on *only* the Japanese internment experience. And it wasn't the first time Germans in America were rounded up! During WWI President Woodrow Wilson required 250,000 German-born men to register at the Post Office. This list resulted in 6,000 arrests and 2,000 Germans sent to internment camps. Furthermore, German language books were removed by patriot groups from public schools and burned. At the time Germans were 10% of the population. The intense anti-German sentiment resulted in many of German descent anglicizing their surnames; Hartmann became Hartley. Answer for yourself why our history books are scrubbed of the full story and completely ignore White European suffering and persecution.

"The frightening thing, he recounted for the ten thousandth time...was that it might all be true. If the Party could thrust its hand into the past and say of this or that event, 'it never happened' — that surely was more terrifying than mere torture and death. And if all others accepted the lie which the Party imposed — if all records told the same tale — then the lie passed into history and became truth. 'Who controls the past' ran the Party slogan, 'controls the future: who controls the present controls the past.' Day by day and almost minute by minute the past was brought up to date. In this way every prediction made by the Party could be shown by documentary evidence to have been correct; nor was any item of news, or any expression of opinion, which conflicted with the needs of the moment, ever allowed to remain on record. All history was a palimpsest, scraped clean and re-inscribed exactly as often as was necessary."

George Orwell, "*1984*"

(Josef Stalin's regime was infamous for re-writing Russian history books to conform to Marxist-Leninist ideology and the communist party narrative, scrubbing names and personalities from the national memory, and more ominously, carefully deleting the faces of murdered dissidents from official — and often famous — national photos). Read the book *Uncovering Soviet Disasters* by James Oberg)

Not only is the past being scrubbed, but the present. While rarely mentioned in textbooks, black-on-black slavery is still common in Africa 150+ years after being outlawed in Western cultures that are largely white. Marxists ignore present day realities because truth shatters their paradigm and undermines their promotion of the Big Lie and the cure — social justice.

America has gone from "Our History" to "Our Histories." This push to be hypersensitive to minorities encourages and legitimizes separatist political agendas, and discourages assimilation. We have gone from pages, to chapters to books to classes, to college degrees on ethnic studies — all taught with a bent to vilify, shun, marginalize and eclipse American tradition and promote Marxist revolutionary thought and dis-assimilation from America's melting pot.

Today there would be less resistance to legitimize Ebonics (a term coined to refer to the prevalent dialect of black Americans and recognized by the Oakland Public School District) in the public school system than it would be to raise the bar by re-instituting Latin into the curricula. The first position is "progressive;" it embraces diversity and weakens America. The latter is viewed as Eurocentric and therefore is considered obsolete and irrelevant.

The annals of history illustrate an enormous disparity in contributions to the advancement of humankind through discovery, invention, exploration, science, engineering, medicine, architecture, and culture given to us by — white men. This is fact.

Hollywood puts its foot on the scale of history to create balance in our minds. It substitutes reality with fiction. It doesn't just sing the praises of minor characters; it composes. The much hyped movie, Hidden Figures, makes my point. The movie would have you believe that three black women mathematicians got us to the moon. The 2016 movie was promoted to be about, *"The story of a team of female African-American mathematicians who served a vital role in NASA during the early years of the U.S. space program."* They did not serve a "vital role."

The truth of the matter is that the heroes of the space program were Jack Crenshaw, and German-born duo Wernher Magnus Maximillian Freiherr von Braun (aerospace engineer), and Albrecht "Alex" Kosmala. Alex was part of a team of white men that made the Apollo Guidance Computer, predecessor to the GPS. That computer had already calculated what Katherine Johnson and the other ladies were triple checking manually. Another white male worthy of front- row recognition is Arthur Rudolph (German inventor of the V-2 rocket).

The movie grossly inflates the contributions of three black ladies from little significance to "vital". Had Katherine Johnson's contribution to the space program truly been vital or pivotal she would have been made the public relations queen of the day. In 1969 NASA was enduring criticism from black activists critical over the cost of sending a man to the moon. The movie is revisionist history and anti-white male propaganda. It discredits white male scientists, physicists, mathematicians & engineers and exaggerates three real, but very minor figures. Black activists of the time wanted the moon landing project scrapped and the money to be spent on welfare for blacks in the USA and to ameliorate poverty in Africa. A song from the day captured the jealous attitude of blacks toward NASA. It was called, "Whitey On The Moon" by Gil Scott Heron.

In the year 2000 we stood at the threshold of a new millennium — a time for reflection, awe, and celebration of the unparalleled inventions and contributions of Western Civilization to the entire world. Instead, the Diversity Movement saw to it that little attention was given to this momentous occasion. It redirected our country's attention to embrace its vision of a "perfected" Ameri_k_a in the 21st Century.

The Diversity Movement views American history as "*his* story" (the oppressive white man's). It sees the U.S. as a product of the evils of Western Civilization. Columbus Day has become hugely controversial.

In an effort to re-write history in the spirit of social justice, relevant, but minor figures like Sacajawea are elevated to the level of major figures like Lewis and Clark.

A gold-colored, one-dollar coin was minted in her honor to celebrate the year 2000. Forty million tax dollars was spent on hype trying to promote public interest in the coin.[5] Minting the Sacajawea coin at the dawn of the 21st Century foreshadowed the anti-American, Marxist paradigm shift that we are suffering from today.

This kind of subtle, persistent indoctrination has a compound effect on the criminal justice system and the court of public opinion. The life, reputation and career of the accused are in the hands of jurors that increasingly process the world not as it is, but through a prism constructed of lies and emotion that call for a reckoning against the white majority who built the country.

Territory only belongs to those strong enough to hold and defend it. This is the history of the world. It is not right or

---

[5]David Noonan, *The Money Nobody Wants*, Newsweek, 3-11-2001

RED BADGE

wrong; it simply is. This will prove no less true in Western Europe, the Ukraine, The United States or Israel. Not that it matters, but I find it ironic and amusing that when we view the history of North America through the Marxist's lens of social justice that new and compelling archaeological evidence turns the self-righteousness of the Left on its head. Europeans were very likely here before the "native" American Indians according to two blasphemous archaeologists, Bruce Bradley and Dennis Stanford.[6] Did the Indians "steal" the land from the white man only to have it "stolen" back?

It is never fun to be on the losing side of history. We have all been taught about the trail of tears. It is a sad story from the losers' perspective and from a purely human perspective. The fact is that the Indians' defeat was inevitable. The Indians lost to civilization. Subsequently, they were taken from the Stone Age to the Space Age in two hundred years. That said, the Indians were not more noble or harmonious with nature than their conqueror – the White Man.

Perhaps the best and most accurate characterization of that truth is reflected in a clip from the 2007 movie, Bury My Heart At Wounded Knee. Fact-based, it dispels the purported virtue of social justice advocates. It obliterates the wistful notion that the "American" Indians lived in harmony with the land and were somehow morally and spiritually superior to the violent White Man.

The clip is of a meeting between Chief Sitting Bull and Colonel Nelson Miles. They sit "Indian style" on the ground. Behind the Chief are his warriors and behind the Colonel are his soldiers. The following is a transcript of that scene.

---

[6]Bruce Bradley and Dennis Stanford, *ACROSS ATLANTIC ICE, The Origin of America's Clovis Culture*, University California Berkley Press, 2012.

Colonel: "Sitting Bull requested this council. We await his word."

Sitting Bull: "Take your soldiers out of here. They scare the game away."

Colonel: "Very well sir. Tell me then, how far away should I take my men?"

Sitting Bull: "You must take them out of our lands."

Colonel: "What precisely are your lands?"

Sitting Bull: "These are the lands where my people lived before you whites first came."

Colonel: "I don't understand. We whites were not you first enemies. Why don't you demand back the land in Minnesota where the Chippewa and others forced you from years before?"

Sitting Bull: "The Black Hills are sacred land given to my people by Wakantanka."

Colonel: "How very convenient to cloak your claims in spiritualism. And what would you say to the Mormons and others who believe their god has given to them Indian lands to the west?"

Sitting Bull: "I would say they should listen to Wakantanka."

Colonel: "No matter what your legends say, you did not sprout from the plains like the Spring grass and you did not coalesce out of the ether. You came out of the Minnesota woodlands armed to the teeth and set upon your fellow man. You massacred the Kiowa, the Omaha, the Ponca, the Otoe and the Pawnee without mercy and yet you claim the Black Hills as a private reserve bequeathed to you by the Great Spirit."

Sitting Bull: "And who gave us the guns and powder to kill our enemies? And who traded weapons to the Chippewa and others who drove us from our home?"

Colonel: "Chief Sitting Bull, the proposition that you were a peaceable people before the appearance of the white man is the most fanciful legend of all. You were killing each other for hundreds of moons before the first white stepped foot on this continent. You conquered those tribes lusting for their game and lands just as we have now conquered you for no less noble a cause."

Sitting Bull: "This is your story of my people!"

Colonel: "This is the truth, not legend!"

Social Justice in the Media

Throughout the Western world, The Socialist State is criminalizing dissent. This endangers free speech. While U.S. courts are indeed compromised by social justice too, for the most part it is the media-fueled court of public opinion that gets its pound of flesh by shunning heretics, i.e. anyone who dares oppose their dogma. It is the media that frame the court of public opinion in favor of the Marxist agenda. It is the media that destroy careers and reputations of anyone that is out of step. It is the media that pressure legislators and the criminal justice system to bend toward social justice.

Media propaganda, using the methods developed by Edward Bernays, convinces much of the public to accept a substitute for reality. Feeding the public heavy doses of the social justice narrative translates to pressure put on legislators, jurors, and judges; prosecutors, and police administrators.

Censorship, the under-reporting of actual crime, and its substitution with sensationalized, lesser stories & non-stories — results in a near "media blackout" on the prolific black-on-black, black-on-white, and female-on-male crime in America. The Marxist-constructed social justice narrative simply does not hold up to the facts of who is doing what to whom, yet it is the prism we govern through.

Consider the following sobering example of selective outrage on part of the media and criminal justice system that are both corrupted by social justice.

U.S. Department of Justice's (DOJ) Bureau of Justice Statistics' (BJS), National Victim Survey (NVS) data on interracial rape shows that in just one year (2005), black males raped 37,460 white women (100 every single day). That same year white men raped ZERO black women. Furthermore, all black female rape victims were violated by black males. Virtually the same statistics were reported in 2003 and 2004.

Equally as astonishing as the number of rapes is the absence of media coverage and DOJ concern.

True to Soviet form, the information above is being buried and harder to find since it was first published. Having it at one's fingertips undermines the State narrative and disproves the Big Lie. From 1996 to 2008 the BJS published very detailed offender/victim information in tables. The most popular was, "Table 42: Personal Crimes of Violence." Data from 2009 on is no longer published in that easy-to-read manner. If there is a chance of uncovering new information, it would require the herculean chore of interpreting raw data. [7]

Taking these federal statistics at face value, if the race of offender and victim were reversed it would have been the lead story in every media outlet in the nation. DOJ task forces would be formed and federal prosecutors would be looking over the shoulders of county jurisdictions, even prosecuting federally.

Black-on-white rape isn't limited to women. The Human Rights Watch report, "No Escape: Male Rape in U.S. Prisons" states:

"White inmates are disproportionately targeted for abuse."

The report continues:

"Inter-racial sexual abuse (rape) is common only to the extent that it involves white non-Hispanic prisoners being abused by African Americans or Hispanics."

PREA (Prison Rape Elimination Act) does not highlight the most common victim of these in-custody rapes. The feds require that jails and prisons put in place reporting methods to stop abuse, but the training hides the reality and scope of the problem.

Where are the ACLU and the other so-called "civil rights" organizations pleading the case for these abused and gang-raped

---

[7] Charles C. Johnson, *Obama's Justice Department Limits Publication of Interracial Crime Stats*, gotnews.com, February 18, 2015

white male prisoners, who more than likely are serving time for a non-violent felony, such as fraud or embezzlement?

What about the U.S. Constitution's 8th Amendment protections against "cruel and unusual punishment?"

Being sodomized and gang raped is clearly cruel and unusual punishment!

In 2008 the United Nations voted to classify rape as a "war tactic", defining it as "a systemic means of spreading terror and encouraging displacement."

Apparently, true human rights and protections against terrorism and displacement from violent rape and gang rape do not apply to white males in U.S. correctional institutions.

In the name of "social justice" do these white female and white male rape victims "have to pay the price" year after year? Is this just more of what Obama's racist, black theology mentor ("Reverend" Wright) would call America's chickens coming home to roost?

Where are the otherwise limitless resources of the DOJ? Where is the media coverage? Where is the National Organization of Women (NOW)? Where are the paragons of virtue: Holder, Jackson, Sharpton and Rangel? Moreover, where are Carol Moseley Braun, Maxine Waters, and the queen of compassion and the self-righteousness, Oprah?

Where are all the leftist "War on Women" activists? They should be screaming at the top of their lungs over the mass rape of white females every year by black males. Yet they are silent as a cemetery. Why?

In addition to the suppression of truth and selective outrage by the media, we had a meddler-in-chief (Obama) whose message was amplified without rebuke when he selectively injected himself in local issues he had no constitutional business or authority to intervene on. He aggravated select local issues and propelled them to the national stage.

In the Cambridge, Massachusetts incident involving Obama's friend, (black) Harvard professor Henry Louis Gates, he said the Cambridge police acted *"stupidly"* and more recently said if he had a son he would look like Trayvon Martin. The stature of the Offices of President and the Attorney General were fully engaged in promoting social justice and punishing their political rivals rather than defending truth and the rule of law.

Recall the Internal Revenue Service using information from the National Security Administration Agency to target the TEA Party. Lois Lerner, Director of the Exempt Organizations Unit of the IRS was not held accountable for something as simple as perjury or obstruction of justice. And, more recently, recall the DOJ going after Dinesh D'Souza — the director of the documentary *2016: Obama's America* so vigorously (seeking jail time over the normal civil fines) for making excessive campaign contributions through four front men. Regardless of the technical "legalities" or the Constitutionality of the Campaign Finance law, the fact remained that in Obama's Amerika, Dinesh D'Souza was a convicted felon (until Trump's pardon) for simply exercising his First Amendment rights and criticizing Obama!

Obama's Attorney General, Eric Holder, was blind to the racist, anti-white knockout game (AKA *"polar bear hunting"*) until the offender/victim roles were reversed in one incident where a white male attacked a black male. The scales then fell off of AG Holder's eyes and the offender was swiftly charged federally with (drum roll please) — a *"hate crime."* We are watching political theater, not criminal justice.

Notwithstanding the refreshing interruption Trump brought, from the Oval Office to elementary schoolrooms the Left conditions us to replace reason with emotion and fact with feelings. They stoke the flames of class envy, racial strife, and a war between men and women by using lies, revisionist history, high-tech faux news propaganda, selective outrage, suppression of truth, and inflammatory rhetoric. They divide the population and fuel unrest, setting the stage for their heavy hand to restore order.

In spite of our warts, this is the greatest nation in the history of the world. Nowhere has there been the social mobility for every kind of person as there has been in the United States. Regardless, Marxists and their attendant *"useful idiots"* in the media and population at large push class hatred, casting everyone into the roles of either victims or tyrant, fueling the final phase of the revolution.

Marxists have moved far beyond demanding equal rights. Now they demand extra rights and *equal results*: a forced redistribution and realignment of society in the name of social justice. Marxists work to disarm the opposition by intimidation and fear. They characterize defenders of tradition and truth as racist, bigot, sexist, rapist, batterer, or a whole raft of other pejorative terms. These labels are the mark of the politically incorrect. They are applied like a pox to anyone on the wrong side of their brand of tolerance as defined under the fast-evolving new regime.

Crime and Punishment

Social Justice usurps 2,500 years of jurisprudence. Let's look at some examples where social justice has corrupted criminal justice in our society:

Duke University Lacrosse Team

Mike Nifong was the district attorney who filed charges after three white members of the Duke University Lacrosse team were accused of raping black stripper/exotic dancer Crystal Mangum. Feminist faculty immediately demanded the team coach resign, as well as demanding that the students be indicted, and expelled. DA Nifong was tenacious in his pursuit of "justice" for Ms.

Mangum. He ignored the facts and stood firmly by Ms. Mangum's side during the whole ordeal.

No matter how loud Al Sharpton cried and how much louder the complicit media amplified his and the feminist ideologues' voices, the facts won out and the hoax was revealed. Eventually, Nifong was disbarred and left office in disgrace. However, Sharpton was given his usual get-out-of-jail free card.

What of the damage to those Duke University students who were snared and pushed into the churning gears of the feminist-inflamed, media-driven court of social justice? Their lives and education were destroyed based on a woman's lie that was embraced as truth by the prosecutor.

And just a year after her false allegations against those three white men, Crystal Mangum murdered her black boyfriend — a real problem for criminal justice — but without any fanfare from the feminists or media.

Ferguson

A year after the Ferguson riots (that followed the justifiable police shooting death of the violent Michael Brown); Municipal Judge Donald McCullin withdrew all arrest warrants generated by the city before December 31, 2014.[8]

This action stemmed from a DOJ report that tainted the Ferguson police and city government as using racially bias policing and revenue generating schemes. Keep in mind the DOJ report followed another DOJ investigation that exonerated Officer Wilson from any and all criminal wrongdoing and furthermore supported his actions. That report was a true investigation. It was hard for Attorney General Holder to swallow, but he saw it coming. No doubt, the order went out for the Civil Rights Division of The DOJ to "find something." The

---

[8]Carey Gillam, *Judge Overhauls Troubled Ferguson*, Missouri Court, Reuters, August 24, 2015

second, broader DOJ "investigation" started with a conclusion and built an argument around it for Holder and Obama to save face. It was as if to say, "We didn't find what we alleged, but look over here! We found all this other stuff." Quashing all misdemeanor arrest warrants in the wake of the DOJ report is social justice from the bench.

Personal versus Public Safety

The U.S. Supreme Court has repeatedly upheld the principle that police forces exist to protect public safety (see Castle Rock vs Gonzales), and have no obligation to ensure personal safety. But that is not sufficient for many feminists who insist that society must provide them personal protection. There is also the problem for them that criminal justice only punishes crime after it occurs and can be proven. Feminists promoting social justice want to punish men before they can commit a crime.

Restraining Orders as a Form of Shunning

In order to do that, they have corrupted the rule of law by instituting a form of shunning known as restraining orders and protection orders. Because this is social justice, no proof is required, hearsay is admissible, and perjury is not punished.

In these cases, a woman only need claim she is in *"fear"* of a man or there is the potential for emotional harm. The court then issues an order that destroys every civil liberty men have fought and died for, including suspending the right to keep and bear arms and driving them from their homes — without due process — as a condition of the ex parte court order. In the past two decades, feminist ideologues have made broad use of this method against millions of men.

I should also note that any legal mechanism to disarm men is an advantage to a State seeking to control the people.

In a question to Ilana Eisenstein, assistant solicitor general, who was arguing about a federal ban on gun ownership for anyone convicted of misdemeanor domestic violence, Justice Clarence Thomas asked:

"Can you give me another area [of law] where a misdemeanor violation suspends a constitutional right?"

Destroying Children, Families, and Marriage for the Cause of Preventing Domestic Violence

Similarly, public concern about violence among intimate partners has led to draconian laws. These laws have been exploited by neo-Marxist feminists to further their agenda of destroying families and marriage.

The Family is the smallest form of government; it is the foundation of society. Once the foundation is fractured Marxists can control the course of society and "*perfect*" it under the umbrella of their ideals.

Broadening the definition of what constitutes criminal domestic violence allows any woman to claim she has been assaulted, battered, strangled, held against her will, harassed, etc. Women can have a man arrested without a warrant or meaningful probable cause.

Few such cases stand up before a jury. The punishment for incurring a woman's wrath is most often accomplished without a trial.

Only rarely does intentional violence between intimate partners rise to the level used to argue the need for these otherwise redundant, zealously prosecuted domestic violence laws. They are being used to promote radical, man-hating, feminist social justice. But those few legitimate cases make excellent propaganda for feminists who ignore the reality that intimate partner violence is gender neutral.

Decades of abuse of criminal law has convinced many men to push back with their own form of social justice. In large numbers, they are refusing to marry or form intimate relationships. And given the refusal of men to marry, more and more women are having children outside of wedlock. Since single mothers are generally not an economically viable unit[9], and most require State support to survive, these actions further the original objectives of the neo-Marxist ideologues to destroy families and marriages, and thereby our Republic.

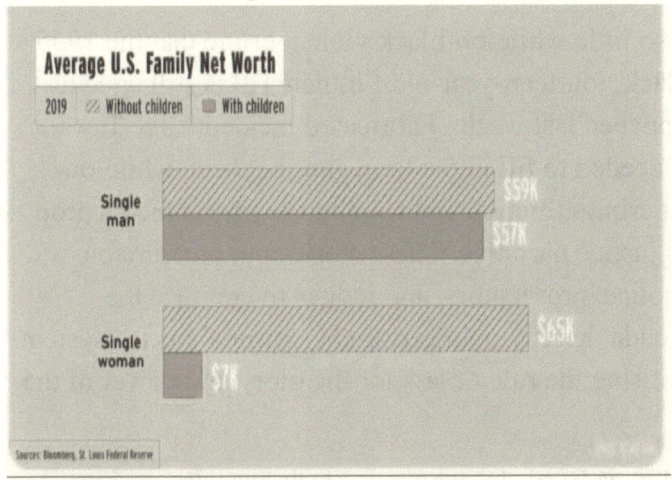

Average U.S. Family Net Worth
2019 — Without children — With children

Single man: $59K / $57K

Single woman: $65K / $7K

Sources: Bloomberg, St. Louis Federal Reserve

Black-On-White Crime

Another area where political correctness and social justice has virtually overwhelmed criminal justice is black-on-white crime as well as black-on-black crime.

Violence by females such as the murder by Crystal Mangum of her boyfriend hardly makes the local news although her lies about being raped by three white men were instantly believed and broadcast to the ends of the earth. The same could be said about the media coverage of other hoaxes like Tawana Brawley, another false white-on-black rape claim used to promote a false narrative of social injustice against blacks. Congressman John

---

[9] https://hdfs.illinois.edu/news/single-mothers-much-more-likely-live-poverty-single-fathers-study-finds

Single mothers are more likely to live in poverty, with **only 15.1 percent of single women working full time year-round**. The study also concluded that single men invested more in education, further widening the gender gap.

Robert Lewis, a black man, who the Left reveres as Civil Rights icon lied about being spit on and racial epithets shouted at him as he walked by a group of TEA Party members. Multiple cameras and cell phones documented the moment and a reward was published for evidence of his accusation: there was none; it was a lie to tarnish the TEA Party as racists.

There is so little white-on-black violent crime that the 1955 murder of black, fourteen-year-old Emmett Till is still cited as though it happened last week. Fabricated incidents like Tawana Brawley are needed to fill in the long gaps between white-on-black violent crimes. Fiction and spin by the liberal media prop up the social justice narrative. These stories put pressure on legislators, police, prosecutors, and judges to embrace the Marxists' agenda thereby politicizing the criminal justice system and compromising the rule of law for the glory and power of the State.

In 1998 James Byrd, Jr., who was black, was dragged to death behind a pickup truck by three white men in Beaumont, Texas. That sickening story made national news and resulted in passage of a hate-crimes law by Congress. But in 2002 when Ken Tillery, who was white, was murdered in a similar fashion by three black men the silence was deafening. It is apparently acceptable social justice when blacks kill whites.

Remember the 2002 Beltway Snipers? How disappointed the liberal media were when the suspects did not match their prejudices and predictions. The social justice narrative called for *"angry white males"* but instead they got two angry black males, one of whom was a Muslim. The story was dropped abruptly.

Remember Don Imus' rude comment where he called a group of black female basketball players from Rutgers *"nappy-headed hos"*? His attempt at *"humor"* was insulting and he had to genuflect and kiss the ring of Grand Inquisitor Jessie Jackson. The Imus non-story was so sensationalized by the media that it all but completely eclipsed coverage of an actual crime that occurred at the same time in Tennessee: a horrific, multiple offender, black-on-white double kidnap/murder/torture/gang-rape/mutilation known as the Christian-Newsome murders.

Channon Gail Christian, 21, and Hugh Christopher Newsome, Jr., 23, was a couple from Knoxville, Tennessee. They were each repeatedly raped, tortured, mutilated and murdered after being kidnapped the evening of January 6, 2007 when Ms. Christian's vehicle was carjacked. Four black men and one black woman were arrested and charged in the case, which received only minor notice in the press.

Liberal media are so anxious to find evidence to feed the narrative of white-on-black violence that they jumped the gun on George Zimmerman. They profiled him. Based on his surname and neighborhood, they assumed he was white. Once the switch was flipped they could not turn it off and Zimmerman was cast — by proxy — in the role of white villain.

But when the facts about Zimmerman's political orientation and racial makeup began to leak, the social justice narrative was in jeopardy. The story line had to morph and conform to the assigned roles of black victim and white killer.

First, NBC (admittedly) spliced police dispatch audio in order to mischaracterize Zimmerman to sound as though Trayvon Martin's race was the lone factor behind his call to police. Then, out of desperation to keep the narrative from derailing, the media resorted to describing Zimmerman as *"White-Hispanic."*

This was the first time ever that "white" was placed before any other descriptor in a newly created, hyphenated ethnic description. By this standard, Barack Obama should routinely be described as a "White-Kenyan."

If Zimmerman had been perceived as a victim, he would have been described simply as *"Hispanic."* If Zimmerman had been accepted to Harvard, he would have been described as

"*Hispanic.*" If Zimmerman had been the subject of excessive police force, he would have been described as "*Hispanic.*"

The Left controls the language. The hyphenated racial adjective, "*White-Hispanic*" was engineered solely to fit the social justice narrative: that white males are anti-social, dangerous racists (Notwithstanding the rare exception, nothing could be further from the truth). If the pieces do not fit, get a bigger hammer.

Enter Angela Cory — the "*special prosecutor*" appointed by the state of Florida. She used a sledge hammer to smash a square peg into a round hole entirely for political purposes after the county prosecutor did the right thing by not filing charges against Zimmerman due to lack of evidence.

While Ms. Cory promised "*justice*" the public was fed heavy doses of misinformation for a year leading up to the trial. Countless times pictures of a cute, all-American-looking, twelve-year-old Trayvon Martin were shown rather than the formidable, seventeen-year-old, tattoo-faced, gold-tooth, self-described thug he was at the time he attacked Zimmerman.

Trayvon Martin was clearly not the next Dr. Ben Carson or Grand Master Chess Player, Maurice Ashley. But you would never have known that from the information censored and then fed to the press by the special prosecutor.

Fortunately for Zimmerman, the Florida jurors did not cave to the immense pressure of media spin, indoctrination, and the self-righteous theatrics of the prosecution. To their credit the jury acted on the facts, not the hype of a corrupt system.

Then there was Michael Richards (AKA "Kramer" of Seinfeld fame) who lost his temper and called a black heckler the "N" word. He had to kiss Grand Inquisitor Sharpton's ring and beg forgiveness. Next, it's Paula Deen's turn in the frying pan. None of these people committed a crime. They used rude language in a variety of contexts, one of them 27 years ago. Then

Phil Robertson of Duck Dynasty fame was raked over the coals for commentary stemming from his religious beliefs that outraged the homosexual lobby. Had he made these comments in Canada or England he could have been jailed for hate speech. Former Los Angeles Clippers owner, Donald Sterling, was fined $2.5 million by the league after recordings of him making disparaging comments about black people were made public by a vengeful ex-girlfriend.

The attack on your First Amendment freedom of speech was punctuated with an exclamation mark just two days after a husband and wife Muslim couple launched a deadly terrorist attack in San Bernardino (12/02/2015). U.S. Attorney General Loretta Lynch put America on notice. She said, "Now obviously this is a country that is based on free speech, but when it edges towards violence, when we see the potential for someone lifting that mantle of anti-Muslim rhetoric or, as we saw after 9/11, violence against individuals... when we see that, we will take action." She didn't put the enemy on notice. She put you on notice! Unpopular speech that the First Amendment was designed to protect is now subjectively protected or prosecuted by the anti-American, Marxist federal government.

In an identical tone US Attorney General for Idaho, Wendy Olson, admonished citizens of Twin Falls, Idaho that they would be prosecuted for being critical of refugees. Emotions ran high in their city after a disabled American girl was raped by three juvenile refugees spawning concerns of what was to come with Obama's plan to bring in thousands more to the state. In the nick of time President Trump stopped Obama's treacherous plan and Olson resigned after Trump's first week in office.

Abetted by media propaganda and the psychological intimidation of political correctness — police, judges, and prosecutors are increasingly pulled into the irrational tide of selective outrage promoted by Marxist ideologues. Consequently, the criminal justice system is increasingly advancing *"social justice*" over actual justice using race, religion and gender as tools to hammer home statist ideology.

CHAPTER TWO

The Reality of Marxism: A Sinister and Depraved Heart of Darkness

"Terror is the basis of Soviet power...Terror is a system of violence, ever ready to punish from above. It is a system of instilling fear, of compulsion, of mass destruction elevated to the status of law."

Vladimir Lenin, first leader of the Soviet Union (U.S.S.R.)

"The misery and oppression of the masses must be intensified to an extraordinary degree."

Soviet Communist Party statement at the Sixth Party Congress in Moscow

"This fear that millions of people find insurmountable — this terrible fear of the state."

Vasily Grossman, war correspondent for the Red Army

"In the Soviet Union the lie has become not just a moral category but a pillar of the state."

Alexandr Solzhenitsyn

"Deception is an arrangement of light and dark...The people must be made to see white where there is black when this is necessary to the progress of the Revolution..."

(From the guidelines for "disinformation" and deceit as an arm of communist secret warfare, offered to Vladimir Lenin by Willi Munzenberg, Jewish-Marxist revolutionary and Propaganda Chief for the Communist International.)

Behind all the lofty slogans and captivating rhetoric of Marxism and their useful idiots on the political Left is a sinister and depraved heart of darkness. Marxism is without question the most murderous ideology in all of human history.

In 1992 (after the fall of the Soviet Union) one of Russia's oldest newspapers – the *Literaturnaya Rossiya* – reported that, including forced starvation and the Russian-Bolshevik civil war, Soviet communism was responsible for the deaths of 147 million people.

What these numbers represent is borderline incomprehensible: 147 million people is almost half the entire population of the United States!

Marshal Georgy Zhukov, the most decorated Army General in Soviet history, spoke of the communists who took over his country thus:

"Sleeves rolled up, axe in hand, they lopped off heads...They packed them off by freight like cattle...If the nation only knew their hands dripped with innocent blood, it would have met them not with applause but with stones."

The Soviet Union was indeed, as President Ronald Reagan observed, an "Evil Empire." Pat Buchanan also accurately described the Soviet Union as a massive "prison house of nations, whose Marxist ideology had been imposed by force and terror."

The Soviet Union covered 11 time zones where over 200 languages and dialects were spoken by more than 100 distinct ethnic groups. It was the largest totalitarian police state in history, and was only held together with the sickest and most brutal force imaginable.

Nearly everything Americans have been taught about Nazi Germany and World War Two is a combination of clever misdirection, gross exaggerations and outright lies to draw your attention away from the much greater evil – the Soviet Union – where atrocities took place on such a scale as to dwarf what happened under Hitler's reign. Establishment history books as well as school textbooks are scrubbed of virtually all of this information.

The U.S. Government, academia, the mainstream media, the major book publishing companies and the organized Left not only ignore the ghastly human rights violations, mass murder and genocide at the hands of successive Soviet rulers and the Communist Party, but actively bury them.

A prime example: *New York Times* correspondent Walter Duranty actively covered up the mass executions and genocide being committed during Stalin's *Reign of Terror* and outright denied in print that the Ukrainian Holocaust of the 1930's even occurred! (The Ukrainian Holocaust or genocide, known as "The Holodomor", is discussed in detail below).

For his handiwork on behalf of the mass-murdering Soviet communists he was awarded the Pulitzer Prize. Adding insult to injury, in November of 1933 President Franklin Delano Roosevelt formally recognized Stalin's government and negotiated a new trade agreement with the genocidal dictator.

When you believe that there is no higher power than the State, and that your rights come from man rather than God, your moral compass fractures and you no longer value nor respect the preciousness of human life. Intimidation, torture, rape, murder and slavery become the norm to control the population.

Anatoli Lunacharsky was a Jewish-Marxist revolutionary and the first Soviet Commissar for Education. In 1917 he proclaimed:

"We hate Christianity and Christians; even the best of them must be looked upon as our worst enemies. They preach love of our neighbors and mercy, which is contrary to our principles. Down with the love of our neighbor; what we want is hatred."

The Soviet Communist Party's willing executioners went on to murder over 300,000 Christian priests, who oftentimes were crucified and had their eyes poked out in satanic rituals. Nuns were mutilated, gang raped and dismembered. The communists destroyed over 60,000 Christian churches, burning many of them to the ground. The churches left standing were often turned into latrines or museums of "state atheism."

Vladimir Lenin sanctioned this mass murder of the Christian clergy specifically, stating: "The more representatives of the reactionary clergy we manage to shoot, the better."

This diabolical orgy of anti-Christian persecution, torture, mass murder and property destruction was official Communist Party policy called "The USSR Anti-Religious Campaign" and was waged throughout all seven decades of Communist Party rule.

The zeal with which the Soviet secret police carried out the "Anti-Religious Campaign" never warned: on November 15, 1966 the secret police demolished the historic Christian Church of the Holy Trinity in Leningrad, considered by many to be the most beautiful church in the Baltic region.

While it is undisputed that Jews were a victim class in Nazi Germany they were at the same time the villainous, bloodthirsty ruling class of the Soviet Union. Ethnic Jews were the founders and architects of the first communist country; they waged the genocidal *Red Terror* and subsequent *Reign of Terror* and were the wardens and administrators of the most massive concentration camp system in history, the Soviet Gulag.

World famous Russian author, teacher, historian, novelist, and decorated Red Army combat veteran of World War Two —

Aleksandr Solzhenitsyn — had this to say regarding who the masters of the Soviet Union really were:

"You must understand, the leading Bolsheviks who took over Russia were not Russians. They (Bolshevik Jews) hated Russians. They hated Christians. Driven by ethnic hatred they tortured and slaughtered millions of Russians without a shred of human remorse. It cannot be overstated. Bolshevism committed the greatest human slaughter of all time. The fact that most of the world is ignorant and uncaring about this enormous crime is proof that the global media is in the hands of the perpetrators."

*(See the biography of Aleksandr Solzhenitsyn in the Endnotes to this chapter for additional information and context)

The following is just a small sampling of the predominant Jewish representation in the first communist government of the Soviet Union:

Communist Party Central Committee: of 12 members, 9 were Jews.

Council of People's Commissars: of 22 members, 17 were Jews.

Central Executive Committee: of 61 members, 41 were Jews.

Extra-ordinary Commission of Moscow: of 36 members, 23 were Jews.

In 1922, the *Morning Post* listed all 545 civil administrators of the Soviet communist government: 477 of them were Jews (88%); only 30 were ethnic Russians (5%).

When 88% of the new "Soviet" government is controlled by a group that makes up less than 2% of the population (ethnic Jews), the violent overthrow of the Russian government in 1917 was clearly NOT a "Russian" revolution, but a Jewish coup d'état.

RED BADGE

But don't take my word for it. Take it from someone in a privileged position to know: Sir Winston Churchill. (**See the biography of Winston Churchill in the Endnotes to this chapter for additional information and perspective)

At the time Churchill wrote the following words he was serving as Great Britain's Secretary for War, a cabinet-level position with access to the highest-level information and most closely-guarded secrets possessed by British Intelligence, whose clandestine operations inside Russia were legendary.

On February 8, 1920, amid the alarming economic chaos and political turbulence that entangled all of Europe in the immediate aftermath of World War One, Winston Churchill authored a lengthy article published in the *Illustrated Sunday Herald* in London, England titled: "Zionism versus Bolshevism: A Struggle for the Soul of the Jewish People." In it Churchill wrote the following:

"From the days of Spartacus-Weishaupt to those of Karl Marx, and down to Trotsky (Russia), Bela Kun (Hungary), Rosa Luxembourg (Germany), and Emma Goldman (United States), this world-wide conspiracy for the over throw of civilization and for the reconstitution of society on the basis of arrested development, of envious malevolence, and impossible equality, has been steadily growing."

"It played...a definitely recognizable part in the tragedy of the French Revolution. It has been the mainspring of every subversive movement during the Nineteenth Century; and now at last this band of extraordinary personalities from the underworld of the great cities of Europe and America have gripped the Russian people by the hair of their heads and have become practically the undisputed masters of that enormous empire."

"There is no need to exaggerate the part played in the creation of Bolshevism and in the actual bringing about of the Russian Revolution, by these international and for the most part atheistic Jews, it is certainly a very great one — it probably outweighs all others...the majority of the leading figures are Jews. Moreover, the principal inspiration and driving power comes from the Jewish leaders."

"In the Soviet institutions the predominance of Jews is even more astonishing. And the prominent, if not indeed the principal, part in the system of terrorism applied by the Extraordinary Commissions for Combating Counter-Revolution (the Soviet secret police) has been taken by Jews, and in some notable cases by Jewesses. The same evil prominence was obtained by Jews in the brief period of terror during which Bela Kun ruled in Hungary. The same phenomenon has been presented in Germany (especially in Bavaria), so far as this madness has been allowed to prey upon the temporary prostration of the German people...the part played by (the Jews) in proportion to their numbers in the population is astonishing."

Frederick Woods, one of the world's leading Winston Churchill bibliographers, has pronounced the article genuine and listed it in his authoritative and groundbreaking book titled, *A Bibliography of the Works of Sir Winston Churchill*.

Winston Churchill's well-informed assessment of the founders and principal players behind Communism, the Soviet regime and its notoriously blood-thirsty secret police has been corroborated by many scholarly sources, but perhaps most significantly by the internationally-recognized and distinguished reference source on Jewish history, culture, and religion: The Encyclopedia Judaica.

The Encyclopedia Judaica writes in its section titled "Communism" that:

"The Communist movement and ideology played an important part in Jewish life, particularly in the 1920's, 1930's and during and after World War II. Individual Jews played an important role in the early stages of Bolshevism and the Soviet Regime."

The Encyclopedia Judaica further reveals, "In some countries, Jews became the leading element in the legal and illegal Communist parties and in some cases were even instructed by the Communist International to change their Jewish-sounding names and pose as non-Jews, in order not to confirm right-wing propaganda that presented Communism as an alien, Jewish conspiracy."

Encyclopedia Judaica admits that Jews held "Many responsible positions in all branches of the (communist) party and state machinery at the central and local seats of power."

The nationally-recognized Bureau of Jewish Education, founded by Lithuanian-born Orthodox Rabbi I.E. Neustadt, states on their website:

"*Encyclopedia Judaica* has been the leading source for information on the Jewish people, the Jewish faith, and the state of Israel. The Second Edition continues the tradition of the Encyclopedia as the best source of coverage of how the Jewish people have influenced history and shaped the modern world. For its all-inclusive coverage of Jewish life, culture, history and religion, the *Encyclopedia Judaica* earned a place on Library Journal's '50 Best Reference Sources of the past millennium'."

Amazon sells a 22-volume edition of the *Encyclopedia Judaica* and its editorial reviews describe it as "a monumental and comprehensive reference work" and a "2007 Dartmouth Medal winner. The landmark *'Encyclopedia Judaica,'* lauded as the standard work on Judaism...has been extensively revised and expanded. Nothing compromised, included are more than 21,000 signed entries on Jewish life, culture, history and religion, written by Israeli, American and European subject specialists."

RED BADGE

Englishman Robert Archibald Wilton was an author and British journalist who specialized in Russian and German affairs. He served in the Russian Army during World War One and was awarded the Cross of St. George for distinguished action in combat. Wilton accepted an appointment as a correspondent for *The Times of London* assigned to St. Petersburg, Russia, and was on-scene during the vicious Jewish-Communist coup of 1917.

Wilton's reports from the field were regarded as incisive, candid and truthful, and he was well-known as a shrewd observer of events. Due to his objectively honest and insightful reporting about who was responsible for the bloody coup in Russia and the savage murders of Tsar Nicholas II, his wife and five children, powerful Jewish interests in England brought immense pressure on *The Times of London*, causing Wilton's reports from Russia to be censored and kept from the public. Wilton subsequently resigned from The Times in disgust and moved to Siberia.

Following the Communist's consolidation of power and the spread of *The Red Terror*, Wilton escaped from the blood-drenched Soviet Union and resolved to write a book revealing all that he learned and saw in Russia before, during and after the Jewish-Communist Coup of 1917.

He authored two books on the topic: *Russia's Agony* in 1918, and *The Last Days of the Romanovs* in 1920. In his second book Wilton writes:

"The thousand and one Jews...continue their work of destruction; having wrecked and plundered Russia by appealing to the ignorance of the working folk, they are now using their dupes to set up a new tyranny worse than any that the world has known."

In describing the cold-blooded "ritual" murders of Russian Tsar Nicholas II, his wife, four daughters and son on July 17, 1918 — the Russian branch of the "House of Romanov" — Wilton observes:

"The whole record of the Bolshevism in Russia is indelibly impressed with the stamp of alien invasion. The murder of the Tsar, deliberately planned by the Jew Sverdlov and carried out by the Jews Goloshekin, Syromolotov, Safarov, Voikov, and Yurovsky, is the act, not of the Russian people, but of this hostile invader."

True to his impeccable reputation for honesty and candidness, Robert Wilton's observations and reporting have been confirmed through further historical investigation conducted by Ivan Plotnikov, a Professor of History at Maxim Gorky Ural State University in Russia.

Jewish-Marxist Yakov Sverdlov was the Chairman of the Soviet Communist Party's Central Executive Committee in 1918. As such, he was effectively the Soviet "Chief of State." It was Sverdlov who publicly announced the *Red Terror* in 1918, and it was Sverdlov who gave the order to execute Tsar Nicholas and his family.

Carrying out that execution order was the blood-thirsty Jewish henchman Yakov Yurovsky, who led the squad of Soviet secret police responsible for the monstrous and grisly murders. When the first round of gunfire failed to kill the Tsar's daughters, the heartless Jewish executioners tried to finish them off by clubbing the critically wounded girls on the head and stabbing them repeatedly with bayonets. Yurovsky himself finally executed two of the girls by shooting them in the head at point-blank range.

Tsar Nicholas II was a nobleman of the House of Romanov and was the last Emperor of Russia. In August of 2000, Nicholas and his family were canonized by the Russian Orthodox Church. Tsar Nicholas is now known as "Saint Nicholas the Passion-Bearer."

Jewish historian Leonard Bertram Schapiro was a professor of Russian Studies at the London School of Economics for many years. He was a scholar of Russian politics and history, and was considered an expert on the subject of Soviet Communism.

His published works include the following books: *The Origins of the Communist Autocracy* in 1955, *The Communist Party of the Soviet Union* in 1960, *Totalitarianism: Key Concepts in Political Science* in 1972, and *Russian Studies* in 1987.

"*Russian Studies*" was a comprehensive collection of articles and essays that Schapiro wrote over the years on Russian politics, history and culture. In an article discussing the early years of the Soviet secret police, known at that time as the "Cheka," Schapiro reports that "Anyone who had the misfortune to fall into the hands of the Cheka stood a very good chance of finding himself confronted with, and possibly shot by, a Jewish investigator."

Dr. W. Bruce Lincoln was an award-winning, best-selling author and professor of Russian history, specializing in early 20th Century Russian history. Dr. Lincoln authored an article published in The Atlantic news periodical in September of 1991 in which he noted that 80% of the rank and file Soviet secret police officers in the Ukraine were Jews.

Many believe that Jews have always been in Russia; not so. There were almost zero Jews in Russia until 1772. That was the year that the Russian Empire annexed part of Poland and with it hundreds of thousands of Jews. Jews were met with mistrust and antisemitism in the Russian Orthodox country's borders. Even so, they were allowed to practice their business enterprises — with restrictions.

In 1791 Empress Catherine outlined a 1.2 million kilometer territory called the "Pale of Settlement." Within that swath of land Jews could move freely and practice their religion. At its peak the territory held five million Jews or 40% of the world's Jewish population at the time. Once outside the Pale, Jews needed special permits to travel elsewhere in Russia. Catherine gave the Jews governing and voting rights in the Pale but deemed them to be "foreigners" in Russia. From 1772 until 1917 (145 years) Jews lived in essence as a separate, but not sovereign nation within Russia. In April of 1917 the Pale was officially abolished. This is the same year a majority of Jews lead a coup that transformed Russia into the Soviet Union. The coup (misnamed the "Bolshevik Revolution") included the ritualistic murder of the Imperial Romanov family that had ruled since 1613.

The word "Bolshevik" means "one of the majority." Using the misnomer "Bolshevik Revolution" conveys that the Soviet Union was born of a popular uprising of the Russian people. Not so. It was certainly popular enough to win and there were Russian people that joined but when you examine who developed the ideology (Karl Marx – a Jew), and who lead the violent overthrow and held the majority of positions in the new (Soviet) government it is more accurate to call it a coup and not a "Bolshevik Revolution."

Without the ruthless leadership, conspiracy and organization from the minority Jewish de facto nation living within Russia's borders for just 145 years there would not have been a USSR. This is a fact that few have the courage to tell.

THE GULAG

The monstrously hellish Soviet Gulag was a massive network of concentration camps which operated throughout the 74-year existence of the Soviet Union, and where the annual prisoner death rate was 70%!

A number of the Gulag's camps were slave labor camps where "enemies of the state" were interned for life and forced to perform excruciatingly hard labor with minimal food, water or sleep in Siberian mines and other areas around the Arctic Circle. Many inmates died from sickness, disease, malnutrition, exposure, and exhaustion.

Due to the absolute failure of Marxism, the Soviet government relied upon the output of up to 20 million slaves in the Gulag to prop up the socialist economy. At its peak there were 53 major camps and 425 minor ones all overseen by a "Commandant." No less than 15 of the Gulag's commandants were Jewish.

In reviewing Nikolai Tolstoy's book *Stalin's War: Victims and Accomplices*, historian Charles Lutton pointed out a little known but shocking fact: The Marxist-socialist Soviet Union was the largest and deadliest "slave society" in history!

Estimates of the number of citizens of the Soviet Union who perished in the Gulag run from a low of 12 million to as high as 80 million!

(With the Soviet archives locked up and the notorious Soviet practice of destroying incriminating government records and otherwise covering up their crimes, the world may never know just how many innocent people this genocidal Marxist regime murdered).

Contrary to what some Soviet apologists might proclaim, the Gulag didn't close after Stalin's *Reign of Terror* – it remained in full operation under all of the Soviet rulers. Even under Mikhail Gorbachev's reign no less than five million citizens remained interned in the camps throughout the 1980's and into the 1990's.

A survivor of the Gulag, Alexander Shatravka, wrote in 1984: "Everything which goes on in the camp resembles one of those films which shows the tortures given by the Gestapo."

Marxist revolutionary Vladimir Lenin, who was a Jew by the standards of Israel's "Law of Return", was the first leader of the Soviet Union. After seizing power in Russia the communists went on a genocidal rampage called the *Red Terror*, which was officially announced by the Soviet government in September of 1918. At the start of the Red Terror in 1917 Lenin proclaimed:

"Terror is the basis of Soviet power. Terror is not an incidental act, nor an accidental expression of government displeasure, however frequently repeated. Terror is a system of violence, ever ready to punish from above. It is a system of instilling fear, of compulsion, of mass destruction elevated to the status of law."

Lenin went on to write: "The scientific concept, dictatorship, means nothing more nor less than power which directly rests on violence, which is not limited by any laws or restricted by any absolute rules."

As the genocide of the middle class was taking place Lenin declared to his Marxist associates in crime, "We are exterminating the bourgeoisie as a class."

On June 26, 1918 Lenin ordered the Soviet secret police to "expand the revolutionary terror."

In St. Petersburg, so many civilians were being executed in the town's courtyard that Lenin ordered his executioners to park trucks nearby and constantly rev the engines to drown out the staccato sounds of gunfire.

The following are excerpts from two of Lenin's 1918 telegrams to the secret police:

"A troika of dictators should be established and mass-terror should be begun at once...We must not wait a single minute! Full speed to the mass arrests! Execute weapons owners!...We have always backed the use of terrorism...The executions should be increased!" (Source: "*Collected Works*", Volumes 29, 35, and 45).

In *The Decision on the Red Terror* of September 5, 1918 can be read the following: "The Soviet Republic must rid itself of class enemies by isolating them in concentration camps..." (Source: Decrees of the Soviet Power, Moscow, 1964, p.295).

Lenin was further quoted by the "Krasnaya Gazeta" on September 1, 1918, saying:

"Without mercy, without sparing, we will kill our enemies in scores of hundreds. Let them be thousands; let them drown themselves in their own blood...let there be floods of the blood of the bourgeoisie – more blood! As much as possible!"

Jewish-Marxist revolutionary Grigory Zinoviev was one of the founders of the Soviet Union, a member of its first Politburo with Lenin, and a longtime head of the Communist International (COMINTERN). Shortly after the communists seized power in 1917 he stated, "The interests of the revolution require the physical annihilation of the bourgeoisie class." (The bourgeoisie were the middle class)

Not to be outdone, Jewish-Marxist revolutionary Leon Trotsky — the founder and first commander of the Soviet Red Army — infamously proclaimed after the 1917 seizure of power:

"We must turn Russia into a desert populated by white negroes upon whom we shall impose a tyranny such as the most terrible Eastern despots never dreamt of. The only difference is that this will be a left-wing tyranny, not a right-wing tyranny. It will be a red tyranny and not a white one. We mean the word 'red' literally, because we shall shed such floods of blood as will make all the human losses suffered in the capitalist wars quake and pale by comparison...we shall become a power before which the whole world will sink to its knees. We shall show what real power is. By means of terror and bloodbaths, we shall reduce the Russian intelligentsia to a state of complete stupefaction and idiocy and to an animal existence...At the moment, our young men in their leather jackets (secret police)...know how to hate everything Russian! What pleasure they take in physically destroying the Russian intelligentsia — officers, academics and writers!"

RED BADGE
(Source: *Memoirs of Aron Simanovich, a jeweler at the court of the Czar Nicholas II*, Moscow, 1993).

And while the Communist Party continuously boasted to the world that the Soviet Union was a "worker's paradise" void of exploitation and oppression, the Soviet Communist Party officially declared at the Sixth Party Congress of the International in Moscow: "The misery and oppression of the masses must be intensified to an extraordinary degree."

Jewish-Marxist Feliks Dzerzhinsky was the founder of the murderous Soviet secret police, serving as its "Director" from 1917 to 1926. Although known by several different names and acronyms throughout its history, the organization itself remained the same, and obediently carried out the most heinous crimes of the 20th Century. From 1954 until the collapse of the Soviet Union in 1991 the Soviet secret police were known as the KGB.

Not only was the founder of the Soviet secret police Jewish, the most blood-thirsty and notorious secret police chiefs in Soviet history were also Jewish, including Yagoda, Yezhov, Beria and Andropov. These Marxist psychopaths were effectively "state-sponsored serial killers." It was they who ruthlessly carried out the constant executions, the wide-scale torture, the "forced famines", the genocide, and the mass internments into the infernal Gulag with cold, calculating fanaticism.

Dzerzhinsky expressed the Soviet secret police's guiding principle in 1918: "We represent in ourselves organized terror – this must be said very clearly."

Lists of the people executed by the secret police were actually published in the weekly newspaper in order to intimidate and terrorize the population into total submission.

Historians can therefore prove that close to two million people were executed during the period of 1918 to 1919. From

January 1921 to April of 1922 another 1.7 million were executed, including Christian priests, nuns, bishops, professors, doctors, lawyers, policemen, nurses, journalists, authors, artists, writers, intellectuals, and farmers.

In addition to the mass executions by gunfire, the Soviet secret police tortured to death countless millions using the most savage and barbaric methods, including: dismemberment, crucifixion, submerging victims in boiling oil or tar, burying victims alive, inserting burning coals into women's vaginas, burning victims to death, forced drownings, flaying, hangings, and forcefully administering slow-acting poisons.

Lenin, Dzerzhinsky, and Communist Party functionaries also deliberately engineered a forced famine in 1921 that ultimately killed over five million peasants. The Marxists were quickly turning the "old Russia" into a human wasteland.

Stalin became the General Secretary of the Communist Party of the Soviet Union on April 3, 1922. The mass executions, forced famines, and mass internments of citizens into the dreadful Gulag only intensified under the rule of Josef Stalin, possibly the greatest mass murderer in history.

A vicious internal power struggle ensued after Lenin's death on January 21, 1924 in which Stalin prevailed and subsequently solidified his near-absolute power. Stalin massively increased the size, scope and power of the Soviet secret police, who became his willing executioners and his primary tool of fear, coercion and oppression.

Referencing Russian historian Nikolai Tolstoy's book *Stalin's War: Victims and Accomplices*, American military historian Dr. Charles Lutton wrote that "It is Tolstoy's contention that Stalin was haunted by the fear that the Communist state was essentially a house of cards that could easily collapse. His overriding concern was to shore up the position of the regime, largely through a policy of terrorizing the various peoples who inhabited the USSR."

One of Stalin's preferred methods of totalitarian control over the population was absolute control of the food supply: "Control the food and you control the people."

Kulaks were former peasants who worked their way up to become independent farmers and relatively large land owners under the Russian Tsars (Czars). Once the Communists seized power however, all land and private property became the property of the State. Under Marxist theory, there is no right to private property of any kind. Therefore, any farmer who refused to turn over all of his grain, livestock, crops and everything else his farm produced to Communist Party officials was labeled a "kulak", a "class enemy" and targeted as an "enemy of the State."

On January 30, 1930 the Soviet Communist Party's Politburo approved the "liquidation of the kulaks as a class." Five to seven million farmers were subsequently identified as "kulaks" and had their farms and all their private property violently seized by the secret police. Anyone resisting the seizures was immediately executed. The rest were shipped via boxcar to concentration camps in the Siberian Gulag, where most of them perished.

The Ukrainian Holocaust or Ukrainian genocide – known as "The Holodomor": literally, "death by forced starvation" – began in 1929 when Stalin ordered all livestock, grain, foodstuffs, silage, and other private property of Ukrainian farmers and peasants confiscated by armed force as punishment for resisting socialist land and farm "collectivization" mandated by the Communist Party of the Soviet Union.

Armed secret police units along with 25,000 young Marxist fanatics of the Communist Party's "Youth Brigades" raided barns and went house to house tearing up cellars and ripping apart walls with axes searching for any hidden food or valuables.

Anyone resisting the raids and search parties were executed on the spot.

Over 500,000 Ukrainian families were forcefully evicted from their homes, packed into rail cars and shipped to desolate areas of Siberia, where they were dumped in open fields exposed to the elements and abandoned there without food, water or shelter. Most of them died on the long, one-way boxcar trip or shortly thereafter.

Military blockades were erected around Ukrainian villages to prevent any food from coming in from outside areas and Red Army patrols prevented anyone searching for food from leaving their village.

In 1932 Stalin issued a decree calling for the arrest or execution of anyone taking so much as a stalk of wheat from a field in which he or she worked.

Thus the Communist Party-engineered "forced famine" cost the lives of at least 7 million ethnic Ukrainians (including 3 million children) who died painful, miserable deaths. At the height of the genocide in June of 1933 over 30,000 people died every day, one third of who were children under 10 years of age!

In 2008 Ukraine's National Security Service published archived documents that prove Josef Stalin and the Soviet Communist Party deliberately orchestrated the Ukrainian Holocaust, and that the death toll was actually much higher than historians have previously estimated. The Ukrainian authorities say at least 10 million civilians died as a result of the communist-engineered famine, while independent Ukrainian historians claim the death toll exceeded 11 million! Even the world-renowned *Encyclopedia Britannica* estimates the death toll higher than before at 8 million.

Similar socialist "collectivization" policies were inflicted upon Kazakhstan, Crimea, and huge swaths of area in the Black

Sea region, with millions more forced starvation deaths and untold human suffering and misery.

Lady Astor of England asked Josef Stalin in 1931, "How long will you keep killing people?" To which Stalin replied, "The process would continue as long as was necessary" to establish a communist society. And continue it did.

During Stalin's 31-year *Reign of Terror* (1922 to 1953) demographic analysts have concluded that the Soviet government murdered over 51 million of its own citizens!

In just a one-year period of *The Great Purge* (from 1937 to 1938) Stalin and his Jewish secret police chief Nikolai Yezhov had over two million people executed in the Gulag.

Jewish historian Simon Sebag Montefiore writes in his book *Stalin: The Court of the Red Tsar* that during the height of The Great Terror while genocide was being waged against the peasantry and mass executions were being carried out around the clock, Stalin was surrounded by beautiful, young Jewish women.

Jewish Commissar Lazar Kaganovich was Stalin's right-hand man. As the chief architect and enforcer of the Communist Party's murderous policies throughout the *Reign of Terror*, he personally oversaw the punitive actions that led directly to the Ukrainian genocide.

Kaganovich fanatically enforced Stalin's execution quotas, which included shooting at least 10,000 Ukrainians weekly. At a 1933 meeting of the Communist Party's Central Committee Kaganovich declared angrily, "We don't shoot enough people!"

As a former ideological enforcer and propagandist for the Red Army, Kaganovich also diligently carried out the Communist Party's "Anti-Religious" propaganda and persecution campaign, which first and foremost targeted Christians.

Marxist dogma mandates "state atheism." Belief in God is prohibited, and any belief in a power higher in authority than the

State is met with ruthless persecution. Almost all of the clergymen of the Russian Orthodox Church and most of its members were shot by the secret police or imprisoned in the hellish Gulag.

In keeping with his fanatical anti-Christian hate, it was Commissar Kaganovich who in 1931 ordered the demolition of the majestic Cathedral of Christ the Savior in Moscow, the tallest Orthodox Christian church in the world!

Jewish-American author and investigative journalist Stuart Kahan aptly dubbed the blood-thirsty Kaganovich "The Wolf of the Kremlin" and the Soviet Union's "Architect of Fear."

In his book *Stalin's Secret War*, Russian historian Nikolai Tolstoy makes a compelling case that of the 30 million Russians who were killed during the chaos of World War Two, over two thirds of them (20 million) were executed by the Soviet government and not by German military forces. These numbers are substantiated by numerous historians and researchers who have documented the fact that Stalin's regime murdered or enslaved over 20 million Soviet citizens before World War Two even started!

"What is so hard to convey about the feeling of Soviet citizens throughout (*The Great Terror*) is the similar long-drawn-out sweat of fear, night after night, that the moment of arrest might arrive before the next dawn...anyone at all could feel that he might be the next victim." {Source: *The Great Terror* by Robert Conquest, 2008}

Even if one were to use the most conservative estimates of the number of Soviet citizens murdered by the Soviet government – 62 million – that number is still more than four times the battle dead of all the nations who fought in World War Two!

Astonishingly, this very "low ball" figure of 62 million citizens murdered by the Soviet communists also exceeds the number of combatants killed in all of the wars of the 20th Century combined!

Historian Charles Lutton accurately described the Soviet Union as "an unrestricted police state, run by perhaps the foulest collection of congenital criminals ever assembled."

Famous Siberian author and novelist Valentin Rasputin wrote in 1990:

"I think today the Jews here in Russia should feel responsible for the sin of having carried out the revolution and for the shape it took. They should feel responsible for the terror – for the terror that existed during the revolution and especially after the revolution...their guilt is great. They perpetrated the relentless campaign against the peasant class whose land was brutally expropriated by the state and who themselves were ruthlessly murdered."

While visiting Moscow's "Jewish Museum and Tolerance Center" in June of 2013, Vladimir Putin pointed out that over 85% of the members of the first Soviet government were Jewish, whom Putin said were "guided by false ideological considerations."

(Source: "*Putin: First Soviet government was mostly Jewish*", Jewish Telegraphic Agency, June 19, 2013)

Jewish nationalist and ardent Zionist Sever Plocker is an Israeli economic advisor, writer, and leading commentator for *Ynet News*, an Israeli publication. In an intellectually honest and highly revealing article titled "*Stalin's Jews*" that Plocker authored on December 21, 2006 for *Ynet News*, Plocker writes in the article's subheading that "We mustn't forget that some of the greatest murderers of modern times were Jewish."

Plocker then goes on to chastise his fellow Jews saying, "Many Jews sold their soul to the devil of the Communist revolution and have blood on their hands for eternity."

Plocker points out that "Lenin, Stalin, and their successors could not have carried out their deeds without wide-scale cooperation of disciplined 'terror officials,' cruel interrogators, snitches, executioners, guards, judges, perverts, and many bleeding hearts who were members of the progressive Western Left and were deceived by the Soviet regime of horror and even provided it with a kosher certificate."

Appearing to admonish his fellow Jews for having a selective memory, Plocker writes: "An Israeli student finishes high school without ever hearing the name 'Genrikh Yagoda,' the greatest Jewish murderer of the 20th Century."

(Genrikh Yagoda was the Jewish Soviet secret police chief from 1934 to 1936 during Stalin's *Great Terror*. According to published statistics, under Yagoda's leadership 38.5% of the most senior posts in the Soviet secret police were held by Jews)

Plocker continues: "Yagoda diligently implemented Stalin's collectivization orders and is responsible for the deaths of at least 10 million people. His Jewish deputies established and managed the Gulag system. After Stalin no longer viewed him favorably, Yagoda was demoted and executed, and was replaced as chief hangman in 1936 by Yezhov, the 'bloodthirsty dwarf'."

Nikolai Yezhov was the Jewish Soviet secret police chief who carried out some of the worst atrocities of *The Great Terror*. From 1936 to 1938, under Yezhov's supervision, most of the original Politburo members from 1917 to 1924 were executed, along with thousands of poets, artists, writers, and intellectuals. Yezhov even carried out executions against 27 Soviet astronomers who presented solar research that was deemed to be "un-Marxist."

Stalin and the Communist Party were so paranoid about maintaining their iron grip on power that they viewed not only the people, but the Soviet Armed Forces as a threat. Therefore, over 30,000 senior officers of the Red Army and Red Navy were executed or imprisoned in the Gulag. Of the first five "Marshals of the Soviet Union" — a rank equivalent to a 6-Star Army General — only two survived *The Great Purge* carried out by the Jewish mass murderer Yezhov.

So unconscionably ruthless and sweeping was The Great Purge of the Soviet military that almost 90% of Red Army Generals and Red Navy Admirals were executed, rendering the Soviet military effectively leaderless and without any experienced senior commanders during the early stages of World War Two.

Plocker concluded his article by saying: "I find it unacceptable that a person will be considered a member of the Jewish people when he does great things, but not considered part of our people when he does amazingly despicable things. Even if we deny it, we cannot escape the Jewishness of 'our hangmen,' who served the Red Terror with loyalty and dedication from its establishment."

What a Totalitarian Police State Looks Like:

(The following is a synopsis of the government forces in the USSR used to monitor, intimidate, surveil, coerce, and terrorize the citizens of the Soviet Union)

- 13 million National Police officers under KGB control (3 million full-time officers with 10 million auxiliary officers)

- 400,000 KGB intelligence officers (secret police)

- 300,000 KGB Border Guard troops

- 75,000 KGB "Special Troops" (elite, military-style Special Forces units directly under KGB command and control)

- 350,000 Interior Ministry troops of the *"MVD"*

*(See below for an in-depth look at this organization)

- 400,000 KGB auxiliary troops (reserve force of armed, Communist Party mobile brigades). These were units made up of young, Communist Party fanatics under KGB command. They played a critical role in the Ukrainian genocide among other Soviet crimes against humanity.

• Total KGB forces: over 1.5 million personnel in addition to a 13 million-man uniformed, national police force!

And don't forget that the government could (and did!) resort to the use of the 5 million active-duty troops of the Soviet Red Army, Red Navy and Red Air Force, which was the largest military force in the world during the Cold War!

*And now we will take a closer look at the MVD because this was the most critically important organization through which the Communist's exercised their absolute, brute-force control over the people in the USSR.

The MVD was NOT a part of the Soviet Army. And while outfitted and equipped identically to the Soviet Army — using the same assault rifles, machine-guns, hand grenades, armored personnel carriers, infantry fighting vehicles, main battle tanks, artillery, attack helicopters, and fast-attack river patrol boats — the MVD was a stand-alone force and was independent of the Soviet Army and the Soviet Ministry of Defense.

The MVD was NOT an Army Reserve, a "National Guard," a federal police force or "gendarmerie" similar to Western European nations. And even though they received military-style training, MVD "troops" were neither soldiers nor police officers. The MVD was literally an "internal army" for the purposes of total control, domination and subjugation of the domestic population. No other country in history has had a force quite like it though Obama may have hinted at creating one as you will see in Chapter Six.

And while technically assigned to the Soviet Ministry of the Interior, whenever called into action by the Communist Party's Politburo, they immediately came under the operational command and control of the KGB. For all practical purposes, they were the KGB's "private army."

And throughout the long, dark nightmare that was life in the Soviet Union, the MVD was often used to quell political dissension and squash rallies, street protests, food riots, and nationalist movements and uprisings.

At a moment's notice the MVD could deploy anywhere inside the Soviet Union as an ominous show of force to intimidate and coerce the people and further, to violently punish them for any outward displays of freedom or individual autonomy, expressions of independence or nationalism, or resistance to totalitarian control.

To maintain this level of terror and totalitarian control, a government must have a standing force of obedient, mindless automatons that do not question the morality of any execution order and are willing to break the bones of their fellow countrymen.

The KGB-MVD nexus were the Soviet Communist Party's willing executioners, and were more than willing to literally break bones, crush skulls and execute unarmed civilians — including women and children — and they did it by the millions.

The KGB also employed over 30 million full-time informants and tens of millions of part-time "rats" who snitched on their neighbors, co-workers, fellow citizens, and family. Furthermore, the MVD, the police and the Communist Party's multiple auxiliary organizations and youth groups also maintained informant networks amongst the general population totaling many more millions of citizen snitches.

Add to those numbers aspiring individuals who didn't mind "ratting out" someone for their own personal gain, as a form of payback to "settle a score" or to draw attention away from their own nefarious deeds, and it's easy to see how one could not have a safe or secure conversation anywhere at any time.

It could be surmised that in any small gathering of family, friends or coworkers, somebody in the group was an officer, agent, employee or informant of the KGB network.

To put this incredibly invasive domestic spying apparatus into perspective, consider the following scenario: two couples are having an otherwise innocuous conversation over dinner with one of the four people present subsequently reporting the topics of discussion as well as any off-handed remarks to the secret police.

Guilty until proven innocent, the accused were arrested and "denounced" for "ideological subversion" and/or "spreading counter-revolutionary thoughts", tortured until they provided a confession, and then sent to the Gulag.

In order to protect yourself from falling under suspicion or being falsely accused, one would have to posture as the perfect "Soviet man" or woman and build a case against a co-worker, inform on him or literally turn in his own brother, sister, mother or father.

In communist East Germany the Stasi secret police and their informant network was even more pervasive than in the USSR! Even in the smallest of households and social gatherings it was entirely possible that someone present was working in some capacity for the secret police.

But East Germany's population of 16 million was tiny compared to the 280 million people of the USSR. Also, East Germany was a very small geographic area in comparison to the vastness of the USSR — the world's largest country! It was quite a feat for the government of a country of such enormous size as the USSR to be able to effectively blanket the population with such pervasive surveillance and monitoring done by humans at a very personal level.

No conversation was safe in either country and people routinely "disappeared" for criticizing the government, the Communist Party and its absurd, virulent ideology.

The "Iron Curtain" of the Marxist Soviet Empire

The Preamble to the "Law of the Border of the USSR" states: "The protection of the USSR state border is a very important, inalienable part of the defense of the socialist fatherland. The USSR state border is inviolable. Any attempts to violate it are resolutely suppressed."

Compare and contrast the seriousness with which communist countries like the Soviet Union, Cuba, North Korea, China, etc. treat their national borders, and the resolute way they protect and defend them with military force against ANY outside intrusion versus the U.S.A., where our government is so grossly negligent in protecting our border from actual hostile threats that they encourage and enable foreign invasion and lawlessness.

However, what most people don't realize in reading the Soviet border law above is that this law was primarily directed at any Soviet citizen who might be thinking of trying to escape the massive socialist prison camp that was the USSR.

Go back and read the Soviet Border Law preamble again — it never articulates a specific concern regarding invasion or intrusion by "outsiders" or "foreigners."

Unlike authoritarian Nazi Germany and many other autocratic regimes throughout history — where almost anybody choosing to leave the country could generally leave — communist governments, like the ones that ruled the Soviet Union, East Germany, Czechoslovakia, Cuba, etc., are uniquely diabolical in that they literally cage the entire population in like prisoners in a concentration camp.

Communist borders are heavily fortified with walls, barbed-wire fences, minefields, trip wires, explosives, vicious guard dogs and machinegun-wielding guards in towers with shoot-to-kill orders. These border fortifications are to keep the native population trapped inside, not to keep foreigners out!

Recall that over 25% of East Germans fled the country before the communists could complete construction of the Berlin Wall and their extensive border fortifications, thus making escape virtually impossible.

Literally nobody is allowed to leave or emigrate from a communist country without specific permission from the government. In practice, this means that virtually nobody gets out alive! People didn't emigrate from the Soviet Union or East Germany – to use their own words – they ESCAPED! Think I'm exaggerating? Continue reading.

Article 64, paragraph 16 of the Soviet Criminal Code states: "Escape abroad, unlawful departure from the territory of the Soviet Union, constitutes treason under the Criminal Code."

(Any form of attempted escape or departure was still considered treason under the Soviet Criminal Code. And every person found guilty of treason in Soviet history was executed)

Article 83 of the Soviet Criminal Code states that "those leaving only because they want to better their way of life" shall be sentenced to "deprivation of freedom" in the Gulag.

Contrary to popular belief, none of this changed under Gorbachev. In fact, Soviet border fortifications were upgraded, modernized and intensified in 1988 and 1989 under Gorbachev's regime. Furthermore, KGB manpower and authority actually increased under Gorbachev's rule.

Likewise, all the way up to the fall of the Berlin Wall in 1989, the communist East German government was constantly upgrading and fortifying the Berlin Wall with additional obstacles, trip wires and more advanced guard towers. In the early 1980's the wall was doubled by a second wall and heightened. In 1987 construction of a third wall was being built in certain areas.

The East German border with West Germany — the "outer perimeter of the Soviet Empire" — was continuously upgraded, improved and fortified with additional mines, obstacles, guard towers, foot patrols, and trip-wire activated explosives.

On August 28, 1986 — five years before the collapse of the Soviet Union — the USSR Council of Ministers passed Resolution No. 31, adding an addendum to the Soviet Border Law which stated:

"Soviet citizens shall not be permitted to leave the USSR on private business."

Of course, the Soviet regime had to allow some people to travel abroad for reasons legitimately related to diplomacy, science, engineering, research, and commercial matters.

The KGB had complete authority to decide who could travel abroad, for how long and for what reason. The KGB also had carte blanche to ban for life anyone's ability to travel abroad. Under Gorbachev's regime, over 90% of Soviet scientists who applied for travel abroad for totally legitimate reasons were denied.

And even though some dissidents, defectors and others successfully escaped the gigantic prison camp known as the Soviet Union, they were not safe.

Throughout their unsavory history the Soviet Communist Party leadership did not hesitate to order special KGB units to travel to various countries around the world to assassinate dissidents, defectors and other outspoken critics of the Soviet regime. No other government in history has done this.

Contrast this with Hitler's Nazis, who not only allowed unrestricted emigration, but actually encouraged certain unwanted groups to leave Germany. In 1933 Hitler's government negotiated a "Transfer Agreement" with organized Jewish groups to facilitate the desire of many Jews to permanently relocate in Palestine. From 1933 to 1940 about 40% of Germany's Jews took advantage of the "Transfer Agreement" and left Germany with all of their wealth and assets intact.

(Source: *The Transfer Agreement: The Dramatic Story of the Pact Between the Third Reich and Jewish Palestine* by the award-winning Jewish author Edwin Black, 1984).

Communist states are truly TOTALITARIAN: the government has TOTAL control over every aspect of your life: political, social, financial, economic, spiritual and cultural. The authorities observe no restraints on their ABSOLUTE POWER.

All Communist states are in reality nothing but gigantic prison camps disguised as countries. Your entire existence is one of being ordered around and dictated to by government — you have NO individual freedom, no rights, and you cannot leave!

And if you try to escape, you will more than likely be shot by border guards, blown up by land mines or mauled to death by attack dogs. The border that divided the Soviet Empire from the "free world" in Europe for 45 years was called the "Iron Curtain" for a reason!

All of this speaks volumes about the Marxist mentality and their oppressively cruel "Heart of Darkness."

At root, Marxism defies human nature and destroys the souls of whole nations, which is why it has utterly failed everywhere it has been implemented. As a governmental system it is a "state monopoly" over everything and everyone, and its power can only be maintained through forced starvation, coercion, terror, torture, secret police, prison camps, and mass murder.

French author, journalist and philosopher Albert Camus observed: "None of the evils which totalitarianism...claims to remedy is worse than totalitarianism itself."

And yet even with this well-documented trail of blood and bones, the Left still tries to maintain that the Soviet Union, home to the world's first Marxist government, was a "champion of the people", a "workers' paradise" and an example of "utopian socialism."

To this day liberals, academics and college professors continue to minimize and white-wash communist genocide, arguing that "you have to break a few eggs to make an omelet." Celebrated author and historian Thomas Sowell responded to that mentality by saying, "Socialism in general has a record of failure so blatant that only an intellectual could ignore or evade it."

The Left's level of denial and deceit regarding the savage cruelty and barbarism of the Soviet regime (and all the world's Marxist-socialist states) is absolutely staggering.

In an article authored by David Horowitz on January 8, 2016 for *National Review* magazine titled, "Is the Left Even on America's Side Anymore?" Horowitz draws attention to a descriptive quote by Jewish Communist revolutionary Leon Trotsky, who once described Stalinism as "the perfect theory for gluing up the brain."

Horowitz goes on to write:

"What he meant was that a regime as monstrous as Stalin's, which murdered 40 million people and enslaved many times more, was nonetheless able to persuade progressives and "social justice" advocates all over the world to act as its supporters and defenders. These enlightened enablers of Stalin's crimes included leading intellectuals of the day, even Nobel Prize winners in the sciences and the arts such as Frederic Joliot-Curie and Andre Gide.

"But brilliant as they were, they were blind to the realities of the Stalinist regime and, therefore, to the virtues of the free societies they lived in. What glued up their brains was the belief that a brave new world of social justice existed in embryo in Soviet Russia and had to be defended by any means necessary.

"As a result of this illusion, they put their talents and prestige at the service of the totalitarian enemies of democracy, acting, in Trotsky's words, as 'frontier guards' for the Stalinist Empire."

Lies, hatred, terror and human suffering are the foundation of Marxist systems. The Marxist leadership's capacity for cruelty and inhumanity knows no bounds. The historical record speaks for itself – the 147 million innocent victims of 20th Century Marxism cry out from their graves for justice and as a dire warning to all future generations: do not go down this Dark Road into the Marxist House of Horrors.

The Marxist mentality is a narrow, inflexible, close-minded pathology and once in power, those possessing this ideological mindset often exercise it with extreme prejudice and homicidal psychopathy. **And this is precisely what is so frightening about Marxism's insidious infusion into American culture, education, academia, and government at every level.**

It is self-evident that Marxism's malignant ideology is absolutely entrenched on American universities and college campuses, and we witness it every day in the anti-social behavior and outrageous disposition of our college students. These brainwashed, young Marxist fanatics will be administrating government at all levels and running corporate America and most businesses in the not-too-distant future. This does not bode well for Americans with traditional Anglo-Saxon Christian values — those of us who believe in God, freedom, privacy, and individual and private property rights in the broadest sense of the term.

Marxists do not seek to make us happier, healthier, wiser, better-off, or freer. Marxists despise love and hate the truth, treating it as a mortal enemy.

This reality was openly acknowledged by Vladimir Lenin, founder of the first Marxist state, when he said, "We must utilize all possible cunning and illegal methods, deny and conceal the truth. A lie told often enough becomes the truth."

(Source: *The Unknown Lenin: From the Secret Archive*, by Richard Pipes and David Brandenberger)

Lenin further emphasized: "The people will be taught to hate. We shall begin with the young. The children will be taught to hate their parents. We can and must write in a new language which sows hatred, detestation and similar feelings among the masses against those who do not agree with us."

Marxism's personification in contemporary America is — **Barack Hussein Obama.**

Obama's nation-destroying actions and unworthy character in office showcased Marxism's sinister heart of darkness: he's a congenital liar who seems pathologically incapable of telling the truth; he's a hateful, racist agitator who has done more to inflict suffering, division, bitterness, and anxiety on the nation than any president in my lifetime.

Obama seemed to rather enjoy harassing and coercing the American people and small business owners with predatory government agencies and he did not hesitate to terrorize his political and ideological opponents with the weaponized IRS, EPA, and ATF. No policy or initiative that he promoted, advanced or decreed made us as citizens or our country as a whole happier, healthier, stronger, safer, or better-off.

Former Reagan Administration official Alan Keyes so cogently described Obama's Marxist agenda as "a better-dressed Soviet-style communism."

Financed, protected and enabled by the American aristocracy and their fellow-travelers in European royalty and the central banking community, Obama's objective of a permanent transformation and disfigurement of America is far from over. The unforeseen Trump presidential victory turned the tables. At breakneck speed President Trump is repairing Obama's damage, shrinking the Administrative State and reversing his anti-American executive orders. Still, the Deep State remains loyal to the revolution and while the visible players like George Soros scramble to discredit Trump and find a worthy opponent to put up against him in 2020. Obama's last year in office was the most revolutionary, lawless and far-reaching in its magnitude. Normalizing relations with Communist Cuba (a literal prison island) punctuates my point. Hillary Clinton was to be his third term.

Notwithstanding the fact that the United States has the highest incarceration rate in the world and one of the largest prison populations, a government doesn't need concentration camps per se to be considered a totalitarian state.

"Totalitarian" refers to TOTAL GOVERNMENT: one that exercises total power and/or total control over the people.

An even more accurate and practical way of defining a totalitarian state is this: Does the government recognize any limits to its power, authority, and sovereignty?

Until Trump's win the answer to the question when asked of the U.S. Government was a resounding "No."

Among other powers asserted by the Obama Administration they claimed to have had the legal authority to assassinate any U.S. citizen, both abroad and inside the U.S., without due process of law or even having probable cause that a crime has been committed. They not only asserted this authority and argued on behalf of it in the U.S. court system; they exercised this power of assassination overseas against U.S. citizens on numerous occasions! This extraordinary declaration of autonomous, self-anointed life and death decision-making and these extra-judicial government executions – without any oversight or accountability – are in and of themselves a totalitarian exercise of power and authority over the citizen.

For all practical purposes, Obama's "Kill List" – the existence of which the government has admitted to and Obama has actually bragged about – is virtually identical to Josef Stalin's "Death List."

And Obama's secret, extra-judicial, trans-national assassinations are strikingly similar to Stalin's executions conducted during his long *Reign of Terror* in the Soviet Union. The only difference is the method of execution. This is highly disturbing.

Likewise, under Obamacare – and the Supreme Court decisions upholding it twice – the government recognizes no limits to its power and its absolute, self-anointed authority to dictate what the citizenry must do or not do. In the words of dissenting Justice Antonin Scalia, under the Obamacare law "The government can make you eat broccoli." Not only can they order you to eat whatever they tell you to eat (with legal and financial ramifications for non-compliance enforced by the IRS), it is the first law to punish a citizen for "inactivity": they can punish you for NOT partaking in commerce or any other prescribed activity. This is totalitarianism by definition. The "Death Panels" and other forms of euthanasia in Obamacare are a reality, and reveal the sinister Marxist heart of darkness inherent in Obamacare and the people who were its architects.

The Food and Drug Administration (FDA) proscribes many things and outlaws many more. The FDA therefore defines for the citizen what they can and cannot put on or in their bodies. Sell or ingest raw milk or food-grade hydrogen peroxide and an FDA SWAT team may come crashing through your front door and arrest you. In so doing unelected U.S. Government bureaucrats essentially tell the American citizen that the government owns your body, not you. If you can't decide for yourself what you choose to eat, drink, ingest into your body or rub on your skin, how can you possibly say you're free? How can a government that exercises that level of intrusion into personal health and decision making not be described as totalitarian?

"If people let the government decide what foods they eat and what medicines they take, their bodies will soon be in as sorry a state as are the souls who live under tyranny." – Thomas Jefferson

The U.S. Government's National Security Agency (NSA) recognizes absolutely no limits to its sovereignty: it has declared limitless, self-anointed authority to eavesdrop and catalog ALL telephone and cell phone conversations worldwide, ALL THE TIME; to intercept, read and catalog all emails, texts, faxes, instant messages, computer activity and electronically-generated comments, writings, postings, documents, and messages worldwide, ALL THE TIME. This operational capability is the very definition of totalitarian government surveillance.

NSA capabilities are so impressive that former officers of the Stasi secret police of totalitarian-communist East Germany have gone on record envying its Orwellian reach and power. Former Stasi officers have been quoted in interviews with the German newspaper *Der Spiegel* describing the NSA's surveillance and eavesdropping capabilities as "extraordinarily vast in scope" and "a surprising capability far beyond what we thought was possible."

Recall that throughout the "Cold War" East German Border Guards apprehended and tortured or shot to death roughly 400 East German citizens every single year trying to flee the communist police state.

And what a thoroughly accomplished police state it was: there were so many officers, agents and informants employed by the Stasi secret police that one could not even have a private conversation in their own home amongst family without the risk that one of them was working for the Stasi!

So evil were the communist Stasi secret police that Jewish Holocaust survivor and world-famous Nazi hunter Simon Wiesenthal called the Stasi, "Worse than the Gestapo."

This is the "End Game" of the Marxist movement in America. We are a well-disguised authoritarian police state quickly advancing toward a high-tech East German/Soviet-style totalitarian one.

There is possibly only one last vestige of power being retained by the people – a critical one – and the one which has thus far prevented the final descent into totalitarianism.

Americans, remember this: the man who would ask you to disarm under ANY pretext is **YOUR ENEMY!** Do not go quietly into the night!

It was George Washington – our great military leader of the War of Independence – who said:

"Firearms...are the American peoples' LIBERTY TEETH and keystone under Independence...When they go, ALL GOES. We need them every hour."

Some additional quotes to ponder...

"It is dangerous to be right when the government is wrong."

– Voltaire

"The ultimate measure of a man is not where he stands in moments of comfort and convenience, but where he stands at times of challenge and controversy." – MLK Jr.

"Law is often but the tyrant's will, and always so when it violates the rights of the individual." – Thomas Jefferson

"Everything the State says is a lie, and everything it has it has stolen." – Friedrich Nietzsche

"From the saintly and single-minded idealist to the fanatic is often but a step." — Friedrich Hayek

"A claim for equality of material position can be met only by a government with totalitarian powers." — Friedrich Hayek

"'Emergencies' have always been the pretext on which the safeguards of individual liberty have been eroded." — F.A. Hayek

"Men are so simple, and so subject to present necessities, that he who seeks to deceive will always find someone who will allow himself to be deceived." – Niccolo Machiavelli, The Prince

"The point is that we are all capable of believing things which we know to be untrue, and then, when we are finally proved wrong, impudently twisting the facts so as to show that we were right. Intellectually, it is possible to carry this process for an indefinite time: the only check on it is that sooner or later a false belief bumps up against solid reality, usually on a battlefield." — George Orwell, "In Front of Your Nose", 1946

"You assist an evil system most effectively by obeying its orders and decrees. An evil system never deserves such allegiance. Allegiance to it means partaking of the evil. A

good person will resist an evil system with his or her whole soul."

– Mahatma Gandhi

The great orator of the War of Independence, Patrick Henry, said it best: **"Give me liberty or give me death!"**

Sources: *Lethal Politics: Soviet Genocide and Mass Murder since 1917* by R.J. Rummel, 1990. *Russia's Agony* by Robert Wilton, 1918. *The Last Days of the Romanovs* by Robert Wilton, 1920. *The Great Terror: A Reassessment* by Robert Conquest, 2008. *The KGB: Masters of the Soviet Union* by Peter Deriabin, 1990. *Chekisty: A History of the KGB* by John Dziak, 1987. *Stasi: The Untold Story of the East German Secret Police* by John Koehler, 1999. *A Century of Violence in Soviet Russia* by Alexander Yakovlev, 2002. *Intrepid's Last Case* by William Stevenson, 1983. *Spy Catcher* by Peter Wright, 1988.

I highly recommend all of Peter Deriabin's books for an incredibly honest, first-person perspective of the sinister Soviet secret police and the equally dark Soviet system as a whole.

See also Aleksandr Solzhenitsyn's illuminating books about the Gulag, the Soviet Union, and the Red Army, especially his last book *200 Years Together: Russia and the Jews* (1996). Unlike his other books, *"200 Years Together"* has not been translated into English and has been successfully suppressed in the United States, which begs the question — with our so-called "free press" — **Why?**

Endnote: As a postscript to Chapter Two I am providing the reader with short biographical sketches of **Aleksandr Solzhenitsyn** and **Sir Winston Churchill** due to the fact that they were both extraordinarily accomplished and influential men.

Both men were awarded the Nobel Prize in Literature back when it was a meaningful accomplishment and actually earned on merit, before the days of Marxist "political correctness" took over.

Due to the weight of their comments and quotes cited in this work it is important for the reader to know that these scholarly men were well educated, earned their unusual wealth of life experiences the hard way, and from it all gained a very unique perspective about their homelands and the world. Both men, but especially Churchill, were privy to information that few citizens ever have the opportunity or privilege to discover. It is therefore important for the reader to deeply consider their words and observations. I highly encourage the reader to research each man more, and consider reading some of their published works.

*Aleksandr Solzhenitsyn** was a famous Russian historian, author, teacher, writer, novelist, dissident, and winner of the Nobel Prize in Literature. He was a Red Army Captain in World War Two who was twice decorated for his actions in combat. He personally witnessed Red Army troops commit war crimes against German and Polish civilians, robbing the elderly of everything they owned and gang-raping young German girls to death.

He became an outspoken critic of the conduct of the Red Army, the Soviet system and its totalitarianism, observing "the heartlessness of our highest-ranking bureaucrats and the cruelty of our executioners."

Before World War Two had even ended, Solzhenitsyn was arrested for "Anti-Soviet Propaganda" and "founding an organization hostile to the Soviet State." He was sentenced to eight years of hard labor in a "Special Camp" of the monstrous Soviet Gulag reserved for political prisoners. After spending eight years in the Gulag he was sentenced to "internal exile for life" and imprisoned in a camp in a remote region of Kazakhstan. The Soviet government was notorious for treating even its mildest critics in this fashion. While imprisoned in the Gulag the secret police recruited Solzhenitsyn as an informant to report on the conversations and activities of other prisoners. According to Solzhenitsyn, he was able to avoid ever having to produce a single report for them. But the secret police have a long memory, and Solzhenitsyn was harassed and persecuted by the Soviet secret police throughout most of his life.

Several years after he was released from his last prison camp he published several books about his experiences, including the world-famous *The Gulag Archipelago*, which helped shine a spotlight on the cruel Marxist-Soviet system and its dark, infernal Gulag.

** **Sir Winston Churchill** was the inspirational and larger-than-life Prime Minister of the United Kingdom during World War Two and again during the early years of the Cold War. He was a prolific writer and an internationally-recognized historian, author, artist, war correspondent, journalist and military and intelligence strategist. He was awarded the Nobel Prize in Literature in 1953 for, among other accomplishments, his six-volume history titled "The Second World War."

Churchill was a former British Army officer who graduated eighth in his class from the elite Sandhurst Royal Military College in England. Captured while on a scouting mission in the Second Boer War in South Africa he spent time in a prisoner of war camp, from which he escaped and became a national hero. He was a combat veteran of multiple military campaigns around the globe, commanding elite army units at the height of the British Empire's military power.

Churchill served in British politics and government for 50 years, holding numerous high-level cabinet positions including Secretary of State for War. As First Lord of the Admiralty during World War One, he was an innovator and forward thinker regarding military tactics and strategy.

Winston Churchill was unique among world leaders in that he possessed a deep understanding of the intricacies and importance of espionage, counter-espionage and deception operations. This was especially useful while serving as a war-time prime minister.

Churchill founded and participated in a high-level secret intelligence and strategic deception organization innocuously named the "London Controlling Section" whose goal was to leave Hitler and the German High Command "puzzled as well as beaten." They succeeded.

Throughout much of his life Churchill maintained an intimate relationship with the highest levels of British Intelligence.

As the secret "eyes and ears of the British Empire" for over 500 years, British Intelligence was the world's first truly global espionage and covert warfare organization and is still considered the "Master Service" by many intelligence professionals and historians.

Paul Greengrass– the famous English film director, screenwriter, former journalist and contributing author – said of British Intelligence:

"They are the master craftsmen. They invented the principles of tradecraft, broke the first codes, ran the best agents, bred the best spymasters, and taught the rest everything they know. Above all, they keep the secrets. In the intelligence world MI-5 and MI-6 are still 'first among equals'."

Throughout much of his professional life, Churchill was privy to the most sensational intelligence, counter-intelligence and deception operations in espionage history. His unique perspective of the world and his view of history was made possible by the fact that he was in possession of highly-guarded secret knowledge – which is why one should pay careful attention to his analysis of major world-changing events like the 1917 coup in Russia.

It was Winston Churchill who coined the famous — and tragically accurate — Cold War term "Iron Curtain" in a speech he gave in Fulton, Missouri in March of 1946.

Dr. Walter E. Williams, George Mason University's Distinguished Professor of Economics and the author of the outstanding book *Liberty Versus the Tyranny of Socialism*, channeled the brilliant F.A. Hayek when he reminded us of the dangerous personalities that gravitate toward authoritarian-type governments, saying:

"Powerful government tends to draw into it people with bloated egos, people who think they know more than everyone else and have little hesitance in coercing their fellow man. Or as Nobel Laureate Friedrich Hayek said, 'in government, the scum rises to the top'."

Alas, I say to the millions of victims of totalitarian regimes around the world who have been tortured — both physically and psychologically; who suffered the never-ending mental anguish of not knowing the status or well-being of a "disappeared" loved one; who had to bear the unconscionable heartbreak of having their family members and loved ones ripped away from them by force and in many cases brutalized in front of their eyes; and for having to endure the unspeakable HELL ON EARTH that is the communist system, my heart and my prayers go out to you and your loved ones — that you all may come together again and find true inner peace and happiness in the next life.

Karl Marx – A Fraud Through and Through

For all his lamentations about the "workers of the world" and the downtrodden, Karl Marx did not come from the "working class" and never even visited a factory during the 30 years he spent in England. In fact, all evidence indicates that Karl Marx refused to perform manual labor of any kind and never held a real job in his entire life! He seems to have believed that work was beneath him. He was born into a wealthy Jewish family and married into wealth, yet always had financial problems. He was financed or supported by others in his writing endeavors, mooching off his friend Friedrich Engels and anyone else who would give him money.

To elude the authorities and evade creditors trying to locate him, Marx frequently used aliases, especially when renting apartments. He was notorious for skipping out before his rent payments were due and likewise failing to pay for other services rendered to him. He even taught his children to call him by different pseudonyms.

Marx and his wife had seven children but only three of those children lived to be adults. Of the three who made it to adulthood, two later committed suicide. Marx's other four children died before they were 18 years old as a direct consequence of living in abject poverty due to Marx's complete failure to provide for them.

Marx is also believed to have fathered an illegitimate son with his live-in maid and housekeeper whom he never paid.

While he clamored for the abolition of all rights to private property, he had his "Communist Manifesto" copyrighted, which is a formal method of legally declaring and protecting one's private property. And while he railed against the profit motive and advocated for the forced redistribution of wealth, he made personal profit off his manifesto and neither he nor his rich family ever re-distributed or shared any of their personal wealth with anyone. Not only was Karl Marx a lazy, heartless deadbeat, he's a colossal hypocrite, parasite and fraud!

CHAPTER THREE

The Purpose of (American) Government and the Role of Sheriff

"The end of law is not to abolish or restrain, but to preserve and enlarge freedom. For in all the states of created beings capable of law, where there is no law, there is no freedom."

John Locke

If you have ever felt small in the shadow of bureaucracy perhaps you asked, "What is the purpose of government?"

The answer is found in one of the four "organic laws" of the United States all of which are codified (law) found in Volume 18 of the Revised Statutes of the United States. Enacted by the 43rd Congress (A.D. 1873-1875) and published by the Government Printing Office in A.D. 1878); it is known as – The Declaration of Independence.

The Declaration is more than an historical document; it is law. It spells out for us binding fundamental truths that define the context and perspective of our nation at inception and the corresponding fundamental purpose of the Republic that emerged.

The document declares: **"We hold these truths to be self-evident…"** Self-evident means that what follows (the truths) are not to be subjected to debate or further examination: **"…that all men are *created*…"** This means that there is an architect and we are His creation: **"…*equal and are endowed by – their creator – with certain unalienable Rights*…"** This means that man did not give us our rights, but God did. Therefore, these rights cannot be separated from us: **"…*to secure these rights, governments are instituted among men* …"**

So we see here the purpose of government. It is not to make sure you wear your seat belt or to protect you from obesity by banning big gulps. **The Declaration tells us the purpose of government is to secure God-given rights.** Whether or not you are a believer in God is irrelevant; this is part of the ethos that distinguishes us as "Americans."

"You have rights antecedent to all earthly governments; rights that cannot be repealed or restrained by human laws; rights derived from the Great Legislator of the Universe." John Adams

Attorney and 2004 presidential candidate, Michael Peroutka, of *The Institute on the Constitution* calls this historical and legal perspective, "The American View." He acknowledges that we, "…do not live there now."

If we are to restore our Republic, we must center up on The American View again or else surrender to the final transformation of moral relativism and state worship.

In a healthy country, it would be inconsequential how vigorously atheists rail against The American View. The only matter of relevance to an atheist's position on the purpose of government is his unalienable right to voice his *wrong opinion* (as measured by the law).

Our founders told us that our republic depends on a virtuous and educated people. Without an agreed fixed standard to measure by we find ourselves adrift and rotting from within. We need a restoration. This cannot be done in the cultural vacuum of moral relativism promoted by the architects of the intolerant diversity movement that has rendered us rudderless and self-destructive.

Despite what you might have been taught in public school or heard in the media, "separation of church and state" is not in the

Constitution. That phrase comes from a letter penned by Thomas Jefferson to the Danbury Baptist Church. What the First Amendment of the Bill of Rights does say is, "Congress shall make no law respecting an establishment of religion, or prohibiting the free exercise thereof..."

The Constitution protects us from a theocracy; NOT from the moral compass of Christianity. The repeated and out of context references to Jefferson's "separation of church and state" rather than Madison's Constitution has confused us.

It was absurd for President Barack Hussein Obama to suggest we are no more a Christian nation than we are a nation of any other faith(s). While the blood spilled by others of different faiths for America is no less real or appreciated, in the balance the crosses in Arlington National Cemetery say it all.

Furthermore, our federal buildings are replete with Biblical references – including the Supreme Court. Look up photo journalist Carrie Devorah's, "God in the Temple of Government" for a snapshot of just some of the evidence. Even though CSPAN, CNN, MSNBC, FOX et al. crop out these Bible inspired images when filming the Capitol or Supreme Court, these bold monuments stand to the naked eye as a testament from our forebears about the inextricable Christian values (mortar) that are the root of our legal and cultural compass. Christian or not, in these times of deception and confusion we must center up on The American View to find clarity about who we are, what we stand for and where we are headed.

We must recognize that when laws conflict with the limits of the U.S. Constitution (the supreme fixed standard) they are usurpations. "...and deserve to be treated as such." — (Alexander Hamilton)

While these usurpations may look like law and are treated as law by "law enforcement" and the courts, they are what the Declaration of Independence describes as, "pretended legislation" or put another way: illegitimate. Case law, executive orders and regulatory violations are examples of this; Congress did not pass them so they **cannot be law.**

The proper role of the Supreme Court is to measure law NOT interpret it or make it. They are to hold the ruler: the fixed standard of the Constitution — to what Congress passes and the President signs.

In its proper and intended role, the Supreme Court would ensure that the Constitution protects us from our best intentions. The Supreme Court's purpose is to defend the Constitution not to treat it as a "living (morphing) document." But, instead it rubber stamps political agendas and makes what lawyers have come to call, "case law." Case law is a misnomer because again — only Congress has the authority to make law. What the court is empowered to do is render rulings; in other words, "measure the law" and rule it constitutional or unconstitutional.

In instances where the Supreme Court settles disputes between states, their ruling is only binding to the parties in the dispute; otherwise they would be "making law" and violating the separation of powers. The Supreme Court is not empowered by the Constitution to interpret the law, only to measure it.

Interpreting law places the Supreme Court as law maker; a constitutional role reserved for Congress exclusively. Not only can the Supreme Court not make law, neither can the President do so unilaterally. Executive orders are NOT law. Although they look like law, they are to apply only to employees of the executive branch and on areas of exclusive federal control like post offices and military bases.

Written in simple language our Constitution makes all of this clear. What turned us on our head is when the Supreme Court acted unconstitutionally and gave itself the (illegitimate) power of judicial review in Marbury vs. Madison. This case made the Supreme Court the law of the land rather than the Constitution.

RED BADGE

The unchallenged and unconstitutional practice of judicial review creates volumes of "case law." Generations of case law argued by lawyers trained in that faulty reasoning takes us more often than not farther away from the fixed standards of the organic law found primarily in the U.S. Constitution and the Declaration of Independence.

Essential to the restoration of the Republic is The People embracing the fixed standards underpinning our legal and cultural foundation. Through this, we can stop further devolution into the subjective, sometimes arbitrary and always prejudicial mire of social justice over criminal justice.

Why is the restoration of the fixed standards important? Think of builders. In ancient days, the fixed standard of measurement was a *cubit* — the length of the king's forearm, from the elbow to the tip of the middle finger. Over time a more precise *fixed standard* evolved — the ruler.

A builder who receives blue prints cannot know how to interpret the intent of the architect without a "fixed standard" of measurement to guide him on the intended dimensions of the design. Our fixed standards of governance (the organic law) have been usurped by the whims of special interests and an occupation government that Professor Edward Erle of UC San Bernardino describes as, an *Administrative State*. This he says is a system where administration and regulation replace politics as the ordinary means of making policy. The Administrative State elevates the welfare of the collective over the rights and liberties of the individual.

The Administrative State has been superimposed over the Constitution; both are visible, but the former has taken over. The Administrative State was built incrementally by the misuse of the Commerce Clause; it is an occupation government. We still see the three branches of government, but it is theater.

Another essential component to restoring the Republic is that peace officers remain accountable locally and that they understand their duty (by oath) to **interpose** themselves between The People whose rights they protect and pretended legislation; much of it from the aforementioned Administrative State (occupation government). The Office of Sheriff is uniquely designed for this purpose.

Interposition stems from Article VI that requires all public officials to take an oath to "…uphold the United States Constitution." Therefore, it is possible for a peace officer to refuse to enforce "a law" and not be breaking the law by committing *perjury* (violating his oath) but, in fact, upholding *the law*. In this instance, his disobedience is obedience (to his constitutionally required oath). Ideally, there would be a moral and educated people in the jury who stand to nullify the charge against him.

Consider the historic Rosa Parks case. Forget that this poor, hardworking seamstress was secretary of the local NAACP and an activist who in 1955, 1956 and 1957 attended summer training sessions at the Highlander Folk School in Mount Eagle, Tennessee. The "school" was founded by James Dombrowski and Myles Horton, both members of the Communist Party (MLK was a fellow student). While her refusal to give up her seat was most likely a scripted event tied to an agenda, she was morally correct to defy state law based on Plessy v. Ferguson (separate but equal). **Plessy v. Ferguson** was erroneously treated as the "law" of the land. This "case law" was pretended legislation. It was produced by the Supreme Court, not Congress; therefore, it was not and could not be law. Article I, Section 1 of the U.S. Constitution says that "all" legislative powers shall be vested in Congress. How much does that leave for the other two branches? Answer: None.

If the responding peace officer stood on his oath and simply refused to enforce immoral and pretended legislation Rosa would not have been arrested for disturbing the peace; she did nothing wrong. This is an example of interposition.

Interposition should have been applied to the enforcement of gun seizures in the aftermath of Hurricane Katrina when federal and local authorities unconstitutionally seized law abiding citizens' weapons. The Sheriff should have stopped the feds and prohibited the local agencies from powering up with them.

The Role of Sheriff

"When Sheriffs Do Not Put Their Oath In Action By Interposing, The Constitution Is Rendered Toothless And Government Is Unrestrained" – **Doug Traubel**

The Sheriff is the <u>only</u> elected peace officer in the country. He answers to his boss: The People; not to judges, not to the president, not to the governor. In most states, it is a constitutional office.

The Sheriff is The Peoples' guardian. The 2014 spectacle on Cliven Bundy's ranch in Clark County, Nevada is an example of what happens when there is a weak Sheriff in office. It should have been through the advocacy and authority of the Office of Sheriff and then the State Attorney General, that Bundy's original grievance was vetted and argued. The Sheriff's late entry on stage caused Bundy's argument to be unclear to the nation. This resulted in a motley band of protesters arriving — most fueled by noble intentions — with a minority in the mix looking for a flash point to a revolution.

A Constitutional Sheriff on the front line with the facts at his side could have brought about a victory for liberty. The Sheriff's absence not only contributed to chaos and confusion, but allowed the unconstitutional Bureau of Land Management to overreact unchecked with grossly disproportionate, unnecessary and illegitimate force against The People.

If I was a Sheriff my mission statement would read something like this:

The Sheriff and his deputies will honor their oath to defend the U.S. Constitution and the State Constitution through keeping inviolate the solemn role of Sheriff as the Chief Law Enforcement Officer of the County and The Peoples' Guardian; by protecting the residents of the County from criminals of all stripes – including agents of an overreaching state or federal government; preserving the peace with grace, mercy and moral agency; and at the same time being courageous in the face of danger as we demonstrate the humble heart of a servant and the protective instincts of a warrior.

The Role of the Citizen

While the Sheriff has a role to interpose, the citizen has a role too. Citizens must understand their authority to nullify (render impotent) pretended legislation and the misapplication of law. Both interposition and nullification are powers that come from the Constitution and Bill of Rights.

Nullification is a right of The People under the 9th Amendment albeit not expressly stated. It is an "unenumerated" right that can be applied to law and pretended legislation. The Supreme Court implicitly recognized The People's right to nullify in Sparf v. United States (1895). The court noted that judges have no recourse if a jury acquits a defendant even when done in the face of overwhelming evidence of guilt. Since the Sparf decision, the Supreme Court has taken the opposite view.

BLACK'S LAW DICTIONARY (2009) defines Nullification as: "*A jury's knowing and deliberate rejection of the evidence or refusal to apply the law either because the jury wants to send a message about some social issue that is larger than the case itself or because the result dictated by law is contrary to the jury's sense of justice, morality, or fairness.*"

Federal and State governments do not want citizens to know about their authority to nullify because it places power where it rightly belongs: in the hands of The People where it could challenge what has to a large extent become a for-profit, self-serving, power hungry court system and government.

Certainly nullification is a problem in the hands of an uneducated and immoral people for example in places like the Bronx borough of New York City where *Bronx Juries* are common. The term refers to a mostly minority jury that refuses to convict minority defendants even when evidence of guilt is overwhelming. Bronx juries can be found in other cities with large minority populations like Baltimore, Maryland.

In Baltimore it is often difficult for black jurors to deliberate a guilty verdict on black defendants as a result of intimidation ("stitches for snitches"), shared gang affiliation, racial loyalty, or out of some odd notion of reckoning shaped by social justice. This brand of Bronx-nullification is not legitimate because its genesis is immorality, but the effect is the same: acquittal. Interestingly, Maryland's constitution recognizes jury nullification in Article 23.

Professor Paul Butler of Georgetown University encourages the misuse of jury nullification by blacks as a tool to fight against (his perception of) a racist criminal justice system. In his essay, **"Racially Based Jury Nullification: Black Power in the Criminal Justice System"** he argues that race can be an appropriate factor legally and morally for jurors to consider when deliberating a guilty verdict. He urges black jurors to be conscious of the political power of nullification, "...in the interest of the black community."[10]

Nullification is distinguished from a mistake by jurors. It requires subjective intent. The most well-known example of the down side of nullification is the O.J. Simpson double murder case. The jury's subjective intent was race-based, arguably to send a political message to white America protesting what they perceive to be rampant police misconduct and disproportional incarceration of black men. These destructive brands of nullification will become more common as the population becomes more Balkanized.

A contrasting example of a proper use of nullification is a case in Detroit, Michigan. Neighbors turned vigilantes and set fire to a crack house. The two defendants confessed to the crime of arson. Their actions followed the transformation of a once peaceful neighborhood where because of the crack house kids could no longer play outside. Police were ineffective, but arson ended the problem. The social condition and the failed attempts by the system to address the chronic and dangerous problem brought sympathy from the jury. They used their moral agency and nullified what they weighed as noble-cause crime.[11]

An example of government's misuse of nullification is sanctuary cities for illegal aliens. This practice of local governments nullifying immigration law is not consistent with the fixed standards because border protection is an expressed constitutional duty assigned to the federal government (Article IV, Section 4). According to the Center for Immigration Studies, there are over 200 cities, counties and states that are sanctuaries based on their respective policies that forbid cooperation with ICE. None of them is being pursued by the DOJ.

---

[10] Paul Butler, *Racially Based Jury Nullification: Black Power in the Criminal Justice System*, 105 YALE L.J. 667, 715 (1995).

[11] Isabel Wilkerson, *'Crack house' Fire: Justice or Vigilantism?* N.Y. TIMES, Oct 22, 1998.

RED BADGE

President Obama's and Attorney General Holder's position on nullifying immigration law by opposing deportation, endorsing executive amnesty and encouraging invasion is unconstitutional and even treasonous in its scope. It is worse than an abdication of a constitutional duty; they are principals to crime by encouraging an invasion of illegal aliens including the 75,000 + reported "juveniles" from Central America sent through the Mexican border in June of 2014.

The Occupation Government (Administrative State) is at war with America. Immigration (legal and illegal) is one of its weapons. It is being used to introduce deadly and disabling diseases once eradicated here, terrorists, and violent criminals including sexual predators, economic sabotage and the dilution of the dominant culture. The lack of quality and quantity control on immigration is intentionally reckless, but sold to us as compassion.

We are not the virtuous, educated and informed people our founding fathers required us to be. If we were we would be outraged. We would have demanded impeachment proceedings in order to bring the abuse of power by the executive branch under Obama to light. Indeed, the abuse was so blatant and the damage so extreme that we would have invited a military coup (d'état) to restore the U.S. Constitution. We would then celebrate the successful use of the constitutional mechanisms at our disposal to have Obama peacefully and lawfully removed from office and even jailed along with former Attorney General Eric Holder. But, predictably there was no accountability. The federal government unconstitutionally nullified immigration law and ignored the U.S. Constitution whenever it suited their agenda. The invasion continued until Trump's election. The destructive executive orders continued until Trump. The people behaved as ignorant sheep, and the media gave the rogue Obama regime a pass.

An example of an area where states could and should properly nullify federal law is the Affordable Care Act. The Supreme Court held that it was constitutional under the power of the federal government to tax under Article I, Section 8. This presents a problem because Article I, Section 7, Clause 1 known as the Origination Clause says that all bills for raising money must originate in the House of Representatives, not the Senate.

The Senate is where Senator Harry Reid took House Resolution 3590, the Service Members Home Ownership Tax Act of 2009, and played a shell game. He removed the content under the "amendment" process replacing it with the Affordable Care Act. His confederates in the Senate knew that if they played by the rules the bill would never have come out of the House where as a tax it was constitutionally required to begin.

The Democrat Party has moved far beyond the classic arguments of liberal versus conservative surrounding how generous government should be. This is no longer JFK's Democrat Party — radical Marxists run the party now. The daily operation of the Administrative State and the way the Affordable Care Act was unconstitutionally passed illustrate that **Marxists are changing the very structure of government behind the Democrat label.** Before Obama's overt efforts to "fundamentally transform" America — in part by taking over 1/6 of the economy through Obamacare — came three equally zealous Democrat Marxists: Woodrow Wilson who inspired the League of Nations (later to become the UN), FDR who gave us the New Deal, and LBJ who introduced the Great Society. The Democrat Party has embraced Marxist ideology for a long time, incrementally transforming the USA into the USSA.

Obama saw his pen as a scepter. His executive orders are Marxist *fatwas*.[12] James Madison's safeguards enumerated in the Constitutional separation of powers did not withstand the personal edicts of Dictator Obama. Unchallenged, he consolidated unconstitutional and autocratic power in the Oval Office.

Obama blatantly and shamelessly refused to enforce or obey a whole host of federal laws: illegal entry into the United States, illegal armed incursions into the U.S. by Mexican Army personnel and drug cartel members, illegal alien VISA violations, federal drug laws (marijuana), the Defense of Marriage Act, selective and arbitrary non-enforcement of the tax laws (dozens of IRS employees not prosecuted nor fined for failure to pay back taxes owed, including Al Sharpton, Bill and Hillary Clinton and former Treasury Secretary Timothy Geithner), Obamacare and the 24 unconstitutional and unilateral executive changes to it.

Just looking at the vulnerability along our borders one must objectively conclude that Obama willfully and knowingly exhibited a treasonous neglect and deliberate disregard to the national sovereignty and territorial integrity of the United States of America.

Yet Obama was not impeached nor removed from office because the Republican Party is filled with co-conspirators and cowards.

Social Security, Medicare and Obamacare are all socialist programs. They are parts of an enormous Administrative State (occupation government) lurching and lording over us. If you agree we have been steadily moving toward socialism domestically why would you think our international policy would not be doing the same?

---

[12]Author's sarcastic reference to *Fatwa*: a rule or legal opinion issued by a Muslim scholar on a matter of Islamic law.

RED BADGE

As many as 70 members of the U.S. Congress are affiliated with the treasonous Democratic Socialists of America (DSA), a sub-group of the Socialist International that actively and subversively works to destroy the independence and national sovereignty of the United States and ultimately submerge our country into an all-powerful, one-world totalitarian government (this is clearly on display with our unprotected open borders, the total lack of border enforcement, the stripping of Border Patrol agents' powers to apprehend and deport illegal aliens, and the various sovereignty-destroying international treaties, partnerships and "agreements" of the last 70 years).

Mikhail Gorbachev called the EU "the new European Soviet" and observed its rule by ex-communists. The U.S. is merging economies through Trans-Pacific partnerships in the same way. The Affordable Health Care Act is designed to offer rationed health care to the evolving *North America Union* (the merger of three populations and economies: Canada, the U.S., and Mexico).

NAFTA/GATT/WTO/CAFTA came first. Then came Obamacare, and soon was to come amnesty for illegal aliens, and the Trans-Pacific Partnership (further integrating national economies to be co-dependent), and the Law of the Sea Treaty (LOST). If Communism is our natural enemy why do China and Vietnam enjoy most-favored-trading status? Trump saved the day by turning the tables on all of this. Say what you will about his style, the man's policies put America first.

Trump challenges the status quo. His first order of business as president was to reject the Paris Accord. He knows we are living under an occupation government (The Administrative State) that is steered by an international communist agenda. President Trump speaking to the UN in October of 2018 rejected the Obama Administration's buy-in to placing us under the purview of international courts and tribunals with the Supreme Court of the United States no longer "supreme."[13]

We were cautioned about government corruption and the consequences of societal devolution by our founders. We were told that our Republic depends on a virtuous, educated and informed people to survive.

We are rotting from within. We need a restoration. This cannot be done in the noxious cloud of moral relativism and ignorance promoted by the architects of the Diversity Movement. The founders gave us the means to fix our problems, but we lack the knowledge and will to do the hard things. President Trump cannot fix this alone.

It is for each of us to decide — today — if we take an active role in the short time we have left and restore our Constitutional Republic through interposition, nullification, recall elections and voting out of office the corrupt.

There is growing support for a Constitutional Convention ("Con-Con"), and this makes me nervous because it could open up the document to potentially dangerous changes that could deal a death blow to individual freedom and national sovereignty. We simply need to strip away the Administrative State and enforce the Constitution we have. We need to behave like citizens, not subjects! We must find and actively support bold candidates, who understand what is and is not Law; who know the purpose of government, its fixed standards, and **will honor their oath**.

Thomas Jefferson said, **"When the government fears the people, there is liberty. When the people fear the government there is tyranny."**

---

[13] Arthur Thompson, International Merger by Foreign Entanglements, John Birch Society, 2014.

There is no doubt at this point in history that the (informed) American people fear their government. A police state was not the intention of the founders or the purpose of modern policing.

Sir Robert Peel is known as the "Father of Modern Policing." His Peelian Principles became the foundation of the Metropolitan Police Force of London.

Peelian # 7:

"Police, at all times, should maintain a relationship with the public that gives reality to the historic tradition that the police are the public and the public are the police; the police being only members of the public who are paid to give full-time attention to duties which are incumbent upon every citizen in the interests of community welfare and existence."

Police are not to replace the citizens' role in maintaining law and order, but to complement it. When London considered establishing a police force, the public's concern was that a police state would evolve that would be "…a curse and despotism…"

Sir Peel's nine principles were made to appease a worried public. **Principle #7 acknowledged that the citizen was no less responsible for protecting the community than an officer.** Furthermore, citizens are not below the police.

The 2005 Minutemen Project on the US/Mexico border; armed Korean store owners on the roofs of their businesses during the 1992 LA riots; militia in Ferguson (August 2015), following violence at the year anniversary of the *justifiable* police shooting death of violent Michael Brown; and armed members of Oath Keepers in front of National Guard recruiting offices (July 2015) to protect our unarmed guardsmen from terrorist attack – these are all lawful, and they are and consistent with Peelian principle # 7. Of course, the federal government views such an expression of grassroots freedom and responsibility as a threat to their evolving tyranny. That arrogant governing attitude is the antithesis of Peelian Principle # 7.

One only has to look at the ominous acquisition of military equipment and hardware by local police forces and federal law enforcement entities, as well as the prolific stockpiling of millions upon millions of rounds of ammunition by alphabet federal agencies to recognize that something sinister is afoot — and it does not bode well for you or what little freedoms you have left.

Edmund Burke warned, *"There is no safety for honest men but by believing all possible evil of evil men."*

It is appropriate to close this chapter with some words from two heroes of the War of Independence, George Washington and Thomas Jefferson:

"A free people ought not only be armed and disciplined, but they should have sufficient arms and ammunition to maintain a status of independence from any who might attempt to abuse them, which would include their own government." (George Washington)

In a speech before the 1st United States Congress, our Nation's first president and military leader of the War of Independence – George Washington – stated the following:

"Firearms stand next in importance to the Constitution itself. They are the American peoples' liberty teeth and keystone under independence…From the day the pilgrims landed to the present day events prove that in order to ensure peace, security and happiness, the rifle and the pistol are equally indispensable…they deserve a place of honor with all that is good. When firearms go, all goes. We need them every hour."

"The greatest reason for the people to retain the right to keep and bear arms is, as a last resort, to protect themselves against tyranny in government." (Jefferson)

Never! Never! Never relinquish your right to bear arms!

CHAPTER FOUR

The Cost of Free "Training"

Necessary austerity measures by local law enforcement administrators have caused them to sign their officers up for free training, frequently advertised by the federal government. This sounds reasonable and the price is right, but there is a danger — propaganda masked as training can bend the minds of officers to find suspicion where there should be none in a free society.

Under the Clinton Administration, U.S. Attorney General Janet Reno ushered in the SPLC (Southern Poverty Law Center) to train federal law enforcement on hate groups. Twenty years later this has evolved into federal law enforcement training local law enforcement with information provided by the SPLC. Often the training material disseminated by the federal agency hosting free workshops is presented to appear vetted or as the legitimate work product of their own resources and analysis, but it is not.

SPLC publications include "Intelligence Report" and the annual "Hate Map." Their elastic definition of what defines a hater or a hate group is ever stretching to target people and organizations that oppose their agenda; including prominent black pastors for their vocal stand on homosexual marriage.

Former Canyon County, Idaho Commissioner Robert Vasquez was featured as a face of hate in one of their magazines, "Klan Watch" for his outspoken views in opposition to illegal immigration.

I was an adviser, bodyguard and speech writer to Commissioner Vasquez during his 2006 run for U.S. Congress. He is a decorated, combat-wounded, U.S. Army veteran and an American patriot. Like many targets of the SPLC, Vasquez is an anchor point for American tradition; this qualified him as a threat that needed to be discredited.

It is a given that I will be featured as a "face of hate" in one of their publications. I look forward to my debut. Oscar Wilde said, "You can always judge a man by the quality of his enemies." And Voltaire said, "'O Lord, make my enemies ridiculous." The SPLC is just that: Ridiculous.

The SPLC is not credible. Their Hate Map claims over 1,000 "hate groups" in the U.S., but it is not reproducible or verifiable. The SPLC is purely agenda-driven, spreading misinformation about the opposition to discredit them and — true to Marxist form — stoking the flames of conflict.

Consider the Department of Homeland Security's 2009 report on right-wing extremists. It branded millions of Americans including former police, veterans, and home schoolers as people of concern. This report is disturbing in its scope and was NOT the result of the limitless investigative resources of the DHS. A public information request made by Americans for Limited Government revealed that the source of the "intelligence" used in the report was none other than: the SPLC. The SPLC has grafted on to the federal government. Its "research" and "intelligence" is parroted by federal agencies and accepted as gospel by many local law enforcement agencies that place SPLC publications in their lunchrooms.

Two instructors at FLETC (Federal Law Enforcement Training Center) are influential members of the SPLC, Richard Cohen and Laurie Wood.

The SPLC is filled with anti-Americans like self-proclaimed Communist Van Jones (President Obama's former Green Jobs Czar). The SPLC recognizes domestic terrorist and accused cop killer, Bill Ayers, as an educator on tolerance and gave Professor Nikki Giovanni an award. Giovanni wrote a poem advocating killing white people. One of her students, Seung Hue-Cho, was the mass murderer at Virginia Tech in 2007. [14]

Not only is this melding of minds in our federal government and in the SPLC alarming and dangerous, but also President Obama quietly signed into law (January 2, 2012) the NDAA, National Defense Authorization Act.

The NDAA declares all of the United States part of the battlefield in the war on terror. It authorizes our military to detain — indefinitely — any American on U.S. soil "perceived" to be a threat without due process or speedy trial. This is dangerously vague language and clearly unconstitutional under the Fourth, Fifth, and Sixth Amendments. President Obama quietly signing this nefarious piece of legislation into law under the Orwellian, Nineteen Eighty-Four banner of "Home Land Security" is frightening given the SPLC's Marxist ideological indoctrination of federal law enforcement and its ever-morphing definition of what it considers a terrorist.

The following is an example of the kind of free training offered regularly. Notice that it is "hosted" by a local agency, but in the print below you see that it is sponsored (paid for) and blessed by the DOJ. Sometimes these free courses are benign, but too often they have a thread of the narrative woven in.

---

[14]William F. Jasper, Senior Editor, *The New American*, "Exposing The SPLC: A Danger to American Liberties." Boise, Idaho November 16, 2011.

RED BADGE
Upcoming Classroom Training

REGISTER TODAY!
Tactical Community Policing for Homeland Security
Instructor Development Program
Boise, ID
March 9 - 11, 2015

Tactical Community Policing for Homeland Security
Instructor Development Program

Hosted by:

Ada County Sheriff's Office

Boise, ID

March 9 -11, 2015

Tuition-FREE!

At its core, effective homeland security is the proactive and tactical practice of community policing - law enforcement and communities working in partnership to be vigilant, resilient, and strong.

Based on this simple but powerful premise, *Tactical Community Policing for Homeland Security* delves into the merits of community policing as a means of thwarting and strategically interdicting terrorism.

This tuition-free, 3-day Instructor Development Program explores:

- Community Partnerships
- Practical Problem Solving Strategies
- Proactive Prevention, Intervention and Interdiction Strategies
- Values Based Policing in the Climate of Terrorism

Designed as a train-the-trainer program, participating law enforcement professionals will leave the class prepared to train others and will receive comprehensive instructional materials designed in a flexible, modular format to be presented during local inservice programs, squad training sessions, or even at roll-call.

Cost: This is a **tuition-free** program supported by the U.S. Department of Justice, Office of Community Oriented Policing Services.. Participants are responsible for travel, lodging, and meals.

A Word to Sheriffs and Chiefs

The training you provide becomes the lenses through which your deputies/officers see the streets they patrol. Forming reasonable suspicion to detain citizens based on propaganda that is represented as truth is a threat to liberty.

Marxists use the hammer of political correctness over the anvil of ignorance to not only reshape our culture and institutions, but also an officer's oath. They want officers to be transformed and feel noble enforcing their counter culture ethos.

Peace officers need to be thinking, active defenders of the unalienable rights of The People. It is up to Sheriffs and Chiefs to make certain their officers' oath is not corrupted. The oath should be an anchor point. It should be in the front of an officer's mind commanding courage and restraint simultaneously as they serve The People within the guardrails of their constitutionally guaranteed rights.

"Don't Tread On Me", "Ron Paul", "912", "TEA Party", "Oath Keepers", "Three Percenter", "NRA", "Malon Labe" or "Open Carry" decals and the like are not indicators of an emerging (racist) "Patriot Terrorist Movement", although your deputies/officers will be subtly and overtly influenced to think otherwise through this repeated free training (propaganda). Through giving grants and free training, the federal government is trying to soften your resistance and enlist you in helping them do what President Obama stated was his objective before taking office. He said, "We are five days from fundamentally transforming America." Think carefully about the "training" you send your deputies/officers to. DHS and DOJ sponsored venues while "free" can be quite costly to liberty.

Sheriff,

Your Office holds a unique power capable of stopping this dangerous trend of federal law enforcement seducing, co-opting and fusing with local law enforcement through grants and free training. You are the ultimate law enforcement authority in your county and in this country. This has been reaffirmed as recently as 1997 in the Supreme Court decision Mack/Printz v. USA.

The federal government knows the truth about the Tenth Amendment and the authority of the elected Office of Sheriff. This is why it is selectively targeting America's most outspoken Sheriff — Joe Arpaio — of Maricopa County, Arizona, with a groundless consent decree. This transparent abuse of power is an effort to crush him and intimidate you by proxy from standing up to them.

These times require courage to uphold your oath. You must know about the organic laws of the U.S. and educate your deputies and county on this trend of federal tentacles wrapping around matters never intended to be within the constitutional limits of their reach.

Visit CSPOA.org, Countysheriffproject.org and Institute on the Constitution to learn more about your unique role.

It has been said that sunlight is the best disinfectant. It is imperative that the relative autonomy of your office be used to shine light on the — quickening evolution of tyranny — that Thomas Jefferson warned us of:

"When all government shall be drawn to Washington as the center of power, it will render powerless the checks provided and will become as venal and oppressive as the government from which we separated."

CHAPTER FIVE

The Thin Blue Line and Media Spin

"The policeman's world is spawned of degradation, corruption, and insecurity. He walks alone, a pedestrian in Hell."

— Violence and the Police: A Sociological Study of Law, Custom, and Morality by William Westley, 1971.

"There is in human nature a resentment of injury against wrong, a love of truth and a veneration of virtue…<u>if people are capable of understanding, seeing and feeling the differences between true and false, right and wrong, virtue and vice.</u>"

John Adams (1775)

Marxism's Big Lie about systemic (white) racism and misogyny in American law enforcement fuels irrational social justice demands for racial and gender parity among the ranks of the *thin blue line* (police).

If a photograph taken of police department personnel does not look like a rainbow of racial and gender parity Marxists find fault. They ask, "Is the entrance exam a product of cultural and gender bias? Is the selection panel made of the Klan in blue? Why are so few minority officers and women in the picture wearing chevrons or brass? Is the promotional test biased too?"

City, county and state governments fold to the pressure of the Big Lie. They legitimize what are usually baseless or exaggerated grievances by answering them with tailored policies, ordinances and law. This has damaged the effectiveness of police service and decimated authentic, masculine leadership required for law and order.

The fault Marxists frame around American law enforcement's employment, promotion, and enforcement practices — while predictable — is a great deception. It is done to discredit local police and form a toehold for federalization. The argument is preposterous in light of our country's history of overcoming real and systemic racial and gender discrimination.

Marxists do not want "equality" of opportunity to compete for the honor of wearing a badge. They want equality of outcomes. **They want a police culture they can control.** To achieve this, they force outcomes in hiring and promotions with less regard to ability, qualifications, performance or merit. The result is malleable, indoctrinated and intimidated police officers and administrators that do not push back political correctness, federal agendas or unconstitutional overreach. The same molding political pressure compromises the oaths of many prosecutors and judges though they may not realize it.

Political correctness intimidates and shapes the minds of government officials resulting in a class of (defacto) commissars.

A commissar is a communist political officer in charge of teaching and enforcing public opinion. More and more our lives are governed by de facto commissars in the roles of police officers, school administrators, human resource personnel, code enforcement officers, prosecutors and judges.

Given that so much of the Big Lie in the media is fueled and justified by America's "original sin" indulge me while we take a necessary detour in this chapter.

The Slavery Crutch

There is no relationship between Selma-1965 and Ferguson-2014. Al Sharpton's media-amplified cries of "institutional racism" are lies, exaggerations, and misperceptions. The fact is that racial discrimination *of any consequence* is unknown outside of textbooks to blacks born after 1965. Yet arguing the legacy of slavery makes it sound as though there are still "black" and "white" drinking fountains. It wasn't too many years ago when the most popular golfer was half black and the most popular rapper was a white guy (Tiger Woods and Eminem). I'd say we've moved on.

It is America's white, Christian majority that ended slavery, championed the Civil Rights Act and funded massive welfare for blacks. Specifically, it was White Christian Republicans and Jews who were the driving force behind the Civil Rights Movement.

The Civil Rights Act of 1964 passed in spite of the Democrats not because of them. Al Gore's father was one of the Democrats that voted against it along with fellow Democrat Robert Byrd (a former KKK member). Today's Democrats use the Act to enforce social justice and create racial and gender division. Despite all of the history and healing since the 1960ies, the likes of Jesse Jackson and Al Sharpton rub the scar, push the Big Lie and count the cash. Ezekiel 34:1-6 addresses such self-serving shepherds who get fat eating off the flock.

The popular media, black community organizers and most universities use slavery as the foundation for the promotion of social justice. From that stage they launch a relentless character assassination of our founders and cultural origins. They feel self-righteous championing atonement by arguing the need to realign society through racial preferences and reparations.

In world history slavery is not an experience unique to blacks. Furthermore, it still goes on today in Africa (Mali, Niger, Chad, Sudan and Mauritania). It might surprise some to know there were American Indian tribes that practiced slavery extensively before Europeans arrived. Their practice expanded when they recognized it as an international commodity.

The length of the African slave trade to the New World spanned 340 years, from 1525 to 1865. At the height of the slave trade less than 10% of Americans were slave owners. And of those that were slave owners, many were blacks, mulattoes, and American Indians.

Of the estimated 10.7 million African slaves who arrived to the New World only 388,000 came directly to North America including territory that either was or many years later became the United States. It is *possible* that as many as 70,000 more came after first stopping in the Caribbean. This would bring the maximum possible estimated total number of slaves brought to North America: 458,000; the rest went to the Caribbean and South America. 4.86 million African slaves went to Brazil alone.[15]

The United States of America did not exist until the ratification of the Constitution in 1789. Slavery had gone on for 264 years in the New World *before* the United States of America was born. This is a fundamental point.

Measured by events on the timeline of history and the number of African slaves brought to "The United States of America"[16] **our country is more hero than villain.** The fact is that the United States of America participated in slavery for 76 years before abolishing it. The number of slaves brought here from our inception (1789) until the ratification of the Thirteenth Amendment in 1865 is far smaller than the hundreds of thousands of white lives killed and maimed in the Civil War.

While no African slaves were forced back to Africa, many indentured servants from Europe were returned for breach of contract or other disqualifiers thereby losing any chance of becoming a U.S. citizen. Indentured servants and White slaves (primarily the Irish) cost less than African slaves. Corporal punishment was carried out on them with less reservation than a

---

[15] Professors David Eltis and David Richardson, *Atlas of the Trans-Atlantic Slave Trade*, reprinted February 16, 2015.
[16] "The United States" is what existed under the Article of Confederation." The United States of America" was created in 1789.

black slave because of their comparatively lower investment cost.

There was a plan to repatriate freed slaves to Africa. Part of the plan involved the creation of Liberia and Sierra Leone. Former (freed) slaves were met with hostility by native Africans. In retrospect, the failure of the plan was a blessing for today's descendants of slaves in the United States. The quality of life blacks have enjoyed here (even during the Jim Crow period and Civil Rights era) was and is superior to that of blacks in any other country on the globe, seconded by — Apartheid South Africa — ironically, based on the UN Human Development Index.

Marxists promote an inverted view of history and have erased White slavery in America from text books. Having black "slave blood" makes one a kind of royal victim in the false narrative. It is as though these descendants have the power to channel the pain of ancestors and wear it on their face for the media that canonize them thereby keeping the transgression alive.

The way the media and public education address the history of African slavery you would not know that it was not a unique experience to them or that the U.S. represented only a sliver of the demand over a blip in history. Looking at slavery from a macro view, the overwhelming African slave trade went to the Middle East where Arab slave traders ensnared not only blacks but Christian Europeans too.[17] Selective outrage is fueled by revisionist history; it twists our self-image and fortifies the casting of characters in the Diversity Movement's Big Lie.

360,000 (white) lives were lost on the side of the North in the Civil War ostensibly to free the slaves, let alone hundreds of

---

[17]Robert Davis, *Christian Slaves, Muslim Masters: White Slavery in the Mediterranean, the Barbary Coast, and Italy*, 1500-1800, Palgrave MacMillan Publishing, December 2003.

thousands more maimed and injured. Reparations and amends have been paid through blood, racial preference in hiring, and over the last fifty years 22 trillion tax dollars spent in welfare and free education; much of it for blacks.

Blacks in America have had many advantages for nearly 50 years, especially compared to blacks from sub-Saharan Africa. Despite all of this black privilege, whites who by and large pay the bill are still cast as villains; why?

When one perceived fault is corrected by the villain, new fault(s) must be found to keep the revolution moving on the rails of the narrative. For instance, when equal results did not occur immediately following the enactment of civil rights laws and Affirmative Action, Marxists then attacked America's proven formula for success as exclusionary.

Marxists all but ignore the modern, systemic and largely self-inflicted causes for failure within the black population such as illiteracy, 70% illegitimacy, absent fathers, high school dropout rates as high as 50% in some cities, rampant criminal conduct and drug addiction. Instead, they advance their agenda by using the failure of so many blacks as a platform to argue fault in America's culture, institutions and white majority as instruments of exclusion and oppression.

Today the black population in the cruel and oppressive U.S. has swollen to 45 million. It would be far larger if not for the already mentioned black-on-black murder, but abortion too. Planned Parenthood kills 800 black babies a day. For instance, in New York City more black babies were killed (31,328) than born (24,758) in 2012; that is 42.4% of the city's abortions. Perhaps Black Lives Matter activists will protest abortion clinics. Hispanic abortions in NYC were 22,917 that year (31%). Hispanic and black abortions combined made up 73% of NYC abortions for 2012. (White abortions in NYC that year totaled 9,704 and Asian abortions were 4,493.)[18]

If the Big Lie is true about the character of America why then do Haitians risk drowning to escape the utopia of two hundred years of self-rule to come to the supposed racist and oppressive United States? Why do Al Sharpton's followers not emigrate from here to Haiti? Under French rule Haiti was once seen as the jewel of the West Indies. Prior to the French genocide by the black population its inhabitants enjoyed the highest per-capita standard of living in the Western Hemisphere. Under black rule the standard of living fell to the lowest.

The "legacy of slavery" is a tired and fallacious argument.

The Media and the White Boogeyman

Due to the small amount of white-on-black crime, and the even smaller number of sustained DOJ complaints against white officers for use of force on minorities, Marxists cannot rely on tangible data to cast blacks as a victim class. Instead, they campaign in the media against the legacy of slavery manifested in the nebulous "vestiges" of hate — those not readily visible as proof, but rather subtle and "institutionalized."

For instance, the media told us that the Sanford, Florida Police Department has a reputation of being "racist." Whose opinion? Based on what evidence? Is this accusation by the media why the lead investigator in the George Zimmerman/Trayvon Martin case recommended a manslaughter charge be filed? Was this a public relations stunt in the spirit of social justice to counter media pressure and placate the angry mob? After all, the district attorney properly did not charge Zimmerman with anything following his first arrest due to lack of evidence.

---

[18] Michael W. Chapman, NYC: *More Black Babies Killed by Abortion than Born,* CNSNEWS.COM, February 20, 2014

RED BADGE

The mainstream media carry the water for the Marxists. They filter and frame the news through the prism of the Big Lie. We do not have a legitimate press. What we have is faux news propaganda and there is plenty of evidence of it.

On August 18, 2009 MSNBC reported on gun-toting, white protesters in Phoenix. The group of about twelve formed to protest President Obama. MSNBC commentators described the group as white, armed and of course "racist" — without evidence. They framed the news with their prejudices and supposition. They talked about fears over these white people showing up with guns so close (miles away) to where the president was speaking and how it is possible that given the anger over having a black president one of them could try to take him out. In order to fit the footage to their commentary MSNBC cropped out the neck, head and hands of the only protester in the group armed with a rifle: A black man!

I can imagine what the MSNBC producer must have thought when he saw the raw footage: "What? A black patriot! This does not fit the narrative!! Crop out his skin!"

America is the new Soviet Union. Many publishers and members of the mainstream media are ideologically aligned with the Marxists; they airbrush history and the news. Together they help the federal government control the masses through misinformation.

ABC recklessly reported the Aurora, Colorado movie theater shooter could be a TEA Party member when they looked on the local TEA Party website and found a member by a similar name as the shooter ("Jim" versus "James" Holmes).[19] What prompted ABC to look at the TEA Party website when doing background on the shooter? This illustrates bias and just how anxious the Media are to connect gun violence with law-abiding

---

[19] Jack Mirkinson, *Aurora Shooting: ABC's Brian Ross Incorrectly Suggests TEA Party link*, Huffington Post, July 20, 2015

whites and conservatives. The reporter, Brian Ross, walked his comments back, but the bell had already been rung.

CNN refutes allegations of altering the social media selfie of Umpque Community College shooter, Chris Harper-Mercer to make his complexion white, his nostrils smaller and his lips thinner. In a similar effort by media to paint the shooter as white, The LA Times on October 2, 2015 described Mercer as having "white supremacist leanings."[20] In fact, Mercer's (unaltered) selfie and his social media page prove the exact opposite: Mercer was a mulatto. His mother, Laurel Margret Harper, is black.[21] On social media Mercer expressed hateful, anti-white sentiments in line with the bloodthirsty, racist rhetoric of the Black Lives Matter mob.

Incredibly, the brainwashed masses believe they are a free people simply because they have a myriad of consumer choices and TV channels to surf. In truth, they are prisoners in a virtual cell made of a substitute for reality constructed largely by media. If you make a cell break by speaking truth you are leaned on by the PC police and called a racist.

"None are more hopelessly enslaved than those who falsely believe they are free." Johann Wolfgang von Goethe.

Damage Control

The rush to judgment by the media on George Zimmerman embarrassed the Marxists. In the wake of the zealous and irresponsible media coverage of that case, they reined in their

---

[20] Michael Muskal, Richard Winton, Marisa Gerber, *Death in a classroom, Oregon Shooter targets his English Class,* LA Times, October 2, 2015

[21] Nancy Dillon, Exclusive: *Mom of Oregon mass killer stockpiles firearms out of fear of stricter gun laws, took son to shooting range,* New York Daily News, October 3, 2015

mouthpieces on another interracial crime that broke on April 8, 2012, in Tulsa, Oklahoma.

The story was a white-on-black crime. Two white males, Alvin Watts and Jacob England, were arrested for killing three black people and injuring two more in a shooting spree. Major Walter Evans of the Tulsa Police Department said it was premature to call this a hate crime, as did special agent Jim Finch of the FBI. Both men were overly cautious in front of the cameras about labeling the crime racially motivated. It was as if they had been coached to pour on thick a posture of restraint to convince the public that they were not rushing to judgment. Both Evans and Finch are black.

These two faces of reason were picked for the camera with the skill of a choreographer. They delivered an unusually tempered reaction to the potential labeling of this spree shooting a hate crime in an attempt to regain credibility lost in the zeal and spin of the Trayvon Martin case by the media, Sharpton, Jackson, Obama, Holder and the New Black Panthers.

Unlike the Martin case the Tulsa case would have fit the Left's narrative perfectly without spin if not for one thing: the aspect of revenge. Two years prior to the Tulsa shootings a black male murdered Jacob England's father. The media's reckless reporting of the Trayvon Martin case contributed to fueling the subsequent uptick in spree violence by blacks targeting random whites. Did the surge in black-on-white violence touch a nerve that pushed the white Tulsa suspects over the edge to their own brand of social justice aimed at a reckoning in the name of Jacob England's father?

Did the white gunmen pursue their own brand of social justice in the form of tribal revenge? Do the media and the likes of Obama, Eric Holder and Al Sharpton have blood on their hands for setting the fire in Sanford, Florida and stoking the flames nationally? The same week as the Tulsa murders an unoccupied Sanford police car was riddled with bullets. In

Gainesville, Florida a white man reported to police that a gang of five to eight black suspects beat him after yelling, "Trayvon!" At the same time, we heard the cries of the New Black Panthers calling for revenge and putting out a $10,000 bounty for the arrest of George Zimmerman.

It is the police that respond to the unrest ignited by these selectively spun stories. Yet, the police are divided too. The false narrative of rampant societal white racism and bigotry has infected the ranks of the thin blue line. Many local law enforcement agencies have *balkanized* (hostile divisions) POAs (Police Officer Associations) that reflect our increasingly balkanized society. This balkanization is symptomatic of buy-in to Marxist propaganda more than it is to anything real. In large cities the fight is as much inside police headquarters as it is on the street. The hallways, breakroom, and locker rooms are like walking through a minefield. There are the Black-POA, Women-POA, Latino-POA, Gay-POA, and others. These groups are Mafia-like in loyalty to their members and almost untouchable to the administration. There is no White-POA.

Whites are deemed the boogeymen in the Big Lie. The protagonists are self-serving, exclusive groups lead by community organizers and crowned by the Diversity Movement and the media as victims. They share a common enemy: The straight-white, conservative/Christian male.

Unappeasable "victim" groups are a product of the division brought about by the saturation of Marxism's Big Lie. Brainwashed, guilt-ridden white people in the media and academia promote the Big Lie. They feel and act morally superior to the rest of the population as they endorse policies and paradigms that justify the forced redistribution of wealth from a singular villain to a plurality of victims. These "enlightened" (brainwashed, useful idiot) whites give the Big Lie credibility.

Eighty-six percent of our nation's peace officers are white; most are male. Plug this fact into the Big Lie and it translates to the premise argued by the media and social science professors that police (based on ipso facto demographics) are an army of racist white men (proxies of white society) that need to be broken, controlled and their purpose redefined.

What took place in Ferguson, Missouri is an illustration of where we are. Across the country Marxists are advancing social justice where the criminal justice system does not render verdicts or rulings productive to their cause. The media help push social justice by mischaracterizing events.

For instance, not only do the media repeatedly describe Michael Brown as "black" but also "unarmed." Being unarmed does not mean "no threat."

In a two-year study beginning in 2011, it was learned that 1,796 people were killed by "unarmed" attackers; 3 of the victims were police officers. Over the last ten years 25 police officers have been overpowered by unarmed people, disarmed and murdered with their own weapon. [22]

Furthermore, the legal standard for police using deadly force does not require the officer put himself at such a disadvantage as to have to "...await the glint of steel..." before he shoots.[23] Rather, what is required is reasonableness from the officer's perspective at that split-second.[24] In addition, the doctrine of mistaken belief protects officers from criminal and civil liability. That isn't to say there are never cases when an officer isn't liable, but they are rare under the 'Could Have Believed' Standard afforded them by the Supreme Court. In the course of performing routine duties, it is extremely difficult to prove intent to murder by a police officer. The politicization of law

---

[22]Brian Willis, *The Most Dangerous Weapon in Law Enforcement*, (International Law Enforcement Educators and Trainers, Dec 8, 2014).
[23]People v Benjamin 51 N.Y. 2d 267 (1980)
[24]Graham v Connor 490 U.S. 386 (1989)

enforcement is threatening this shield of relative immunity that gives police the benefit of doubt.

In 2018 Washington State the people passed Initiative 940, a police reform measure voted in by 360,000 brainwashed Washingtonians. The initiative is purported to repair strained police relations and "save lives." It requires more police training on mental health and de-escalation techniques. I-940 also requires an independent investigation of any police use of force that results in death or serious bodily harm. Moreover, the initiative lowers the standard of proof to charge officers criminally. Washington is the first state to do this and it will spread.

When you decode the Orwellian language of I-940 it boils down to this: Police will more easily and more often be charged with murder and aggravated battery — after a subjective social justice investigation — of the police shooting. Framing that investigation will be the unrealistic expectation on officers to use de-escalation techniques before shooting. The soft shields of the reasonableness standard and qualified immunity have been removed in Washington.

Contrary to the argument in favor of I-940, police do not have a license to murder. I agree that someone does need to police the police. Yes, there are rare and isolated cases of police brutality (Use of Excessive Force under the color of law 42 U.S.C. § 1983). Criminal intent is easier to prove in those cases as opposed to situations when an officer overreacts in the emotion of the moment in the performance of his duty or mistakes something as a weapon in good faith. Think of a dark alley and furtive movement by a suspicious subject. Decisions are made at The Speed of Life. Granted, the consequences of police overreacting with deadly force can be just as serious as malice. Until now establishing criminal intent by an officer has been difficult. I-940 will cause Washington police officers to retire early or quit for fear of being sentenced to prison on the altar of social justice. It will discourage others from applying to be an officer and those that remain will become almost entirely reactive (retired on duty). Crime will soar because police will be too afraid of being prosecuted for performing their duty.

Political pressure for police reform is running on emotion and incomplete facts spun by the media, activists and politicians. Police officers are paying the price with their careers and lives. With increasing frequency, they are being attacked or assassinated. In addition, and as troubling, they are being indicted purely out of political pressure. This is an extremely dangerous slippery slope for society with real consequences far worse than the make believe crisis. The rare case when an officer is *legitimately* charged with murder — as appears to have happened to Chicago Officer Jason Van Dyke in the shooting death of Laquen McDonald on October 20, 2014 — does not retroactively validate public opinion spun by Black Lives Matter Et al. Furthermore, that case proved "the system" worked.

In Baltimore, following the post-arrest death of Freddie Gray Prosecutor Marilyn Mosby said,

"To the people of Baltimore and demonstrators across America, I heard your call for "No justice, no peace…This is your moment…You're at the forefront of this cause and as young people, our time is now."

(This is the same social justice, revolutionary sentiment expressed by Obama while on the campaign trail November 2, 2012 when he told a predominantly minority audience in Ohio that voting is the best "revenge.")

Is this not a revolutionary, social justice tone that tainted the chance for the officers to have a fair trial? The accused rolled the dice. They chose a trial by judge rather than jury. The lack of evidence could not bend the mind or oath of the judge and all of the officers were acquitted. Black Lives Matter were dismayed.

They thought the social justice fix was in with a black judge presiding.

The Baltimore prosecutor's comments prove she has no objectivity and that a particular national (communist-funded) agenda is more valuable to her than the oath of office and pursuit of the truth.

The Saint Louis County Prosecutor, Robert P. McCulloch, played it a bit smarter in the Michael Brown case. He found political cover behind the Grand Jury. He had seven witnesses that corroborated Officer Wilson's account. In addition, there was physical evidence including Michael Brown's DNA on Officer Wilson's gun. But, McCulloch suspended reality.

He knew how the opinion of a lone white-male prosecutor clearing a white-male police officer would go over in the media. Rather than show the courage his oath requires and appropriately decline prosecution he punted to the Grand Jury that found "No True Bill" (no probable cause to indict).

McCulloch knew there were no civil rights violation and no criminal misconduct by Officer Wilson. He knew Brown was a violent criminal. McCulloch's eloquent comments made after the Grand Jury's decision, while true, convicted him of being under the influence of political correctness. Using the Grand Jury did not teach him anything he did not already know. This political decision legitimized the Big Lie by giving the perception that McCulloch thought there was some criminal misconduct by Officer Wilson worthy of a Grand Jury's scrutiny.

Further evidence of the effect of political correctness on law enforcement and government is how ineffective police and National Guard were during the riots. They had the means, but not the will to restore order. There is a leadership vacuum throughout this country from the bottom to the top.

In New York, the influences of political correctness and social justice has the state's attorney general, Eric Schneiderman, advancing the creation of a special state prosecutor whose only purpose is to prosecute cops who use deadly force. This is an effort to appease protesters and rioters. We now expect violence whenever a police officer shoots a black person — regardless of how violent the attack on the officer.

Rioters are *not* protesters; they are a combination of criminals, terrorists and agents of communist revolution! These elements in places like Ferguson destroyed businesses of productive, contributing members of society. They should have been crushed. Instead, the timid police response emboldened them and inspired sympathetic, anti-police demonstrations in other large cities. Reverse the players in Ferguson:

It is unlikely you heard of unarmed, twenty-year-old, white male Darin Taylor who was shot and killed by a black Salt Lake police officer just two days after Michael Brown died. If the KKK was organizing demonstrations and riots in Utah — Martial Law would be declared without hesitation. The purveyors of social justice afford a double standard of grace and mercy to its pet victim classes (so much so that they do not distinguish lawful protesters from criminal rioters).

There is a pattern of discrediting white police by wrongly persecuting them in the media and through the Department of (Social) Justice. The resulting pressure is breaking the back and spirit of law enforcement and will transform America's police forces.

When truth and due process no longer matter — who in their right mind will apply to be an officer? In 2014 murders of police officers spiked 89% from the previous year: 27 to 51.[25] Fewer and fewer whites will apply and fewer and fewer deserving candidates as a whole will apply. America's police departments

---

[25]FBI National Press Office, May 11, 2015

will come to look like and behave like the corrupt and inept agencies of the Third-World.

In other words, there is a self-fulfilling prophecy of sort being played out. The remedies and reactions to the media's and DOJ's fictitious crisis of an open season on black males by white police will in fact create real problems of police corruption and brutality.

Diversity in recruiting will be valued more than competence and character. The applicant bar will be lowered. The ranks will be filled with underqualified people of questionable character. Predator and police will be indistinguishable in many areas. These "perfected" police forces will be unscrupulous and easily controlled by the federal government to do their bidding.

Attorney General Loretta Lynch is who Baltimore Prosecutor Marilyn Mosby and Mayor Stephanie Rawlings-Blake interfaced with in the wake of the Freddie Gray controversy as they invited a DOJ consent decree over the Baltimore Police.

Freddie Carlos Gray, Junior

On April 12, 2015 Baltimore police arrested Freddie Gray; a 25-year-old black male on probable cause for carrying an illegal knife. On April 19, 2015 Gray died of a spinal cord injury. A cursory review of circumstances raised concern that police misconduct was the cause of death. Without a thorough investigation Baltimore's State Attorney, Marilyn Mosby, hastily charged six officers (three white and three black) involved in the arrest and/or transport of Gray.

The hasty filing of charges ignored professional expectations and due process required of Mosby's oath. Mosby acted on emotion and political activism. She moved so fast that there was no time to study the autopsy or Gray's medical history. There was no use of the Grand Jury to probe and vet the facts. There was no probable cause to charge the officers. The prosecutor was anything but fair and objective. It was Mike Nifong's Duke

Lacrosse case all over again. In this case what makes the political aspect of this misuse of power more egregious is political incest. Mosby's husband (Nick Mosby) is on the Baltimore City Council. Furthermore, Billy Murphy, the attorney for the family of Freddie Gray donated $4,000 to Marilyn Mosby's campaign.

Who will apply to be a police officer in places like Baltimore where due process is ignored and criminal charges are filed on officers by social justice? Already we see the results of fear turned to apathy in the ranks. Gun violence is up 60% in Baltimore over last year with 32 shootings just over the (2015) Memorial Day weekend alone marking the most violent month in 15 years.[26] In the first half of 2015 murder is up 19% in 35 big cities and Chicago in the lead with 252 as of August 2015 (up 20%). Baltimore had 45 murders in July alone. Saint Louis and Milwaukee have seen murder increases of 64% to 88%. All of this after 2013 marked a fifty-year low in murder according the Major Cities Police Chiefs Association.[27]

The media and the Obama Administration intentionally created a powder keg across the country.

Violent crime is up dramatically in Seattle due to a social justice inspired DOJ consent decree on Seattle Police stemming from complaints carried in the media about use of force on minorities.

In the first two months of 2011 Seattle had two murders. In the first two months of 2012 (following the consent decree) Seattle had nine murders and three more by April. Mayor McGinn agreed with the suggestion that there is a cause-and-effect relationship between Eric Holder's DOJ scrutiny and the rise in violent crime. He seems to understand that previously

---

[26]Heather Mac Donald, *The New Nationwide Crime Wave*, The Wall Street Journal, May 29, 2015
[27]Judy Woodruff, *After Declining For Decades, Homicides Surge in Cities Across the Country,* PBS News Hour, August 4, 2015

proactive officers fear a politically correct administration more than they do dangerous criminals.

Following the DOJ's fabrication of a systemic problem with racist, white officers in places like Ferguson, Missouri (stemming from the August 9, 2014 shooting death of an "unarmed black teen", Michael Brown, by a "white" police officer, Darren Wilson) — the Ferguson, Mo. Police Department will be descended upon by a bullying consent decree. Violent crime will rise there. The same theme keeps repeating itself across the country.

In April 2001 black riots broke out in Cincinnati, Ohio. The riots were supposedly triggered by the fatal police shooting of an "unarmed black teenager" (sound familiar?). The suspect was, in fact, an adult.

At the time of the officer-involved shooting, the 19-year-old suspect was fleeing police in Cincinnati's most crime-ridden and drug-infested neighborhood. Additionally, the suspect had fourteen outstanding warrants for his arrest.

A brave officer cornered the suspect in a dark alley. The suspect responded by reaching into his waistband at which point the officer shot him once in the chest.

In incidents like this the media emphasize the "victim" was unarmed. This becomes the litmus test of public opinion rather than the facts and the relevant legal prism surrounding police use of force.

In *People v. Benjamin* the court's opinion recognized that it is common knowledge that the waistband is where a handgun is often carried. Although reaching into the waistband "…could be considered innocuous behavior, it would be unrealistic to require (the police) to assume the risk that the defendant's conduct was in fact innocuous or innocent. **Indeed, it would be absurd to suggest that a police officer has to await the glint of steel before he can preserve his safety."**

Cameras fanned the flames helping the cause of race hustlers in Cincinnati that had been stirring the pot for quite some time, accusing the Cincinnati Police of institutional racism.

The facts tell a different story though, one which is egregiously ignored by the media: a Cincinnati police officer is 27 times more likely to die at the hands of a black male than a black male is to die at the hands of the Cincinnati police.[28]

Keep in mind that well over 95% of police shootings nationally are ruled justified and are initiated as acts of self-defense.

No matter though: Cincinnati neighborhoods were looted and torched by black mobs, and blacks destroyed millions of dollars of property. The Cincinnati Police Department came under a consent decree by the DOJ which crippled their desire and ability to fight crime and do their job. Crime soared and effective law enforcement ceased to exist as a result of race politics played in the media.

On April 30, 2012 the DOJ's Civil Rights Division announced that it is exercising its authority to investigate the county prosecutor's office in Missoula County, Montana. Missoula County Prosecutor Fred Van Valkenburg said that this is the first time ever that the DOJ has used its federal authority to investigate a local prosecutor's office. He said that the heavy hand of the federal government is sending a message to all local prosecutors in America that the Feds can second guess every decision they make.

Van Valkenburg has received no explanation from the DOJ for the intrusion. Therefore, he was left to speculate that an allegation of gender discrimination had been made, tied to rape cases that were properly declined for prosecution due to lack of

---

[28]Heather Mac Donald, *What Really Happened in Cincinnati*, City Journal Summer 2001.

probable cause (in violation of social justice).[29] There was no push by the press to vet the DOJ's motives.

Gatekeepers

Police are the gatekeeper to a criminal justice system being manipulated. Intimidated and "trained" police are expected to feed the system. When police buy into Marxist propaganda in the name of "public safety", "national security" or "social justice" they find no objection to the damage and injustice they inflict because they are programmed to feel noble or self-righteous doing it.

There are still many peace officers that think clearly and desperately want to work for Sheriffs and Chiefs who understand their oath and know that for good or bad our conduct sets the example for the officers coming behind us. Honoring one's oath is made difficult when police CEOs codify political correctness in policy and enforce it in performance evaluations. Folding to media pressure there are Chiefs who have told their officers, "We are arresting too many blacks."

Marxists use organizations such as the Southern Poverty Law Center and rabid feminists in NOW (National Organization of Women) to manipulate the public perception of society and police. Their attendant media frame and amplify their arguments through selective outrage. Marxists use the power of the media to provoke and divide the population, and intimidate and indoctrinate police.

The fact is that police will never be more professional than they are today. Furthermore, it will never be better for minorities in America than it is right now. They should respect

---

[29] http://johndavis.gonevis.com/how-many-rape-accusations-are-false/ U.S. Department of Justice, FBI study –2012 "False Allegations of Adult Crimes". The study found that 60% of rape cases in the U.S. are "false accusations", 15% end in acquittal of the accused, 8% the accuser recants, and 17% end in conviction. **In summary, 83% of rape investigations nationwide result in no conviction** due to false accusations, recantation by the accuser and acquittal.

the system, for it has served them well in the balance of history. Instead, most blacks (based on voting patterns) are tools for its destruction. Other blacks (the minority within the minority) who defend the American Way are shunned and insulted by race hustlers that call them "Uncle Toms" or "house niggers."

Just after World War One Willi Munzenberg, the Propaganda Chief for the Communist International, stated: **"All news is lies and all propaganda is disguised as news."**

CHAPTER SIX

Policing the New Majority

"Government-imposed 'tolerance' merely masks true bigotry."
— Mike Adams

"From the moment the organizer enters a community he lives, dreams, eats, breathes, sleeps only one thing and that is to build the mass power base of what he calls the army." – Saul Alinsky, *Rules for Radicals*.

The mantra of *"strength through diversity"* smacks of Orwellian-Newspeak. Diversity can be defined as "a state of division." There is no unity in a state of division. Division does not strengthen a country, but only the political interests of those who promote it.

Yes, it is important to know about the Buffalo Soldiers, the Tuskegee Airmen, the Navajo Code Talkers and other inspiring American stories. The contributions, sacrifices and bloodshed by minorities for America are real, measurable and valued, but they are also incidental — when compared — to that of the white majority over the course of our history.

Whites are the only group that could not have been removed from our history and there still be a United States of America.

The unparalleled contributions marked by generational sacrifices, creativity, inventions, innovations, faith, courage and experiences of the European majority (Northern and Western Europeans in particular) over epoch periods are the origins of what was observed by Alexis de Tocqueville and others as American culture.

This is the culture and character immigrants (regardless of expanded European immigration or race) had sought to assimilate to at least in their public face. This is also the culture and character that black Americans modeled before President Johnson's Great Society replaced the father with welfare. Over the last fifty years that norm, that standard, that identity has been debased, diluted, vilified and now rejected by every group including much of today's white generation.

American culture is broken. It is in full retreat making it nearly impossible to rally the nationalism needed as the antidote for our suicidal cocktail.

A rhetorical question asked by Pat Buchanan in his book *Death of the West* captures the essence of our time, "Are we a nation or are we an economy?" This is the intended consequence of the Diversity Movement — to blow a hole in our identity so big that we cannot muster the clarity, nationalism, and unity of outrage necessary to rally in self-defense from tyranny.

It is no wonder so many young whites have an identity crisis and that white male teens have the highest suicide rate. Many walk around with ear buds listening to gangster rap, wearing sagging pants and have their hat on backward. They abandon the glory and substance of American culture for a morally and intellectually bankrupt substitute that Hollywood and the music industry glamorize and sell as *black culture* (Though I hear no objection to that depiction in the media from "black leadership," I know that the minority within the minority — namely black Southern Baptist pastors and conservatives — have something to say about it, but are ignored).

More and more young whites operate on the most base of human instincts marked by any combination of promiscuous, intemperate carnal feasting; illegal drug use, narcissism, materialism, selfishness, money worship, and gang life — all of which are seductively packaged and marketed by the entertainment industry. **There is an epidemic of white trash in America!**

Diminishing the regeneration of culture and patriotism within each subsequent generation is the key to weakening resistance to the transformation of our culture and institutions.

Targeting white youth accelerated the collapse of the American mainstream through corrupting the moral fiber and identity of its principle trustees. The Marxist architects know it is counter-productive to "social progress" for white youth to have a strong cultural and guilt-free connection with American history, Christianity and Western Civilization. Reverence for these breeds patriotism, nationalism, moral absolutes and cultural bias; all obstacles to "progress." Such reverence translates into points of resistance to Stalinist re-education efforts.

The Diversity Movement is pushing the culture and character that built the American Nation to the back of the bus. The fact that the pledge of allegiance, prayer in school and English as the national language are all topics of debate in America shows how unraveled we are. The objective of Marxists is a transfer of power through the destruction of our culture and institutional framework. The Diversity Movement has sown the seeds of white guilt and self-hate effectively weakening resistance in each subsequent generation.

Destroying American culture is essential, but not enough for Marxists. A new majority must be formed to fill the vacuum; one with no ties to the past. The new majority will feel no nostalgia for what has been taken away because they will have no "American" frame of reference.

The Marxists are using unrestricted Third World immigration as a weapon of war and as a tool for societal "ethno-engineering."

The policies of open borders and the expansion of the welfare state are rapidly changing America's demographics and culture. By 2043, the majority of the U.S. population will be non-white.

There are 147 Latinos, 43 Asian-Americans, 41 African-Americans, and 6 Caucasians born every hour in the United States.[30] In just over one generation (twenty-seven years), whites will no longer be the majority, but only a plurality. There are enormous and intentional consequences for this that are being seen and suffered now and will intensify each year.

Immigration law is meant to protect what and who is already here, not to put our needs and security second to any portion of what a 2014 United Nations report tallied as 51 million refugee and asylum seekers. The U.S. takes in 70% of the world's

---

[30] National Journal, *The Economic Impact of Changing Demographics in the United States*, September 5, 2015.

emigrating refugees annually rather than just help them in their home countries.

In addition, the U.S. allows one million aliens in legally annually and many more millions *illegally* by looking the other way — nullifying immigration law, until President Trump took office. In the next ten years, 10 million more legal immigrants alone will enter the United States. According to the Senate Subcommittee on Immigration, this number is equivalent to the combined populations of seven cites: Dallas (1.2 million), Denver (650,000), Boston (65,000), Chicago (2.7 million), Los Angeles (3.9 million), and Atlanta (450,000). Again, this number does not account for refugees and millions more *illegals* and their children born here.[31]

The subcommittee projected that in the next 8 years the percentage of our country that is foreign born will reach 1 in 7. Contrast that to what it was in 1970: 1 in 21. Since 1970 the foreign-born population in the U.S. has quadrupled to 42.1 million in 2013.

Jeff Session as a senator (R-AL) wrote in an op-ed, "What we need now is immigration moderation: slowing the pace of new arrivals so that wages can rise, welfare rolls can shrink and the forces of assimilation can knit us all more closely together." What the honorable Mr. Sessions failed to recognize is that most of these immigrant groups resist assimilation or at best are discouraged to do so by a media and federal government under the influence of the Diversity Movement.

The Mexican population is the largest and fastest growing minority group in the United States. A population must have a 2.1% birth rate to maintain a steady population. The U.S. birth rate is 2.0. When broken down ethnically the Anglo birth rate in the U.S. is 1.6 %, (below replacement levels) while the Hispanic

---

[31] Caroline May, *U.S. To Admit in More Legal Immigrants in Decade Than The Combined Populations of 7 Major Cities*, Breitbart, April 13, 2015

birth rate is 2.7%. In California Hispanics are the majority representing 31% of the population. Among the 35.5 million Hispanics in the U.S. (up 13 million since 1990), Mexicans represent the largest group followed by Puerto Ricans and Cubans.

Hispanics in Idaho comprise 11% of the population – excluding illegal aliens. Hispanics make up 15.6% of Idaho's adult prison population and 12.2% of the rider program (Idaho Department of Corrections Inmate Population Mix File Sept. 2017). Whites are 89% of the state population and make up 74.6% of the prison population and 76.1% of the rider program. This disproportionate Hispanic prison figure is cause enough to look more closely at this burgeoning immigrant group.

Despite what we were told by President Bush, Mexican culture is substantively different from American culture. There are no economically thriving, low-crime, desirable neighborhoods in the U.S. where the Spanish language and Mexican culture are dominant. The character and quality of life in these neighborhoods has changed to an unrecognizable degree from what it was before the former majority moved out.

I want to be perfectly clear about some important distinctions. When I use the term, "**Americans of Mexican descent**" I am referring to fully assimilated Americans as opposed to "**Mexicans in America**" (an entirely unassimilated population) or "**Mexican-Americans**" (a partially assimilated population).

Americans of Mexican descent are successful because they adopted the authentic American culture as their own. Many have served in the U.S. military. Many own businesses and are productive, law abiding, patriotic Americans. They are not conflicted by a dual allegiance or insist on the prefixed title "Mexican-American." They leave the barrio (Mexican neighborhood) and abandon cultural handicaps to live with other Americans of like-mind and values, thereby giving the next generation a better chance to succeed as Americans. This is the American experience, each generation doing better than the preceding one. A measure of assimilation that I look for is a self-deprecating sense of humor. Take my friend Tony (Antonio) for example. Not only will Tony laugh at a Mexican joke I tell him, but also he will respond with a Mexican joke or act out a parody that is funnier. To the detriment of our country, Americans of Mexican descent like Tony are eclipsed by the volume of the other two groups mentioned above and by their hyper-sensitive, reactionary cultures.

ASSIMILATION

Assimilation of Mexicans to American culture is slowed in part because of culture, in part because of proximity to Mexico, in part because of the numbers flooding into the U.S. and in part due to separatist activism encouraged by Marxists here who promote a collective identity.

My home state of Idaho is a refugee resettlement receiving area. Since 1980 The College of Southern Idaho has helped resettle 5,000 refugees. From 2001 thru 2011 Idaho received 5,341 refugees. In 2013 Idaho received 920 refugees (1.32 percent of the total of refugees arriving to the U.S.). Beginning in October of 2015 (the new fiscal year) 300 more refugees are coming to Idaho from Syria. By 2017 the cities of Boise and Twin Falls are to receive up to 2,000 more refugees from Syria, Iraq, the Democratic Republic of the Congo and Somalia. Boise will take 70% of the refugees and Twin Falls 30%. Idaho's refugee population comes from 18 countries and speaks as many or more languages. Being marked a refugee by ICE is the premier immigrant status; it qualifies one to receive welfare with a fast-track to citizenship within five years.

Resettlement agencies start with small numbers. Prior to President Trump's policy changes Boise was positioned over the next twenty years to become unrecognizable; its lack of diversity "problem" would have been "cured." A small city cannot integrate these numbers to the degree that more densely populated areas might. Thank you President Trump!

Idaho's refugee resettlement program began in 1975. It had moral intentions narrowly aimed at Southeast Asia in part to integrate children fathered there by our servicemen. Today the program is much broader and translates to new voters and the further dilution of our dominant and defining culture. Refugee integration, assimilation and self-reliance are not concerns of the power hungry elite. They and their children live away from the earthshaking consequences of their self-serving policies.

Nationally, 30 percent of "English-learner" students are third-generation American citizens![32] **Third generation!!** This is the result of government programs designed to discourage assimilation. The reality is that a significant part of our population is comprised of "American citizens" who are not "*Americans*;" the terms are no longer synonymous. There is no argument against the fact that speaking English is essential to absorbing the culture and inculcating all things "American." Hispanics have the highest dropout rate and the highest teen pregnancy rate. They are the largest users of government healthcare. There is much to be concerned about within this emerging new ethnic majority.

But consider Dearborn, Michigan — home of one of the largest and fastest growing Muslim population in the United States. Sharia Law is challenging state and U.S. law there. In the Twin Cities area of Minnesota there is a population of 100,000 Somali Muslims. This unassimilated group is the largest Somali population outside of Somalia and is proving to be a ripe recruiting ground for ISIS. Similarly, the U.S. is home to the largest Nigerian population outside of Nigeria. We take more Nigerian immigrants than any other country.

The U.S. is taking larger numbers of immigrants and refugees than we did before 1970, but from fewer countries due to Ted Kennedy's *Immigration Reform Act of 1965*. The Act for the first time placed a limit on immigrants coming from the Western Hemisphere. For 50 years now (two generations) the U.S. has been giving preference to third-world immigrants. This switch in preference brought counter cultures to the U.S. not

---

[32]Heather MacDonald, *Practical Thoughts on Immigration*, Imprimus, February 2015.

well suited to assimilate. This change was by design. Our cultural backbone is being broken. **There is no more important crisis to our national survival than immigration.** Colonization is well underway and not only from Mexico anymore.

What will happen to the streets of America when there are more tax takers than taxpayers and the government nipples begin to run dry? Already half of the population pays no income tax; they are either the working poor trying to survive or the dependent "looter" as Ayn Rand so aptly refers to them in her book *Atlas Shrugged*. We are taught that the looter is nobler than the producer; he is "disenfranchised" — a victim of the haves. It is insensitive and hateful to criticize the virtuous looter. Shut your mouth and pay up "haves"! *"From each according to his ability, to each according to his need."* — Karl Marx

The *Immigration Reform Act of 1965*, the *Immigration Reform Act of 1986* (allowed illegal aliens who were granted amnesty to sponsor others — referred to as "daisy chain immigration"), the *Voter Reform Act of 1964* (eliminating the literacy requirement to vote) and President Johnson's (cradle-to-grave) *Great Society*, all combined: have damaged our national identity and caused the looter population to swell, while the number of taxpayers shrinks.

The objective of Marxists is for the productive, traditional society to become a minority; slaves too small to ever vote American culture back in power but yet large enough to provide a steady stream of taxes to support the Marxist State. The producers will be large enough in number to pay the bills, but small enough to control. This is why they must disarm us — another agenda item of tyranny. This was the aim of the failed Fast and Furious operation and the United Nations Small Arms Treaty (July 27, 2012).

RED BADGE

When the ratio of taxpayers to looters becomes even more grossly imbalanced the tone of our self-righteous, nanny state will change dramatically. It will begin to beat the sacred cows. Government will have to become efficient. The once honored looters will become a liability to the elite that their dependence brought to power.

The first group to go will likely be poor blacks and blacks with violent criminal records. It is a business decision for the Marxists. The State will look at the small return on investment of tax dollars spent generation after generation and eliminate them.

It is tragic that twice, 97% of black voters cast their ballot blindly and voted for race. For president they voted for a person (Obama) that does not share their pedigree; an elitist whose paradigm holds no love, no loyalty and soon no use for them despite his posturing to the contrary from the free throw line.

Under Obama the black poverty rate was 27%; up from 25% in 2009. Black unemployment was 11.6 % (double that of whites). Black unemployment for ages 16 to 19 was 36.8%. From 2010 to 2013 the net wealth of blacks has declined 34%.

Government will have to stretch the confiscated wealth of a diminished tax base to cover a growing dependent population. The least productive will be the target of scrutiny and accountability never before seen. The targeted groups will have no moral ground to argue in their defense because they stood idle and cheered the injustices carried out on White America as it was dispossessed and the society it built was forcibly redistributed in the name of social justice.

With the reorganization of society and transfer of power complete the voting bloc of blind followers and looters (who Vladimir Lenin referred to as "useful idiots') will have served their purpose; they will act like spoiled children. During the revolution, they demanded "justice" and "democracy." They worked to subvert our institutions and dispossess the bedrock, old guard culture. As a result, social justice and mob rule corrupted Due Process and the Rule of Law.

After the Marxists declare victory this element will demand more and become unruly when "entitlements" are rationed and they are told "no" for the first time by the State they've worshiped as the great arbitrator. When they are given less and when they are made to report for menial public works jobs for the money that once magically appeared in their bank account each month — they will revolt. Police will finally be unleashed. The media will do a 180. They will champion the police to crush the rebellion. For the moment, police remain the villain and the looters are bribed into obedience with welfare because they are still useful idiots in the Marxist Cultural Revolution underway.

Much of the funding for the looters comes from transfer payments in a Ponzi scheme larger than anything Charles Ponzi or Bernard Madoff could ever have dreamed of: Social Security. With the oldest of the 80 million baby boomers already collecting in 2012, the collapse is near. Trump's economic policies are stalling the collapse.

The well is going to run dry. For the moment the looters strut, many of them "with their pants on the ground" (as the song goes), carefree about tomorrow. The gravy train provides "Obama money", food, clothing, housing, bus tokens, and cell phones: all "free" for them. They can "Occupy Wall Street" on your dime and promote fault, envy and resentment toward you (the haves).

It is the police and ultimately the military under the unconstitutional authority of the NDAA that will restore order with brutal force and FEMA detention camps. The Occupy Wall Street Movement and operation Jade Helm each foreshadowed the unrest to come and the solidification of an evolving police state rising to meet resistance from either end of the political spectrum.

RED BADGE
"Civilian National Security Force"

On July 2, 2008, while campaigning in Colorado Springs, Colorado, then-candidate Barack Hussein Obama made a disturbing and cryptic statement in a speech.

In talking about his plans to double the size of the Peace Corps and nearly quadruple the size of AmeriCorps, he made a shocking pledge:

"We cannot continue to rely on our military in order to achieve the national security objectives we've set. We've got to have a civilian national security force that's just as powerful, just as strong, just as well-funded."

The statement was ignored and even suppressed by major media outlets.

Obama did not elaborate on what he meant by "a civilian national security force" and to this day he has never elaborated or explained what he was referring to.

It is important to realize that every totalitarian government, dictatorship, monarchy and tyrannical regime throughout all history has created and employed some form of domestic "security force" or secret police to monitor, intimidate, control and terrorize the civilian population into forced obedience and subservience to the ruling regime. For instance, ancient Rome under Emperor Augustus had its Praetorian Guard.[33]

In the 20th Century all the world's totalitarian regimes, dictatorships, etc. nationalized their domestic police organizations (effectively putting them under centralized government command and control) and usually referred to them

---

[33] This internal army operated against Roman law. Under Augustus' direction it slowly evolved from an invisible force (intentionally un-uniformed) to 9,000 uniformed, armed soldiers patrolling the city in formation as if there was a pending invasion. There was no such threat. *They* were the threat.

as "security forces," "national security forces," various "guard" units, or "security services." This pattern continues into the 21st Century, with U.S. military and intelligence agencies often training other nations' "security forces" (secret police).

Refer back to Chapter Two on the mechanisms of totalitarian government control in the largest and most murderous police state in history: the USSR. The primary tool used by the Soviet Communist Party to control and terrorize the people was the MVD "interior troops." By definition, the MVD could accurately be described as a "civilian national security force" in that they were not the military, they were only used inside the borders of the USSR, and they were under the civilian control of the KGB. In a frighteningly accurate way, the Soviet MVD was — to use Obama's own words — "just as powerful, just as strong, just as well-funded" as the Soviet military.

Now recall that the MVD carried out many of the most heinous crimes against the people in the long dark history of the Soviet Union: mass murder, mass arrests, wide-scale torture, genocide, etc. The blood of millions of innocents is on the hands of the Soviet MVD.

Throughout his formative years Obama was mentored and schooled by bona-fide Marxists — Frank Marshall Davis, Bill Ayers, etc. — and by his actions and statements it is obvious to anyone with critical thinking skills that Obama is an avowed Marxist.

Is Obama's cryptically described yet undefined "civilian national security force" a Soviet-style MVD?

It is self-evident that the U.S. Department of Homeland Security (DHS) has absolutely nothing to do with our security or safety: there have been more terrorist incidents on our soil since the creation of DHS than ever before. Our borders are not only unsecure, they're wide-open! Anyone with hostile intent can easily slip into our country over the Mexican border.

RED BADGE

Even more troubling is the fact that the DHS continuously acquires more authority, more personnel, more weapons and more military equipment. As increasing numbers of federal agencies come under its organizational umbrella, it is obvious that the DHS has everything to do with securing the totalitarian police state that is being erected all around us.

With all of this in mind, Obama's allusion to a "civilian national security force" and its obvious implications do not bode well for America, for individual freedom and for the free exercise of human and constitutional rights.

In George Orwell's seminal work, *1984*, protagonist Winston Smith is given a horrifying picture of life under a tyrannical regime:

"But always – do not forget this, Winston – always there will be the intoxication of power, constantly increasing and constantly growing subtler…If you want a picture of the future, imagine a boot stamping on a human face – forever."

"There is no safety for honest men, but by believing all possible evil of evil men, and by acting with promptitude, decision, and steadiness on that belief." — Edmund Burke

"There is no crueler tyranny than that which is perpetuated under the shield of law and in the name of justice."

— Montesquieu

"Government is not reason, it is not eloquence – it is FORCE! Like fire, it is a dangerous servant and a fearful master."

George Washington

"The price of liberty is eternal vigilance."

Thomas Jefferson

Now that you see where the population is headed let's look at the devolving police culture that currently serves them.

Local law enforcement is the part of the public sector most scrutinized by the oligarchs of the Diversity Movement. They need the police to submit to their paradigm (co-opted) or be replaced (federalized). Marxists need to intimidate and control local police to abandon their oath and do their bidding. This is being accomplished by:

- Discrediting them in the media
- Calling for federal oversight
- Changing the demographics in the ranks
- Replacing alpha male recruits with beta male recruits
- Reshaping police culture
- Militarizing police
- Redirecting policing priorities
- Altering their view of the streets they patrol

The Diversity Movement negatively impacts police hiring and promotional practices. These social justice-inspired changes are touted as necessary to combat racism in the ranks. The resulting internal reconstruction compromises police effectiveness and public safety. Round table discussions about comprehensive strategies to effectively combat crime are all but worthless when limited by the guardrails of the Politically Correct discourse between intimidated and mediocre officers. *For the moment*, the Marxists do not want the number of criminals and welfare cheats decreased any more than they want the U.S. – Mexico border controlled. These useful idiots — dependent on government — serve a purpose. They grow to form the new (un-assimilated) balkanized majority needed to vote for the Left and collapse the system under the weight of their dependence.

Rational Profiling

(The adjective **ra·tion·al** means, "based on or in accordance with reason or logic.")

Nationally, law enforcement administrators are leery of media attention on allegations of racial profiling. This fear resulted in the San Diego Police Department adopting a policy that requires officers to document the race of every motorist stopped. Say nothing of the disproportionate amount of violent crime, drug sales, and theft committed by minorities: this policy is aimed at hobbling proactive cops (86% of whom are white nationally) by treating them as though being proactive is criminal. Furthermore, it is not "over policing" for officers to go where the 911 calls for service take them and then arrest who the evidence points to.

Profiling which also considers race, when done *rationally*, is a wise practice for daily living. We all do it. It is unfortunate that actor Danny Glover could not hail a cab in New York City, but cab drivers are familiar with being disproportionately cheated out of fares and robbed by black males. These drivers, exercise rational profiling based on a demonstrated pattern of behavior. Similarly, a young black person being followed by loss prevention in a store is not persecution. It is reasonable for business owners or the public in general (black, white or other) to have an elevated level of concern given theft offender demographics. A substantive contributing factor to this is a person's public presentation.

In an article titled, **"Is Racial Profiling Racist?"** Dr. Walter E. Williams, a distinguished professor of economics at George Mason University, and who is himself a black man, stated the following:

"If racial profiling is racism, then the cab drivers of Washington, D.C., they themselves mainly blacks and Hispanics, are all for it. A District taxicab commissioner, Sandra Seegars, who is black, issued a safety-advice statement urging D.C.'s 6,800 cabbies to refuse to pick up 'dangerous looking' passengers. She described 'dangerous looking' as a young black guy ... with shirt tail hanging down longer than his coat, baggy pants, unlaced tennis shoes."

In his highly acclaimed book *Suicide of a Superpower*, Pat Buchanan states:

"After a cabbie in New York City was shot four times by a robber wearing a hooded sweatshirt, identified by police as Hispanic, the president of the New York State Federation of Taxi Drivers Fernando Mateo (who is himself black and Hispanic) advised his drivers to profile blacks and Hispanics for their own protection."

"Said Mateo, 'the God's honest truth is that 99% of the people that are robbing, stealing, killing these drivers are blacks and Hispanics'."

Let's be intellectually honest. A black male, U.S. Marine age twenty, dressed in uniform can enter a convenience store, buy chewing gum and not elicit concern from the clerk whatsoever. The same person can return to the store the following day dressed in a hoodie, with pants sagging and feel the clerk's eyes on him. He chose to present himself in thug-wear on his day off. The reaction he gets from the *clerk* (white, black and other) is not racism; it is reality. No different than whites, law-abiding black people practice rational profiling every day for survival.

The December 2014 edition of People magazine included an interview with the Obamas about race and what they teach their daughters on the subject. Their examples of racism were absurd. First Lady Michelle (supposedly) went to a Target store in disguise. Someone asked her to get something down from a shelf. She offered this as an example of racism. How ridiculous! She projects racism on to every white person. I'm sure she would feel insulted if she walked by an occupied car and heard the power locks activate. Hypersensitive and seeing "racism" everywhere, she lives in a substitute for reality constructed by Marxists in Academia.

On weekends I do not wear a tie. I am a pretty good handyman and often look the part. I have been mistaken as an employee in hardware stores and other places. I wasn't offended and if I could help I did.

Another comment in the People magazine article from the president was about stereotypes and how black males should not be perceived as more dangerous. But statistically speaking they are more dangerous Mr. President! And if they dress in thug wear they will get the reaction they are after.

Domino's Pizza franchises were accused of racism after announcing the discontinuation of service to predominantly black neighborhoods that were deemed too dangerous. This action stemmed from a string of pizza delivery robberies within the area in question. There is nothing arbitrary about this kind of racial profiling; it is rational and warranted in the face of reality.

It is unfortunate that law-abiding, responsible black people are sometimes caught in the middle of *rational* profiling. **But, is it the victims that give young black men a bad name?** <u>Negative perceptions will not change until the underlying behavior changes.</u> Marxists have laws passed and lawsuits filed to stop the use of reason and reality. In the name of social justice and pizza for all, they would deny a working person the right to apply what they know and discriminate for their safety.

Dr. Walter Williams points out the following in the same article referenced above, "Is Racial Profiling Racist?"

RED BADGE

"*The Pizza Marketing Quarterly* carried a story of charges of racial discrimination filed in St. Louis against Papa John's pizza delivery services. Papa John's district manager said she could not and would not ask her drivers to put their lives on the line. She added that the racial discrimination accusation is false because 75 to 85 percent of the drivers in the complaining neighborhood are black and, moreover, most of those drivers lived in the very neighborhood being denied delivery service."

In other words, black pizza drivers refused to deliver pizzas IN THEIR OWN NEIGHBORHOODS out of a well-founded fear for their personal safety!

It is immoral and unlawful for police to stop someone just because they are of a certain skin color and for no other reason. I would turn a fellow officer in for doing that. I do not doubt it happens, but it is less likely to be done by white officers in recent decades given the higher scrutiny they face. I do not believe it is nearly as common as the media would have you think. In fact, I believe it is quite rare. The vast majority of (white officer) police contacts of minorities are professional. The aftermath of one such contact went viral after a post on Face Book. Motorist William Stack, a twenty-two-year-old black male critiqued his April 2015 stop in South Carolina by a white officer. He made some refreshing and mature comments on not broad brushing all police officers as racist villains or the people they use force on as their undeserved victims.

Profiling rooted in reasonable suspicion (not race) is essential for effective, *proactive* (seeking out the criminal) police work, but fear of an accusation of stopping someone for "driving-while-black" turns many officers from proactive to *reactive* (They become "AAA with a gun": Armed report takers driving with blinders on). My motives as a patrolman were never

RED BADGE

questioned for making *pretext stops* [34] on possible or known outlaw motor cycle club members or Skin Heads; only black, Asian and Mexican gang members. Below is a letter from the Civil Rights Division of the U.S. Department of Justice clearing me of a criminal complaint filed with the FBI. It is an example of the kinds of empty, knee-jerk complaints that proactive officers get and that the feds are all too eager to investigate.

---

[34] "Case Law." If police have reasonable, objective grounds to make a traffic stop any underlying motive to stop the subject, as pretext is irrelevant. (Pg. I-26 State vs. Law, 115 Idaho 769,769 9.2d1141 (ct. app 1989).

U. S. Department of Justice

Civil Rights Division

DLP:RWR:bbm
DJ 144-22-293

Washington, D.C. 20530
September 03, 1996

Mr. Douglas E. Traubel
~~[redacted]~~
~~[redacted]~~ Idaho ~~[redacted]~~

Dear Mr. Traubel

The Civil Rights Division, Department of Justice, recently completed its review of an investigation as reported by the Federal Bureau of Investigation. This matter concerned allegations that you were involved in a criminal violation of civil rights statutes regarding the deprivation of the civil rights of Tariq Quinn McWilliams.

After a careful review of the investigative reports in this matter, and based upon the information currently available to this Department, we have concluded that this matter should be closed and that no further action is warranted.

Sincerely

Deval L. Patrick
Assistant Attorney General
Civil Rights Division

By: *[signature]*

Richard W. Roberts
Chief
Criminal Section

The year was 1996. I asked the Sheriff if I could work a temporary assignment as a one-man gang unit on the streets of Boise over the summer. My sergeant and peers joked and treated me like Don Quixote. They did not share my background as a gang officer from Southern California, but to the Sheriff's credit he approved it. On the first day I made a pretext traffic stop for a mechanical violation. As I approached the car I saw that the three occupants were dressed in gang attire.

On the back seat was a pistol grip shotgun with a blue bandana draped over it. I ordered the occupants to place their hands above their heads. The rear seat and front seat passengers did so immediately. The driver did not comply with this reasonable and necessary command.

I struck the driver on the left side of his face with the back of my left hand as I pointed my gun at him and repeated my command; he complied. A search for additional weapons revealed brass knuckles concealed under the driver seat and gang paraphernalia. The passengers were white.

The driver, McWilliams, was a light-skin mulatto, age 18. His mother — a white woman — was the complainant. She had no interest in my account or concerns about her son's obvious interest or involvement in gang life. I was the enemy.

Fast forward. In 2009 McWilliams committed a murder. He stabbed a man in front of a Boise bar. I was assigned the follow-up investigation: He is in prison. Mom should have listened to me. I have had my share of complaints for similar proactive policing; none have been sustained, but waiting for the outcome each time is stressful.

Detective Traubel with the fruits of the traffic stop

Intimidated white officers reduce the numbers of minority contacts, even though probable cause or reasonable suspicion warrants action. This renders minority neighborhoods in particular more vulnerable. This was a part of the reason I left California for Idaho. To my disappointment nothing was different.

Officers everywhere come to realize that they are paid the same whether they make an arrest or not. Many become RODs (retired on duty). Arrests in Baltimore were down 56% in May

2015 compared with 2014 (following the Freddie Gray media spin).[35]

Sitting in the Captain's office feeling guilty until proven innocent for their motives is a haunting memory that influences officers to be less proactive. More and more officers ignore the black juvenile wearing gang clothing and smoking on the corner during school hours. Surviving your politically correct administration to retirement is more challenging than surviving a violent run-in with a criminal.

Institutional cowardice in police administrations empowers race hustlers while severely hampering effective law enforcement. Today the police are pushed back on their heels, not the crooks. I have seen this in Southern California when activist groups throw out the race card, rally the media and complain to the mayor and Chief — for profit — under the guise of calling for justice.

"Community Organizers" understand the power they have to put officers on the defense. They teach provocateurs to cry wolf and throw out the race card. They draw attention to themselves by dramatic antics and shouting words and phrases that might convince passersby that they are being brutalized, and their rights trampled.

Police need "reasonable suspicion" to detain a person and investigate potential criminal conduct. Reasonable suspicion is defined as "…specific and articulable facts that the suspect has been, is, or is about to engage in criminal activity."

When I worked as a peace officer in Southern California, there was a black man in San Diego known as "The Walker." The Walker would set up police and sue for civil rights violations. He would wear his hair in long dreadlocks, dance alone crazily and carry on in public, drawing attention to himself.

---

[35] Heather Mac Donald, *The New Nationwide Crime Wave*, The Wall Street Journal, May 29, 2015

His behavior was lawful but purposefully bizarre, thus arousing public and police suspicion.

When out of character, "The Walker" proved to be an articulate man — with an agenda. He set out to prove that reasonableness is a subjective test based on institutionalized white cultural norms. He was one of the early foot soldiers of the Diversity Movement. He set out to find fault, manufacture victims and challenge the Old Guard's cultural standard of measuring "reasonable suspicion" — while getting paid from out-of-court settlements. It is the success of Leftist efforts like this that lead us down the slippery slope of relativism.

The American legal system is based on subjective reasonableness rooted in what was a dominant and mostly shared cultural prism. In order for a peace officer to detain someone, he must be able to articulate reasonable suspicion. In order for a peace officer to arrest someone, the higher standard of probable cause must be met. Although different, both standards are based on subjective reasonableness.

Everyday peace officers make judgments and decisions whether or not to take action and if so, what action to take. A jury of presumably reasonable people and a judge later determines if they agree with the officer. The minds of many jurors and judges are infected with political correctness. Fixed standards and a shared cultural prism are no more.

Consequently, hypersensitive judges and jurors are irrationally suspicious of the officer's motives. Granted, the defendant is presumed innocent, but political correctness makes it increasingly difficult for juries to render a well-reasoned verdict. Today, what constitutes a jury of peers may include a segment sympathetic to the subculture of the defendant (perhaps even resulting in jury nullification based on racial loyalty, counter-culture or even Sharia law). America is broken along many fracture points. The rapidly forming new majority will not rally to restore the binding culture of what is being lost; America is foreign to them.

The Duty to Apprehend

Police are taught that there are three categories of people: "Yes people," "No people," and "Maybe people." These distinctions suggest the obvious — that officers cannot talk everyone into handcuffs.

"Yes people" are compliant to a uniformed police presence. "No people" are fighters, runners or both. "Maybe people" can go either way. It is the last category where there are the most variables effecting the direction of a police contact.

Certainly the conduct and abilities of the officer are among the many variables. Each officer has a different background, intelligence, communication skills, command presence, temperament, education and limitations; they all perform differently. Yes, they all go through the same standardized basic training, but competence and character differ from officer to officer.

Some have athletic prowess and played contact sports growing up. Some come to the ranks with a frame of reference for physical confrontation limited to wedgies suffered during childhood. All, however, take the same oath. They must respond to 911 calls with different tools in the toolbox — outcomes will vary. A fit, 6'3", 220-pound officer might use a control hold to subdue a "no person" instantly. Given the same circumstance a 5'3", 135 pound, soft officer might necessarily use a Taser or deadly force.

In light of the controversy in Ferguson, Missouri surrounding the August 9, 2014 justified police shooting death of an eighteen-year-old, unarmed, violent black male, Michael Brown, by white officer, Darren Wilson, there are three facts to consider: First, every fight an officer is in involves at least one gun; the one he/she is wearing and must defend. Second, most eighteen-year-old males can out-last and ultimately overpower the average thirty-year-old man; this is in part why eighteen-year-old males are subject to the draft. Lastly, the premise launched by the media of an open season on young, black males by white police officers is outrageous. This myth is dispelled by DOJ reports on law enforcement officers killed and attacked (LEOKA studies), combined with year-to-year violent offender demographic information.

Public trust is a fragile treasure. Officers know that any use of force places their safety, career, and agency's reputation in jeopardy. Still, unnecessary escalation by police does happen. With that said, it is the least frequent of the variables in play leading to use of force.

Police walk a tightrope of laws, policies and moreover public opinion. Despite earnest recruiting efforts to increase diversity in the ranks over the last four decades, 86% of America's peace officers are white; most are male. Conversely, despite racial preferences and generous generational economic and educational assistance from taxpayers in the trillions of dollars earmarked for non-Asian minorities — **the fact remains: the overwhelming amount of violent crime in America year after year is committed by (young) black and Hispanic males** (Sources: yearly DOJ uniform crime reporting and *The Color of Crime; Race, Crime and Justice in America*: Second, Expanded Edition, New Century Foundation 2005).

NYPD is frequently attacked by the media for being a racist organization. In fact, "Unlike the Ku Klux Klan, the NYPD is not a whites-only organization. According to the latest edition of the department's *Crime and Enforcement Activity in New York City*, as of December 31, 2013, the NYPD's 34,584 uniformed officers were 51.8 percent white, 26.5 percent Hispanic, 15.8

percent black, 5.9 percent Asian, and 0.1 percent "other." If NYPD practices white supremacy, it's remarkably rusty."[36]

The reality (nationally) of who makes up the majority of police and who makes up the majority of violent offenders is used by the incredulous media to construct a false conclusion that modern law enforcement is nothing more than the Klan in blue. This is irresponsible. It is an insult to a noble profession. In 2014 the issue is not white vs. black, but police vs. criminal.

Certainly, there are cases of police brutality on minorities — just as there are on whites. In the interest of public trust, all of these incidents should come to light. Excessive use of force under the color of authority (perceived or real) always gets traction in the media when the perceived victim is non-white; not so when the roles are reversed: On August 11, 2014 (just two days after the death of Michael Brown) a black Salt Lake City police officer shot and killed an unarmed twenty-year-old, white man, Dillon Taylor. There was no media blitz and to-date the DOJ has not descended on Salt Lake.

The Obama Administration worked with the agenda-driven media and race hustlers the likes of Al Sharpton and Jesse Jackson to promote selective outrage, dividing the population along racial lines and convicting police in the court of public opinion — before the facts are in. Sharpton visited the White House over 80 times; he had Obama's ear. Another esteemed White House guest invited by Obama was a rapper named "Common" whose song "Assata" celebrates cop killer/fugitive Assata Shakur. She was a member of the Black Liberation Army and killed New Jersey Trooper Werner Foster in 1973. After her conviction she escaped and fled to Cuba where she remains.

---

[36]Deroy Murdock, *An Assassination of Truth*, National Review Online, January 8, 2015

RED BADGE

Thomas Sowell opined on why we spend so much money on a criminal justice system if we are holding court in the media with the mob as jury.

When black people are killed or harmed at the hands of whites the media feed us 24/7 spin the likes of which we saw in the Trayvon Martin case and the police shooting death of Michael Brown. There is no objectivity.

When Eric Holder came to St. Louis in the wake of Michael Brown's death, he said, "I am the Attorney General of the United States. But I am also a black man." Like President Obama's comments on Trayvon Martin and the Cambridge, Massachusetts (Brandeis University) case before, the knee-jerk, racially biased assumptions by this duo echoed from pulpits of stature is divisive. Their positions afford them credibility to the ignorant — dividing the country racially without regard for the truth. Obama and Holder are washed in racial bias and social justice ideology. Their irresponsible commentary injected into local issues usurps the Rule of Law and Due Process they took an oath to defend.

Cameras are wielded like swords pushing police administrators back on their heels. An intimidated police administration creates timid cops. Timid cops make minority communities less safe. Police learn that being reactive pays the same with half the risk to limb and livelihood. Rather than be proactive and work to prevent violent crime in these neighborhoods, some demoralized officers elect to drive in circles with blinders on. They show up after the fact to draw a chalk line around another tragic victim of black-on-black crime.

Today police are under a microscope like no other time in American history. This is not altogether undeserved or an entirely bad thing. Surely, police misconduct does happen. Someone needs to police the police. A responsible media could help, but they — like the DOJ — have lost all objectivity.

In this climate an officer's mind is distracted by worry of job loss and civil or criminal federal charges, retarding reaction time. While the suspect is deciding between fight-or-flight, the officer may be under-reacting due to analysis-paralysis.

When it comes to making an arrest or a detention the bottom line is this: the suspect has an obligation to submit, and the officer has a duty to apprehend.

There is no nice way to take a "no person" into custody. Even a peaceful protester using only *passive resistance* in the form of dead weight requires some level of force to arrest. It can look bad to a passerby particularly when the suspect is animated. The next level of resistance is a term coined, *"egressive resistance"* where a suspect is not trying to overpower an officer, but is trying to break free and escape. On the opposite end of the resistance spectrum is *active resistance.* The *"active aggressor"* attacks the officer to overpower and harm him.

Tragically, officers are murdered with their own guns when active aggressors overpower and disarm them. How many police murdered by minorities are in some part the result of a literally paralyzing amount of worry implanted into the officer's psyche by their administration, giving the advantage to the attacker during a life and death struggle?

All of this begs the question: What kind of police culture do you want? Do you want a double-minded police administration that reins in the real cops preferring armed report takers who never get a complaint, look the part, but can't deliver? Do you want Sheriffs and Chiefs to genuflect to external forces like the ACLU, the Southern Poverty Law Center, Al Sharpton, media spin and self-serving special interest groups?

I imagine that you want a culture of professional, competent, courageous and constitutional-minded officers.

I imagine that you want officers whose actions are motivated by a sense of duty balanced by the golden rule.

I imagine that you want officers armed with discretion, grace and mercy selected on meaningful criteria that hold the line on our quality of life.

I imagine that you want officers who seek out real criminals as opposed to criminalizing harmless behavior by being overzealous with no thought given to the spirit of the law, only the letter.

I imagine that you want officers whose performance is not graded by the number of tickets they write.

I imagine that you want officers with a sense of duty so strong that their oath trumps their prejudices.

I imagine that you want officers who although they know not all people contribute the same value to society, treat every human being as an equally precious life.

How is that kind of culture made? Not by Sheriffs, and Chiefs genuflecting to external forces and allowing their oath to be reshaped by the hammer of political correctness over the anvil of ignorance and fear.

It comes from bold leadership rooted in truth. It comes from coaching a culture. It comes from hiring officers with a servant's heart. It comes from holding cops and criminals accountable without regard to political forces undermining truth and the Rule of Law. And, it comes from holding on jealously to local control. Consider the conduct of BLM agents in Clark County, Nevada in 2014.

Forget whether or not the Bundys' argument was right or wrong. The use of force by armed federal bureaucrats playing cop was excessive. The late entry of the Sheriff on-scene prolonged the abuse. Where is the accountability? For the Sheriff it is in the hands of the voters. For the feds it sits in the in-box of a sleepy, senior bureaucrat across the country in D.C.

Praise President Trump for pardoning the Bundys, for disarming the FWS, and taking away their police powers. Trump is one man against an infected, bloated and unconstitutional Administrative State that is defended by Deep State operatives. Will Trump be a speed bump to the Marxist revolution or a pivot point back to the Republic? Time will tell.

In the meanwhile we are far from a restoration of the Republic. I have many concerns about the changing police culture in America, including the line between local and federal being blurred.

Irrespective of my concerns, local police — in their traditional role — deserve the benefit of doubt when they meet physical resistance doing a job most citizens would not entertain the thought of doing. The public should beware of media spin, hasty conclusions and false witnesses. They should suspend judgment until all of the facts are in. These brave men and women deserve that much consideration.

Duty to Apprehend Part II

There are three kinds of resistance an officer face: *Passive, "Egressive"* and *Active.*

Passive: Dead weight; an abortion protester for example.

Egressive: This is a term coined to describe a subject's efforts to break free from police and escape.

Active: This is the most serious level of resistance. The subject is trying to overpower an officer with the intent to harm or kill him.

- In Ferguson, Missouri evidence from three independent investigations is conclusive that Officer Wilson was faced with active resistance.

- In the Staten Island, New York officers were faced with low-level egressive resistance from Eric Garner.

Police can lawfully use force to:

- ✓ Effect an arrest
- ✓ Prevent escape
- ✓ Overcome resistance
- ✓ Maintain order

The amount of force used must be reasonable as measured by the totality of circumstances. Contrary to public opinion, when there is a complaint regarding police misconduct in general or excessive force in particular, police can and do more often than not properly police themselves. Of course, this requires integrity-centered leadership in the organization. Today's call for police reform argues a need for citizen review boards and/or federal oversight. Citizen review boards and federal oversight do not guarantee impartiality, morality or accountability.

I sat on a police peer review board. The board's findings resulted in a ruling of negligence for excessive force and the termination of an officer. Bad apples and the incompetent have short careers. The problem is that too often these officers are recycled. Unless decertified by the state it is common that they are hired by another agency resembling the game whack a mole. Background checks do not always reveal the truth surrounding the circumstances of an officer's "resignation" due to tight-lipped Human Resource managers.

In light of the unrelenting, biased media coverage against white male police officers, one must know that it is no truer that all white male officers are bad than it is that all minority officers are good or somehow better. **It is racist toward whites to suggest that by merely diversifying the ranks – in favor of minorities – the alleged problem will be fixed.**

RED BADGE

Misfits and predators of all races wear badges. In my police career I found that criminal police offenders mirror offender demographics in the civilian world. It stands to reason that lowering hiring standards in order to increase diversity for diversity's sake will actually increase the amount of police misconduct. **Standards must matter over diversity.**

More to the point, there is no evidence to prove the premise of a systemic problem of "white male, racist cops." DOJ figures from 2009 through 2012 show that 34% of people shot by police were black and 61 % of people shot by police were white. Furthermore, many blacks shot by police are shot by black officers. The purported cure for the Big Lie is itself the danger. In this case the poison is the medicine because it will be prescribed to a misdiagnosis.

To help illustrate the outright lies of the media and White House look at the latest data from the NYPD's 2013 Annual Firearms Discharge Report; it tells the opposite story. "The Department has made restraint the norm," this document explains:

> "NYPD officers shot and killed 93 criminal suspects in 1971, when such annual statistics began.
>
> In 2013, NYPD mortally shot a grand total of 8 people. This tied the NYPD's 2010 low-water mark for fatal shootings.
>
> The eight whom the NYPD killed in 2013 were all males.
>
> Two were Hispanic. Six were black. One of these black men wielded a knife. The other five were armed with handguns.
>
> One of them had been arrested 13 times before he fired six shots at two cops on a subway car, non-lethally striking both, as well as a passenger. One policeman then dispatched the criminal. Another subject had been arrested nine times and spent more than 25 years in prison before triggering a bullet-filled street

altercation. He aimed his gun at two officers, one of whom cut him down.

> That same year (2013), the NYPD reports 335 New Yorkers were murdered, and 63 percent — or 211 of them — were black.
>
> The FBI's *Crime in the United States* 2013 specifies that over 90 percent of black murder victims nationally are killed by black assailants. If those figures apply locally, black New Yorkers killed 190 black murder victims in 2013 — roughly one every other day.
>
> Strangely, this mass carnage generates neither protests, chants, nor even a letter-writing campaign by the "'Black Lives Matter" crowd.
>
> So, Gotham's cops have shot and killed just six black men in 2013, all of whom were armed and dangerous. Where, exactly, does one find the NYPD's brutality and murder — "day in and day out?"
>
> Once again, these slanderous claims turn out to be another gift-wrapped pack of lies.
>
> One painful truth is that blacks are staggeringly over-represented in the areas of gunfire and murder.

According to the U.S. Census Bureau, New York City's population was 23% black (12% black males) in 2013.

NYPD found that blacks were 63 percent of murder victims and 55 percent of murder suspects.

Blacks were 74 percent of shooting victims and 75 percent of shooting suspects.

Of the criminal suspects who shot at police officers that year, 100% were black." [37] (Black males are 12% of the NYC population)!

The "Hands Up, Don't Shoot" and "Black Lives Matter" dolts ignore this black-on-black holocaust and black-on-police officer violence.

Instead, these demonstrators portray all blacks as mere innocents terrorized by a bigoted legal system and its sadistic enforcers. They are part of the Black Liberation Movement. It is a farce; another Marxist revolutionary group calling for social justice.

"Police killings of blacks are an extremely rare feature of black life and are a minute fraction of black homicide deaths," argues Manhattan Institute fellow Heather Mac Donald.

"The police could end all killings of civilians tomorrow and it would have no effect on the black homicide risk, which comes overwhelmingly from other blacks." (Mac Donald)

Based on spotty but best-available numbers from the FBI, USA Today reported in August 2014 that, on average, white police officers killed 96 blacks annually between 2006 and 2012. This included both armed and unarmed individuals.

In 2013, the FBI indicates, 12,253 Americans were murdered. Among them, 51 percent — or 6,261 of them — were black.

And over 90 percent of them (5,635) were killed by other blacks, almost all of whom were (black) males.

So, if we assume that the trend from 2006 to 2012 continued into 2013, white cops killed 96 blacks — including many who were armed and/or dangerous — while black killers annihilated 5,635 black people.

---

[37]Deroy Murdock, An Assassination of Truth, National Review Online, January 8, 2015

Incredibly, 1.7 percent of the supposed problem receives 100 percent of the attention.

If there is a War on Black America, it is black murderers who mass-murder other blacks.

The media and DOJ have framed a context of discourse around police that is inverted. Without regard to truth and reason white male police officers are cast the villain. **The ignorant have digested the false narrative**; they feel righteous in their protests. **They are unwittingly ushering in changes that will destroy professional police agencies.**

Nobody in their right mind with the desirable qualities and traits long expected of police will apply. Who does that leave to wear the badge? Lowering the bar in recruiting will bring increased crime on the streets, police corruption and federal tyranny as the "fix." Using the street vernacular of those carrying signs or wearing t-shirts that say, "Hands Up Don't Shoot", "Black Lives Matter", or "I Can't Breathe" — these protesters are "tools" being "clowned" and "played" to promote the Big Lie. To use Lenin's term, they are useful idiots.

The federal government wants a big footprint in local police departments. The media's character assassination of police is built on a false crisis; one most recently footnoted by a rogue DOJ's findings in Ferguson. The resulting spin will be used to argue federal oversight nationally. Federal "fixes" will destroy professional policing and local control. They will bring about truly systemic problems of increased crime, police corruption and incompetence. The duped pubic will then cry for yet more federal help. Over time this merger will evolve into the de jure or de facto federalization of police with no local accountability.

Use of Force

A good use-of-force policy is written loosely so as to allow some flexibility for unusual or extreme situations. For example, striking a subject in the head with a rock would generally be against policy, but if an officer tumbles down a hill fighting a suspect, breaks his strong-side hand, and is losing the fight to the point he feels he could go unconscious or be killed, then making an improvised weapon from anything could and should be within policy.

The Staten Island situation where Eric Garner died is an example of the use of an unauthorized technique. There is no question that force was warranted. Officers were making an arrest and overcoming resistance. The question is whether or not the totality of circumstances necessitated the unauthorized choke hold. The trivial nature of the offense is irrelevant to the ensuing struggle. Like any lawful police contact the suspect has a duty to comply and the officer has a duty to apprehend: therein lies the conflict.

An officer cannot argue qualified immunity as a defense for using an unauthorized technique unless other force options were not available, not justified, or used and proved ineffective. Were other force options available to officers facing Eric Garner? It appears so. Let's look at the options.

Taser: NYPD does not issue Tasers to every officer. If an officer on-scene was armed with a Taser, its use would have been unwise. Mr. Garner was an obese man. Being shot with the Taser would cause him to fall. He could have broken his skull on the sidewalk and died. Not using a Taser was wise.

Baton: Mr. Garner's level of resistance did not warrant that level of force. Not using a baton was wise. Furthermore, consider for a moment that Mr. Garner's level of resistance did justify the use of a baton(s). Imagining the optics of the media (blending Rodney King footage) would have caused officers to second guess that option.

Empty hand control holds: This was tried twice, but Mr. Garner effectively parried away those consecutive attempts by two officers.

Pepper spray: Pepper spray followed by a common peroneal strike and an arm bar take down was an appropriate option, but was not used. Perhaps the plain clothes officers were not carrying pepper spray. Hindsight is 20/20. Maybe waiting a short time for a uniformed, fully equipped officer to arrive could have made this option available. We know that uniformed officers were nearby based on how quickly they arrived once the struggle ensued. There was no urgency to go hands-on by the first officer, but when he initiated the arrest things became fluid due to Mr. Garner's resistance.

The Grand Jury's decision stands, but officer Pantaleo could still face internal discipline, a civil suit for wrongful death and federal charges. Officer Pantaleo used an unauthorized technique. Again, he can argue a defense of qualified immunity *if* he can prove that other options were not available to him and that he had to act immediately.

One relevant point not yet raised in the media is details about Mr. Garner's arrest history. We know he was arrested thirty times over thirty-four years. Did any of those arrests include a violent offense or resisting arrest? Did the officer(s) know Mr. Garner's potential for violence based on his criminal history and previous police contacts? Conversely, did his record show no violent history despite his many arrests?

Police dispatch alert officers about the "highlights" of a subject's arrest record that come up on the screen in order to caution them about the potential for resistance, flight or attack. The kinds of information shared are: wanted status, no contact orders, assault, battery, resisting arrest, eluding, and carrying a concealed weapon. Knowledge of Mr. Garner's arrest history could be a reason why officer Pantaleo took swift action against this "no person."

RED BADGE

The media continue to call officer Pantaleo's action an "illegal" choke hold. Words mean things. The hold was not illegal, it was unauthorized. In other words, it was not on the list of NYPD approved techniques permitted in normal or common offender encounters.

What Really Happened to Mr. Garner

The decision to initiate the arrest was not made by Officer Pantaleo. It was the short officer in the black t-shirt with "D.D." on the back that initiated the arrest. He tried to grab Mr. Garner's right wrist. Mr. Garner used egressive resistance to break free.

Officer Pantaleo then followed up on the first officer's failed effort. Officer Pantaleo attempted to control Mr. Garner by grabbing his right wrist from behind. When Mr. Garner defeated that attempt Officer Pantaleo immediately attempted to apply a head-and-arm rear choke. He did this by sliding his right arm deep under Mr. Garner's right arm and then placing his left arm around Mr. Garner's neck. The interference of police bodies in front of the camera does not make clear when or if Officer Pantaleo was able to complete the intended technique. What is clear is the completion and effectiveness of the intended hold was compromised due to Mr. Garner's unruly mass and height disparity relative to Officer Pantaleo.

The choke hold attempt turned to a clumsy take-down that was frustrated when the intended direction was reversed by Mr. Garner's opposing body mass. Still, Mr. Garner's fall was softened by Officer Pantaleo's body. I could see no frames of footage that showed the head-and-arm rear choke hold was completed in text-book fashion, but it is clear in the video that once on the ground, Officer Pantaleo is holding on firmly around Mr. Garner's neck. At that point you can see that Officer Pantaleo's right arm had changed position. It is no longer under Mr. Garner's right arm.

Officer Pantaleo's right hand fingers are clasping his left hand fingers (hooked) in a modified *LVNR* (lateral vascular neck restraint). Officer Pantaleo is not on top of Mr. Garner, but behind him, chest-to-back. This is an important point to note because it argues against chest compressional asphyxia; one of the causes of death in the coroner's summary.

Officer Pantaleo releases his grip and uses his right hand to grab Mr. Garner's extended right arm in a failed effort to place it behind his back to be handcuffed. Officer Pantaleo then releases his left arm from around Mr. Garner's neck and transitions to his knees. He uses both hands to hold Mr. Garner's head down against the pavement. You can hear Mr. Garner say repeatedly, "I can't breathe." Were either the head-and-arm rear choke hold or the LVNR applied successfully Mr. Garner would not have been able to speak at all.

The city coroner called Mr. Garner's death a "homicide." Most people erroneously equate that word to mean murder. Ignorance of the legal definitions and distinctions between the two words has caused emotion to run away and unwarranted criticism of the Grand Jury system. Homicide is the killing of one human being by another. Not all homicides are crimes. Homicides that stem from self-defense, pure accident, act of war and capital punishment are non-criminal. Murder is the intentional, unlawful killing of one human being by another person.

The city coroner determined the cause of death was compression of neck and chest combined with Mr. Garner's positioning on the ground. Additional contributing factors were acute bronchial asthma and hypertensive cardiovascular disease.

Prior to reading a summary of the coroner's findings and only viewing the video it looked to me as though Mr. Garner's death might have been "positional asphyxia" due to the duration and position of his obese body on the ground. Though officers were standing over and around him, I saw no additional body weight on him to argue "compressional asphyxia" to the chest.

Mr. Garner's own weight on his chest under any circumstance would certainly make it difficult for him to breathe. What is being argued in the media is intentional, "mechanical asphyxia" (air choke) as the cause of death. The coroner's summary supports mechanical asphyxia, but the aggravating factors are being ignored or marginalized; without those Garner would not have died. I have to wonder if the pressure for social justice influenced the coroner to switch the order of the primary and contributing causes of death.

As opposed to the head-and-arm rear choke hold, the LVNR is authorized by some agencies, but many have removed it as a force option in favor of the Taser. This is a mistake because Tasers are overused, not fail-proof and can cause more damage than an LVNR when the subject free falls to the pavement.

When used properly an LVNR will prevent a subject from talking. In fact, when fully applied the LVNR results in the subject passing out due to disrupting blood flow. The failed choke hold on Mr. Garner no doubt compromised his airflow, but did not stop it as evidenced by his ability to speak. In addition to positional asphyxia, aggravating factors in Mr. Garner's death were no doubt his obesity, his excited state and other health problems.

There is no argument that this was a preventable death, but it was _not_ murder. Misdemeanor manslaughter was as close as the Grand Jury could have come to a criminal charge, but they weighed the evidence and circumstances deciding otherwise; we must accept their decision.

Mr. Garner was not "killed" by police. Saying police "killed him" implies the officer(s) had intent. The unauthorized techniques by Officer Pantaleo (the attempted head-and-neck rear choke, followed by the attempted or modified LVNR), were effective. These unauthorized techniques ultimately did place Mr. Garner on the ground and stopped his further resistance. He did not die on the pavement.

In my opinion, the primary factor that led to the death of Mr. Garner has been conspicuously overlooked by the media: negligence on behalf of the police supervisor on-scene. The sergeant did not alert on the signs that the arrest was turning to a medical emergency. The sergeant was not supervising.

Mr. Garner's repeated and strained admonishments to officers, "I can't breathe" were ignored. The sergeant should know that the first of the sixteen cues of high-risk individuals for sudden and in-custody death is a big belly (John G. Peters, Jr. Institute for the Prevention of In-Custody Deaths, Inc. 2005). Why has this NYPD sergeant been spared the scrutiny of the media and DOJ?

Do you recall the name Stacy Koon of Rodney King fame? He was the white male, LAPD sergeant on-scene. If Sergeant Koon was a black female, like NYPD Sergeant Kizzy Adoni who stood over the gasping Mr. Garner, would he have dodged media scrutiny too and not gone to federal prison? Nobody died in the Rodney King case. In fact, King's injuries were far less serious than what his attorney embellished.[38] Mr. Garner died. Yet, the media's finger of scrutiny has not pointed beyond Officer Pantaleo.

Truth and reason are being choked out by the emotion and the political bias of the media and DOJ; byproducts of the Big Lie. Like the Ferguson incident, the media have spun the Staten Island incident and mischaracterized Officer Pantaleo's conduct as a racially motivated murder.

---

[38]Daryl Gates *CHIEF, My Life In The LAPD*, (Bantam Books 1992), 316-317.

Race had no relevance to the police contact.

It was Mr. Garner's *behavior* that caused police to contact him.

It was Mr. Garner's *behavior* that caused force to be used on him.

It was Mr. Garner's *behavior* that caused him to be obese.

Would it be relevant for me to always describe the on-scene Staten Island, NYPD supervisor as the "black, female sergeant?" No. The sergeant's race and gender had no more to do with Mr. Garner's death than did his race and gender (*unless it can be proved her chevrons are the product of social promotion rather than merit and competence).

Yet the media spin race when it suits their agenda. In the Ferguson case they referred to Officer Wilson as white and Michael Brown as black when there was no evidence of racial bias. In Ferguson like the Staten Island case and thousands of police contacts daily across the country, everything that unfolded was initiated by the suspect's behavior. For Mr. Garner, first it was his petty criminal act and then resisting arrest. Race has no relevance in the analysis of police conduct in either case. No matter though, the media spin it that way.

Until Trump the media was in bed with the White House and DOJ trying to break the back of police in this country. The Marxist revolution has entered a violent phase. Selective outrage is the fuel. It is spun by Obama, Eric Holder, Loretta Lynch, New York Mayor Bill de Blasio, the likes of Al Sharpton, and the media. Facts are inverted. Lies look like truth. Rebellion looks righteous.

Wrongfully discrediting police will have devastating consequences to our future. Nobody in their right mind will apply to be a police officer. Through attrition the courageous, professional officers will disappear including command staff.

RED BADGE

The recruiting bar will have to be lowered in order to fill the ranks. We will suffer the unscrupulous with a badge. Police and gangster will be weighed as the lesser of two evils. The pool left to promote from will become shallow. It will yield inept, under qualified police administrators. Their lack of competence and lack of confidence will steer them to be directed by the federal puppet masters. They will look the part in a photo with stars and bars on their epilates, but always have an eye to the feds for direction.

Police will never be perfect. That is an impossible bar. Improvements can always be made and police need to be held accountable. But, on the whole **we will never have a more professional (and accountable) police force than we have today across the United States.** Enjoy it because it is going away.

At the same time, **minorities today – blacks in particular – will never have it better than they do right now in terms of professional police, due process, government favoritism, freedom and social mobility. Crying wolf is going to turn everything upside down.**

What happened in Staten Island was truly a tragedy. It was an unintended consequence of three factors: Mr. Garner's resistance, one police officer's arguably wrong force option, and the big one: an incompetent sergeant's inaction.

Policing the new majority will bring more and more claims of police brutality and racism. Do not allow the Marxists in the media and Washington DC to recast tragedies like Eric Garner's death as something it is not. The Marxists' goal is to find as many justifications as they can to argue the need to federalize police. Keep law enforcement local. Support your Sheriff!

CHAPTER SEVEN

Securing the Border is Hateful?

Not only have our local law enforcement officers become less proactive due to intimidation, division, confusion, and fear of wrongful prosecution, but also the United States Border Patrol has been banged with the Politically Correct gavel. The 9th U.S. Circuit Court of Appeals (United States v. Montero-Camargo (208 F.3d 1122 [9th Cir. 2000]) ruled that a person's "Hispanic appearance" could not be considered as a factor in stopping motorists near the United States – Mexico border. Hurting someone's feelings is more important than national security

This ruling is an example of Leftist judicial activism. To consciously ignore that our Southern border is porous, and that most of the people who live in Mexico share common physical attributes, and further, to forbid our federal border agents to protect us by including physical/ethnic attributes among profiling factors is absurd.

Weak law enforcement emboldens the enemy. On March 14, 2000 in El Paso, Texas, U.S. Border Patrol agents were fired upon from Mexican military vehicles that crossed into the United States. With the exception of FOX News Channel, this alarming story was not covered on major broadcast or cable TV news outlets.

The Border Patrol agents did not return fire, but only detained the Mexican soldiers briefly. It might surprise you to know that since 2004 there have been 300 military incursions by Mexico into the U.S. according to the Department of Homeland Security.[39] These incursions involve the trafficking of drugs and who knows what else in this time of war.

---

[39]Caroline May, *300 Military Incursions since 2004*; Breitbart.com, May, June 17, 2014).

Complementing Mexico's overt military efforts at defeating our border are untold numbers of tunnels coming from Mexico into the United States through which aliens, contraband and terrorists pass. It has been well established that Afghanis have been found with genuine Mexican passports. "Muhammad" becomes "Manuel", yet speaks little or no Spanish.[40] On top of all of this is a disturbing trend of American citizens being kidnapped in Mexico or abducted from the U.S. and taken to Mexico. In the case of women kidnapped, it is believed by law enforcement officials that they are offered as "gifts" to drug cartels. What we call a "border" does not hold up to the definition; in that it is so easily defeated.

The U.S. Government Accountability Office reported that the Border Patrol embellishes its effectiveness. Furthermore, the GOA estimated that **70% of illegal border entries go undetected**. OTMs (Other Than Mexicans) are among those entering our country. How many terrorist cells are here waiting for orders to strike?

Mexico is not our friend. Mexico is not our ally. Yet our government shows no leadership on the border save dog and pony shows for the press that showcase our capabilities but that are never sustained. We have the means, but not the will to effectively police the border. Why?

Immigration is being used as a weapon. Marxists want a new majority made of a permanent underclass married to government. Based on Emperor Obama's federal policy, legal immigration alone will outpace the American population 7 to 1 through 2065.[41] For every *net American birth* (births minus deaths) seven more naturalized citizens will be added. The new majority

---

[40]Todd Bensman, *Afghanis caught with genuine Mexican passports bought in Mumbai, a U.S. Security Vulnerability in Mexico's Foreign Offices?* The San Antonio Express-News, March 2008.
[41]Exclusive – *Senate Immigration Subcommittee Releases Chart Proving Immigration Will Outpace American Population 7 to 1 Through 2065*, Breitbart News, October 4, 2015

will dilute the culture and overwhelm the infrastructure creating crisis after crisis that will be used to justify a larger federal government.

Article I, Section 8 of the U.S. Constitution delegates power to Congress to establish a Uniform Rule of Naturalization. Obama made his own rules unchecked by Congress as he upset the racial and ethnic composition of the country to meet his destructive ends.

Stats from across our land:

- 22% of ALL felony crimes committed in Phoenix, Arizona are committed by illegal aliens.

- 22% of ALL violent crime in Collier County, Florida is committed by illegal aliens.

- 19% of the prison population in Chicago, Illinois is illegal aliens.   (Source: FOX news channel, February 24, 2009)

Three very different venues in three very different areas of the United States, yet they all have something in common and one glaring consistency: an illegal-alien crime wave.

In 2010, New York state prisons held over 4,000 prisoners from 10 Latin American and Caribbean countries and fewer than 150 prisoners from all of Western Europe (many of those were likely non-European, Muslims).[42]

Under the Obama regime, the southern border was symbolic; it was literally wide open. Realistic estimates of the number of illegal aliens (mostly Mexican) that have colonized America since 1980 are at least 50 million.[43] If that figure is accurate

---

[42] Ann Coulter, Townhall.com, *Immigration Advocates Frightened by 99-Pound Blonde,* June 3, 2015

[43] W. Gardner Selby, *Republican Group says 9 million to 50 million Illegal Immigrants Live in U.S.*, Austin American Statesman, February 1, 2013.

20% of the entire population of the United States is made of illegals!

By the near total lack of enforcement of federal immigration laws under the Obama regime and its' constant calls for widespread amnesty, illegal aliens know that their lawlessness was not only tolerated but condoned. There was no deterrent to breaking our immigration laws. Enter President Trump who enforces the Rule of Law protecting the American people and he is called a "racist."

The fifty-plus Mexican consulates peppered across the United States are aligned with an army of Marxist, anti-American, immigration "rights" lawyers. They represent any illegal alien who feels like confronting our laws and system of justice.

In 2012 ICE deported only 19% of the over 400,000 illegal aliens jailed by local authorities and placed on an ICE detainer under the authority of the *Secure Communities Program*.[44] The program allows local authorities to hold the alien for ICE rather than releasing him/her on bond or after serving time for the offense(s). Furthermore, about 50% of those that ICE chooses to not deport — reoffend! In 2014 the deportation rate of illegal aliens not explicitly targeted by ICE was one half of one percent.[45] **Until Trump there was virtually no fear of deportation from the interior of the United States even after arrest by local police.** This encourages more (illegal) entry.

While Obama was in office illegal aliens have been responsible for 611,234 criminal charges in Texas including

---

[44]Heather MacDonald, *Practical Thoughts on Immigration*, Imprimus, February 2015.
[45]Heather MacDonald, Practical Thoughts on Immigration, Imprimus February 2015.

2,993 murders and 7,695 sexual assaults.[46] **This is just one state in the union.**

Since 9-11-2001, 63,000 Americans have been killed by illegal aliens. That does not take into account the tens of thousands more American victims that live with the physical, emotional and financial scars from surviving being victims of: Assault, aggravated assault, battery, aggravated battery, robbery, burglary, theft, rape, child molest, DUI, aggravated DUI, hit & run and property damage. You disqualify yourself as an American if you oppose enforcing immigration law and securing the border. Yes, you can be an "American Citizen" and be an Open Border/Sanctuary City advocate, but no "American" would put another nation's people before the safety and wellbeing of their own. If half the population is hostile to our founding ethos, the Rule of Law (including immigration law) and embrace (knowingly or unknowingly) Marxist dogma, then we are on course for Civil War. Google "President Trumps talk to Angel Families" (survivors of victims killed by illegal aliens). It is very sobering.

During President "W" Bush's first term, he gave his State of the Union Address and identified our relationship with Mexico as the most important international relationship we have. When we were attacked on September 11, 2001 Mexico did not as much as posture to support us. Since then the U.S. Government has made absolutely no substantive effort to secure our southern border.

Since that time more American citizens have been killed by illegal aliens (most of them from Mexico) in the U.S. than the total number of American soldiers in Iraq and Afghanistan combined. Curiously, the U.S. Department of Justice does not keep tally of the number of Americans murdered by illegal aliens, but a 2006 report released by U.S. Congressman Rep. Steven King (R-Iowa) showed 4,380 Americans murdered

---

[46] J. Christian Adams, *Illegal Alien Crime Wave in Texas: 611,234 Crimes, 2,993 Murders,* PJ Media, July 22, 2015

annually (twelve per day) by illegal aliens. Multiply that figure by the number of years at war (at the time of the report, seven) and we had 30,660 Americans killed by the hands of "people here to do jobs we won't do", versus 4,851 U.S. soldiers killed (4,221 in Iraq and 314 in Afghanistan) over the same length of time policing foreign borders.

*Note: the murder-by-Illegal-alien rate of 4,380 annually has been consistent over the last 10 years. Significantly, that figure does <u>NOT</u> include another roughly 4,500 American citizens killed every year by illegal alien drunk drivers in motor vehicle collisions. This brings the fatality rate into sharper focus: over 9,000 American citizens are killed at the hands of illegal aliens every single year.

Also not included in these disturbing statistical numbers are the alarming number of American women who are raped every year by illegal aliens, and the huge number of people feloniously assaulted (maimed or brutalized) but not killed.

If you scoff at these murder figures, consider this hard fact about illegal aliens and crime: One out of three inmates (29%) in U.S. federal prisons are illegal aliens.[47] These aliens are not in prison for jumping the border.

According to the Pew Research Center Illegally present foreign nationals are estimated to be 3.5% of the population. In fiscal year 2014 they made up 37% of all federal sentences cleared and officially recorded.

A report from the U.S. Sentencing Commission stated:

"Broken down by some of the primary offenses, illegal immigrants represented 16.8% of drug trafficking cases, 20% of kidnapping/hostage taking cases, 74.1% of drug possession

---

[47] *Offenders in Federal Justice System 2010/Overview/revised; U.S. Department of Justice, Bureau of Statistics*; page 10, October 12, 2013.

cases, 12.3% of money laundering cases, and 12% of murder convictions."[48]

*These figures do NOT include offenders convicted for whom no sentences were yet issued, convictions where sentences are issued but not yet recorded, and federal cases initiated but for which no convictions were obtained.

Additionally, these figures do NOT include death penalty cases or state criminal cases (significant in that the vast majority of criminal convictions come at the state level).

The first thing any national government does when it is worried about hostile infiltration from abroad is secure their land borders. One only has to look at Cold War Europe for a stark example: even on the Western side of the Iron Curtain, there was 24/7 around-the-clock military and police patrols on the ground and in the air along the international borders. The land border as well as its accompanying airspace was under constant guard and continuous surveillance by armed government personnel. Nobody could pass over the "Iron Curtain" in either direction without being detected and apprehended by military or police personnel (U.S. and NATO forces on the Western side and Warsaw Pact forces on the Eastern side). Total border security is entirely possible!

For those who question the effectiveness or feasibility of deploying the U.S. Armed Forces to patrol and guard our own national borders, let's not forget that the U.S. military has a wealth of experience effectively securing and guarding borders: the Cold War "Iron Curtain" in Europe and the 38th Parallel in Korea are just two very visible examples of successful implementation of total border security.

While the Mexico border is a huge concern, our border with Canada is overlooked by most Americans. According to Customs

---

[48]Caroline May, *Illegal Immigrants Accounted for Nearly 37% of Federal Sentences in FY 2014,* Breitbart News, July 7, 2015

and Border Protection Commissioner Alan Mersin the Canadian border is a greater threat from invading terrorists than Mexico.[49] Canada is more socialist than the United States. It stands to reason that their brand of tolerance is even more radical than ours and that they have sleeper cells exploiting loopholes to get here legally.

Besides, what's the point of having a "Department of Homeland Security" if you are not going to secure the homeland? Which begs the question: Is the federal government's fear mongering about terrorism a sham? Is there something much bigger at work here?

If the U.S. Government was truly worried about terrorists committing horrific acts inside the United States and harming American citizens, why haven't they secured our border and maintained a constant military presence on land and in the air along it, and why haven't they deported all of the foreign-born "security risks" known to be residing here? President Trump is right to build a wall and take seriously immigration enforcement.

Why did the Obama Administration remove from the citizenship oath the requirement to defend the United States? Now naturalized citizens can refuse service altogether, including non-combat and non-military support roles in times of war.[50]

Why in 2013 did the Obama Administration release from deportation hearings 36,000 people to include 193 convicted murders, 426 convicted sex offenders and 16,070 drunk drivers?[51]

Why did Obama not condemn and prosecute sanctuary cities like San Francisco where 32-year-old Katie Steinle was shot and

---

[49]Colin Freeze, *U.S. Border chief says terror threat greater from Canada than Mexico*, The Globe And Mail, May 18, 2011

[50]Katie Pavlich, *Obama Administration Strips Requirement to Defend The United States From Citizenship Oath,* Townhall.com, July 22, 2015

[51]Jessica Vaughan, *ICE Document Details 36,000 Criminal Alien Releases 2013, Center for Immigration Studies*, May 2014

killed on July 1, 2015? This beautiful, vibrant and accomplished woman was walking with her father on Pier 14 when she was shot and killed by Francisco Sanchez, an illegal alien deported five times with seven felonies to his credit. It should be no surprise Katie was killed by an illegal alien in our largest sanctuary city where since 2011 there has been a 55% increase in arrests for murder and a 370% increase in arrests for rape.[52] Obama zealously stepped into select local issues like Ferguson where he had no business, but abdicated his constitutional duty to protect our borders.

The U.S. Government brags about its ability to detect, locate, arrest and deport some 90-year-old alleged Nazi war criminal that has lived in the United States for over 50 years and has fully assimilated into our culture — and effectively looks like somebody's grandpa, yet under Obama they claimed they were unable to locate, arrest and deport people of Arabic, Latino, or North African descent, who have foreign-sounding names, speak a foreign language with a noticeable accent, and who don't look and act like most assimilated Americans.

Under President George W. Bush (like Obama), our immigration and border enforcement was intentionally weak in order to realize the Marxist One-World plan of a borderless region called the "North American Union."

The North American Union, which plans on merging Mexico, the U.S.A. and Canada into one large borderless, nation-less mass, is well on its way to reality. The North American Union is being financed by the international banking cartel; its legal documents and framework are crafted by the Council on Foreign Relations, with its titular front man being George Soros. It has been co-championed by successive Mexican, U.S. and Canadian

---

[52]Matt Vespa, *San Francisco Sees Spikes In Murder and Sexual Assault Arrests*, Townhall.com, September 14, 2015

presidential administrations. Trump is stalling this agenda and flexing our sovereignty.

A critical part of the plan includes the "norming" of laws and currency (goodbye U.S. dollar!). Mexico and Canada have some of the most restrictive gun laws in the world, and both countries have handgun bans. Where do you think the U.S. is headed? Does this help explain the all-out assault against our 2nd Amendment right to keep and bear arms?

Imagine what life will be like in America when Mexican drug cartels and street gangs no longer have a border to cross and can roam freely and legally inside the United States? Mexico currently has one of the highest murder rates in the world, and has more kidnappings than any country in the world! Further, imagine having to live in a country like that with no ability to protect yourself or your family with a firearm. It is essential That President Trump get a second term and that the right person is groomed to be his third and fourth term.

(Over 40,000 people have been killed in drug-related violence in Mexico since December of 2006 — less people have been killed in the civil war in Syria!)

On May 9, 2005, the U.S. GOA (Government Accountability Office) released a report on a study of 55,322 illegal aliens incarcerated in 2003. This number represented 459,614 arrests, averaging eight arrests per alien in this group. These figures alone are staggering, but consider the obvious: that one's criminal record only documents the crimes they were caught for.

In 2006, the Violent Crimes Institute in Atlanta released the results of a one-year study and found that there were at the time 240,000 illegal alien sex offenders in the U.S., each with an average of four victims.

According to a CNN report 318, ten-year-old girls gave birth in Mexico in 2011! The source for the information is the Network for the Rights of Children which also reported that in

Jalisco, Mexico alone, 465 girls between 10 and 14 years old were mothers[53]. **Culture matters.**

"In all of Western Europe, the United States, Canada, Australia, and New Zealand combined; there have been eight reported births to girls aged 10 or younger. Seven of the eight involved Third World immigrants."[54] **Culture matters**

Every crime an illegal alien commits, from driving uninsured and without a license to drunk driving, to hit-and-run, to drug sales, to battery, to theft, to robbery, to child molestation, to rape, to murder — would not have happened here if they were not here.

It is a lie that illegal immigration is a victimless crime or not a crime at all and that these people are only here as "citizens of the earth" to do jobs that Americans won't do. That is the sales pitch we heard echoed by the Bush dynasty and Obama.

The mantra is always about how noble and family-oriented the "migrant worker" is with a blind eye to Americans brutalized by illegal aliens and burdened by taxes to support them. It is a case of the seen versus the unseen. We are shown one endearing angle with the subliminal message: "Harmless; nothing to see here. Move along. Enjoy your vegetables."

The media usually cover up when the offender is a minority illegal alien by being intentionally vague i.e. "*Man* pleads guilty to rape of twelve-year-old…"

Bush's blind eye toward crime caused by illegal aliens was an abdication of his constitutional duty to secure the border

---

[53]Belen Zapata, *Autoridades de Jalisco indagan caso de una nina de 9 anos que tuvo un hijo*, CNN Mexico, February 7, 2013
[54]Ann Coulter, *Trump Opponents Take Nuanced View of Child Rape*, Townhall.com, July 23, 2015

(Article IV, Section 4). Obama continued Bush's symbolism over substance, smoke and mirrors border policy aimed at amnesty.

Perhaps siding with the business community to satisfy the demand for cheap labor, Bush waited until the last day of his presidency before commuting the sentences of two former Border Patrol agents, Ramos and Campean. These agents were sent to prison for shooting a fleeing drug smuggler in the buttock after a struggle where one of the agents was bloodied. Eight hundred pounds of marijuana was found in the smuggler's vehicle.

The U.S. government actually offered this drug smuggling, repeat-offender immunity and flew him back on your dime so that he could be the star witness against the agents who were protecting us from him. Nothing the agents did that was wrong warranted criminal prosecution, but an argument could be made that they should have been disciplined or fired for not following Border Patrol policy. It seems the prosecution had a politically correct agenda. The fact that Bush waited so long to commute the sentences of these men and did not grant them a pardon demonstrates his lack of commitment to border security and played to the agenda and narrative.

Bush's support of amnesty and his lack of support for border security weakened and demoralized the Border Patrol making our European cultural rudder (hegemony) more vulnerable. With a birth rate nearly twice that of whites; Hispanics are more than transforming the face of America. By design, their numbers are growing at a rate too fast to assimilate. The result: colonization.

We have the means to find and deport every illegal alien (including an estimated 50,000 illegal aliens from Ireland), but not the will. The Marxist Diversity Movement oligarchs call the shots. They characterize the notion as impossible, ridiculous, unnecessary, and of course — racist.

Marxists support amnesty. They align themselves with the Aztlan Movement and brown berets who seek to colonize and take back states that were once part of Mexico. They see their circumstance as equivalent to the Palestinians in Israel. Their slogan reeks of social justice: "We didn't cross the border, the border crossed us!"

Hats off to The Minute Man Project! Americans — of all colors — took part in exercising their rights to assemble and bear arms in defense of their country. They worked as force multipliers for a demoralized Border Patrol, who I am told from inside sources admired and respected them and their capabilities.

Do you recall the media scrutinizing this law-abiding group while Marxist agitators sat on them like prey with cameras? Both the media and the illegal alien activists characterized these patriots as racists while at the same time President Bush called them "vigilantes." The news did not report the diversity of the group because it would contradict the narrative.

Obama did not begin the dismantling of the United States, but he put it in top gear. He was running the last leg of the race to our ruin. He more than nullified illegal immigration. He encouraged invasion. There was no regard to quality or quantity control. He wanted to destroy our bedrock culture. This is not the behavior of a president who loves this country. In contrast, Trump stands strong on border security and resolute on building a wall. Using the military he stopped (in December of 2018) what would have been an invasion of many thousands from Honduras. Consequently, Mexicans in Tijuana felt the burden of illegal immigration when the caravan became a log jam and backed up on them to process, support and absorb. I watched Mexican news channels. The comments of Mexicans about the invaders were identical to what Americans say of illegal aliens from Mexico. How Ironic.

CHAPTER EIGHT

The Truth You Are Programmed to Dismiss as "Crazy Talk"

The 1919 "Communist Rules for Revolution"

In May of 1919 Allied military forces that were occupying Germany following the armistice of World War One captured a secret, underground manual titled "Communist Rules for Revolution" in Dusseldorf, Germany. In the course of their investigation Allied military intelligence personnel secured material witness testimony from a secret agent of the Communist Party's underground revolutionary movement.

During the debriefing the secret agent confirmed that the captured revolutionary manual was genuine and that the list of primary goals to be implemented to affect the overthrow of the countries of Western Europe and the United States remained the grand strategy of the communists' "World Revolution."

The goals listed in the 1919 "Communist Rules for Revolution" manual to be achieved are as follows:

1. Corrupt the young; get them away from religion. Get them interested in sex. Make them superficial; destroy their ruggedness, self-reliance and individuality.

2. By specious argument cause the breakdown of the old moral virtues: honesty, integrity, sobriety, continence, faith in the pledged word, strong work ethic, ruggedness.

3. Encourage civil disorders and foster a lenient and soft attitude on the part of government toward such disorders. (Think of the LA riots; Ferguson, Missouri riots; Baltimore riots, etc.)

4. Divide the people into hostile groups by constantly harping on controversial matters of little or no importance. (Rebel flag)

5. Get peoples' minds off their government by focusing their attention on athletics, sexy books, plays, and other trivialities. (Twitter, Facebook, texting, smart phones, iPads, pornography, sex scandals)

6. Get control of all means of publicity (media).

7. Destroy the peoples' faith in their natural leaders by holding the latter up to contempt, ridicule and disgrace.

8. Cause the registration of all firearms on some pretext, with a view to confiscation and leaving the population helpless.

Take a look at the above list and ask yourself if any one of these goals have not been partially or fully achieved in the U.S. today.

What is especially alarming is Item #8 – which further validates the necessity of our 2nd Amendment right and the warnings of our Founding Fathers about domestic tyranny.

I ask the reader to compare the above list from 1919 to the following list drafted by the *Frankfurt School* communist revolutionaries. One can see that this plot has been a long time coming. The Frankfurt School was a well-financed and sophisticated branch of the communist revolutionary movement that simply refined tried and true methods of subversive warfare and agitation propaganda. And most importantly, recall that our current occupant of the White House is a stealth radical Marxist, steeped in the ways of subversive revolution.

A Primer on "The Frankfurt School"

The "Frankfurt School" was the informal name given to the Institute for Social Research, a group of radical Jewish Marxist revolutionaries who operated out of Frankfurt University in

Germany from 1923 to 1934. The organization was originally called the "Institute for Socialism." It was then changed to the innocuous sounding, "institut für sozialforschung" (Institute for Social Research) in order to obfuscate and deliberately mislead followers, dupes and investigators. When Adolf Hitler came to power they were forced to leave Germany. They came to the United States and set up their operational headquarters at Columbia University (Obama's alma mater) in New York where its founders and later its protégés spread to other Ivy League schools influencing radical movements in the 1960s and today. They later set up a second branch of their revolutionary society at Berkeley University in California, so as to have an operational headquarters on each coast of the United States.

The founding members included Herbert Marcuse, Erich Fromm, Max Horkheimer, Wilhelm Reich, and Theodor Adorno.

They were responsible for the creation of the neo-Marxist "New Left" phalanx, which helped create, mold, finance and direct the feminist movement, "Women's Liberation" movement, the LGBTQ ("gay pride") movement, the transgender movement, the various Black Power movements such as the militant Black Panthers, and Hispanic colonization movements such as La Raza ("The Race") and Aztlan (militant Mexican re-conquest /supremacy movement).

There are various off-shoots and sub-groups of those front line groups, such as Black Lives Matter, Occupy Wall Street, ACORN, Center for American Progress, SEIU, and many, many more.

Financed from its inception by the international banking houses of Europe, with Lord Rothschild at the head, the Frankfurt School's primary goal was the overthrow and destruction of Western Civilization from within by criticizing, degrading and subverting every aspect and pillar of our culture.

The complete subversion of American society and culture could not be accomplished without successfully attacking and uprooting the traditional faith-based belief system (religion) of the people. Therefore, well-funded and organized Marxist and communist front groups, spearheaded by the Soviet KGB, have relentlessly attacked Christianity, the Christian Church, Christian holidays, as well as Christian organizations throughout America.

The subversion of major Christian church organizations as well as Biblical scripture itself has been accomplished through the successful infiltration of the National Council of Churches (NCC) by operatives of the Soviet KGB's Foreign Intelligence and "Active Measures" arms, which have also successfully infiltrated and subverted the NCC's parent organization, the World Council of Churches (WCC).

Many of the major Christian denominations throughout the United States are affiliated with or are members of the NCC. This is why you see so many Christian denominations and groups falling in line with Marxist dogma on issues including sanctuary cities, open borders, homosexuality and same-sex marriage.

The successful infiltration and subversion of the WCC and NCC — and Christianity as a whole — is beyond the scope of this book. However, I highly encourage everyone, my Christian readers especially, to investigate this further on their own.

The Marxist millionaire Felix Weill was the House of Rothschild's agent and front man in the early days, playing virtually the same role that billionaire, Hungarian-born George Soros plays today.

Instead of the old-fashion frontal assault (violent, armed revolution) the Frankfurt School conspirators decided they would advance their goals through "quiet revolution" and "stealth attacks" upon the foundational pillars and anchor points of the dominant culture by creating upheaval, division, disarray, and confusion, and discontent.

The primary stealth tactics advocated by the Frankfurt School for attacking, subverting and destroying the host peoples' culture and society included the following:

1. The creation of "racism offenses" where only the dominant cultures' creators (White people) could be guilty and only minorities (non-Whites) could be victims.

(This has morphed into federal and state "hate crimes" which in reality criminalizes unapproved thoughts, a true manifestation of Orwellian "thought crimes," which are zealously prosecuted against Whites the overwhelming majority of the time, despite the sobering truth to the contrary found in victim/offender statistics).

2. Continual "change" to create confusion, discontent and disarray in society and subvert the acceptable norms of conduct.

(Sound familiar? "Gay Pride" and the transgender movement, homosexuals and trans-genders in the military; the War against Christianity, American heritage, our Founding Fathers, Southern Heritage and symbols of that heritage, etc.)

3. Introduction to sex and homosexuality at a very early age in school and teaching about homosexuality in the primary grade levels of education.

4. The undermining of schoolteachers' authority.

5. Massive, uncontrolled immigration in order to destroy national identity and national cohesion.

6. The promotion of excessive drinking and drug use.

7. Relentless attacks against Christianity and its leaders.

8. Creation of an unreliable and arbitrary legal system with bias against victims of crime and those in the majority (Whites).

9. Create an entrenched, divisive, and re-distributive welfare state; encourage minorities and immigrants to sign up for welfare; promote permanent dependency on the State and State benefits.

10. Control all of media (news, entertainment, books, etc.).

11. Control and continually dumb-down education.

12. Promote the overall breakdown of the traditional family unit by: Relentless attacks against the institution of marriage; encouraging divorce and making it socially acceptable, legally expedient and incentivizing its monetary rewards for women; encouraging children and wives to rebel against fathers/husbands as the "head of the household."

One of the dominant themes promoted by the Frankfurt School was the concept of "pan-sexualism", a construct that originated with Marxist subversive and Frankfurt School fellow traveler Sigmund Freud.

"Pan-sexualism" involved the self-centered search for pleasure with absolutely no moral restraints ("If it feels good, do it!"), exploiting the differences between the sexes and attacking their traditional roles in order to create gender confusion, hostility and inter-gender warfare; and the re-defining of the traditional relationship between men and women, with an emphasis on "female empowerment", the masculinization of women and the feminization and emasculation of men.

To further their aims, they would:

• Attack the traditional position and authority of the father as the 'Head of the Household"; attack, undermine and ridicule the traditional roles of father and mother; and use the power of the State to negate the rights of parents to be the primary educators of their children.

- Abolish differences in the education of boys and girls; teach about sex and homosexuality at all grade levels, starting in primary school, while emphasizing that homosexuality is not a perversion or deviant behavior, but an "alternate lifestyle choice"; encourage femininity in boys, masculinity in girls, gender confusion, and role reversal.

- Quietly declare war on masculinity and the male gender: abolish all forms of male dominance and hierarchy and replace the patriarchal society with a matriarchal one; force every male-only institution and organization to open themselves up to women, homosexuals and trans-genders; disguise the war against men as "women's liberation" and "women's empowerment" by declaring women to be an "oppressed class" and men, especially White men, as their "oppressors."

- Feminize all aspects of the culture and transform society into a female-dominated one by artificially elevating women into all fields of power, influence and authority.

The Communist International's propaganda Chief, Willy Munzenberg, summed up the Frankfurt School's long-term program and method of operation thusly:

"We will make the West so corrupt that it stinks."

Look at the massive increase of women in police and fire departments, the military and various traditionally all-male institutions, clubs and military academies, and now the revolutionary change of not only allowing but advocating for women in military combat roles Special Forces units; there is an ever-increasing female presence in executive leadership and decision-making positions in both government organizations and the corporate world. Many of these positions were obtained through unfair, affirmative-action promotions which creates further hostility, bitterness and resentment between men and women in the workplace and society. Look at the forced opening up to women and "trans-genders" of traditionally all-male military academies, combat units and institutions (i.e. West Point, Annapolis, ROTC, Virginia Military Institute, Army Special Forces, Army Rangers, Navy SEALs, Marine infantry school, etc.). But it's never the reverse.

{Virginia Military Institute (VMI) was an elite, all-male military college known as the "West Point of the South." It was the last military college in America to open its doors to women. VMI was sued by the Department of Justice in 1990 for "discrimination." Their case went all the way to the U.S. Supreme Court, where American tradition lost to the Marxist Frankfurt School. VMI, like every other military college in the U.S., is now "co-ed"}.

Saul Alinksy openly expressed his admiration for Lucifer in his book. Thus, if Barack Obama regularly employs Alinsky tactics to subvert, divide and destroy the United States as we have traditionally known them, a case could be made that Obama is a Satanist. The same could be said of another Alinksy follower, practitioner and protégé, Hillary Clinton.

At the beginning of his 1971 book *Rules for Radicals*, Saul Alinsky recognizes and lavishes praise upon Lucifer:

"Lest we forget at least an over-the-shoulder acknowledgment to the very first radical: from all our legends, mythology, and history (and who is to know where mythology leaves off and where history begins – or which is which), the first radical known to man who rebelled against the establishment and did it so effectively that he at least won his own kingdom – Lucifer."

Alinsky was a radical communist revolutionary and father of the modern neo-Marxist "community organizer" movement, of which Barack Obama is a disciple.

Did America hit the tipping point when it elected Barack Hussein Obama as president? A country that would willingly elect somebody as utterly corrupt and deceitful as Barack Obama is essentially morally bankrupt.

To re-"elect" such a vile and depraved individual who appears pathologically incapable of telling the truth and who is so radically Marxist, racist, malignantly narcissistic, psychologically damaged, and morally compromised was probably America's death sentence.

America is living on borrowed time, especially economically. That which cannot continue, will not continue.

We no longer are a true "nation." We no longer agree on anything or have any ties that bind us together. Every issue further separates and tears us apart.

It is exciting to watch President Trump work to change course and I support most of his policies. Nonetheless, I fear a new Dark Age is about to descend upon us from which America and the world will probably never recover.

The Origin of the Race Card

A Racial Program for the 20th Century was a book written in 1912 by Israel Cohen, a founding member of the revolutionary socialist *Fabian Society*.[55] The book reveals the Communist "Grand Strategy" to subvert and destroy America using the race weapon. The following is a quote from the book:

"We must realize that our party's most powerful weapon is racial tensions. By propounding into the consciousness of the dark races that for centuries they have been oppressed by whites, we can mold them to the program of the Communist

---

[55]Fabian Society: British socialist organization that advanced the principles of socialism through soft, persistent methods in democracies, rather than by violent revolution.

Party. In America we will aim for subtle victory. While inflaming the Negro minority against the whites, we will endeavor to instill in the whites a guilt complex for their exploitation of the Negroes. We will aid the Negroes to rise in prominence in every walk of life, in the professions and in the world of sports and entertainment. With this prestige, the Negro will be able to intermarry with the whites and begin a process which will deliver America to our cause."

Rep. Thomas Abernathy read this passage into the Congressional Record on June 7, 1957 (Vol. 103, p. 8559, top of page.)

Israel Cohen (1879-1961) was the General Secretary of the World Zionist Organization and a co-founder of the Fabian Society along with Israel Zangwill and George Bernard Shaw. Israel Cohen was a significant and influential player in most of the communist and Fabian Socialist movements in England.

The international central banking cartel, the royal bloodline families of Europe along with various secret societies were the financiers and organizational brains behind the Fabian Society, which promoted gradual, creeping socialism as the means to achieve the End Game of One-World Dictatorship, step-by-step.

These same bankers, royal bloodline aristocrats and secret societies were the money, power and organizational acumen behind Communism and the "World Revolutionary Movement."

For additional documentation and proof of the communist strategy of "racial tension" and ultimately, racial warfare, read on.

Former FBI Director J. Edgar Hoover stated the following regarding Communist methods and objectives in America:

"Communists seek to advance the cause of communism by injecting themselves into racial situations and exploiting them:

(1) To intensify the frictions between Negroes and Whites to 'prove' that discrimination against the minorities is an inherent defect of the capitalistic system,

(2) To foster domestic disunity by dividing Negroes and Whites into antagonistic, warring factions,

(3) To undermine and destroy established authority

(4) To incite racial strife and riotous activity, and

(5) To portray the Communist movement as the 'champion' of social protest and the only force capable of ameliorating the conditions of the Negro and the oppressed."

In 1935, the Communist Party USA published a pamphlet entitled **"The Negroes in a Soviet America."**

It encouraged blacks in the USA to "rise up" against the government and against whites in general, and assured them that all American communists (of any color) would support them. The pamphlet encouraged blacks to overthrow their white oppressors and promised blacks that a Soviet-style communist government would confer greater rights and benefits on blacks than on Whites and that "Any act of discrimination or prejudice against a Negro will become a crime under the Revolutionary law."

In 1922, the Communist International (COMINTERN) provided its members in America $300,000.00 for the purpose of spreading agitation-propaganda amongst American blacks and inciting them to rise up against White rule.

In 1925, Communist Party U.S.A. (CPUSA) instructed its members:

"The aim of our Party in our work among the Negro masses is to create a powerful proletarian movement which

will fight and lead the struggle of the Negro race against the exploitation and oppression in every form and which will be a militant part of the revolutionary movement of the whole American working class... and connect them with the struggles of national minorities and colonial peoples of all the world and thereby the cause of world revolution and the dictatorship of the proletariat."

In The Communist Party: A Manual on Organization, J. Peters writes:

"The other important ally of the American proletariat is their mass of 13,000,000 Negro people in their struggle against national oppression. The Communist Party, as the revolutionary party of the proletariat, is the only party which is courageously and resolutely carrying on a struggle against the double exploitation and national oppression of the Negro people, becoming intense with the developing crisis, [and] can win over the great masses of the Negro people as allies of the Proletariat against the American bourgeoisie."

In *America's Road to Socialism,* James Cannon states that American blacks "...will play a great and decisive role in the revolution ... And why shouldn't they? They have nothing to lose but their poverty and discrimination, and a whole world of prosperity, freedom, and equality to gain. You can bet your boots the Negro will join the Revolution to fight for that – once it becomes clear to them that it cannot be gained except by revolution."

Leonard Patterson, a former black American Communist Party member who was trained in Moscow, U.S.S.R., has confirmed J. Edgar Hoover's statements regarding the Communist Party's methods and objectives and has also revealed that the Communist Party effectively infiltrated and manipulated the black Civil Rights Movement in the 1960's.

Patterson testified on November 18, 1950:

"I left the Communist Party because I became convinced ... that the Communist Party was only interested in promoting among the Negro people a national liberation movement that would aid the Communist Party in its efforts to create a proletarian revolution in the United States that would overthrow the government by force and violence through bloody full-time revolution, and substitute it with a Soviet form of government with a dictatorship of the proletariat."

Manning Johnson was an American black man who achieved the highest rank in the Communist Party USA that could be held by a Negro. Below I quote extensively from his 1958 book *Color, Communism and Common Sense:*

"During the three decades which have elapsed since the Sixth World Congress in Moscow (U.S.S.R), the American Communist Party has conducted many campaigns and formed and infiltrated a large number of organizations among Negroes. From the bloody gun battles at Camp Hill, Alabama (1931), to the present integration madness, the heavy hand of communism has moved, stirring up racial strife, creating confusion, hate and bitterness so essential to the advancement of the Red cause."

Johnson goes on to list a wide array of national black activist organizations (the NAACP being the biggest and the most well-funded) that were all "formed, directed, controlled and led by Reds (communists) and fellow travelers."

He said all of these organizations exposed millions of American blacks to communist agitation-propaganda and ideology.

Johnson remarked on the extent to which the communists were able to hoodwink, manipulate, and brainwash the black elite, saying: "The list of sponsors, officers, and contributors reads like a Who's Who in the Negro intellectual, professional, labor and religious circles."

Johnson continues:

"Through the aforementioned organizations and many others, Negro institutions of higher education like Howard University were penetrated to subvert teachers and students and thus politically contaminate the intellectual stream of Negro life."

"White leftists descended on Negro communities like locusts, posing as "friends" to come help "liberate" their black brothers. Along with these white communist missionaries came the Negro political Uncle Toms to allay the Negro's distrust and fears of these strangers. Everything was inter-racial, an inter-racialism artificially created, cleverly devised as a camouflage of the red plot to use the Negro."

"Many Negro intellectuals, artists, professionals, etc., were carried away with this outburst of inter-racialism. Here was an opportunity to be accepted by the other racial group. Secretly, they had always wanted to get away from the other Negroes. Moving around among whites would somehow add to their stature and endow a feeling of importance. So they went after communist inter-racialism like a hog going after slop."

Johnson then laments that "there are numerous examples of the harmful and deadening effect of communist inter-racialism (integration) on any proposal for constructive Negro projects."

Here is the highest ranking black communist party official in America confirming the communist origins of inter-racialism, de-segregation and "integration", which has morphed into the modern day diversity cult, multiculturalism movement, and the "anti-racism" and "tolerance" campaigns.

RED BADGE

The following are some illuminating quotes from Chapter 7 of Manning Johnson's 1958 book *Color, Communism and Common Sense*. Chapter 7 is called "Creating Hate" (think LA Riots, Ferguson, Baltimore, etc.).

Manning Johnson:

"The placing of the repository of everything, right and just, among the darker races is a dastardly Communist trick to use race as a means of grabbing and enslaving the whole of humanity.

"Moscow's Negro tools in the incitement of racial warfare place all the ills of the Negro at the door of the white leaders of America. Capitalism and imperialism are made symbols of oppressive white rule in keeping with instructions from the Kremlin.

"To one familiar with Red trickery, it is obvious that placing the blame for all the Negroes' ills at the door of the white leaders in America is to remove all responsibility from the Negro. This tends to make the Negro:

1. Feel sorry for himself
2. Blame others for his failures
3. Ignore the countless opportunities around him
4. Jealous of the progress of other racial and national groups
5. Expect the white man to do everything for him
6. Look for easy and quick solutions as a substitute for the harsh realities of competitive struggle to get ahead

"The result is a persecution complex — a warped belief that the white man's prejudices, the white man's system, the white man's government is responsible for everything. Such a belief is the way the Reds (communists) plan it, for the next logical step is hate that can be used by the Reds to accomplish their ends."

In 1953 Manning Johnson testified before the Committee on Un-American Activities of the U.S. House of Representatives, 83rd Congress. Robert L. Kunzig, chief counsel for the committee, asked: "Was deceit a major policy of Communist propaganda and activity?"

Manning Johnson answered, "Yes, it was. They made fine gestures and honeyed words to the church people which could be well likened unto the song of the fabled sea nymphs luring millions to moral decay, spiritual death, and spiritual slavery."

Manning's quotes clearly illuminate the Communist Party's racial tension and agitation grand strategy, validating the veracity of Israel Cohen's 1912 *A Racial Program for the 20th Century*.

Manning Johnson ultimately quit the Communist Party USA because he came to believe that he and his fellow blacks were being deceived, lied to and exploited. He also feared that the Communists would incite American blacks to initiate an armed, bloody revolution where as many as five million blacks would die.

Just prior to the LA Riots of 1992, the Los Angeles Police Department gathered intelligence that showed the Communist Party USA, Socialist Workers Party, Revolutionary Socialist Party, Black Panthers and other Left-wing radical groups were behind a massive agitation-propaganda leaflet distribution inciting blacks to riot, commit arson, and exact "payback."

In the aftermath of the LA Riots it was reported that over 600 buildings had been torched or otherwise damaged through arson, 52 people were killed and over 1,000 seriously injured, and over $1 billion in property damage was inflicted by rioting blacks and Hispanics. There were similar incidents reported in other major cities around the country.

RED BADGE

Witness the recent (2014-2015) events in Ferguson, New York City, and Baltimore – riots that were every bit as horrific in their violence and wanton destruction as LA in 1992 – and all committed at the hands of incited, inflamed and falsely outraged blacks.

Witness the current racial tensions and the militant and murderous anti-police movement taking hold amongst minorities, but especially blacks, which is being organized, financed, and exacerbated by Left-wing radical groups: the racially-inspired "Hands Up, Don't Shoot" movement along with the "Black Lives Matter" movement, both of which are financed by Rothschild front man George Soros and both of which are based on deceit and a false narrative.

The communist grand strategy of racial tension, especially black vs. white, is alive and well, and might possibly be the match that ignites a second civil war in America.

Writing in the September 1994 issue of "American Renaissance" distinguished historian, poet, essayist, and syndicated journalist, the late Dr. Samuel Francis wrote:

"For perhaps the first time in history, certainly for one of the few times in history, we are witnessing the more or less peaceful transfer of power from one civilization and from the race that created and bore that civilization, to different races.

"...the transfer of power in almost every dimension of public and private life...is clear in the rise of multi-culturalism, Afro-centrism, and the other anti-white cults and movements in university curricula, and in the penetration of even daily private life by the anti-white ethic and behavior these cults impose."

The recent attacks on Southern culture and heritage, and especially the all-out attack on the Confederate battle flag and the Orwellian-cleansing of Confederate history and its heroic figures, is only the latest coordinated Leftist assault primarily on the people who founded and created American identity, heritage and culture.

Dr. Francis continued:

"What we are witnessing on the official level of public culture in the attacks on these traditional symbols and their displacement by the symbols of other races is the effective abolition of one people and the gradual creation of another.

"The erasure and displacement of official cultural symbols and the similar process in elite-produced, mass-consumed popular culture represents the expropriation of cultural norms, the standards by which public and private behavior is legitimized or condemned and a culture defined...the new norms that are being constructed and imposed are...not only explicitly racial but also explicitly and vociferously anti-white."

Dramatically and presciently, Dr. Francis expounds on the death of America and the West that is the only possible outcome without its founding peoples:

"The civilization that we as whites created in Europe and America could not have developed apart from the genetic endowments of the creating people, nor is there any reason to believe that the civilization can be successfully transmitted to a different people. If the people or race that created and sustained the civilization of the West should die, then the civilization also will die. A merely cultural consciousness, then, that emphasizes only social and cultural factors as the roots of our civilization is not enough, because a merely cultural consciousness will not by itself conserve the race and people that were necessary for the creation of the culture and who remain necessary for its survival."

In other words, the distinctive institutions and unique traditions of Western Civilization, and especially of the United States of America, some of which include: constitutional and representative government "of the people, by the people and for the people," government recognition of the natural rights of the individual and minorities (in the broadest sense of the term), democratic and popular elections, rule by consent of the governed, freedom of religion, freedom of speech, the right to keep and bear arms, protections against government searches and seizures, and the Rule of Law, etc. – will all come to pass.

Realize that Dr. Francis wrote these thoughts 21 years ago! His predictions have so accurately manifested themselves that his foretelling of a future America without its founding stock should alarm everyone – regardless of race – who loves his/her country and enjoys his/her constitutional and human rights.

In Their Own Words

Zbigniew Brzezinski is the former National Security Advisor to President Jimmy Carter. He was also a founding member of David Rockefeller's Trilateral Commission in 1973 and sat on the Board of Directors of the Fabian Socialist Council on Foreign Relations.

Brzezinski was the impetus behind the creation of the Federal Emergency Management Agency (FEMA), a true "Shadow Government" in waiting.

If the U.S. Government declares a "State of Emergency" for any reason or activates the National Incident Command System, the unknown and unelected bureaucrats of FEMA assume total control over not only all agencies and entities of the U.S. Government, but all land, airspace, waters and waterways under U.S. Government control and all property, natural and human resources within the United States (that means you and everything you own!).

This has all been "legalized" through successive presidential Executive Orders and "National Security Decision Directives."

During the 9/11 attacks, major news outlets reported that Vice President Dick Cheney was spirited away to an undisclosed underground, nuclear-proof command bunker – managed and operated by FEMA – somewhere in the vicinity of Washington D.C.

If you doubt any of this, I urge you to do some research of FEMA and presidential executive orders. What you find out will surprise and alarm you.

Many knowledgeable sources say that as a Professor of Russian Studies at Columbia University in the early 1980's, it was Brzezinski that initially spotted the young Marxist Barack Hussein Obama and decided to recruit and cultivate him for future political use. From that point on, Obama was groomed for years by the political elite to be sprung on an unsuspecting America at a later date. (Recall that Columbia University is the headquarters of the Frankfurt School and is also the recipient of massive funding from the Rockefeller Foundation. "The borrower is servant to the lender.")

In a similar vein to Orwell's *1984* and Huxley's *Brave New World*, Zbigniew Brzezinski wrote a book in 1976 called *Between Two Ages: America's Role in the Technetronic Era* which prophesied a nightmare totalitarian future.

Even though this book was published on October 28, 1976, it remains quite expensive to buy. Hardcover versions are almost impossible to find and paperback versions, if located, cost around $50.00. Somebody doesn't want you reading this book!

In it, among other things, Brzezinski foretold of the end of national sovereignty, the dissolution of the Nation State, and intimated that the future America would be governed by a "ruling elite." Additionally, Brzezinski touted the greatness of Marxism.

The following excerpts are quoted directly from Zbigniew Brzezinski's *Between Two Ages*:

"Marxism represents a further vital and creative stage in the maturing of man's universal vision ... Marxism is simultaneously a victory of the external, active man over the inner, passive man and a victory of reason over belief ... Marxism, disseminated on the popular level in the form of communism, represents a major advance in man's ability to conceptualize his relationship to the world."

Here Brzezinski reveals the coming Orwellian "1984" society:

"The technetronic era involves the gradual appearance of a more controlled society. Such a society would be dominated by an elite, unrestrained by traditional values. Soon it will be possible to assert almost continuous surveillance over every citizen and maintain up-to-date complete files containing even the most personal information about the citizen. These files will be subject to instantaneous retrieval by the authorities."

"In the technetronic society the trend would seem to be towards...effectively exploiting the latest communications techniques to manipulate emotions and control reason."

"In the technetronic society...human beings will become increasingly manipulable and malleable."

"Power will gravitate into the hands of those who control information. Our existing institutions will be supplanted by pre-crisis management institutions, the task of which will be to identify in advance likely social crises and to develop programs to cope with them."

"This will encourage tendencies through the next several decades toward a Technotronic Era, a dictatorship, leaving even less room for political procedures as we know them. Finally, looking ahead to the end of the century, the possibility of biochemical mind control and genetic tinkering with man, including beings which will function like men and reason like them as well, could give rise to some difficult questions."

RED BADGE
Brzezinski on sovereignty:

"Today we are again witnessing the emergence of transnational elites ...Whose ties cut across national boundaries ...It is likely that before long the social elites of most of the more advanced countries will be highly internationalist or globalist in spirit and outlook ... The nation-state is gradually yielding its sovereignty... Further progress will require greater American sacrifices. More intensive efforts to shape a new world monetary structure will have to be undertaken, with some consequent risk to the present relatively favorable American position."

Bold predictions of secret weather warfare and covert bacteriological warfare on page 57:

"By the year 2018, technology will make available to the leaders of the major nations, a variety of techniques for conducting secret warfare, of which only a bare minimum of the security forces need be appraised. One nation may attack a competitor covertly by bacteriological means, thoroughly weakening the population (though with a minimum of fatalities) before taking over with its own armed forces. Alternatively, techniques of weather modification could be employed to produce prolonged periods of drought or storm..."

Predictions of space warfare, deep-sea military bunkers, lethal laser weapons, and again – weather warfare:

"In addition...future developments may well include automated or manned space warships, deep-sea installations, chemical and biological weapons, death rays, and still other forms of warfare – even the weather may be tampered with."

Below is a revelation that by the mid-1990's governments will have advanced mind control weapons and the ability to manipulate and exploit human behavior over very large populations for extended periods of time:

"In addition, it may be possible – and tempting – to exploit for strategic-political purposes the fruits of research on the brain and on human behavior. Gordon J. F. MacDonald, a geophysicist specializing in problems of warfare, has written that timed artificially excited electronic strokes could lead to a pattern of oscillations that produce relatively high power levels over certain regions of the earth.... In this way, one could develop a system that would seriously impair the brain performance of very large populations in selected regions over an extended period.... No matter how deeply disturbing the thought of using the environment to manipulate behavior for national advantages to some, the technology permitting such use will very probably develop within the next few decades."

More revelations of the planned American police state and society's domination by elite governing overlords:

"Society would be dominated by an elite...which would not hesitate to achieve its political ends by using the latest modern techniques for influencing public behavior and keeping society under close surveillance and control."

Remember that this was written in 1976! And not by just anybody, but by a former member of the National Security Council, counselor to president Lyndon B. Johnson, and the former Chief Advisor to President Jimmy Carter on National Security Affairs. Brzezinski remains a top level behind-the-scenes national security and foreign policy advisor to President Obama.

Now think about the incredible, revolutionary advances in high technology over the last 40 years, especially scientific, electronic, and computer technology, all of which have military applications.

In the late 1970's and throughout the 1980's Soviet military journals spoke of a "Military Technical Revolution" (MTR). In the early 1990's U.S. military experts declared that a "Revolution in Military Affairs" (RMA) was well underway. U.S. military research analysts and shadowy organizations such as the "Defense Advanced Research Projects Agency" (DARPA) said the RMA would come in several stages or phases of development in which increasingly "dramatic" and "brilliant" weapons systems would fundamentally transform the nature of warfare.

In 1995, U.S. military strategists were openly boasting that the revolutionary advances in U.S. military capability that had already been achieved since Operation Desert Storm in 1990 (where the U.S. Armed Forces destroyed the 4th largest army in the world in 96 hours) would "soon be dwarfed by even more fundamental transformation."

(See *Strategy and the Revolution in Military Affairs: From Theory to Policy* by Steven Metz & James Kievit, June 27, 1995).

Enter the "High-Frequency Active Auroral Research Project" (HAARP) and the Pentagon's strategic goal of "Full Spectrum Dominance": total military control over all land, sea, air, and space of planet earth, as well as outer space, cyber space, and the weather. While this topic is far beyond the scope of this book and too vast to be adequately addressed here, I will provide a brief glimpse into the super-weapon world we are presently living in, although few seem to be aware of it.

In April of 1997 U.S. Defense Secretary William Cohen was speaking at the "Conference on Terrorism, Weapons of Mass Destruction, and U.S. Strategy" in Athens, Georgia. During a question and answer session Cohen said,

"There are some reports, for example, that some countries have been trying to construct something like an Ebola Virus, and that would be a very dangerous phenomenon, to say the least. Alvin Toeffler has written about this in terms of some scientists in their laboratories trying to devise certain types of pathogens that would be ethnic specific so that they could just eliminate certain ethnic groups and races; and others are designing some sort of engineering, some sort of insects that can destroy specific crops. Others are engaging even in an eco-type of terrorism whereby they can alter the climate, set off earthquakes, volcanoes remotely through the use of electromagnetic waves."

In 2002 the International Affairs and Defense Committee of the Russian State Duma (parliament) stated the following regarding the Pentagon's HAARP:

"Under the HAARP program the USA is creating new integral geophysical weapons that may influence the near-Earth medium with high-frequency radio waves...The significance of this qualitative leap could be compared to the transition from cold steel to firearms, or from conventional weapons to nuclear weapons...The HAARP program will create weapons capable of breaking radio communication lines and equipment installed on spaceships and rockets, provoke serious accidents in electricity networks and in oil and gas pipelines, and have a negative impact on the mental health of people populating entire regions."

As one would expect in any civilized country, there are federal laws on the books in America that cover "War and National Defense": U.S. Code Title 50. As a U.S. citizen and American civilian, you probably assume that you are safe from HAARP testing and experimentation and trust that the U.S. Government would never use the HAARP "super weapon" on the American people, especially without their consent. But you would be wrong on both accounts.

U.S. Code Title 50, Chapter 32, Section 1520 (a) prohibits the Defense Department from experimenting or testing chemical and biological warfare agents on human subjects or civilian populations. However, there is a gigantic loophole in the law, and it is SIGNIFICANT:

Under Subsection (b) titled "EXCEPTIONS", the law does not apply to a test or experiment carried out for purposes related to "medical, therapeutic, pharmaceutical, agricultural, industrial, or research activity." The law also does not apply for purposes related to protection against weapons of mass destruction. But **most alarmingly, the law does not apply to "Any law enforcement purpose, including any purpose related to riot control."**

Additionally, the "informed consent" requirement contained within the federal law is suspended due to HAARP being classified as a "research project." Therefore, HAARP can legally be used against the American people and against the territory of the United States without anyone's knowledge or consent.

HAARP is a weapon far superior to nuclear without the lingering radioactive side effects. This is why a pious Obama — like previous presidents — can comfortably posture moral superiority to our people and to the world by boasting of reductions in the number of nuclear warheads we have. The U.S. hasn't given up anything nor has Russia.

On November 4, 2008 the Strategic Studies Institute of the U.S. Army War College issued a document titled "Known Unknowns: Unconventional 'Strategic Shocks' in Defense Strategy Development." This virtually unknown document discusses the dangerousness of potential "catastrophic" domestic, economic and social "shocks" inside the United States and warns that if "home-grown domestic civil disorder and/or violence" occurs, the Department of Defense would be "forced...to radically re-role for domestic security and population control."

Ladies and gentlemen, welcome to the New World Order!

CHAPTER NINE

Dispelling the Mythology behind Tailor-Made Laws, Race & Crime, and Multiculturalism

Domestic Assault and Battery

Mandatory and pro-arrest policies regarding domestic violence has nearly eliminated officer discretion on the matter throughout the country. Fear of consequences for using discretion has officers in a headlock. In the face of institutionalized social justice few officers have the moral courage to exercise discretion resulting in many unnecessary arrests that damage the American family.

Scenario:

A woman has been drinking adult beverages throughout the evening. Her husband and she argue over finances. She walks to the car. He grabs her by the wrist in order to prevent her from driving drunk. She screams, pulls away and falls; twisting her ankle in the driveway while the children look on.

The neighbor calls 911. Upon arrival, officers separate the couple, and interview them individually. The woman is crying. She has a red mark on her wrist and a swollen ankle consistent with her account of events and those of the neighbor, husband, and children. The injuries are minor. She refuses medical attention.

There is no history of domestic violence on file between the couple and the "victim" does not want her husband arrested. With no regard to the victim's protest he is arrested for domestic battery and the *enhancement section* — for committing the "offense" in the presence of children.

This scenario illustrates how unnecessary arrests set in motion a chain of events more damaging than anything that took place prior to law enforcement being called: The husband is unnecessarily arrested in front of his family and neighbors. A NCO (No Contact Order) is issued forbidding him from seeing his kids and wife or contacting them by phone, text, mail or through a third-party. He has to pay for bond or will miss work. He must spend more money living out of the home or risk arrest and even more money for an attorney unless he qualifies for the public defender. He cannot possess a firearm or ammunition while the NCO stands — even though they are not evidence of the alleged crime. Peace officers sometimes seize these items stripping the defendant of his Second Amendment right without Due Process; as if a man is less deadly without a gun. Shouldn't his chainsaw, shoelaces, kitchen knives, hammers, dumbbells, and baseball bats be seized too?

The humiliation, family separation and financial burden brought about from unnecessary, social-justice-inspired arrests are a strain on the family.

Pro-arrest policies are adopted by law enforcement administrators out of fear of expensive tort claims, fear of the Feds de-funding grants and fear of bad press. Fear is inculcated in officers through yearly in-service training. Arresting for the slightest, explainable injury is fail-safe. In cases of mutual battery police are expected to identify the "primary aggressor" and make an arrest. That is usually the male even if he was defending himself from his hysterical wife by overpowering her attack. The wife can corroborate his story, but still an arrest is made often time with the enhancement charge stacked on top if children were anywhere they could have conceivably heard the quarrel. Stacked charges make an unnecessary arrest more likely to result in a plea. That is easy money for the state. This is how the game is played. The man is neutered and fleeced. The policies surrounding how these laws are enforced are bias against men and profitable to the system in court costs and fines. Actual evidence matters less in domestic assault and battery than any other kind of crime.

Pro-arrest policies cause officers to not think. One size fits all. They pass the buck to prosecutors, placing them in an untenable position. Many of these cases are resolved by a plea to the lesser charge of disturbing the peace. The majority of defendants take a plea deal often times only to expedite the reunification of family, the restoration of rights, and stop the financial bleeding of separation and attorney fees. At $300.00 an hour for an attorney, how much "justice" can the average person afford?

In 2003, twenty-one-year-old Angie Leon of Nampa, Idaho, was murdered by her estranged husband, Abel Leon — a known criminal alien. Over a five-year period, Abel Leon had fifty-nine contacts with law enforcement; almost all resulted in arrest. Thirty-five of the fifty-nine were for domestic violence.

Angie told authorities numerous times Abel would kill her. Angie's murder was as much the result of the failure of ICE as it was the prosecutor's office for not fighting to keep Abel in custody after a felony charge of eluding police — despite priors for three failure-to-appear warrants, twenty protection order violations and the state's knowledge he was a danger. ICRMP (Idaho's self-insured communities risk management plan) paid out $925,000 to Angie's mother, Sylvia Flores.

Cases like Leon are rightfully referenced in domestic violence training, but to such an extreme that the interests of city and county Risk Management offices have collided with justice, leaving a chalk line around discretion.

In 2011, there were seventeen deaths in Idaho related to domestic violence. Like Angie, those victims were not saved by domestic violence laws and pro-arrest policies. In fact, there is no way to know if domestic violence laws and the elimination of officer discretion reduce the number of injuries and murders or contribute to them — by holding victims hostage to their circumstances. Could a victim's past experiences with overzealous arrest policies and prosecution make her less likely to call 911 when all she wants is for officers to preserve the peace while she collects her toothbrush and leaves?

The argument in support of domestic violence laws is built on the premise that the pre-existing, non-tailored misdemeanor and felony assault and battery laws are insufficient given the unique psychological aspects of a (female) victim trapped in a cycle of domestic violence. The state argued it needed more power to intercede and prosecute on behalf of women paralyzed by fear, confusion and control.

Sometimes the state does know best. Nonetheless, **very few cases prosecuted as domestic assault or battery fit the kinds of controlling abuse that proponents of the law argued it was intended to address.**

The pre-existing (and now co-existing) assault and battery laws are sufficient tools in the hands of competent peace officers empowered with discretion.

What makes matters worse is when the unwilling victim turns hostile to an overzealous arrest/prosecution and recants saying she lied to police. In an already weak case that should have been declined, this makes it difficult to prosecute a future (legitimate) case because the victim's credibility is damaged.

In addition, the underlying premise for the law may be flawed. The media ignore studies like, Domestic Violence: The Male Perspective, where research supports: "Domestic violence is often seen as a female victim/male perpetrator problem, but the evidence demonstrates that this is a false picture." This and other studies show men are nearly as often the victims of domestic violence (40%) as are women, but they under report.

I watched this area of law and police policy evolve from its inception in San Diego, California. It became the national model. Today, across the country domestic violence assault and battery laws are redundant and *gender biased* in their investigation and prosecution. In the absence of compelling physical evidence or an independent witness, "trained" police are left with one person's word against the other.

Police taught to value a woman's statement as having more veracity than a man's statement is no different than valuing the statement of a white over a black or the rich over the poor.

There is no doubt that good has come from some of these arrests, but that does not change my opinion that across the country (and in other Western countries) domestic violence laws are unnecessary and over zealously enforced. Too often these arrests damage the families they are purported to protect.

Compounding the damage to the family is the double standard found in the kinds of injuries that distinguish a misdemeanor domestic battery from a felony domestic battery; they are lower — and far more subjective — than the kinds of injuries that typically distinguish non-domestic misdemeanor batteries from non-domestic felony (male-on-male) batteries. The injury threshold for a man to be charged with felony domestic battery is far lower than the injury threshold for the same man being charged with felony battery from a common street fight.

The existing statutes for misdemeanor battery, misdemeanor assault, aggravated (felony) battery, aggravated (felony) assault, stalking, phone harassment and intimidating a witness are sufficient to address the very real issue of spouse-on-spouse, and other intimate partner assaults and batteries.

Repealing domestic violence law is unlikely. What is the alternative? Restore discretion.

RED BADGE

The relative autonomy of the Office of Sheriff is pivotal in modeling this change. Yes, the feds could investigate and prosecute a select few cases under federal domestic violence law. Yes, the Department of Justice could de-fund grants to Sheriffs who honor their oath and row against the federally adopted, radical feminist narrative. Yes, the press will spin the move toward discretion casting the Sheriff a Neanderthal. So be it. Sheriff, did you take the job to be popular or to honor your oath?

Most Sheriffs and Police Chiefs take the path of least resistance for fear of the potential negative consequences of being controversial. Going with the flow is damaging enough. Others take it a step beyond. In Canyon County, Idaho, Sheriff Kieran Donahue plays the domestic violence mantra to his political advantage by promoting his *Man Up Crusade Against Domestic Violence*. It sounds so unobjectionable. Domestic violence is as safe an issue to tie your reelection campaign to as anything that is for the children. There are purple ribbons, purple bandanas, purple stickers, purple t-shirts, rodeos and lots of positive free media coverage of the Sheriff who promotes a compassionate, zealous and *gender bias* message that in my view endorses the devastating absence of discretion by police in our homes.

Peace officers are the gatekeepers of who goes to jail. Decisions based on facts, reason and discretion must be restored. By department policy, a decision to not arrest for domestic battery could require a second opinion from a sergeant. Short of a crime report, an information report could be filed in-house describing what happened and why an arrest was not made. Such a report could be useful for call history in the event that some unforeseen tragedy does happen.

The existing pro-arrest practice aimed at eliminating all exposure to liability by making unnecessary arrests is fear driven; it advances a Marxist objective to damage the smallest form of government: the family.

The discretion I advocate is not license for peace officers to be lazy and leave a scene when they should make an arrest. Until crystal balls are issued to peace officers, *reason and facts*, not fear of special interest groups, tort claims and bad press — should steer their actions in our homes.

Hate Crimes and so-called Hate Speech

"To learn who rules over you, simply find out who you are not allowed to criticize." — Monsieur Voltaire

Hate crimes are another category of tailor-made law. They are the absolute manifestation of Orwellian "thought-crimes." If you are a civilian or public official and argue against hate crime legislation, you are cast as a racist.

Hate crime laws have never been about suppressing crime or protecting minorities. If legislators wanted to impact crime, they would address the prolific black-on-black and black-on-white crime that has plagued society for decades.

Hate crime laws actually contribute to rampant crime because out of fear of being snared themselves by a biased and racially-charged Justice Department police made fewer self-initiated, proactive contacts with blacks and other minorities leaving communities less safe. Police officers know that accusations of "racial profiling" against blacks or Hispanics could find them on the receiving end of a full-blown federal civil rights and criminal investigation by the Justice Department. This was particularly so under Obama.

From a strict legal analysis, hate crimes are not crimes at all. They should be nullified by jurors. Hate crime "laws" are invalid because they cannot stand on their own. They must be subjectively affixed to a host crime. The definition of a crime is "…an act committed or omitted in violation of a law forbidding or commanding it."

Every crime has specific elements (corpus delecti) that must be satisfied in order to be prosecutable. Without a host crime, hate crimes are merely hateful or unpopular thought. Hate crime law can only be applied after an actual crime has taken place, and then they are selectively piggybacked as an enhancement thereby coloring the offender.

In Chapter One I mentioned the March 2012 (lawful) killing of Trayvon Martin in Sanford, Florida by neighborhood watch member George Zimmerman. The zeal to get into Zimmerman's head and criminalize his thoughts shows how close we are moving to the Canadian social justice model where one can be arrested for merely making disparaging comments about protected ("victim") classes like homosexuals.

When someone says you offend them what they are really saying is that you must agree with them. And so it is with The State. Codifying dissent as a crime by using (subjectively charged) hate crime laws is dangerous to liberty. Government should punish harmful acts, not ugly or dissenting thoughts and opinions.

Robert Moon of the *Conservative Examiner* nailed the Left's motives in codifying dissent as a crime in this excerpt from his October 25, 2014 piece titled, *Democrats working to silence dissent*:

"…this is the signature of a party with time-disproven ideas that cannot compete on a level playing field. It is why Fox News always crushes its competition in the ratings. It is why liberal talk radio always fails. It is why liberals regularly try to impose speech-trampling attacks on dissent like the Fairness Doctrine…

"It is why Democrats campaign endlessly to give amnesty to millions of illegal immigrants (future Democrat voters). It is why liberals always turn toward unaccountable, un-elected activist judges to work around the will of The People.

"It is why they constantly have to lie, cheat, and steal their way into power (i.e. felons, illegal aliens and dead people voting only for Democrats in the tens of thousands in every election).

"And it is why they will never stop trying to suffocate and criminalize conservative speech online. Allowing multiple sides of the story to get out prevents liberals from burying scandals, misrepresenting the facts, and misinforming the public at every turn. Their only option is to silence everyone but themselves."

The True Intent of Tailor-made Law

The true intent of tailor-made law is not protection, but *division* (i.e. woman against man and Black against White). Consider that every state in the union already has a law against rape. Rape laws exist to protect women, agreed? Why not pass a tailor-made law making it a separate crime to rape a white woman? Would this be an unnecessary duplication of law? Why would white women deserve more protection than women of any other race?

DOJ Bureau of Justice Statistics show black males rape over 37,000 white females a year while white men rape **zero** black females. I suppose it is "racist" that white males do not rape black females. (I can hear it now from Whoopi Goldberg on The View: "I see how it is. Whitey don't want to get up in here! Dat's racist. Dhey so racist dhey won't even rape us." That is how sick the mindset of these dividers is.) Satire aside, why is there no outrage in the DOJ and the media of the astronomical number of white women raped every year by black males?

No victim regardless of race or gender should be treated as if he or she is of less value than another, but silence on this long-standing black-on-white rape epidemic suggests otherwise. Year after year these black-on-white rape statistics are staggering.

Following the Marxists' rationale used to argue the need to create special victims through domestic violence laws and hate crime laws; do these sobering rape statistics not plead the case that white women deserve their own social justice inspired law to give them extra protection from prolific targeting by black male predators?

How about lesbians? Some studies show that lesbian relationships have similar levels of violence as heterosexual relationships, while other studies report that lesbian relationships exhibit substantially higher rates of physical aggression. Do we need to pass a domestic violence law to protect women from women?

How about peace officers? It is already against the law to kill an officer. Black males disproportionately murder peace officers. Black males are 6% of the population, but are responsible for 44.3% of officers murdered by use of guns and knives according to a study from 2003 thru 2012.[56] The fact is that (nationally) a police officer is six times more likely to be shot by a black than the opposite;[57] in many areas the odds are much higher than that. Do we need a special tailor-made law to protect our nation's peace officers from black males who kill or attempt to kill them?

If we are going to tailor make "social justice" laws that carve out special classes of victims i.e. Homosexuals, blacks and women, what would happen if we based them on reality rather than the mythology carried in the state narrative?

What would tailored-laws look like if we considered the truth over the narrative about who the pattern of victims and suspects are year after year after year?

The intent of tailor-made laws has never been about public safety. They are born of selective outrage married to a substitute

---

[56]Richard R. Johnson, Ph.D., *Factually Examining Deaths From Police Use Of Force, Legal & Liability*, Risk Management Institute, May 2015
[57]Jason L. Riley, *Race Relations and Law Enforcement*, Imprimis, January 2015

for reality; one used by Marxists to divide our country and vilify our culture.

With few exceptions (i.e. protecting the elderly, the gravely disabled and children) I support repealing tailor-made laws and holding everyone equally precious and accountable under one Rule of Law. **The goal should be equal protection for all, not extra protection** found in social justice that divides society by race, gender, religion and sexual orientation.

Repealing domestic violence laws and hate crimes laws is unlikely, but local law enforcement agencies (Sheriff Offices in particular — given their relative autonomy) can change their policies and procedures to eliminate the Robocop approach and model discretion and moral agency over how these laws are applied.

Tailor-made laws have always been about Marxist social engineering. More and more Police, Prosecutors and Judges are becoming pawns of a compromised criminal justice system used to advance and enforce an agenda. In Mecklenburg, N.C. Chief Magistrate Judge Khalif Rhodes led a policy (2018) to stop issuing arrest warrants for violent crimes. Instead, the court is issuing summonses. Judge Rhodes spoke in dangerous social justice language when he defended his actions saying, "We as a county have a bail policy that has fundamental issues that directly affect poor people, and if we want to change racial and ethnic disparities...we have to make changes in policy."

In Ada County, Idaho, Sheriff Bartlett took a total of $1,300,000 from the MacArthur Foundation over a three year period, 2015 through 2017. Part of the Foundation's mission is to promote "social justice" as it relates to research and policy aimed at remedying perceived inequities in incarceration time for the poor and minorities.

Social justice is undermining the criminal justice system with policies and practices aimed at fairness that ignore realities of offender demographics.

In January 2019 Boston's new District Attorney, Rachel Rollins, stopped prosecuting a list of 15 crimes. Among the list are: minor in possession of alcohol, trespass, shoplifting, possession of a controlled substance and resisting and obstructing a police officer. Obviously, this black woman has been indoctrinated to view the mission of her Office through the lens of social justice as she looks at the usual suspects coming before the judge. These charges will be dismissed prior to arraignment or diverted for community service or free job training. The cancer of Social Justice is metastasizing and will embolden the criminal.

Race and Crime

"What sort of 'truth' is it that needs protection?"

Auberon Waugh

Black males comprise only 6% of the U.S. population. Yet on average year after year black males commit: 62% of robberies, 57% of murders, 42% of forcible rapes, 48% of aggravated assaults, 48% of auto thefts, 45% of burglaries, and over 50% of all violent crime in the United States.

There is a great deal of misinformation about black incarceration rates. The common argument is that blacks get longer sentences for possession of crack cocaine while whites get lighter sentences for powder cocaine.

The congressional black caucus was the driving force in favor of longer sentences for crack because it was damaging black neighborhoods. Now, years later we are told by the same camp that the results are racist. Facts frame an entirely different picture.

90% of America's prisoners are in state prisons. Blacks comprise 37.5 % of the states' prison populations. If you subtract the number of blacks in prison for possession of drugs the percentage drops only a half percent to 37%.[58]

The fact is that black males are not disproportionately incarcerated due to racism in drug sentencing.

Black males are disproportionately incarcerated because they are only 6% of the population yet commit over 50 % of ALL violent crime.

Between 1976 and 2005 Blacks committed 52% of ALL murders in the USA.

Black males between the ages of 13 to 24 constitute only 1% of the population, yet this 1% commits over 20% of ALL violent crime in the United States!

This same 1% of young black males is responsible for 21% of all murders of police officers in the line of duty, 86% of whom are white. This statistic alone warrants officers being extra-vigilant for their safety around young black males.

Federal Bureau of Investigation (FBI) "Uniform Crime Reports" for 2012 determined,

"In the year 2008, black youths, who make up 16% of the youth population, accounted for 52% of juvenile violent crime arrests, including 58% for homicide and 67% for robbery."

The U.S. DOJ's Justice's Bureau of Justice Statistics annual report shows that 85% of all interracial crime is black-on-white. Curiously though, in 2002 whites were marked the offenders of "hate crimes" 61.8% of the time compared to blacks at 21.8%. Why the discrepancies in applying hate crime laws when whites

---

[58]Jason L. Riley, *Race Relations and Law Enforcement*, Imprimis, January 2015.

are clearly the victims of interracial crime the overwhelming majority of the time?

In order to fuel the revolution, the state narrative must portray whites as villains not victims. This is why Hispanics are categorized as "white" in government crime statistics when they are criminal offenders (to artificially inflate the "White" contribution to crime), yet are deceitfully categorized as "Hispanic" only when they are victims of crime.

This is also why the Associated Press coined a new term by describing George Zimmerman as "White-Hispanic" when the facts about his race threatened to undermine the narrative.

In 2002, the U.S. Department of Justice Uniform Crime Report data documented 100,111 violent, "white"-on-black crimes versus 466,205 violent black-on-white crimes. Apparently, there is a crisis of hate, but the perpetrators are mostly black and the victims are white. The narrative is inverted. Eric Holder is correct. Americans are cowards on the topic of race; especially him.

Let's look at facts verses the false narrative. 93% of blacks murdered year after year are murdered by other blacks – not by whites. Marxists try to take the sting out of that fact. They counter with fiction claiming that 84% of whites murdered are killed by other whites. Not true. That figure is taken from the DOJ that often tallies Hispanics as white or places them in a "white" sub-set. Consequently, *white* (Caucasians of European descent) offender numbers are skewed and inflated across the board in the aggregate. For instance, if two rival Hispanic gangs clash the deaths are likely to be tallied as white-on-white murders. As unflattering as it is, the 93% figure of black-on-black murder stands as a sobering distinction from any other group.

Significantly, 50% of white and Asian murder victims are murdered by blacks. "White"-on-black murder from 1995 thru

2002 totaled 1,676. During this span of time black-on-white murder totaled 4,044. **Blacks are 22 times more likely to kill whites than whites are to kill blacks.** The FBI in 2012 found that of the 2,648 black murder victims, some 2,412 were killed by fellow blacks and only 193 by "whites." Truth is not allowed traction. Consequently, the narrative remains inverted.

2002 Justice Department data shows that whites robbed blacks 7,111 times, while blacks robbed whites 49,714 times. Looking at this same crime over a six-year period (1996-2002) "whites" robbed blacks 104,092 times and blacks robbed whites 855,260 times. In 2002, the number of multiple-offender white-on-black crimes was 61,993. For the same year, the number of multiple-offender black-on-white crimes was 500,338. Truth does not matter to the media or the government. The narrative is a lie.

According to Department of Justice Crime Victimization Surveys, in 89% of single-offender and 94% of multiple-offender inter-racial crimes it is blacks who are attacking whites.

The Obama Administration stoked racial tension and anger. Through both police interviews and anecdotal evidence, it is clear the lopsided interracial crime numbers grew worse over his two terms.

Just look at one recent phenomena: "flash mobs." That term is an Orwellian euphemism for groups made up almost exclusively of violent young blacks that routinely terrorize and brutalize lone white victims or white couples (See author Colin Flaherty's books documenting extensively this exclusively black violence directed against whites).

{And one must remember every time they read these statistics that persons of Hispanic and Latino heritage (mostly from Mexico, Central and South America) are listed as "white" in these crime stats, artificially inflating the white crime rate. It is also worth noting that white street gangs are virtually non-existent in the United States. Therefore, when you look at the government statistics for "multiple-offender white-on-black crimes", it is all but guaranteed that this represents some Hispanic/Latino gang attacking an individual black or black street gang}.

In order to give these staggering numbers some texture here are snapshots of just a small number of the kinds of routine black-on-white crime you might have missed in the national news that have occurred over my police career alone. To warm you up to the truth I will begin with a list of whites set on fire.

Angela Turner, a guest contributor for Doug Giles' Clash Daily.com published in December 2012 the following list of whites set afire by blacks. She wrote:

Robin and Mani Aldridge – Just last week, a beloved special needs teacher and her high school junior daughter from Charlottesville Virginia were beaten before they were burned in a house fire. Police arrested a black man named Gene Everett Washington and charged him with two counts of first-degree murder. (2014)

Michael Brewer – 15-year-old Michael from Miami had burns over 60% of his body after three black students poured alcohol on him and set him on fire. All three are serving time in prison. (2009)

Allen Goin – A 13-year-old from Kansas City, his two black teen attackers put him in a bear hug, poured gasoline on him and set him on fire saying, "You get what you deserve white boy." (2012)

Gabriela Penalba – A 23-year-old teacher in Knoxville Tennessee was set on fire by a 15-year-old black student. She briefly turned her back to the class when the student lit her hair and shirt ablaze. (2013)

Kathryn "Kit" Grazioli – Colorado Springs firefighters found Kit's 87-year-old body burning on a trail after a nearby resident called to report the fire. Officers arrested a black 21-year-old, Marcus Smith, and charged him with 1st degree murder. Kit was a deacon at her church and loved by the community. (2011)

Jonathan Foster – In Houston, Mona Nelson, a black 44-year-old woman abducted and killed 12-year-old Jonathan with a blowtorch on Christmas Eve, later dumping his body in a ditch. She was found guilty of capital murder and sentenced to life in prison. The story was getting mainstream media coverage until they arrested a black woman. (2010)

Kenneth Athey – Beaten with a hammer, stabbed, doused with chemicals and set on fire, 87-year-old Kenneth survived to testify against his black male attacker. (2008)

Luke Fleischman – a black teenager, who was prosecuted as an adult and sentenced to seven years for the hate crime, set the 18-year-old on fire while sleeping on a bus in San Francisco. (2013)

Richard Michael Carter – Two black brothers were arrested for shooting and burning Richard, a father from South Carolina. (2013)

Flo "Violet" Parker – The 67-year-old homeless woman from California was set on fire by a black man as she slept on a bench. (12/27/2012)

Nancy Harris – The 76-year-old grandmother was killed when a black man set fire to her while she was working at a convenience mart. She was loved in her Texas hometown and known as Grandma to everyone. (2012)

Melinda McCormick – A black woman and two black men beat and burned Melinda to death. (2013)

Jimmy Sanders – Shot and burned after stopping to help two black men, Erik Ellis, 28, and Malcolm Melton, 22, with car trouble. "He didn't answer his phone. I called about eight or nine times. About an hour after he wouldn't answer I got really, really nervous and upset," Betty Sanders said. Jimmy was 65 and also from Mississippi. (2010)

Raymond Vasholz – Raymond died after his black neighbor, Terrance Hale, attacked him and his wife and set them on fire. Elizabeth and Raymond were married 58 years."[59] (2014)

Add to this list two more: In December 2014, 19-year-old **Jessica Chambers** was murdered. She was doused in gasoline and suffered 98 percent burns. The investigation went on for a year and resulted in 27-year-old Quinton Tellis being charged with murder.

In August 2016, 85-year-old Korean War veteran **Gene Emory Dacus** was found by a neighbor on fire in the backyard of his Birmingham, Alabama home. 18-year-old Thomas Sims was arrested for murder.

If the race of offender and victim were reversed in just one, let alone seventeen, of these horrific crimes media coverage would be unrelenting and the full weight of Obama's Department of Justice would land right in the middle of it. Do white lives matter?

Continuing:

- November 2015, three black males (members of "The Killing Gang") committed a home invasion where they robbed, raped and murdered (by a bullet to the head) Amanda Blackburn, the pregnant wife of a pastor. Amanda's one-year-old was present during the attack. Amanda and her baby died.

---

[59] Angela Turner, *SAVAGE: Is Burning Whites the New 'Knock Out Game' for Blacks?* Clash Daily.com, December 12, 2012.

- January 31, 2014 Charlottesville, Virginia: Reserve police captain Kevin Quick was carjacked, kidnapped, robbed and killed by four members of a gang. This good citizen and father volunteered as a peace officer. He was a "random" victim killed by people with the street names "K-Gunns", "Big Homie" "Black Wolf", and "Lady Guns."

- September 2014, Moore, Oklahoma: Alton Nolen was suspended from his job at a food processing plant for making inflammatory statements about white people. He returned the same day and slashed the neck and face of his accuser, Traci Johnson before beheading Collen Hufford.

- June 25, 2014 Essex County, New Jersey: Another "random" victim, 19-year-old Brendan Tevlin, was stopped at a red light. Self-proclaimed jihadist Ali Muhammad Brown fired ten rounds striking Tevlin eight times killing him.

- March 21, 2013 Brunswick, Georgia: De'Marquise Elkins and a second (black) unnamed accomplice tried to rob random victim, Sherry West. When she refused to surrender her purse Elkins shot her in the leg and then shot her 13-month-old baby in the face execution-style as he slept in his stroller.

- August 2013 Spokane, Washington: Delbert Belton, an 88-year-old WWII veteran, and random victim was bludgeoned to death with flashlights by two black male teens who robbed him as he sat in his car.

- In 1993 on the Long Island subway six whites were murdered and 19 additional white passengers were shot by a black man, Colin Ferguson. His defense (representing himself in court) was "Black Rage." The theory held that he was the product of hundreds of years of white oppression. The murders were the justifiable product of emotional release. Congress did not reference this crime in its argument to pass hate crime law. It was the dragging death of James Byrd in 1998 that was the inspiration.

• There is a reason why the videotaped beating of white truck driver Reginald Denny by a group of black males during the 1991 LA riots is not recorded in the annals of The Southern Poverty Law Center's Klan Watch publication as a hate crime; it does not fit the narrative.

• In 1998 black robbers killed a German-speaking tourist in Santa Monica, California when he did not understand the commands. If the suspects were skinheads and the victim a Spanish-speaking Hispanic, we would all have known about it.

The reason you may not have heard of these crimes is because the popular media cherry pick stories that fortify the false reality and then determine the life span of coverage. Showing the grossly disproportional, brutal crimes at the hands of black criminals toward whites would conflict with their policy of subjective reporting aimed at promoting the inversion of reality known as the Big Lie. It is impossible to find an equal number of these kinds of crimes day after day committed by whites against blacks. White-on-black crime is very rare.

In a nation of short attention spans, sound bites, and one-second images, the media are powerful propaganda machines capable of artfully molding the world-view of an increasingly dumbed-down citizenry.

Why are the arsons of Asian-owned and White-owned businesses during the 1991 LA Riots not in the media's annals of hate crimes? Businesses with "Black Owned" signs in the windows were spared. Where was the outrage in the media? Like Ferguson, Mo. in 2014, are we to chalk this up to social justice? Why are these incidents not showcased as clear examples of intolerance and the need for hate crime laws? The reason is that the perpetrators were black. The liberal media almost exclusively portray white males as the perpetrators of hate and non-Asian minorities and homosexuals as their victims.

The followers of black (cult) leader, Yahweh Ben Yahweh, beheaded and mutilated their white victims. One follower, Robert Rozier, a former professional football player, was arrested in 1986. He was linked to the murders of six white people and slicing off the ears of two of the victims to offer Yahweh Ben Yahweh as proof of the kill. This is the stuff movies are made of, but have you heard of it?

We are not supposed to associate blacks as the perpetrators of hate, but only its victims. The media's biased coverage and selective outrage facilitates the strategy of promoting a false reality to support social justice. Truth does not matter. The narrative is inverted.

Wilkinsburg, Pennsylvania, March 1, 2000. A black man named Ronald Taylor shot and killed three white victims and wounded two other whites. The news covered this incident live until the police standoff ended. Once the suspect was identified and his motive revealed – hate for whitey – the story was dropped after a recap in the newspapers the following morning. On the day of the incident there was brief coverage of local law enforcement's intent to pursue a hate crime charge against the black suspect. There was also brief coverage of a segment of the black community voicing their disapproval of applying the hate crime law to the suspect. Had the suspect been white and the victims been black, the media would have over-reported the crime and there would be no debate over whether or not to apply the hate crime charge.

Another example of selective outrage by the media was the lack of coverage in 1999 of the sexual molestation and murder of a 13-year-old boy by two homosexual suspects in Arkansas. The story received very little coverage in the shadow of the murder of the drug dealing, homosexual Matthew Shepard and disappeared more quickly than the Wilkinsburg case above. We are not supposed to associate this kind of predatory violence with homosexuals.

In Chapter One I mentioned the Christian-Newsome murders that took place in 2007 and how the Don Imus non-story controversy eclipsed this horrific crime. Examples like that and those listed above are voluminous and on-going, but either ignored or under-reported by the media.

According to the Bureau of Justice Statistics' National Crime Victimization Survey, in 2013 whites were documented as victims of violent crime 2.2 million times. Non-whites target whites as their victims of violent crime 60% of the time. But white victims report less than half (47%) of the violent crimes perpetrated against them. This brings the estimated total number of violent crimes committed by non-whites against whites to several million each year. **The crime narrative is inverted.**

The same survey showed for the year 2012-2013 that blacks chose whites as their victims of violent crime (battery, rape, robbery, murder) 38.6% of the time. **In contrast, whites almost never choose blacks as their victims** of violent crime at only 3.6% in 2012-2013. The number of white-on-black rapes and robberies is so small that when rounded to the nearest whole number was zero in 2010 — and this is the norm. Whites choose other whites as their victims 82.4% of the time. However, blacks attack whites almost as often as they attack other blacks: 38.6 % to 40.9%. A black is 27 times more likely to attack a white and 8 times more likely to attack a Hispanic than the reverse.

Political commentator Bill Whittle points out that the DOJ's presentation of statistics are misleading because America's black and white populations are not equal in size.

Whittle says that when you consider that 38 million people (the U.S. black population) commit five times as many violent crimes on 197 million people (the U.S. white population) what you discover is that blacks violently attack whites 25 times more frequently than vice-versa. Furthermore, looking just at the crime of aggravated assaults, **black-on-white offenses are 200 times higher than white-on-black offenses.**

On the topic of the supposed epidemic of white police officers hunting black males, Mr. Whittle handily dispels this myth with hard facts and common sense. He points to the number of robberies in 2009. From that he extrapolates that one thousand times a day in the U.S. police respond to robberies. Despite this enormous volume, it is very rare to find a controversial police shooting and of those most include extenuating circumstances that justify the police action. In short, he asks, "If there is an epidemic where is the epidemic?"

Data from the FBI's annual report on law enforcement officers killed and assaulted (LEOKA) for a ten-year period (2003 -2012) show 576,925 felonious assaults on law enforcement officers. 191,225 of those involved some kind of weapon (i.e. baseball bat, gun, car, brick...).

Narrowing armed assaults on police to those attacks involving guns and knives alone the number is 32,767 for that ten-year period. This translates to a yearly average of 3,277 officers attacked by guns and knives.

Based on that yearly average the public should expect police to be justified in using deadly force to protect themselves as many times as they are attacked with guns and knives: 3,277/year.

Of the police officers murdered in this manner over the ten-year period, 44.3% (1,452 of the 3,277) of attackers were black males. **Yet, black males make up only 6% of the population.**

But the gross imbalance is worse than that. Certainly, not all black males are killing almost half of police officers murdered each year. Their full 6% of the 320 million U.S. population is not taking on the nation's 800,000 officer population.

If we subtract elderly black males, non-criminal black males and pre-teen black males from the 6% aggregate we would discover the percentage of black males responsible for the 44.3% of police murders is even more grossly disproportionate than 6%.

It follows logically from the 44.3% figure that we should expect police to be legally justified in using deadly force 1,452 times/ year against those black males who disproportionately attack and/or kill them with guns and knives.

Police use a lot of restraint. 800,000 police officers representing 18,000 agencies kill 429 people a year. 316 are non-black. 113 of them are black.

In summary:

Annually, in almost 50% of the incidents in which police officers are feloniously attacked and/or murdered the assailant is a black male.

The fact is that only about a quarter of people killed by police yearly are black. Police use tremendous restraint.

There is no epidemic of police officers killing black males; and much less unjustifiably so.[60] **On the contrary, there is an epidemic of black males feloniously attacking and murdering police officers (and white people in general). The media never headline any of these murders, "White police officer killed by black male."**

Van Jones, President Barack Hussein Obama's former green jobs czar and a self-professed Marxist Revolutionary and radical black activist, confirmed these findings.

In an October 5, 2005 article titled "Are Blacks a Criminal Race?" Jones, in a moment of factual honesty wrote: "African American youth represent 32% of all weapons arrests [and] were

---

[60] Richard R. Johnson, Ph.D., *Factually Examining Deaths From Police Use Of Force, Legal & Liability,* Risk Management Institute, May 2015

arrested for aggravated assault at a rate nearly three times that of whites."

The implications are shocking: Nearly 50% of all black males and 38% of white men will be arrested by the age of 23.

These statistics, compiled by four college professors between the years 1997-2008, were published in the January 6 edition of the journal *Crime & Delinquency*.

The biggest question one takes away from this study is what types of crimes are these young adults committing? Not surprisingly, there exists a great deal of variance depending on the perpetrator's race.

A 2012 study by the Department of Justice's *Office of Juvenile Justice and Delinquency Prevention* revealed that in 2010 black youths committed six times more murders, three times more rapes, 10 times more robberies and three times more assaults than did their white counterparts.

Colin Flaherty is an award winning writer, whose work has been published in more than 1,000 places around the globe, including in *The New York Times, The Washington Post, The Los Angeles Times, The Boston Globe, The Miami Herald, Bloomberg Business Week, Time* magazine and others.

Flaherty is the author of two Amazon #1 Best Sellers: *White Girl Bleed a Lot: The Return of Racial Violence and How the Media Ignore It* and *Don't Make the Black Kids Angry: The Hoax of Black Victimization and Those Who Enable It*.

In Flaherty's third book: *Knockout Game a Lie? Aww, Hell No!,* he documents yet another disturbing black-on-white violent crime trend, where blacks actually HUNT white people and violently surprise attack them for fun and sport, which blacks call "The Knockout Game" and the racially-charged "Polar Bear Hunting." (Shades of black-run South Africa?)

Flaherty's books expose what he calls "the biggest lie of our generation: that black people are relentless victims of relentless white violence, often at the end of a badge – for no reason whatsoever."

Flaherty proves through painstaking documentation that "just the opposite is true. Black crime and violence against whites, gays, women, seniors, young people and lots of others is astronomically out of proportion."

Flaherty states that the anti-White false narrative and media Big Lie ignoring and suppressing the fact that blacks are the main perpetrators of violent crime "Just won't quit. Neither will the excuses. Or the denials. Or the black-on-white hostility. Or those who encourage it."

Flaherty expresses his grave concern for the country due to "the people in the media and government who ignore it, condone it, encourage it, and even lie about it."

This black-on-police murder epidemic begs the questions: Are white police officers under reacting to black males when it comes to officer safety? Are officers' reaction times slowed due to analysis-paralysis born of worry and fear planted in their psyche by the media, their own police administration and a biased Attorney General, and Department of Justice?

Yes, there are rare and isolated cases of *police brutality* (Use of Excessive Force under the color of law 42 U.S.C. § 1983). Criminal intent is easier to prove in those cases as opposed to situations when an officer overreacts in the emotion of the moment in the performance of his duty. Granted, the consequences of police overreacting with use of force can be just as serious as deliberate brutality, but establishing criminal intent is far more difficult.

To illustrate this point, consider the April 7, 2015 shooting death of Walter Scott by South Carolina police officer Michael

Slager. In my opinion, the officer does deserved prosecution for manslaughter (not murder) and decertification as a peace officer.

Why charge manslaughter and not first degree murder? Let's break it down: Scott's first illegal action (fleeing from a traffic stop) dictated that Officer Slager give chase. Scott's second illegal (and violent) act was committed on Officer Slager as he attempted to disarm him of his Taser. Despite Scott's blatant unlawful and escalating criminal conduct — **deadly force was the wrong force option**. Prosecution of the officer is warranted.

Scott was no longer a threat to officer Slager when he was shot. Nor was Scott a violent fleeing felon whose escape presented an imminent danger to the community. As a certified law enforcement firearms trainer I find Slager's overreaction to Scott's criminal conduct disturbing to watch and tragic. At the same time, I understand the anatomy of a foot pursuit. I understand and have experienced the emotions, variables, psychology, human physiology, and sequence of foot pursuits followed by hand-to-hand combat.

As ugly as the videos are to watch there are mitigating factors. Furthermore, nothing that happened can be used retroactively to validate the allegations in the media and by the Obama White House of a systemic racist, criminal (white) police culture. Race was not a factor in the shooting; behavior was.

Scott's criminal conduct set in motion what followed. Although Scott had significant culpability for the outcome; Officer Slager had more. Officer Slager's defense will be manslaughter, not murder. A jury will be challenged to suspend the conditioning by the media spin in recent police use of force controversies and look at this one in a vacuum weighing the totality of circumstances.

Obviously, it is imperative for the public trust that we police the police. When we get it wrong I call my profession out and when one of us acts criminally I support prosecution of officer and the ceremonial melting of the badge worn.

On 10/05/18 Chicago police officer, Jason Van Dyke, was in my view properly charged with the crime of murder in the second degree connected to an on-duty, use-of-force incident where he shot and killed Laquan McDonald (age 17) 16 times. Video shows Laquan brandish a knife. Like so many news stories where police shoot black criminals the coverage makes it sound as though the crime was a white officer killing a black or worse — a black teen. Nowhere in the country is there a crime in the respective state penal codes that forbids the murder of a black teen. "Murder" is a crime. "Murdering a black teen" is not a crime. The media are intentionally misleading in the way they title stories and carry a political narrative into an event. This kind of coverage suggests race was a motive and that white police are evil and that black "victims" of police use-of-force are innocent. The rare illegal use of force by police is just that: Rare.

Furthermore, half of the "victims" of fatal police shootings are white and 26 percent are black, but you would never know this from the slanted and selective news coverage of police shootings. Also, more Hispanics are killed by police than blacks. The premise of BLM is a lie. In fact, according to two reports from 2015, one from the DOJ about the Philadelphia Police Department and the other from the University of Pennsylvania, black officers are 3.3 times more likely to fire a gun than other cops.

To better explain my point about racially charged headlines the reader must understand what a crime is. A crime is: An act or omission in violation of a law requiring or forbidding something. Every crime has "elements" that must be met in order for a charge to be filed by the prosecutor. Nowhere in the elements of the crime of murder is there a subsection element to include a particular human victim described as a black or black teen. The media selectively and deceptively inject race in headlines involving police use-of-force in order to shape public attitudes and perceptions.

Seldom do I comment on a police shooting before all the facts are in. The October 24, 2014 Chicago case involving Officer Jason Van Dyke shooting to death Laquan McDonald was an exception. Below are my comments made exclusively to TVOI (The Voice of Idaho) news on December 1, 2015. In it I explain why I said in my opening paragraph that Officer Van Dyke was "properly" charged criminally.

As a preamble to my comments I must emphasize that police video never captures the whole story. Body cameras record in 2-D a three dimensional event from one angle. Video is subject to interpretation together with other evidence (i.e. the veracity of witness statements, off-camera contextual factors that must be weighed in the totality of circumstances to include pre-attack body cues (often undetectable by camera), and a suspect's prior violent acts immediately preceding the use of *deadly force [1]* by police.

Ten limitations about body cameras the public should know come from the **Force Science Institute**:
- Camera speed differs from the speed of life.
- A camera doesn't follow your eyes or see as they see.
- A camera may see better than you do in low light.
- Some important danger cues can't be recorded.
- Your body may block the view.
- A camera only records in 2-D.
- The absence of sophisticated time-stamping may prove critical.
- One camera may not be enough.

- A camera encourages second guessing.
- A camera can never replace a thorough investigation.

In the Chicago case there is one question that must be asked 16 times by the prosecutor; once for each bullet fired: "Officer, why did you fire the *first* time? Why did you fire the *second* time? Why did your fire the *third* time? ...Why did you fire the *sixteenth* time."

If you watch the video carefully the suspect (with knife in hand) does appear to pivot toward the officers ever so slightly at an apparent distance that has been proven to be deadly in edged weapon attacks. This is when the first shot is fired.

It takes time for the body to send signals to start and stop an action. A threat can change faster than the signal from the brain to the trigger finger to stop shooting. With that said, the first shot can possibly be explained. Each subsequent shot in this instance becomes less defensible to the point of criminal charge(s) against the officer.

This case does not retroactively validate the faux outrage, ignorance and lies of Black Lives Matter and their echo chamber in the media. I have done significant research on the topic of police use of force. In addition, I have sat on peer use-of-force review boards resulting in termination from the ranks of one officer. Incidents like Laquan's death are extremely rare. They are politicized to girder the Big Lie of a systemic problem of racist white cops killing young black men — as though they are operating by proxy as Klansmen on behalf of an equally racist white-majority America that gives its tacit approval.

RED BADGE

The DOJ and the media ignore the gross disparities in interracial crime because the truth undermines the Marxist tactic of promoting the myth of black victim status at the hands of the oppressive white majority and by extension: police as their supposed agents. The Big Lie of the racist, oppressive white majority shapes the context of public discourse. It advances the need to change ("perfect") our culture and institutions. The Obama Administration aggressively promoted the narrative amplified by a chorus of voices in the media, creating a national echo chamber of misinformation.

Remember how quickly Obama's Department of (Social) Justice inserted itself in the middle of the Sanford, Florida case involving Trayvon Martin and George Zimmerman. In contrast, Attorney General Eric Holder refused to prosecute The New Black Panthers that intimidated white voters at the polls by carrying clubs and wearing paramilitary uniforms. Nor did he go after the Panthers for putting out a $10,000 bounty for Zimmerman's arrest.

Daily, black criminals target and brutalize whites disproportionately across the country but, Eric Holder turns a blind eye to this actual epidemic. The DOJ is a political apparatus. It serves the Marxist agenda not justice.

This is what Holder did when he pressured Ferguson police to not release the footage of Michael Brown strong-arm robbing a fist full of cigars before he violently attacked Officer Wilson. Certainly, the footage is relevant to show the "gentle giant's" state of mind and criminal character on the day of the shooting death. Holder was replaced by Loretta Lynch who is cut from the same social justice cloth.

Proof of this came two days after a husband and wife Muslim couple launched a deadly terrorist attack in San Bernardino (12/02/2015). Lynch put America on notice that our First Amendment has been reined in. She said, "Now obviously this is a country that is based on free speech, but when it edges towards violence, when we see the potential for someone lifting that mantle of anti-Muslim rhetoric or, as we saw after 9/11, violence against individuals... when we see that, we will take action." One anti-American, Marxist wrecking ball in charge of the DOJ was replaced by another.

The Marxist agenda is not transparent to most people because the public are constantly fed a substitute for reality on TV, in the movies, in schools and in the news. The majority of the **American people are literally programmed to suspend reality**. They process the world through the altered lenses of the narrative fed to them. Take black serial killers for example.

Between 13 and 16 percent of known American serial killers this century have been black (Hickey, Eric, Serial Murders and Their Victims, Monterey, Ca: 1991). During this same period, blacks represented 10 to 12 percent of the population (and black males half of that). Further evidence of the disproportional involvement of black suspects in serial murders is a study of 337 serial killers. The study found that 22 percent of the suspects were black (Hickey, 2nd Ed. 1997:136). Another study included mass-killers and spree-killers along with serial killers, putting the involvement of black suspects at 20 percent. Hence, for the percentage they represent in the population blacks are over-represented as serial killers, but under reported in the media.

A compelling example of the nexus between the liberal media and political correctness is the case of two serial murders in Philadelphia in the mid-1980s. One killer was white and the other was black. Both killers kidnapped, imprisoned and tortured their female victims in basements before killing them. The white killer, Gary Heidrick, was launched into the spotlight of the national media and became the subject of television reports and books. The black killer, Harrison Graham, received little media attention, yet killed four more people than Heidrick.[61]

When we think of serial killers, we think of white males like Jeffery Dahmer and David Berkowitz. Why don't we think of names like Coral Watts, Milton Johnson or Louis Wallace? These three men were black serial killers active in the same era whose number of victims each exceeded those of Dahmer and Berkowitz.

One reason suggested for this imbalance of media coverage is that pejorative terms like "primitive," "monsters," and "animals," are adjectives commonly used to describe serial killers. These terms would be considered racist if applied to blacks or other minority serial killers (Jenkins, 1994:173). Therefore, fear generated by political correctness results in the non-reporting of information (de facto censorship) and the subsequent manipulation of public opinion.

"History is created, manipulated and written by those who are predominantly on the victorious side of the nation which has supreme political and especially military dominance. Any 'truth' which has the slightest potential of weakening their total hold over the masses is not tolerated. Any truth which can impact their power is squelched or cunningly hidden by them, usually in a manufactured media release to the unsuspecting public, often in a jovial manner to render the information a laughing matter and display it as harmless."

Clark C. McClelland, Retired NASA astronaut

---

[61] Jenkins, Philip, *Using Murder: The Social Construction of Serial Homicide,* New York, Aldine De Gruyter, 1994, p.169.

Race

"There is not a truth existing which I fear, or would wish unknown to the whole world." Thomas Jefferson

In 21st Century America no topic is more taboo and more off limits to open discourse – and especially for white people – than race, especially telling the uncomfortable truths about the prevalent and distinct differences in the various races in all things: crime rates, propensity to violence, impulse control, IQ, athletic prowess, credit ratings, neighborhoods, scientific and cultural advancements, historical achievements, inventions, establishment of Great Civilizations, etc.

There is no topic discussed with more dishonesty and outright deceit than race. It is the one topic where an individual's public pronouncements and private opinions are legions apart. When race enters any conversation, otherwise courageous individuals reveal themselves as absolute cowards.

Racial truths are self-evident however, no matter how much they are openly resisted and ruthlessly suppressed. It does not matter how many millions of deluded imbeciles and socially engineered dupes clamor mindlessly in support of the "false narrative." On race, the inconvenient truth about the size and scope of differences, abilities, and accomplishments is a truth most people in America cannot handle.

"Truth never damages a cause that is just." Mahatma Gandhi

Defending Western Civilization, freedom and the Rule of Law are "just" causes. These just causes require that I have the courage to write on the very uncomfortable truth about race, in particular the Negroid (black) race, as it has been made the primary focal point of disinformation fueling the Marxist revolution in the United States.

Long before the days of "political correctness", banned words and forbidden speech, famous German philosopher Arthur Schopenhauer said,

"All truth passes through three stages: First, it is ridiculed. Second, it is violently opposed. And third, it is accepted as self-evident."

Those who speak the truth on race, especially those who point out <u>ANY</u> uncomfortable truth about blacks, are ridiculed or violently opposed.

To paraphrase authors Frank Borzellieri and Jared Taylor, when anyone on the political Left states that they want to "have a conversation about race", what they really mean (and intend) is for white people to sit down, shut up, and be preached to. The true intent of this call for a "conversation" is for whites to be scolded and severely admonished in an uninterrupted minority monologue void of any actual "discussion" or any intellectually honest assessment of the facts and data about race.

Likewise, when you hear the liberal cliché "celebrate diversity," what the Left really means beneath that Orwellian euphemism is to take delight in the state-sponsored racism and officially-sanctioned discrimination directed against white people, especially white males, and to jubilate in the on-going dispossession and disenfranchisement of white America and the dissolution of the country and culture they created.

I highly encourage the reader to check out Frank Borzellieri's books "*The Unspoken Truth*" and "*Don't Take It Personally*." With laser precision, he absolutely destroys the lies about diversity, multiculturalism, race and crime, IQ disparities, and much more. Mr. Borzellieri is a brilliant and fearless reporter of the truth. His two books mentioned above can be used as companion volumes to this book to shine the bright light of truth on the many taboo subjects that plague contemporary America.

Not only is it a lie to assert that the unenviable condition of the majority of blacks today in the U.S. is a symptom of racism and oppression by Whites, it is also a lie asserted about the black condition internationally.

The truth is that—universally—the great majority of blacks suffer most of all from their own prevalent deficiencies and self-destructive propensities—independent of any society they live in.

Even more tragic is the fact that the chronic crime, violence, destruction and chaos originating from so many unprincipled blacks are suffered by all others in their presence.

"There Goes the Neighborhood"

This truth becomes more obvious the denser the black population and only compounded under black-run government: be it Zimbabwe or Baltimore; Haiti or Detroit; Somalia or Chicago; Sudan or D.C.; Rwanda or New Orleans etc. Blacks suffer most where they govern themselves. A dysfunctional majority elects a dysfunctional government. The media suppress this truth and you are a racist or an Uncle Tom for observing and commenting on the self-evident, empirical evidence spread over centuries. Truth has been inverted.

Reality Check

Under the Rule of Law every life regardless of race, creed or social station is to be treated as equally precious and valuable. Nonetheless, not all people, races, religions and cultures give equal value. One can measure and rank cultures and people (tribes) by their accomplishments and contributions to society or their lack thereof.

Where did nearly every comfort, convenience, technological/scientific advancement, engineering feat, medical advance and art enjoyed by the world come from? Close your eyes and point in a random direction. Open your eyes and research the inventor of whatever you are pointing to. What was his last name? What did he look like? What country did his invention come from? Whether it is the conveyor belt, the gun, eyeglasses, electricity, motion pictures, the light switch, remote controls, the battery, infrastructures, fundamental and cutting-edge scientific theories/processes, vacuum cleaner, camera, radio, television, computer, satellite, telephone, locomotive, planes, the rocket, automobiles (and all its parts from the tires to ABS brakes to the variable speed windshield wipers), air conditioner, microwave oven, western medicine, the light bulb, etc. A Marxist would answer, "Humankind invented it all." No. It wasn't "humankind" rather it was one kind of human that brought everything of consequence. White men invented nearly everything of consequence that surrounds you.

That's right, "evil white men" imagined it, invented it, engineered it, manufactured it, and distributed it without prejudice, for self-satisfaction and profit. In the process millions of jobs were created, income taxes paid and the quality of life for all humankind rose significantly around the world. The list of White-guy inventions is so incredibly lopsided compared with any other racial group it is mind boggling.

Some tribes are capable of reverse engineering. They can copy these White-male inventions and make variations from the original to compete with in the free market. Others merely enjoy them, covet them as status symbols and depend on them daily, but their tribe cannot reverse engineer so much as the zipper, toothpick, or rubber band.

As America's Occupation Government continues to orchestrate radical demographic change, the self-evident truth about race, culture and who needs whom will become undeniable as society crumbles around us. Two generations of suspending reality by social promotion and government-*forced* preferences/outcomes in education and employment has weakened us and not changed the truth. Notwithstanding man's sinful nature, we are not all the same. Person to person, culture to culture, and tribe to tribe we are all very different. We should treat one another as equally precious in our daily walk and under the law even though it is undeniable that we do not all contribute the same value to society. That is the ideal, but such a tolerance and Christian attitude is by and large a one-way street.

<u>Warning</u>: Objects in Your Rearview Mirror May be Closer than They Appear

Reality is gaining on us. The United States is headed down a horrific and violent road given the balkanized, rapidly growing, unassimilated and hostile minority ethnic groups here juxtaposed to the aging, shrinking and vilified, Old Guard white majority. A prediction for America can be made by looking at the illustrative economic and crime trends in parts of Africa.

The fast-changing United States population as a whole and Whites in particular will suffer unprecedented horrors — the likes of what is taking place in southern Africa and post-apartheid South Africa. It is instructive to study the region in some depth as it is a bellwether for the pending demise and total breakup of American society; a demise orchestrated on-cue by the handlers of Obama. Even with Obama out of office he is given a voice while the media work to make President Trump's election appear illegitimate and his America-first agenda appear racist.

South African-born Ilana Mercer, author of *"Into the Cannibal's Pot: Lessons for America from Post-Apartheid South Africa"* said — "More people are murdered in one week under African rule than were under the detention of the Afrikaner government over the course of roughly four decades."

South Africa's population is 14 million black and 6 million white. White people in general, and white farmers in particular, are being systematically dispossessed, brutalized and mass murdered in southern Africa to an extent not seen since the Soviet Communist genocide committed before, during and after World War Two against the Germans and Eastern European peoples.

Nowhere is this more widespread than in black-run Zimbabwe (formerly White-run Rhodesia until 1980) and the "new" black-run South Africa.

Since the dawn of black majority rule in South Africa in 1994, an all-out genocide has been carried out by blacks against the native Whites (people of Dutch descent known as "Afrikaners"), with the full support of the black-run government.

News coverage of this modern-day holocaust is ignored and actively suppressed throughout the world, but especially in the U.S. media. In fact, this black-on-white genocide is the one and only case that exists anywhere in the world where a minority group is actively persecuted, brutalized, systematically dispossessed and mass murdered by the thousands without so much as a peep from the media or the plethora of "human rights" organizations around the world and other so-called advocates for the persecuted and downtrodden (i.e. Human Rights Watch, the Red Cross, Doctors Without Borders, Amnesty International, etc.).

Culture Matters

Since the Zimbabwe government-enforced seizure of white-owned farms and the subsequent genocide against white farmers began under black rule, the agricultural-based economy has collapsed, and the country is now starving to death.

Historically, the extremely small population of white farmers literally fed the entire country. In what is one of the most extreme and personified cases of "biting the hand that feeds you", black Zimbabweans are literally KILLING the hands that feed their country (30% of the population is now starving).

The black Zimbabwe authorities (police, military, provincial officials) refuse to investigate the theft, robbery, and murder of white people, and the expropriation of their houses, farms and land in black-run Zimbabwe, because this is state-run and state-sanctioned persecution and violence directed against whites.

Robert Mugabe, the racist black dictator, also banned whites from owning businesses in the "new" black-run Zimbabwe. Due to the on-going persecution, dispossession and rampant violent crime against whites, the "professional classes" — doctors, nurses, economists, scientists, engineers and farmers — that are able to leave, flee the country. And they literally "flee for their lives" — being forced by the black government to leave their wealth and real estate behind.

The exodus and mass murder of whites has created a national "brain drain." Its effects can be dramatically felt in the hollowed-out hospitals and medical care facilities that have virtually ceased to operate under black-run incompetence and mismanagement.

A further side-effect of the "white removal" of medical professionals is the rapid spread of disease, which has become rampant. Due to poor medical record keeping, a large but unknown percentage of the population suffers from AIDS. What is known is that 20% of black Zimbabwean adults are HIV positive.

The following are some vital statistics for black-run Zimbabwe:

- The unemployment rate is estimated to be 94%!
- Life expectancy is just 30 years of age.
- Most of the country suffers from shortages of basic foodstuffs and fuel.

- Most dwellings have no electricity or running water.

Shortly after the official confiscation of privately-owned white farms by the black government began in the late 1990s the Zimbabwean economy experienced record hyper-inflation.

The black takeover of the previously white-owned farms resulted in a sharp drop in food production and an immediate steep decline in exports of agricultural goods. This had a massive negative impact on the money flow into the national treasury. It didn't take long for the agricultural-based economy to collapse.

Under black government rule and black-operated farms, about 30% of the country's 13 million people are now starving to death.

Zimbabwe now has the worst ranked economy in the world, reaching a record 80 BILLION PERCENT inflation rate in November 2008!

From 2008 to 2009 the hyper-inflation reached such epidemic proportions that the Zimbabwean government stopped keeping official inflation statistics.

At one point the government actually printed a 100 Trillion "Zim dollar" bill, the highest denomination paper banknote ever printed in any country.

The 100 Trillion Zim dollar bill wouldn't get you far though: it was good for daily bus fare and not much else.

Prices doubled every 24 hours and the annual rate of price growth was 11 million percent!

In 2009, Zimbabwe abandoned its totally worthless currency, literally not worth the paper it was printed on.

As of today, Zimbabwe still has no national currency. The country uses currencies from other countries as a medium of exchange, with the currency of choice being the U.S. dollar.

RED BADGE

The Reserve Bank of Zimbabwe has officially declared that it has no intention of bringing back a national currency (which the people have no faith in anyway).

There is only one radio station in the whole country, which is owned and controlled by the government, and disseminates nothing but "party propaganda" 24 hours a day. It is the only source of information for most of the nation's people.

Possession of a short-wave radio capable of picking up foreign or unauthorized broadcasts is illegal and Zimbabwean police have a history of conducting house-to-house searches for short-wave radio possession. Possession of a cell phone can also land one in jail.

In 1994 Nelson Mandela's black communist revolutionary movement, the "African National Congress," assumed all governmental and institutional power in South Africa (Remember, this is the man held up as a saint and awarded the Nobel Peace Prize the year before and who was adored by President Obama).

Since that date, almost 10% of the 40,000-strong white farming community has been murdered. The glorification of Mandela by Hollywood and TIME magazine ignored this horrific truth. But it is worse than that.

Another 300,000 innocents have been murdered since the dawn of black rule. This "ethnic cleansing" and extermination of whites continues unabated.

The "new" black-ruled South African government has instituted an attack on private property, personal wealth and business called "Black Economic Empowerment" (BEE), which includes, among other things, a series of anti-white laws that forcefully redistribute profit, business ownership, and labor. BEE is literally state-sanctioned racism and discrimination directed against white people, and white males in particular.

Even Great Britain's elite, left-wing journal "The Economist" called South Africa's Black Economic Empowerment "The world's most extreme affirmative action program."

Ilana Mercer, a native of South Africa, had this to say about the effects of BEE:

"...such a coercive transfer of private wealth from those who create it to those who consume it is that societal institutions – state and civil – are being hollowed out like husks. South Africa's gutted institutions serve as a harbinger of things to come in the U.S., where affirmative action is still dismissed as a 'minor irritant', but ought not to be. **South Africa is a microcosm of what America could become, unless it returns to the principles that made it great."** Culture matters.

The black crime wave that has engulfed South Africa since the dawn of Black Rule is so out of control that ghastly events have become an everyday occurrence. The black government has actively covered-up this on-going holocaust by releasing its highly flawed and fraudulent national crime statistics only once a year.

Reputable international organizations including Interpol, the Institute for Security Studies, the Crime Information Analysis Center, and United Christian Action have all done independent analysis of crime in South Africa and found it to be far in excess of what the black South African government has reported officially.

Regarding the crime of murder, an excellent barometer of a nation's level of violence and criminal pathology, South Africa's (murder) rate was found to be in some cases DOUBLE what the black government had reported officially.

Robert McCafferty of United Christian Action, who studied and analyzed crime in South Africa and collated information from various domestic and international sources said, "What sets

South Africa's crime apart from basically every other country on earth is the incredibly high levels of violent crime."

Independent estimates on the murder rate run from a low of 89 per day to as high as 130 people murdered EVERY SINGLE DAY! Compare this with Chicago — America's "Murder Capital" — which has about one homicide a day.

In black South Africa, a rape is committed every 26 seconds!

And as horrific and unconscionable as statistics like this are, they tend to gloss over an even more brutal reality: most of these black male-committed rapes involve violent assaults, body part mutilations and permanent disfigurements of the victim.

Disturbingly, individual cases of extreme human depravity inflicted on violent crime victims are a regular occurrence in black-run South Africa.

For instance, it is commonplace to hear news of an infant being raped, both vaginally and anally. In black African culture it is a fact that many men believe that "baby rape" will cure them of AIDS (an extreme version of their own "virgin cleansing myth").

Writing in the "Child Abuse Review", Linda M. Richler states that the rape of infants in South Africa has reached "epidemic proportions" and "occurs with unacceptably high frequency."

Richler continues, "To penetrate the vagina of a small child the perpetrator must first create a common channel between the vagina and anal canal by forced insertion of an implement."

Ilana Mercer documents that "Roughly 10% of all rapes in the country — **52,425 a year** — are **committed against children under three years of age!"**

Ilana Mercer further points out that in black South African culture, "Young men consider rape a form of recreation"— so much so that they have even coined an expression for recreational gang rape: "Jack-rolling."

Starting in 1999 — just five years after the black takeover — rape became so prevalent and was so out of control in black-run South Africa that the Lloyds of London insurance company (known as "the Rolls-Royce of insurance coverage") began underwriting rape insurance policies for South African women.

The "Rape Care" insurance package includes benefits for surviving victims who contract HIV or AIDS as a result of being raped. Recall that a violent rape is committed every 26 seconds in South Africa and 34% of the adult population of southern Africa carries the AIDS virus!

Mercer again:

"Add to this what are known as "muti-murders" (African ritual killings, which include genital mutilation, castration, and human sacrifice), and "necklacing", the black African custom of placing a diesel fuel-doused tire around someone's neck and igniting it, and one has an idea of the level of black criminal pathology that is commonplace in black-run, "democratic" South Africa."

Mercer documents crimes committed by black against whites that are beyond comprehension to Americans. Seven times a day white farmers are murdered and often times their families too. Many of these murders take place on Sunday when the patriarch is attending church. He returns home to discover his elderly or infirmed in-laws or parents have been gang raped, tortured, mutilated and murdered. He might also discover his wife and children have suffered the same barbaric brutality and are alive just enough to be abused more as he is forced to watch them suffer and die. The torture includes having knives stuck in their vagina and their eyelids cut off. He then meets a similar grizzly fate of torture and mutilation to include his penis being cut off. These ritualistic and frenzied rapes, mutilations and murders do not make the news in the U.S. but it would if the roles were reversed. The Christian-Newsome murders in Knoxville, Tennessee was of the same kind of crime and happened here, but got almost no coverage.

Prior to black rule, the rape of women, especially white women, was a rare occurrence, and perpetrators were swiftly and severely punished. No more.

Ilana Mercer on black South African crime and corruption: "In a country in which crimes are seldom prosecuted, the newly-installed President Zuma has the dubious distinction of having stood trial on 783 charges of corruption, racketeering, tax evasion, and rape."

Daniel Etounga-Manguelle, a native-born black Cameroonian and former advisor to the World Bank, had this to say about black Africans: **"What Africans are doing to one another defies credulity. Genocide, bloody civil wars, and rampant violent crime suggest African societies at all social levels are to some extent cannibalistic."**

The only fix he argues is fundamental cultural change. This abhorrent behavior is not a product of colonialism. He rejects the stock answer that disparities in crime and the downward spiral in quality of life are symptoms of the legacy of colonial rule, saying that African traditions stayed intact during that period. (See Chapter 5 of *Into The Cannibal's Pot* by Ilana Mercer for an in-depth deconstruction of the colonialism argument)

"Do White Lives Matter?"

By their deafening silence it is obvious that to the media and human rights groups around the world, White lives mean nothing.

Whether it be an adolescent white girl or a frail, elderly white woman who is savagely gang raped, brutalized, throat slit and shot full of holes by a group of black men, in the eyes of all the self-proclaimed civil rights advocates, women's rights activists and other human rights groups, it's about as significant as a cockroach being squished on pavement.

For all the governments around the world that pontificate endlessly about "human rights" and self-determination, most especially the United States, it is obvious by their inaction that White lives and the ongoing genocide against Whites in South Africa and neighboring Zimbabwe do not matter. The U.S. government does care plenty about Cecil the lion being killed by a white male, American dentist on safari July of 2015. Where are the media on the real stories? Where are the U.S. and the United Nations' Commission on Human Rights?

Under United Nations General Assembly Resolution 260, the "Convention on the Prevention and Punishment of the Crime of Genocide," adopted in 1948, what is being perpetrated against the White people of South Africa and Zimbabwe clearly meets the criteria and definition of "genocide."

If the United Nations was created to prevent war and stop genocide, why are they "missing in action" on this rampant White genocide?

Where are the calls for stiff sanctions against the black South African and Zimbabwean governments by the various "humanitarian," "civil rights," and other non-governmental organizations (NGOs) to try to bring those blood-thirsty tyrannical governments to heel for their genocidal practices?

Where are the calls for an international boycott of the black South African and Zimbabwean governments by the World Bank and International Monetary Fund (both UN organizations)?

Where are the calls for UN troop intervention to stop the killing and to "save the women and children?"

Why is the U.S. Congress not advocating for a humanitarian intervention?

Where was Obama calling for airstrikes, drone attacks and NATO boots on the ground to stop the terroristic African National Congress? Finally, under Trump the topic is getting some notice.

A Glaring International Double Standard

Clearly, for all the undeserved venomous hate and false propaganda directed against them, White people constitute the only race and "group" – in the world – that can be persecuted, systematically dispossessed, mass murdered and exterminated as a people with no repercussions to the perpetrators.

There is not one word of concern nor any human-rights advocacy emanating from the world's media, the world's governments, the various international aid and human rights groups, and the one international organization invested with the global reach and military power to bring a stop to these types of atrocities: the UN.

Who is Committing the Genocide?

It is a combination of corrupt, racist black police officers, common black criminals, black gangs, black militias, and black communist revolutionary groups like the African National Congress (ANC).

Groups like the ANC and other organized black militias committing the white genocide are in some cases armed, funded and encouraged by elements in the black government. These groups are effectively acting as a covert proxy force for the government, carrying out their genocidal policies while giving them "plausible deniability."

Because the crimes are committed by or with the tacit approval of a racist, sympathetic black national police force, the police seldom make any attempt to solve the crime.

The murder victims include men, women, children and babies — no white person is spared — regardless of age, infirmity, innocence, or defenselessness. Again, these crimes are rarely if ever investigated.

To further degrade and defile their white victims, the black perpetrators oftentimes repeatedly stab and hack the bodies of their victims with large knives and machetes and mutilate, dismember and/or castrate them before their untimely deaths.

Most of the women and young girls are repeatedly gang raped before being hacked, mutilated, dismembered and shot to death.

And many of these barbaric murders also involve a high degree of torture before the final grisly act.

The almost-all-black South African Police Service (SAPS) is so systemically corrupt and incompetent that virtually none of the murderers of the nation's white people is ever identified, let alone apprehended or prosecuted.

This is well known by black criminals, encouraging further dispossession, theft, robbery and murder of white people.

Just like everywhere else in the world where blacks and whites live amongst each other, virtually all of the inter-racial violence in South Africa is one-way: black-on-white.

Dr. Gregory Stanton, head of "Genocide Watch" warns of preparation for government-sanctioned genocide against white farmers and their families. But it is already underway when you consider the on-going slaughter of whites by black gangs and South Africa President Jacob "Juju" Zuma openly advocating mass-murder of European-descendent South Africans.

Dr. Stanton confirmed in a June 2003 interview that, **"The rates at which the (white) farmers are being eliminated, the torture and dehumanization involved — all point to systematic extermination."**

Dr. Stanton points out that while the crime of murder is rampant throughout black-run South Africa, whites specifically are murdered at four times the rate of the rest of the population (which includes blacks, Asian Indians, Mulattos and others).

Due to the on-going genocide against white farmers, statistically, farming in South Africa is now the most dangerous occupation in the world.

The Republic of South Africa <u>under White-rule</u> had the highest standard of living and the strongest economy on the African continent. It <u>was the *only* African country with a space program and a nuclear program.</u> It alone had modern skyscrapers in the major city business districts and its beautiful, largely crime-free cities were international tourist attractions. **Culture matters**.

If White-run South Africa was so racist and evil, why did the country experience constant black immigration but NO black emigration? By "voting with their feet," blacks all across the African continent clearly demonstrated that they preferred to be second-class citizens in a First-World, White-run country than first-class citizens in a backward, Black-run, and Third-World country.

Devolution — When Fact and Fiction Collide

Ironically, the plight of blacks in South Africa under Black-rule is far worse than it ever was under (minority) White-rule.

Under White-rule, blacks in South Africa had the highest standard of living on the African continent, and a much higher standard of living than in any Black-run country. **Culture matters**.

Historians and the media criticize apartheid as immoral and racist. At first glance, who could argue to the contrary? Many would be surprised to know its origins were economic. It was brought about by organized white laborers forcing a wedge between black laborers and white industrialists and merchants. Clearly, apartheid evolved beyond economics to protect Afrikaners from violent, predatory black-on-white crime. As unpopular as segregation became in the international community, in retrospect it cannot be denied that the apartheid system provided a stable, effective and mutually beneficial economy and form of government for both races.

Under apartheid there were many wealthy blacks, crime was low, criminal justice was effective, trains ran on time, there was low unemployment, and there was the best health care on the continent. The standard of living for both black and white was very high. **Culture matters.**

Compare that stable picture to today's violent, murderous, disease-ridden and starvation-plagued South Africa under black-rule. **Culture matters**.

Shortly after blacks took over the South African government the unemployment rate DOUBLED, with almost half the nation unemployed. Black-run South Africa currently has a 48% unemployment rate. **Culture matters**.

The white poverty rate, which was literally non-existent under white-rule, now runs at 7% to 10% every year (which is strikingly similar to Obama's America!).

Under Black-rule, the amount of people subsisting on $1.00 a day (yes, that's ONE U.S. dollar a day!) also doubled, to roughly one out of eight black South Africans.

In 2006, only 5,000 of the 35 million black South Africans earned more than $60,000 a year.

Fully 25% of the people live in shacks without electricity or running water. Another 25% do not even have access to clean drinking water.

Almost half the nation's schools have no electricity (40%), and half the country lives without telephone service of any kind.

The HIV/AIDS infection rate is 20%. In other words, one in five South African blacks is either HIV positive or has full-blown AIDS.

Under Black-rule, South Africa has the distinction of being the "crime capital of the world" (with a higher violent crime rate than countries engulfed in civil war, such as Syria, Iraq, Afghanistan and Mexico). **Culture matters.**

More police officers are murdered in South Africa than in any other country in the world!

South Africa also has the highest rate of rape and gang rape in the world – a crime one could argue is the worst dehumanization possible, leaving the victim to endure the physical, psychological and emotional scars for the rest of her life.

"At his best, man is the noblest of all animals; separated from law and justice he is the worst." Aristotle

More disturbing still, an offender's chances of being brought to justice and held accountable for the crimes of rape, robbery or murder are almost nonexistent.

South Africa also is the world's leader in the "non-violent" crimes of fraud, identity theft and child pornography.

Crime is so out of control and has become such a national embarrassment that the Black-run government stopped keeping crime statistics for several years, lest they fall into the "wrong hands."

If we are to believe the current regime's own statistics, less than 8% of violent criminals are ever brought to justice.

In other words, more than 9 out of 10 criminals who commit murder, rape, robbery, home-invasion burglary, and/or aggravated assault get away with the crime!

"For in all states of created beings capable of law, where there is no law, there is no freedom." John Locke

All of this is well known by the media, especially the mainstream media in the United States. However, not a word is spoken of this violent, crime-ridden, murderously racist, backward, Black-run country.

Every day there is news of new atrocities and new horror stories committed against whites that come across the international wire services like Reuters and the Associated Press, only to be ruthlessly suppressed by the American media establishment.

Censorship protects the selective outrage in the "false narrative" making it easier to manipulate Americans' perception of reality; blacking out the horrible truth that would shatter the Left's Big Lie.

Most Americans have no idea that any of this is taking place, and if one listened to the American mainstream media, or read the Orwellian "Newspeak" propaganda on Wikipedia, they would think all is well in South Africa since the blacks took over the government and pillars of power. Nothing could be further from the truth.

And let's not forget about the all-black African nation of Rwanda, in which inter-tribal warfare erupted in 1994.

The Hutu majority (84%) sought to completely exterminate the Tutsi minority (15%). With utmost savagery, over one million Tutsis were slaughtered in 100 days, mostly with machetes!

Out of a population of 7.3 million people, the official figures published by the Rwandan government estimated the number of victims of the genocide at 1.2 million people. This calculates to **10,000 people murdered every day. Put another way: 400 every hour or 7 every minute!**

An estimated 500,000 women and girls were raped, gang-raped, beaten and brutalized. And to finalize and give lasting memory to their degradation, their genitalia were mutilated by their attackers.

Are these sorts of horrors the future that awaits White Americans as they fall from the majority?

But it is already happening! The media censor the prolific black-on-white crime in America just as they do in South Africa. As whites in America become a minority they will be brutalized in larger numbers and greater frequency by unassimilated groups taught to hate them. As the demographics and culture of local police forces, judges, prosecutors and juries change, accountability, justice and fairness will be a crap shoot.

It usually takes a foreigner to hold the mirror for us to see our condition. Patrick Sheehan, who was employed by the *Morning Herald* newspaper in Sydney, Australia, wrote an article in 1995 that you would never see in an American newspaper.

Mr. Sheehan analyzed U.S. Department of Justice crime data documented in the FBI's Uniform Crime Reports over a 30-year period, from the enactment of the Civil Rights Act of 1964 to 1994.

What Mr. Sheehan discovered shocks the conscience and is one of those astonishing truths that dare not be spoken in America. Based on his research Mr. Sheehan wrote:

"The longest war America has ever fought is the Dirty War, and it is not over. It has lasted 30 years so far and claimed more than 25 million victims. It has cost almost as many lives as the Vietnam War...yet the American news media do not want to talk about the Dirty War, which remains between the lines and unreported...When all the crime figures are calculated, it appears that black Americans have committed at least 170 million crimes against white Americans in the past 30 years (1964 to 1994). It is the great defining disaster of American life and American ideals since World War II. All these are facts, yet by simply writing this story, by assembling the facts in this way, I would be deemed a racist by the American news media. It prefers to maintain a paternalistic double-standard in its coverage of black America..."

Twenty-three years have passed since Sheehan's article and the Dirty War continues. It has been 50 years since the Civil Rights Act was passed and since "The War on Poverty" was declared. Blacks have been given complete political freedom, preferential hiring, preferential economic and educational opportunities (mostly at the cost of Whites and Asians), special civil rights protections ("protected class" identification in law and employment), and over 22 TRILLION dollars has been forcefully extracted through taxation from the majority white population to be largely redistributed to blacks in the form of welfare and tailor-made government programs. **This figure is more than the national debt!**

Since the inception of LBJ's *War on Poverty* in 1965, means-tested welfare spending has increased 16 times over what it was.[62] Today, over one-half of the population receives some form of welfare benefit with blacks and Hispanics grossly over-represented as recipients.

---

[62]Romina Boccia, *Opportunity For All. Favoritism For None*. Heritage Foundation, P. 144, January 23, 2015

What is the return on investment? Nationally, approximately one-third of black males less than 35 years of age are convicted felons, currently charged with a felony, in jail or prison, on probation or parole, or have an active felony warrant for their arrest.

In our nation's capital, Washington D.C., the problem is even worse. The Washington Post has reported that 50% of black males between the ages of 18 and 35 are "incarcerated, on parole or probation, awaiting trial or being sought on an arrest warrant on any given day."

As disturbing as these numbers are they do not include the following: the unknown number of black males who have evaded police detection and apprehension for their crimes, the multitudes who have been arrested by the police but were never charged by prosecutors, and also those who have completed their jail or prison time and the terms of their probation or parole.

When one contemplates the magnitude of this crime rate reality, it becomes crystal clear that a significant majority of the young black male population of Washington D.C. are in fact criminals. And most major cities echo these same alarming statistics.

One only has to survey the wanton violence, arson, destruction and chaos inflicted on the city of Ferguson, Missouri following the death of violent felon Michael Brown by police to see that lurking in the shadows of the night is an ever-present army of black criminals waiting to spring themselves on the *innocent, law-abiding community* at large (white, black and other).

Due to the suppression of these inconvenient truths by our Marxist media establishment, most Americans are not aware of this terrifying reality. But what they do know is what they feel in their gut, what they personally see and hear and what they themselves experience.

And what they feel and experience was illuminated by none other than Jesse Jackson when he stated the following: *"There is nothing more painful to me at this stage in my life than to walk down the street and hear footsteps and start thinking about robbery — then turn around and see somebody white and feel relieved."* (Source: Dr. Walter E. Williams, "Is Profiling Racist?" August 3, 2010)

As one of the so-called "leaders of the black community," it was Jesse Jackson again who pointed out the uncomfortable truth that more blacks are murdered and assaulted by other blacks in ONE YEAR than all the blacks murdered and assaulted by white people in the last 100 years.

Even more disturbing is the fact that more white people are murdered and raped by blacks each and every year than all the blacks lynched by white people over the last century. I can think of no two crimes that are more hateful and degrading than murder and rape.

While some observers point out that 93% of blacks murdered are killed by other blacks, what they never discuss is that over half of all the white people murdered in the United States every year are murdered by blacks. Equally ignored is the astonishing fact that interracial rape is almost exclusively a black-on-white crime. In 2010 there were 37,000 white women raped by black males. Significantly, an additional 36,000 black women were raped exclusively by black *males* (the term "males" implies adult and juvenile offenders). Over a two-year period from 2012 to 2014 the number of black-on-white rapes spiked even higher to 44,000 a year!

It is estimated by the FBI that as many as a third of all rapes go unreported, so the number of white women raped by black males every year (and black women raped by black males every year) is surely many thousands higher than even the grim statistics document.

Combing through the DOJ's Bureau of Justice Statistics reports, **in any given year it is not uncommon to discover that not a single white-on-black rape was reported anywhere in our country of over 300 million people.** Even in the rare case a white-on-black rape is reported it is unlikely that the offender is actually white. For instance, a Spanish-speaking Negro born in Cuba who rapes a black woman in Florida will be tallied as a "white-on-black rape" due to the DOJ classifying offenders from "Hispanic" countries as white. In fact, such a rape is a black-on-black crime. That same offender raping a white victim would be tallied as a "white-on-white rape" when in actuality it was a black perpetrator both times. These statistics deflate black offender numbers and artificially inflate white offender numbers. This shows the systemic level of deceit emanating from the Department of Justice and their statistical compilations.

At 6% of the U.S. population, black males not only commit a grossly disproportionate amount of violent crime, they commit a substantial majority of ALL violent crime in the nation!

The criminal justice system is not racist toward blacks.

Blacks are arrested at a rate equal to the rate victims identify them as suspects.

Between 1976 and 2005, 52% of murders in the USA were committed by blacks! Prolific.

While only 3% of white crimes are committed against blacks, well over 50% of black crimes are directed against white people. And even this figure of 3% is highly misleading; as law enforcement data classifies Mexicans, Puerto Ricans, Cubans, and other non-white Hispanic/Latinos as "Whites" in their crime reports (this is standard operating procedure in FBI Uniform Crime Reports).

According to the *LA Times*, 95% of outstanding homicide warrants in Los Angeles are for Hispanic illegal aliens (mostly Mexican nationals) many of whom are gang members. Yet statistically these wanted murderers are listed as "white" in FBI Uniform Crime Reports. This is a great deception. To illustrate just how little crime is actually committed by Caucasians (White Americans of exclusively European descent) one need only look at our largest city, New York, with over 8 million people.

Heather Mac Donald, J.D., a John M. Olin Fellow at The Manhattan Institute in New York, a distinguished author and contributing editor of the urban affairs quarterly magazine *City Journal*, has extensively researched national crime statistics, police tactics, and the mother of all taboos, the racial component of crime — with a special focus on New York City.

She notes that official NYPD reports document that 89% of crime victims in New York City identify their attacker as a "black or Hispanic male."

Blacks commit 75 percent of all shootings in New York and make up 23 percent of the city's population.

Furthermore, based on victim and witness statements provided to the NYPD, 83% of all gun-brandishing assailants are black, yet black males make up only 12% of the city's population. Another 15% of armed assailants are identified as "Hispanic" by victims and witnesses. So blacks and Hispanics are responsible for 98% of the crimes involving a firearm in America's largest city. This means that a mere 2% of gun-related crimes are committed by a combination of Whites, Asians, Indians and "others."

Other studies have shown that whites commit about 1% of the homicides in New York City, where they are 45% of the population. What does this mean in practical terms?

If you are assaulted, robbed or murdered while going about your business in America's largest city, there's a 98% chance that your attacker will be a black or Hispanic male.

That is not racist rhetoric — that is reality. The numbers prove that if all black and Hispanic males moved out of New York City it would be safer than Boise, Idaho. And New York is hardly an anomaly.

Crime statistics in most cities and especially in the larger cities reflect a similar pattern. Chicago's Hyde Park neighborhood, which is mostly white, has a homicide rate of 3 per 100,000 people.

In nearby Washington Park, a neighborhood whose population is 98% black, the homicide rate is 78 per 100,000 people – over 25 times higher!

The Englewood neighborhood on Chicago's South Side, which is almost entirely black, consistently has the highest number of shootings and murders in the whole city.

Even "white collar crime" — which liberals and the media love to falsely claim is largely committed by whites — is predominantly perpetrated by blacks.

In fraud, forgery, counterfeiting, embezzlement and trafficking in stolen property, black arrests outnumber white arrests by 300%. (Source: FBI UCR)

Rarely has a social epidemic been so one-sided in regards to who the victims and perpetrators are — as crime. Yet whites continue to be inundated with deceitful propaganda about their history and are brainwashed into looking upon themselves with guilt, shame and self-loathing. They have lost the ability to express collective outrage over being the preferred targets of crime.

Conversely, Marxist agitators continuously pound into the heads of the collective black and Hispanic populations the concepts of: racial pride, victimization, grievance, tribal solidarity, militant ethno-centrism, revenge and hate.

RED BADGE

Is it any wonder blacks perpetrate a grossly disproportional number of ghastly crimes including gang rapes and murders?

According to the Negro Almanac the total number of blacks lynched between 1882 and 1962 was 3,442 (the number is 1,294 for whites lynched over that same span of time). However, from 1947 to 1961 black lynching averaged less than one a year. It is important to remember that lynching was almost always employed against criminals and was a community's response to the commission of a heinous crime such as rape or murder. Although criminal, lynching was normally done in pursuit of justice outside the established system.

Consider the comparatively small number of blacks lynched to the number of unprovoked, unconscionable, and predatory violent crimes (on-going now for 50 years), committed by blacks against millions of innocent white victims. Realize that many of these innocent victims are women, children, and the elderly.

Without even taking into account the staggering number of murders, aggravated assaults and robberies committed against whites every year (which number over half a million) — if one looks at just rapes alone, black males rape 11 times more white females **EVERY SINGLE YEAR** than the total number of blacks lynched by whites from 1882 to 1962.

Lynching is long gone in the USA but there is no end in sight to the predatory savagery of black criminals and the staggering number of despicable crimes they commit against whites every year.

As the Australian reporter Patrick Sheehan said, it truly is a "Dirty War" — and one that has been ignored and covered up by the policy of selective outrage in the media and U.S. government for two generations now.

RED BADGE
International white genocide & America's 50-year Dirty War beg the question, "Was Thomas Jefferson right?"

On the third panel of the Jefferson Memorial you will see only the first sentence below quoted from Thomas Jefferson's autobiography. It is the words following that sentence from the original text that have virtually been airbrushed away from public view that gives the reader pause:

*"Nothing is more certainly written in the book of fate than that these people (the Negroes) are to be free. **Nor is it less certain that the two races, equally free, cannot live in the same government. Nature, habit, opinion has drawn indelible lines of distinction between them.** It is still in our power to direct the process of emancipation and deportation peaceably and in such slow degree that the evil will wear off insensibly, and their place be...pari passau filled up by free White laborers. If on the contrary it is left to force itself on, human Nature must shudder at the prospect held up."*

And so it goes. America is "shuddering at the prospect" of a **black crime epidemic** that has "forced itself" on, just as Thomas Jefferson predicted.

In 1867, just two years after the Civil War concluded, President Andrew Johnson stated the following in his annual address to the U.S. Congress:

"... (Blacks) have less capacity for government than any other race of people. No independent government of any form has ever been successful in their hands. On the contrary, wherever they have been left to their own devices they have shown a constant tendency to relapse into barbarism."

Look at the world. Look at black Africa. Compare American cities. Does President Johnson's observation hold true?

Stop the excuse making! The black demographic in the USA is afforded the highest level of grace for failure and the lowest threshold of self-control (think of riots and looting) for anti-social and violent criminal behavior. **If Presidents Jefferson and Johnson are to be proven wrong that burden must be placed squarely on black shoulders. In the meantime, (perhaps forever more) orderly society must respond to reality by supporting proactive policing and rejecting The Big Lie.**

One of the obstacles to disproving Jefferson and Johnson and to ending the Dirty War is the self-proclaimed, media-baptized, black "leadership." They reject truth. They teach hate and victimhood for power and profit.

Accomplished, intellectually honest and independent-thinking black Americans like Dr. Ben Carson, lawyer/radio personality Larry Elder and others know there is no connection between Selma-1965 and Ferguson-2014. They love America as she is, scars and all, but the media work to discredit and shun them from getting much traction.

In contrast the media seek out dividers, deceivers, enablers and real haters the likes of Al Sharpton, Jeremiah Wright, Jesse Jackson, Oprah (who said "Old white people have to die" when referring to ending racism), Louis Farrakan, Eric Holder, and former New Orleans Mayor Ray Nagin (whose dream it was to rebuild a "chocolate city" after Hurricane Katrina). These frauds and their army of unappeasable followers see racism everywhere. But, THEY are the haters! They invert reality. They will not live without a crutch and compete in peace and harmony under a mutually respected rule of law, and shared affection for our history and ethos. These "leaders" do not want an honest discussion about race or the causes of the black crime epidemic. Race hustling is easier and more profitable than having a real job or producing anything.

Another obstacle to ending the Dirty War is the psychological self-flagellation of white guilt. This programmed guilt causes many whites to accept, justify or excuse prolific black crime as a reaction to oppression. It is 2019! There is no black oppression! "Shake off the psychological hold of the Big Lie, Whitey!" There is no just cause for the generational black criminal tribalism perpetrated on American society and whites in particular. **Standing up for law and order does not make you a racist.**

Former prison psychologist Marlin Newburn says:

"Black street predators are merely living their preferred lifestyle where property destruction and primitive brutality bring them the sadistic entertainment and power they enjoy…

"What's worse is that there is nobody in the mainstream media or in political office willing to step up in the light and call the community-killing exactly what it is. Worse yet, they outright lie about these black crimes by using some Orwellian newspeak to redirect accurate descriptions of the predators...

"Cowardice by the power elite fuels the carnage while hastening the death of business and communities. And more blacks will end up dead or in prison...

"As a prison psychologist I've talked with hundreds of young black predators who simply said they 'was just havin' fun.' They did not have a recognizable conscience, no thoughts of personal responsibility or feelings of guilt or empathy for their victims, nor did they remotely have a grasp of the pain and community destruction they and their 'homeboys' caused.

"Having the emotional maturity level of a pre-adolescent, age 8 to 12 inclusive, they act on emotions, not thought. They are completely infantilized due to never being held accountable for their actions. Because of never having been taught delayed gratification and consideration of others, they also live and act on impulse, never thinking of possible consequences.

"They are classic narcissists where the world must conform to their impulses or demands.

"That the media and political powers are willing to turn a collective blind eye on the pathology helps black crime grow. It demonstrates a tacit acceptance of the mayhem.

"Not accurately reporting the willful destruction and assaults of others by black street predators is a form of caring in their eyes, but its pathological altruism at its sickest. It's a very sick form of 'understanding' under the belief that they are being compassionate toward their imagined put-upon black people as said black people live a libertine lifestyle.

"All they're doing is helping increase the insanity as the black predator knows he is covered with a blanket anonymity, and that there is no one in power who will hold him personally responsible. Until they end up dead or in prison, they enjoy the predator lifestyle." — **Dr. Marlin Newburn**

The black-on-white crime wave in the U.S. is not a reaction to real injustices blacks are suffering at the hands of the white majority. Furthermore, social justice is not tied to righteousness, but revolution and opportunism. The terrorist chant, "No Justice, No Peace!" is born of fiction not virtue. Offender-victim demographics over fifty years prove the Dirty War is the reality. White Americans have long suffered from black predatory tribalism. Nevertheless, speaking truth on race and crime necessarily brands one a racist. I am amused by the complicit media propping up a substitute for reality by calling footage of young black mobs rioting and looting "teen violence." It is such an absurd euphemism. If the viewer sees and calls it what it is he is labeled "racist." Stop playing along by suspending reality.

Recognize the label for what it is. Do not run from it; that is what the Marxists want. Push through it. The patented use of the words "racist" and "racism" are a Marxist construct. These words did not exist in the English language prior to the 1930s. They are the product of the *Frankfurt School*.

The creation of the words *racist* and *racism* in essence replaced the words "kind" and "kindred" with a negative connotation. They are applied selectively to whites for the intended purpose of pushing tradition back on its heels. Labeling whites "racists" intimidates them into silence from promoting order and defending standards, expectations and tradition. Ultimately, this created the moral relativism and identity vacuum we see today. The term(s) leave the false impression that the naturally defensive side of tribalism or a kindred spirit is unique to whites. In fact, the kindred spirit of tribalism is natural and universal. In benign form you see it in high school and college cafeterias and libraries where ethnic groups self-segregate, or in racially exclusive churches, cultural events, clubs and celebrations.

An adult conversation about race must recognize common tribal characteristics and differences. Not all peoples can be metabolized by a nation. Some tribes are like oil and water; they will never mix or peacefully co-exist like the Israeli Jews and the Palestinians. There will not be peace in the Mid-East until there is an undisputed victor. However, more similar tribes can co-exist with their harmless differences. Sometimes there is crossover (assimilation) through shared ideals, intermarriage and the binding power of a common faith that can for the most part transcend minor differences. Marxist leaders are not interested in a constructive conversation because they are all about being divisive and destructive under the guise of championing tolerance.

Healthy minds would process the facts about race and crime I have assembled, sweep the lies of Marxism aside and demand a substantive analysis and response. But political correctness has literally paralyzed the power of reason and outrage in the majority. A momentum of survival must be initiated through a demonstration of courage by speaking truth. Courage is contagious when demonstrated by a leader.

The last obstacle to ending the Dirty War is cowardice. Courage must be demonstrated by leaders in law enforcement as much as by true leaders in the black population. Sheriffs, Police Chiefs, Prosecutors, Judges and Black Pastors must cast off political correctness. They must see things and say things as they really are. They must operate in reality no matter how uncomfortable that may be. Leadership must not flinch. It must not show any regard to the inevitable false cries of institutional racism. One such voice worthy of familiarizing yourself with is Sheriff David Clarke of Milwaukee. Sheriff Clarke is a realist and a leader who happens to be black.

The Myth of Crime and Poverty

I have spent considerable time and research on facts about race & crime. The reason for this is that I had to debunk two generations of propaganda that built an aversion to truth in the population and perpetuated the Big Lie of a systemic and consequential white racism. It is that lie that fuels the Marxist subversion of American law enforcement and culture. I anticipated how Marxists will respond to the irrefutable facts in this book. They will counter my argument first by attacking the messenger as a racist and also by excusing and justifying the black crime wave as a reaction to poverty and economic oppression.

I credit Heather MacDonald for assembling much of the following information that I extracted from her January 4, 2010 essay, *A Crime Theory Demolished*.

The black crime rate was lower in the 1940s and 1950s when discrimination was legal and black poverty was much higher than it is today. Black crime has increased under the supposed good intentions of liberal policies — independent of poverty.

The poverty-crime theory was born in the 1960s and has steered public policy ever since. The premise is that recession is a predictor of increased crime. In other words, there is a cause-and-effect relationship between poverty and crime. The underlying theory was contrived by sociologists Richard Cloward and Lloyd Ohlin. Both professors argued that juvenile crime was a "social criticism" over upward mobility being a sham. These sociologists served three left-wing presidents: Kennedy, Johnson and Carter. Their bogus theory became the basis of government policies for the massive redistribution of wealth from mostly white working class people to unemployed and unemployable blacks ("unemployable" due to lack of skills and a criminal record).

If crime was caused by poverty, then government could correct it through directed social services and community investment (redistribution of tax dollars). Police bought into this theory because it took pressure off them. It offered a straw man to blame crime on. This relieved them of any ownership of rampant crime. After all, soaring crime was not the result of soft or ineffective policing, but rather it was a social disease out of their control.

The economic facts of the 1960s disprove the premise. Murders rose 43% in a robust economy with expanded government jobs for inner-city minority residents. In fact, if the theory were true would we not have seen unprecedented crime during the Great Depression? Crime rates dropped over that long and most difficult period.

In 2000 Andrew Karmen of New York's John Jay College of Criminal Justice restated Cloward's and Ohlin's premise. In his book *New York Murder Mystery*, he wrote that crime is "a distorted form of social protest." He, like Cloward and Ohlin offers an excuse for criminal behavior. He misplaces the responsibility for crime on the larger (oppressive) society, thereby endorsing social justice as the remedy. Apparently, rioting in Ferguson, Mo. that set a police car ablaze and nearly killed two officers with gunshot wounds deserves grace as it was merely a "distorted form of social protest." The offender is actually the victim don't you see? Advocating individual responsibility, adherence to societal norms of behavior and accountability for blatant criminal acts is backward and ..."racist."

In late 2008 an editorial in the *New York Times* warned that "The economic crisis...has clearly created the conditions for more crime and more gangs among hopeless, jobless young men in the inner cities." Arguing the need to be proactive, the paper encouraged President Obama to pour tax dollars in after-school programs, summer jobs and social workers. The tea leaves had been read, but before any of these measures could be engaged or take effect, the underlying theory proved wrong — just as it did in the 1960s. The FBI's Uniform Crime Report showed that murder dropped 10% nationwide in the first six months of 2009. Violent crime dropped 4.4%. Car thefts dropped almost 19% and property crime dropped 6.1%. All of this good news on crime was reported in the midst of a recession and housing collapse. In Los Angeles murders dropped 25% in 2009 while unemployment in California was 12.3%. Precisely the opposite of what was predicted happened rendering the assertion that poverty is the root of crime invalid.

Leftists who criticize incarceration rates as racist cannot deny the correlation between the five-fold increase in state and federal prisoners between 1977 and 2008 from 300,000 to 1.6 million and the decrease in crime nationwide. Black incarceration saw a spike in the 1970s and 1980s in black-run cities like Chicago, Detroit, Philadelphia and Cleveland (some of the most violent places in the country). It takes some mental gymnastics to argue racism when the Mayor and/or Police Chief are black.

Successful policing in New York City and Los Angeles reduced crime throughout the recession (from the mid-1990s to present). Success was attributed to a process developed in the mid-1990s by NYPD Commissioner Bratton. It relies on interpreting crime statistics to direct the deployment of police resources combined with holding accountable precinct commanders for results. The process is called *Compstat*.

Compstat was used by NYPD Commissioner Ray Kelly resulting in a 16-year 77% crime drop. Murders fell 19% to their lowest level since 1963. Adhering to Compstat, L.A. in 2009 saw a 17% drop in murder, an 8% drop in property crimes, and a 10% drop in violent crime.

The evidence shows the opposite of the Left's assertion and excuse making for criminals. "Community investment" and make-work projects do not decrease crime. The opposite is true: by crushing crime urban reclamation and the local economy boon. People feel more confident investing in businesses, shopping, eating out and buying homes where crime is low.

Based on offender demographics already documented in this book it stands to reason that recommitting to an on-going process of crushing crime will result in a disproportionate number of police contacts and arrests of black and Hispanic males. Sheriffs and Chiefs need to get in front of the predictable reaction of the Left and lead! They must disarm the Marxists with truth and take back the country. Otherwise Marxists will continue advancing the false conclusion that policing is "racist" and we will continue our descent to chaos and the "remedy" of federal tyranny never before seen here.

Multiculturalism, Crime and Revolution

More broadly, to save our Western culture requires that same kind of courage in leadership nationally. We must reject the Marxists' deadly brand of tolerance and multiculturalism beginning with the immediate overhaul of our immigration and border enforcement policies.

We must be aggressive and unapologetic at saving America's Western European cultural dominance. In the best sense of the word, we must "discriminate."

For example, favoring immigration from India over Mexico is better for America. India is a former British colony and the culture respects education. They are English-speaking and assimilate quickly. Indians typically have a darker complexion than Mexicans. My position is not based on skin color, but cultural preference. **Culture matters.**

Pat Buchanan has rightly pointed out that no dominant majority ethnic group has ever been able to transfer its culture on to a different (replacement) majority ethnic group. China would no longer be China without a Han Chinese super majority (91.9%). America is somewhat different in that we are not a race, but an idea. Nonetheless, that idea has a cradle, an origin, a cultural framework. Our immigration policy (and educational template) must reflect that fact and the fact that not every culture and creed is equally suited to be absorbed into America, least of all — Islam; the translation of which means "submission."

We must learn vicariously through Europe. Western Europeans are suffering the reality that the state religion of tolerance is no match for the intolerant religion of Islam. A nation owes to posterity a posture of jealously — centered on its one legitimate and defining culture (cradle). Law and policy should be built on that plum line. A nation practicing discrimination in its immigration policy is not hate. A nation expressing a preference for one group or religion over another is not hate, it is a prerogative. Americans defending our sovereignty, our heroes, our heritage, the English language and the cultural rudder of Western Civilization is not hate.

Multiculturalism is cultural anarchy. It brings deep divisions, hostility toward the host nation, grievance politics, the welfare state, and moral relativism. It is the plague. It is the death of the West and the native stock of people that created an extraordinary and unparalleled civilization. This suicidal brand of tolerance reflected in immigration policy of Western countries is intentional. Marxists put it there. Marxists must render impotent the freedom-loving spirit unique to Western people for international communism to succeed. Diluting the native and traditional population does just that.

A sane immigration policy defends our Western cultural dominance and benefits those living here. "What can you do for us?" is the question immigration screening need ask of the applicant.

Defending our host culture is not hate. All cultures are not equal. It is okay to make a judgment; some cultures are better than others. In Mexico it is legal in 31 of 32 states to have sex with girls as young as 12 years old;[63] this is wrong. **Culture matters**.

Between 2000 and 2005 almost 100 Hmong men were charged with rape or forced prostitution of girls in Minneapolis-St Paul. Most of the victims were 15-years-old or under and a quarter of them were not Hmong.[64] **Culture matters**.

Americans do not stone women to death for "adultery." **Culture matters**.

Americans do not permit genital mutilation or the rape of boys (a practice called "bacha bazi") as cultural imperatives. **Culture matters**.

---

[63] Ann Coulter, *Ramos Can Stay, But Matt Lauer Has to Go*, Townhall.com, May 27, 2015

[64] Ann Coulter, *Ramos Can Stay, But Matt Lauer Has to Go*, Townhall.com, May 27, 2015

Americans do not rape infants to cure AIDS. **Culture matters**.

Americans do not throw homosexuals off of buildings to their death. **Culture matters**.

Victor Davis Hanson (author of *Mexifornia*) says immigrants to the U.S. vote with their feet. In other words, they agree life is better here, but do they fully understand why? No. They are not taught why. They cross the border and are then discouraged from assimilating by the divisive, Marxist state that seeks to dilute the host culture and render it defenseless.

Compare the orderly, dignified and honorable behavior of the Japanese people following the earthquake on March 11, 2011 to the helplessness, chaos and the opportunistic, predatory criminal behavior in New Orleans following Hurricane Katrina. **Culture matters**. Japan's 9.0 magnitude earthquake triggered a tsunami that then caused a level 7 meltdown of the Fukushima Daiichi Nuclear Power Plant. This was far worse than Hurricane Katrina. To this day there are 300,000 Japanese living peacefully in temporary housing, but through it all there was no rape, looting or murder. **Culture matters.**

In December 2013 Iceland's police shot and killed a suspect for the first time ever. The Republic of 320,000 (93% homogeneous Icelandic) is a very gun-friendly country with almost non-existent violent crime. **Culture matters**.

America is exceptional *because* of our origin and culture, not in spite of them. Without leadership that recognizes, values, promotes and jealously protects America's Western and unique cultural rudder, our circumstance is on course to devolve into unprecedented tribal violence and a tyrannical government.

Civil unrest is just beginning. A race war is being stirred up by the Marxists. They need chaos to seize power. A nation-wide leadership vacuum and identity vacuum have emboldened provocateurs; their momentum is growing in the absence of nationalism, accountability and rebuke. Eventually the rioters (and vigilantes that could rise to counter them) will literally be in the crosshairs of the federal regime's Department of Homeland Security. The regime will respond to this orchestrated crisis as the savior. It will answer the people's cries for safety — at the cost of freedom. Fear plays into the hands of the Marxist state.

The U.S. has reached the saturation point of unassimilated people in many neighborhoods and cities. Some social scientists put the tipping point at 18%. When groups opposed to assimilation reach that mark is when they change from docile to hostile. London is not an English city anymore; Paris will follow. Here, look to Dearborn, Michigan and the Twin Cities of Minnesota as the canaries in the mine.

"No people in history have ever survived who thought they could protect their freedom by making themselves inoffensive to their enemies." Dean Acheson U.S. Secretary of State, 1949-1952

Following the January 2015 massacre in Paris at the satirical weekly *Charlie Hebdo* France's Prime Minster, Manuel Carlos Valls said, "We will do everything to protect our freedom, our democracy and our *tolerance*." The last word in that sentence is the cause of the death of the West. In an identical suicidal tenor Germany's Chancellor Angela Merkel said, immigration is a "gift for all of us."

Madam Chancellor, Islam is a gift from hell! Western leaders will not publically recognize that immigration has become a weapon: Marseille is now 40% Muslim. It is considered the most dangerous city in Europe. Gangs control the city to the point of having their own checkpoints. Police have lost control adding it to the list of "no-go" zones in France, where whites and non-Muslims dare not go and police do not respond. The city was the cultural capital of France. In the 9th Century, Muslims took the city; they still believe it is theirs. If Napoleon Bonaparte were alive he would surround the city and recapture it with fire, bullets and bayonets.

Following 130 murdered and 352 injured in Paris on November 13, 2015 the French government and the media blur reality. French officials identified Abdelhamid Abaaoud as the mastermind behind the attacks. Repeatedly they describe him as a "Belgian man." He might be a Belgian citizen, but he is not a Belgian man. He is an Arab and a Muslim. Similarly, another person believed to have been involved in the attack, Salah Abdeslam, is called a "French National" another misleading term.

Muslim immigrants in Sweden make up 5 % of the population, but commit 77% of its crime.[65] Hail diversity! There is an epidemic of native Swedish women being raped and gang raped by Muslims. In the first seven months of 2013, **Muslims raped 300 Swedish children and 700 Swedish women.** These prolific predator Muslims come primarily from Africa and Saudi Arabia with others arriving from Turkey and Bosnia. While the rapists might be Swedish "residents" or even granted Swedish "citizenship" they are NOT Swedish men as the press has reported. After 40 years of Sweden embracing multiculturalism, violent crime has increased 300%! As a direct consequence of Sweden's liberal immigration policies and allowing into its midst massive numbers of African and Arab Muslims, Sweden now has the distinction of being the "Rape Capital of Europe." [66]

Germany censored the gang rapes of German women by Muslim men on New Year's 2016. In one night there were hundreds of victims of violent crime committed exclusively by non-European Muslims against native German people in 12 of the 16 states. The German government's response: Pamphlets.

---

[65]Bethany Blankley, *As Christianity exits Europe, 'Criminal Muslims' fill void with rabid violence,* The Washington Times, December 29, 2014,
[66]Ingrid Carlqvist and Lars Hedegaard, *Sweden: Rape Capital of the West,* Gatestone Institute (International Policy Council), February 14, 2015.

Chancellor Merkel distributed pamphlets to these "refugees" of a cartoon with a circle and line through it depicting a man groping a woman. The pamphlets are a symptom of the degree of mental illness that Marxism brings to those under its spell. The brain denies itself the natural right of self-defense and national survival as though they are evil acts. The calls for tolerance and diversity by Marxists turn louder while the continent is being sodomized. Make no mistake; these so-called "refugees" are an invading force. They are an army. They are colonizing Europe and rape is one of their weapons of displacement and psychological attack. Merkel's pamphlets emboldened the enemy who laugh at Europe's suicidal mindset. The same government effort to cover-up the prolific rapes of German women by African and Arab Muslims is being repeated in Sweden and Britain.

For native German, French and Swedish husbands, sons, brothers, uncles, fathers, grandfathers and policemen these attacks will restore their sanity. When they look in the eyes of their women who have been raped, gang raped and sodomized it becomes crystal clear that the state's suicidal tenets of tolerance, diversity and acceptance are no longer virtues. The common denominator of the offender cannot be ignored. **Righteous anger is the proper emotional response. War with the Muslim invaders is the only answer.** These backward merciless, savages must be repelled swiftly and with extreme prejudice! These rapes cannot be handled as a criminal justice matter as if the perpetrators are a part of our civilization. The frequency is so great and the scope so wide that native German women will not go outside to attend annual festivals for fear of being raped. The scale of rape and other violence is so brazen and widespread throughout Western Europe it is beyond the ability of civil authorities to handle it as a criminal matter. It is an act of war. Order and respect must be restored. There must be a reckoning. They must fear the West. The honor, dignity and safety of European women as well as the bedrock principles of Western

Civilization must be defended from future attacks. Europe! Where are your men? Rise Up! Protect, defend and cherish your land and your Kind. Quoting author and nationally syndicated radio personality, Dr. Michael Savage, "Borders, Language and Culture" must be defended!

A tribe needs a fertility rate of 2.1 to sustain it. The overall non-Muslim fertility rate of Europe is 1.5. The average Muslim fertility rate for Europe is 2.2. Non-European Muslims are simply out breeding the native populations and colonizing. In Southern France there are more mosques than churches. Germany's Federal Statistic Office has already admitted that the fall in the German population cannot be turned around and that by 2050 Germany will be a Muslim State. The same holds true for all of Europe. The Anglo population of the United States will follow without immediate action.

"If you are not prepared to use force to defend civilization, then be prepared to accept barbarism." Thomas Sowell

Contrast Western Europe's suicidal behavior with Russia's Vladimir Putin whose expansionist policy and the revitalization of the Russian Orthodox Church are aimed at uniting the Russian people. Putin is overtly tribal in his policies and celebrates a birth rate reversal for Russians. In 2014 births of ethnic Russians reached 1.7, passing the death rate. White (ethnic) Russians who have three or more kids pay no taxes. In the West we see "leaders" embracing the demise of their tribes and culture as enlightenment — and then there is Putin. He champions his tribe and points out unequivocally to non-Russian minorities that they need Russia, not the other way around. His sentiment is reflected in the adage, "When in Rome, do as the Romans do."

Pegida — Patriotic Europeans Against the Islamization of the West — understand Putin and know that Islam is incompatible with the West. In his 2015 Christmas address Czech President Milos Zeman said, "I am profoundly convinced that we are facing an organized invasion and not a spontaneous movement of refugees." He said that the integration of Muslims "...is practically impossible" and sited Muslim culture as the cause of the 2016 New Year's rapes in Cologne, Germany.

Astonishingly, European (tribal) nationalist movements that are clearly motivated by self-preservation are rebuked by France's Valls, Germany's Merkel and Great Britain's Cameron with stronger language than they express over colonization by violent and hostile Muslims with birthrates double the native populations. These incoherent, double-minded heads of state exhibit symptoms of Stockholm syndrome.

It is suicide to ignore trends highlighted in many places like Brussels where for four years running the most common birth name is Mohammad. At the same time Muslim leaders zealously advance Sharia. Yet — "tolerance" — not survival remains the European Union's highest virtue. In other words "suicide" not survival remains the European Union's highest virtue. Muslim leaders boast that within 15 years Brussels will be theirs and in time all of Europe. American cities are vulnerable to the same trends destroying Europe. Vulnerability here and across the ocean is brought about by a leadership vacuum that does not defend against challenges to cultural hegemony.

What would leadership sound like? *"The next terrorist attack on the USA or any Western country will result in the Islamic pilgrimage site of Medina becoming a crater and then Mecca if necessary."* Some of my readers will be appalled and say that we are too good for that. They do not cherish Western Civilization. This is how they've been programmed. Western Civilization is literally being killed in front of us by the cabal of international communists and Islam, yet like Merkel they call for more tolerance. These are extreme times and require extreme measures. Tolerance only gives quarter to the enemy.

Western Europe is the canary in the mine. America's black & Hispanic violent crime waves combined with colonizing counter cultures, and unbridled immigration create well-founded feelings of hopelessness among Anglos for the future. This is causing their birthrate to decline and white flight. What follows is the decline of neighborhoods and once great cities like Detroit falling like dominos and creating a vacuum to be filled by counter cultures and a larger federal authoritarian (Marxist) footprint.

Like in Europe something must be done to save our culture and institutions! The media-fueled escalation of black-on-white crime has turned to police being attacked and assassinated in the wake of well-funded provocateurs chanting, **"What do we want?" "Dead Cops!" "When do want it?" "Now!"** and **"Fry like bacon! Pigs in a blanket!"** Marxists cast the police as oppressors at home just as they cast the U.S.A. as the oppressor on the world stage. Our criminal justice system and Western Civilization are in peril. Police are pushed back on their heels at home while America's occupation government projects weakness abroad inviting attack.

The unappeasable portion of America's black population has proven to be a productive recruiting ground for conversion or alliance to Islam illustrating what Sun Tzu wrote in *The Art of War*, "The enemy of my enemy is my friend."

The swelling unrest in the U.S.A. comes from the same communist playbook being followed in other Western countries. The Diversity Movement's vilification of tradition is fracturing, diluting, intimidating and displacing host cultures. This creates an identity vacuum.

Islam is exploiting the identity vacuum made by the embrace of multiculturalism in Europe and the United States. Journalist Brigitte Gabriel warns of the danger of falling into the tolerance trap. Like a reflex Americans police their tongue by defending Islam the second after they muster the courage to express anything critical about Muslims. In the next breath they submit that the "radical" element within Islam is only a "minority." Ms.

Gabriel emphasizes that "the peaceful majority are irrelevant." She does the math.

There are 1.2 billion Muslims in the world (1/5 of the world population). According to the world's premier intelligence services it is estimated that between 15 and 25% of Muslims are radicals.

This translates to the world's largest army consisting of **180 to 300 MILLION radical Muslims dedicated to KILLING Westerners and waging war against Western Civilization!**

The radical "minority" is so huge that it nearly equals the size of the United States population! Parroting the tolerance mantra of the peaceful majority in the face of growing and relentless attacks by radical Muslims is naïve and deadly. This attitude has placed Western culture in a vulnerable, reactive position. Yet, as Commander-in-Chief Obama coached Americans to embrace that very mantra.

In September of 2015 Obama did not step in to save 15 Iraqi Christians (Chaldeans) detained by ICE in San Diego from deportation. The Chaldeans committed immigration fraud to enter the USA from Mexico after already having been granted safety in several European countries. Their deportation means certain death if Europe will not take them back. In contrast Obama in November of 2015 opened his arms to receive 10,000 Muslim "refugees" from Syria with no means to vet them.

It should be of grave concern to Americans that president Obama said before the United Nations on September 25, 2012, "The future must not belong to those who slander the prophet of Islam." Imagine during WWII FDR saying, "The future must not belong to those who slander Nazism." Whose side is Barack Hussein Obama on? Who is this supposed "man of the world?" He has already told us, but most are too indoctrinated in the false reality to hear it, or doped up, or obsessed and distracted with entertainment to see what is in front of them: Pure Evil.

Referring to Muslims in America on page 261 of Obama's book *The Audacity of Hope* he writes "...I will stand with them should the political winds shift in an ugly direction." Obama described the Muslim call to prayer as "one of the prettiest sounds on Earth at sunset." He also recited with perfection in Arabic the opening lines, seemingly impromptu. In a 2008 interview with George Stephanopoulos Obama referred to, "My Muslim faith" only to be corrected when interrupted and prompted by his handler, George.

Obama expressed more heartfelt praise and pride for the "courage" of NBA player Jason Collins for coming out of the closet as a homosexual than he did for the Americans who stopped Ayoub El-Khazzani from committing a terrorist attack on a French train August 22, 2015.

According to Egyptian magazine, Rose El-Youssef (Dec 22, 2012) Obama's cabinet included associates of the Muslim Brotherhood: **Arif Alikan** (Assistant Director for Policy Development for DHS), **Mohammed Elibiary** (Homeland Security Adviser), **Rashad Hussain** (Special Envoy to the Organization of the Islamic Conference), **Salam al-Marayati** (Obama Adviser and founder of the Muslim Public Affairs Council where he is also its executive director), **Imam Mohamed Magid** (Obama's Sharia Czar and member of the Islamic Society of North America), and **Eboo Patel** (Advisory Council on Faith-Based Neighborhood Partnerships).

As Secretary of State, Hillary Clinton's top aid was **Huma Abedin**. Huma has ties to the Muslim Brotherhood.[67] In addition, her mother, Saleha Abedin, is dean of Dar al-Hekma University in Saudi Arabia. Saleha is an Islamist activist and a

---

[67] Andrew C. McCarthy, *Michele Bachman has every right to ask question*, National Review July 25, 2012

member of the Muslim Sisterhood. Is it Huma's influence that tipped U.S.A. policy in favor of the Muslim Brotherhood during the Arab Spring and beyond?

In August of 2014 while Congress was on recess, Obama appointed civil rights activist and Muslim, **Fatina Noor**, as a special policy assistant for Immigration Policy & Rural Affairs at the White House Domestic Policy Council. This position is in the Office of the Director of the U.S. Citizenship and Immigration Service under the Department of Homeland Security. **We are in deep trouble**. Infiltrators have been installed and are driving policy.

Turkey is an influential member of NATO (North Atlantic Treaty Organization), the most powerful military conglomerate in the world. Turkey is the only Muslim and non-European member of NATO. Turkey is (on paper) our ally.

In 1919 Turkey killed 1.5 million Armenian Christians. The Armenian Christian population in Turkey at the time was 2 million. This horrifying historical fact has been all but airbrushed from history. This wouldn't be new information to most readers if the roles were reversed in the annals of history and a Christian country killed 75% of its Muslim population. *(If The Crusades come to your mind remember that they were in response to the Muslim invasion of Europe. Europe should be channeling the spirit of the Knights Templar today for its survival).

Today Turkey is supplying food, fuel, firepower and vehicles to ISIS. Clearly, Turkey is not our ally, but it may well be Obama's ally. Is there an alliance between leaders of the New World Order and radical Islam? In the face of ISIS Obama preached tolerance. He emphasized to us that "radical" Islam represents only a minority of the world's Muslim population.

History shows that the peaceful majority does not matter. Look at past regimes controlled by radical minorities: 11 million killed by Nazi Germany, 147 million killed by the Soviet Communists in the USSR, 72 million Chinese killed by Communist China's *Red Guard*, and 12.5 million Chinese killed by Imperial Japan. History is repeating itself. It took only 19 hijackers (and possibly a few more conspirators to place explosives in the Twin Towers before the attacks) to kill almost 3,000 people on 9/11. The radical "minority" had help from Obama.

Rush Limbaugh brought attention to a very important fact; one that you've heard and perhaps wondered about. Obama and his mouthpieces always used "ISIL" when referring to what the rest of us (even the media) call ISIS. Obama emphasized the "L" in ISIL. So what's the difference and why did he do it? ISIS stands for Islamic State in Iraq and Syria. ISIL stands for Islamic State in Iraq and *Levant*. Levant refers to the land bridge between Turkey and Egypt that includes Israel right in the middle. Limbaugh says that Obama is not talking to Americans when he uses the term, but to Iran. Opting for ISIL over ISIS is deliberate. It sends the message to Islam that Obama does not recognize Israel and is dragging his feet doing only the minimum he must to appease Congress while allowing ISIL to grow and win.

Islam is colonizing the West in part because Obama helped them and in part because its leaders are not double-minded. Muslims know who they are. They know what their objective is. The West is the opposite. The multi-cultural identity vacuum in the West is created by intimidation, ignorance and the indoctrination of a suicidal brand of tolerance. It is in this identity vacuum where fundamental transformational changes are forced upon institutions and culture. Without the vanguard of jealousy found in nationalism the West's institutions and host cultures are defenseless to the parasites of Islam and Marxism. Rallying nationalism for survival is of course…racist. You see this accusation in the riots and media attacks surrounding (then) presidential candidate Donald Trump, the one man (an outsider) who unapologetically holds up the singular greatness of America as worthy of defending and restoring.

Even with evidence over his lifetime to the contrary, President Trump is called a hater and homophobic by Leftist commentators like on The View. In reality, he threatens to unite what they have divided by upholding some absolutes and by putting Americans first.

With so much of the Left's "Hate America" rhetoric riding on homosexuals, I must digress and address that subject specifically.

Several years ago Pepsi gave $1 million to promote the homosexual agenda. This money was divided between the Human Rights Campaign (HRC) and Parents, Families and Friends of Lesbians and Gays (PFLAG).

HRC, financially supported in part by Pepsi, gave $2.3 million to defeat California's Proposition 8 that defined marriage between a man and a woman.

Pepsi is a huge corporation interested in profit. Ask yourself what is in it for Pepsi to throw this kind of money at these Leftist groups. Do you think that Pepsi really believes in the agenda of this tiny market of the population? Answer: This money is looked at as overhead. It is like paying protection money to the mob so that they won't break your store windows.

This money, coupled with placing homosexuals in management positions, and spending advertisement dollars in homosexual magazines becomes an insurance policy and an affirmative defense to costlier civil judgments and bad press. This is the cost of doing business in America today. Fear has changed the culture of corporations to make extortion appear philanthropic. This is largely how the Left "finances" its efforts to transform our society. Race hustlers like Sharpton do the same thing.

It is interesting that while Pepsi supports "tolerance" by donating money to HRC and PFLAG it will not support any pro-family organizations. Which camp do you think buys more soda, homosexuals or heterosexuals? Put another way, is it the normal or the abnormal that PEPSI makes a profit from?

Let's put homosexuality in perspective. Not everything that occurs naturally is normal. There is an intended design. Natural and normal are not synonyms. These are not equivalent words.

Among naturally occurring abnormalities are homosexuals. The homosexual lobby intimidates and indoctrinates the normal (heterosexual) population to accept them as equal to the intended design.

The normal majority is being forced through law, public schools, the media, Hollywood and government policy to accept homosexuality as normal.

"Normal" is self-evident. Being born without four fully formed fingers and a thumb on each hand occurs naturally, but like being born a homosexual is not the intended & expected design, therefore it is — in fact — abnormal. Are glove manufacturers haters? Should they be made to stop manufacturing five-digit gloves and force everyone to wear mittens?

It is the abnormal that must adapt to the normal. Albinos are abnormal. I can't pretend not to notice one and they probably notice me noticing them and become used to it; they adapt and become well-adjusted. There is a subconscious, natural reaction to the abnormal; perhaps in the form of a stare, expression of curiosity/disbelief, surprise or a raised eyebrow (what Leftist thought police coin "microagressions"). A natural and benign reaction to the abnormal or even just the different isn't necessarily scorn and if it is, so what? Get over it. There are no safe zones in reality. It is the abnormal that must adapt. Part of that is accepting their abnormality by becoming well-adjusted to it as opposed to militant.

The leap from homosexual to transvestite to transgender is a leap from abnormal to outright freakish and mentally ill. The freakish will elicit a stronger reaction from normal people and even other (lesser) abnormal people. Again, get over it. Not everyone has to like you or accept you. You are not a victim. You are on the scale of abnormal. If you are abnormal you know it. Expect to be noticed and reacted to.

If the abnormal are intentionally harmed materially or physically by the normal we have a crime, but not a "hate crime." **Hate crimes are a Marxist construct.** These laws are tools of thought control. Assault is assault. Battery is battery. If a "straight" batters a homosexual the victim should not receive extra protection by enjoying the state's call for a higher penalty on the offender. Conversely, when a homosexual batters a heterosexual the (normal) victim shouldn't receive less protection. The abnormal should be equally precious under the law, not extra precious with their own special laws.

In our daily walk the abnormal should be treated lovingly and as equally precious human beings. Nonetheless, they remain — abnormal. Tailored laws and demonstrations calling for tolerance cannot change truth and nature.

When it comes to homosexuals I am libertarian. I am pro-love. In most cases I wouldn't know about the invisible birth defect of homosexuality if not for the lengths so many of them go to make it visible and put it in my face in flamboyant and militant ways.

Many homosexuals make an effort to draw attention to the invisible. They have parades, display decals, flags, mannerisms, other modes of recognition, public conduct, speech, or cross-dress to draw attention to their abnormality. The more outrageous ("flaming") their behavior the more difficult it is for the normal to mask a natural reaction.

It is not "hate" for the normal to have a reaction to the abnormal. There is a predictable reaction to the abnormal. So long as it isn't violent it isn't a crime. After all, "Queer" means odd, strange, bizarre, and unnatural.

While I am on the topic of defining words, it is not hate for me to insist on the precise definition of marriage that necessarily requires two elements: One man and one woman. Marriage is an institution that belongs to heterosexuals exclusively.

Being pro-love, I have no objection to homosexuals having an equally binding civil union, but I will not call it a "marriage" because it is NOT nor could it ever be. Words mean things. A wife cannot have a wife. It is crazy talk. A husband cannot have a husband. It is nonsense. We need to defend the English language. Words mean things.

The abnormal and the normal are as different as their distinctions and cannot hold equal space in law, logic or life.

No matter how convincingly you repress this truth and fool yourself under the self-righteous tenets of tolerance, diversity and acceptance the truth is immovable.

A homosexual who projects self-loathing on to the normal majority rather than adapting to reality merely makes a spectacle of him/herself. These people are not victims. They are simply abnormal people navigating a normal world in denial of their abnormality. The most animated and flamboyant homosexual activists ultimately stoke a natural and visceral reaction from the normal. They even embarrass well adjusted, invisible homosexuals that happily live among us.

I agree with the homosexual lobby about one thing. While homosexuality can be learned especially in this era of promotion, I believe it is usually predetermined genetically and for those it is NOT a choice.

Being born a homosexual is as abnormal as being born without thumbs. Homosexuality is an invisible birth defect. By that I mean a same-sex relationship is obviously not the intended design of the architect of the universe. It is absurd to argue otherwise. It is self-evident what normal is. Normal and abnormal are not judgments, they are nouns and adjectives.

Consider Hermaphrodites. They too are a naturally occurring abnormality. It doesn't mean we (the normal) shouldn't love them. The intended design is to be born one sex or the other with the corresponding plumbing genetically assigned to a male or female accordingly. There is no ambiguity in the intended design of the two sexes and the purpose of sexual intercourse — procreation.

Homosexuals prefer to be called "gay." The high jacking of that word as a substitute for the precise term "homosexual" is very often a misnomer. If homosexuals were universally gay (happy) why then is there a high suicide rate among them? Navigating a normal world as abnormal can be painful. Furthermore, some of the most violent domestic violence cases I've seen have been homosexual couples to include a literal scalping (two lesbians) and another case where an arrow was shot through the back of the head and out the mouth (two homosexual males).

The laws of nature dictate that the abnormal adapt to the normal environment to survive, but in the U.S. the Marxists have succeeded in forcing the normal majority to adapt to the estimated 1.5% of the population that is homosexual. Listening to the "news" or watching TV you'd think one in four is a homosexual. The mentally ill "transgender" population is even smaller, yet it commands media attention and brings into question a serious debate about bathroom access. How much more unraveled can the Marxists make us? I do not care who you love. What I do care about are the consequences of substituting reality with fiction.

At every turn the Marxists are chiseling away at the anchor points of our society. I did not say one hateful thing, but I'll be treated as though I did. Truth tellers and rational thinkers are a threat to the revolution underway.

I can find no more appropriate close to this chapter's effort to illuminate the magnitude and consequences of lies and deception that craft our current suicidal condition, than this salient quote of warning by the longest serving former director of the FBI:

RED BADGE

"The individual is handicapped by coming face-to-face with a conspiracy so monstrous he cannot believe it exists. The American mind simply has not come to the realization of the evil which has been introduced into our midst."

J. Edgar Hoover — "Masters of Deceit" (1958)

FBI Director 1935-1972

BOI Director 1924-1935

CHAPTER TEN
Reclaiming Liberty

Over my thirty-two years as a peace officer, I have had a front row seat watching the growth of all levels of government. Correspondingly, I have watched the citizen's freedom and rights shrink. The pace of government expansion has been incremental for most of my career, but since the Twin Towers/Pentagon attacks on September 11, 2001 it has accelerated.

The size of the federal government today and the reach of its tentacles have so eclipsed the states that most people would have to look in a history book to know it was the states that gave birth to the federal government, not the other way around.

Power is supposed to flow up from the people. Instead, we find ourselves covered by the weight of an intricate web of federal regulations and armed bureaucrats that justify their existence under the unobjectionable-sounding banner of "public safety." Many of these bureaucrats call themselves, "Law enforcement" and no doubt feel noble carrying out their assigned role, but a lot of abuse can come under that banner.

The federal government "cares" so much about our public safety that the USDA has made armed raids of family farms for the "crime" of selling raw milk and organic vegetables.

It is wise to question the motives and constitutionality of this level of intrusion in our lives. Government that seeks to remove all risk removes all rewards of liberty. The "safety" of the nanny state is a prison.

They "cared" so much that in the aftermath of Hurricane Katrina in 2005 that FEMA, with the help of duped local law enforcement, set a dangerous, unconstitutional precedent. Abandoning their oaths they disarmed law-abiding citizens leaving them vulnerable to roaming bands of violent predators.

RED BADGE

Boundary County, Idaho (1992) was the site of gross federal abuse of authority in an incident named "Ruby Ridge" by the media. The name describes the ridge where the Weaver family built a modest home to live away from society and practice their lawful, but politically incorrect beliefs.

Rather than take charge and wait to arrest Randy Weaver on the federal warrant during a low-key traffic stop, the Sheriff yielded to the feds who unnecessarily escalated things and made a blood bath followed by a cover-up.

Hundreds of federal agents descended upon the Weaver family's home. About half of the feds used military rules of engagement to serve an arrest warrant on a trumped up charge. The matriarch of the family, Vickie Weaver, was shot in the head by a brave federal deputy marshal while carrying her ten-month-old baby girl, evidently in a threatening manner. Prior to her murder Vickie's fourteen-year-old son was shot once in the arm by an FBI agent when he walked outside of the cabin with a rifle to investigate why his dog was barking and then finished off with a second bullet in the back as he ran to Vickie for safety. He too was murdered by the federal government.

Then there were the unnecessary deaths of 76 men, women and children after the FBI took over a botched and overzealous BATF warrant service in Waco, Texas (1993) at the Branch Davidian church for suspected violations of federal firearms laws. Again, the Sheriff there yielded to the feds and there was a blood bath — on both sides.

The federal government has a history of using disproportionate force and then getting a pass.

The feds are in our backyards more and more. Much of the power and influence the federal government enjoys over the states has come about through the repeated misuse of the Commerce Clause in the Constitution.

The original intent of the Commerce Clause on the states was simply to regulate commerce with other nations, Indian tribes and the respective states in the union. But, since FDR there have been Supreme Court decisions generated by its unconstitutional power of "judicial review" and tied to the Commerce Clause. The expanded meaning given to the Commerce by the Supreme Court has become the primary source for regulatory expansion over the states, un-doing the framers' original structure of limited and delegated powers. When the Supreme Court is allowed to determine how much power the federal government has there is a conflict of interest. This unconstitutional judicial power came from Justice John Marshal in the 1803 Supreme Court case Marbury v. Madison. Since then the SCOTUS has by decree told us what the law *is* and what it *ought to be*. The Supreme Court acts beyond its intended role of measuring laws passed by Congress against the fixed standard of the US Constitution. It has become a law-making branch.

Consequently, the federal government has jumped the guardrails and is drunk on power it was never intended to drink.

Through intimidation, ignorance, and fear of losing federal funds, states comply rather than nullify unconstitutional regulation thereby surrendering the principle of balanced power known as dual sovereignty — where each part, federal and state, is sometimes superior and sometimes subordinate to the other.

States do not have rights. Only citizens have rights. States have powers. When states do not assert the powers reserved for them under the Tenth Amendment against federal overreach the citizen shrinks. The Tenth Amendment was given to us as the rampart separating the states from federal tyranny.

As the term suggests, "Dual Sovereignty" has two parts, but one part is sitting out. State sovereignty must be asserted for the proper balance of power between the states and the federal government to be restored.

To "restore" means to return to a former state. This is what is needed in the United States, a restoration. We need a return of balanced powers and with it a return to the form of government we once had.

James Madison said, "...A healthy balance of power between the states and the federal government will reduce the risk of tyranny and abuse from either front." We have lost that balance of power.

Dennis Prager said, "The bigger the government, the smaller the citizen." We are there.

Thomas Jefferson warned, "When all government shall be drawn to Washington as the center of power it will render powerless the checks provided and will become as venal and oppressive as the government from which we separated." We are there.

When I consider the web of regulations and regulatory agencies spun over the states, one of the grievances in the Declaration of Independence resonates: *"He has erected a multitude of new offices and sent hither swarms of officers to harass our people and eat out their substance."* We are there.

TSA alone has grown from 16,000 agents to 56,000 agents in ten years. They have grown beyond airports and have done 8,800 unannounced check points.[68] Then there are these sister bureaucracies: HUD, USFS, USDA, FDA, FCC, Department of Education, DHS, EEOC, OSHA, EPA, DEQ, BLM, IRS, DEA, BATFE, FBI, IRS, ...etc. None of them fall within the enumerated powers granted in the Constitution, but they lord over us nonetheless.

"When the United States was founded, the essence of the government was the diffusion of power between the states

---

[68]Ron Nixon, *T.S.A. Expands Duties Beyond Airport Security*, New York Times, August 5, 2013

and the federal government. At the outset, state attorneys general were the engines that drove law enforcement, as the U.S. attorney general was involved exclusively with governmental relations between the states and the feds and protecting federal interests – which included federal property and federal currency. The job came with a small office and a handful of remotely venued prosecutors. The states checked federal law enforcement excess by not cooperating with it or even judicially invalidating it. Today, the attorney general – often called "General" by law enforcement – commands an army of 90,000 lawyers, FBI agents, investigators, clerks, pilots, even troops."

Judge Andrew Napolitano November 13, 2014

I would find it impossible to survive a career today if I were just starting out given the intense pressures of political correctness and the misinformation police are handed by the federal government. The old game was the "War on Drugs." June 17, 2011 marked 40 years since President Nixon declared the war on drugs; how are we doing? After September 11, 2001 the new game became the "War on Terror." If past performance is indicative of future results, the feds have no intention of winning as our borders still stand open, but the American people find themselves surrounded by virtual barbed wire. Our government has not been in it to win it since World War Two. It has turned against us using crisis after crisis to justify its growth and overreach.

On both "war fronts" federal law enforcement is becoming more intrusive in local matters, militarized, and aggressive under the banners of "Public Safety", "The Patriot Act", and "Homeland Security."

Could the real objectives of the wars on terror, drugs, guns, domestic violence, "hate", "global warming" and raw milk be less about protecting us and more about social engineering and conditioning us to submit to a bloated anti-American federal bureaucracy, and the incremental emergence of a police state? From seat belt laws, to motorcycle helmet laws, to police enforcing smoking bans on private property, to school lunch inspections, to overzealous Child Protection Services, to the tyranny of the EPA and OSHA, to the molestation of our daughters and wives by TSA, we would all be better off with government on every level that "cared" less about us.

The only things protecting The People from a police state is the local control of police and peace officers honoring their oath to operate within the limitations of the respective State and U.S. Constitutions they swore to uphold. The federal government is trying to pierce local law enforcement with nose rings in the form of grants, indoctrination (free training), intimidation (via 30 police departments under consent decrees), *JTTF* (Joint Terrorism Task Force) cooperatives, and fusion centers. The photograph on the cover of this book is of an auxiliary police officer's badge from the Soviet Union. This is what our federal government wants local police to become — its weak stepsister. To accomplish this objective, they must romance, indoctrinate and intimidate state, county and local government to yield to their will. This was the aim when Obama's predatory DOJ targeted of Maricopa County's Constitutional Sheriff, Joe Arapio.

Many so-called federal "crimes" are just regulatory violations. The standard of proof is often lower, and the fines and penalties are higher, than state crimes.

The average defense attorney charges $300.00 an hour. At that rate, how much "justice" can you afford when snared by a robotic bureaucrat playing cop who justifies his existence to someone in DC? It is cheaper to plead guilty and just pay the fine than it is to fight for your innocence and challenge their legitimacy.

Incredibly, the U.S. Constitution mentions only three federal crimes: Treason, Piracy, and Counterfeiting, but today there are literally more federal laws and regulations than can be counted; it has been tried. There are so many that it seems we can be in violation of something at any given moment. Many of these laws are a duplication of state laws, some are the product of politicians grandstanding on issues and putting their name to legislation while others are made so that the federal government can step into local affairs and persecute rather than prosecute when they disagree with what a local jury or prosecutor did.

If you order a copy of the US Constitution (at a cost of $130) from the federal government you receive with it 2,800 pages of SCOTUS precedents. Precedents are NOT law nor are they amendments to the Constitution. Juxtapose these 2,800 pages with this quote from Justice Scalia, **"The Constitution that I interpret and apply is not living but dead, or as I prefer to call it, enduring. It means today not what current society, much less the court, thinks it ought to mean, but what it meant when it was adopted."** It is no wonder questions surround his untimely death.

As you know, the Tenth Amendment of the Bill of Rights reaffirmed that any power not explicitly granted to the federal government was explicitly withheld from the federal government. The Constitution is NOT a living document. Of course Marxists want you to believe that so that through judicial activism they can use the courts to make law and rapidly transform the country as they have been doing. This is why they were so unhinged in their opposition to Justice Kavanaugh to the Supreme Court. He will be less likely to view the constitution as a living document. There was a good reason to not confirm him based on his record with respect to his fingerprints on the Patriot Act, but his opponents chose the low road of slander and false accusations because they are not opposed to the unconstitutional power the Patriot Act gave the federal government.

The federal government has become what professor Edward Erle of UC San Bernardino describes as an *"Administrative State."* This is a system where administration and regulation replace politics as the ordinary means of making policy. The administrative state elevates the welfare of the collective over the rights and liberties of the individual. The overreach of the administrative state is seldom challenged by state government because they depend on federal money.

Sometimes state officials cite the "Supremacy Clause" to their constituents as political cover for standing down to federal overreach. The Supremacy Clause is not a federal trump card over the states.

State officials reference the Supremacy Clause as an out to justify standing down to the federal government on its apparent interest in gun confiscation. The fallacy in this argument begins with the fact that the words, "Supremacy Clause" — do not exist in the constitution. They are a descriptor used to refer to Article VI, Section 2.

The popular use of this descriptor has become a substitution for the very section to which it refers. Subsequently, "The Supremacy Clause" has evolved into a life of its own apart from the very authoritative clause it was coined to reference. Although only a balloon tied to the section it references, it has come to have its own gravitational pull intellectually taking us off course. The use, over use, and misuse of that term has intoxicated the federal government into believing it has limitless "supreme" power over the states and conditioned the people to believe the same. Consequently, its use has changed the scope of the very constitutional source it references and knocked it out of alignment with the expressed intent behind it — as found in Federalist papers 33 and 44 respectively.

Using the term, "Supremacy Clause" is much like the popular misuse of, "separation of church and state" (as if it were found in the Constitution); we are seeing something that is not there.

This misinformation over the meaning and scope of the Supremacy Clause has intoxicated federal bureaucrats with an attitude that they have absolute power over the states and has conditioned the people to believe the same when they do not see their state government flex and stand up jealously to federal overreach.

Jealousy is the fear of losing something you love to someone else. Jealousy is the tenor we need in our elected representatives when it comes to state sovereignty and individual liberty.

Alexander Hamilton made clear that when U.S. law is not pursuant to its constitutional (limited and delegated) powers it would be "merely a usurpation and will deserve to be treated as such."

Certainly, the founders agreed that a supreme law was required for any proper government to function, but the federal government would be limited in its scope and supremacy to only the laws pursuant to the Constitution.

Judicial Activism

Justice Robert Bork, in his book *The Tempting of America, The Political Seduction of the Law*, explains the importance of the philosophy of original understanding. "The abandonment of original understanding in modern times means the transportation into the Constitution of the principles of a liberal culture that cannot achieve those results democratically."[69] In other words, reading the Constitution out of context and without regard to supporting documents like the Federalist Papers has caused the U.S. to abandon its original intent. What was once a clear road map has become a game of political scrabble.

---

[69]Robert Bork, The Tempting of America, The Political Seduction of Law, p.9, Simon & Schuster Inc., 1990.

Activist judges ignore the principles of the Constitution that should control them. They transform the Constitution into "malleable texts that judges may rewrite to see that particular groups or political causes win" (Bork, p.2). In fact, today they make law by interpreting the Constitution as they see fit, even ruling on issues such as Roe vs. Wade. Bork points out that abortion is a legal and moral matter for the individual states. Likewise, he points out that the Supreme Court ruled on the death penalty, suspending it for five years, a matter specifically and repeatedly mentioned in the Constitution for individual states to decide.

Bork says that the perception of law by Americans has become de-legitimized. "… **Americans increasingly view the courts, and particularly the Supreme Court, as political rather than legal institutions**" (Bork, p.2).

A glaring example of this is the 2015 SCOTUS ruling on homosexual "marriage" as acknowledged in the two following dissenting opinions:

"**…By imposing its own views on the entire country, the majority of this Court facilitates the marginalization of the many Americans who have traditional ideas. If a bare majority of Justices can invent a new right and impose that right on the rest of the country, the only real limit on what future majorities will be able to do is their own sense of what those with political power and cultural influence are willing to tolerate. Even enthusiastic supporters of same-sex marriage should worry about the scope of the power that today's majority claims.**"   Justice Samuel Alito

"**Today's decree says that my Ruler, and the Ruler of 320 million Americans coast-to-coast, is a majority of the nine lawyers on the Supreme Court.**"   Antonin Scalia

"Recently we have seen judicial activism on steroids at the Supreme Court. We-a-slim-majority-of-the-Court have spoken. And there it is. To me the big issue boils down to authority. By what authority did a majority do this? As Chief Justice Roberts himself said, you can celebrate this decision if you want to, but the bottom line is it had nothing to do with the Constitution. If the Constitution means whatever the justices want it to say, then the nation is like a great ship set adrift without a rudder – or worse, with a rudder forcing us to go on its inexorable way toward a great waterfall. Thus, (the majority's decision) has turned the Constitution on its head, granting a right not found there that will trump rights explicitly spelled out there. Those who applaud such an imposition of power may not be so enthusiastic if another arbitrary authority arises which doesn't share their values. ISIS marked the Supreme Court's decision over the weekend by throwing alleged homosexuals off tall buildings in Syria, as crowds below cheered on. I'm sure those poor victims received no due process."

Jerry Newcombe, Townhall.com columnist, July 1, 2015

Let's dispense with the charade that the Supreme Court is independent or judicial — it is neither. It has become just another political and legislative branch of government, effectively a third chamber of Congress, except for the fact that its officials are unelected, operate in strict secrecy, and hold office for life — similar to the inner core of the Presidium in the communist U.S.S.R. The Court's members are no longer there to "judge," but to "vote." The radical Left enjoys a distinct and permanent voting bloc on the Court consisting of four justices, meaning they only have to influence, coerce or sway one other member to get every "vote" to go their way, and seal victory for their radical, revolutionary transformation of the country.

While still a young nation, it was in 1821 that Thomas Jefferson warned the American people, *"The germ of dissolution of our federal government is in...the federal judiciary."*

On the heels of the radically unprecedented Supreme Court decisions on same-sex marriage, Obamacare, and racial preferences in federal housing law, best-selling author and former presidential candidate Pat Buchanan commented in a June 29, 2015 column titled "Does Moral Truth Really Change, America?"

"America has never been more disunited and divided — on politics and policy, religion and morality. We no longer even agree on good and evil, right and wrong. Are we really still 'one nation under God, indivisible?"

The most lasting mark a president can leave on the country is nomination(s) to the Supreme Court. Under President Obama the Constitution suffered irreversible damage. He nominated Elena Kagan to replace John Paul Stevens and before that Sonia Sotomayor to fill David Souter's spot. Obama made it clear before selecting Sonia Sotomayor (a self-admitted judicial activist) that he intended to nominate a woman or minority to fill the position.

Because race, sex and now gender are valid social justice qualifications for the bench in Leftist ideology perhaps had Hillary Clinton been Obama's third term she would have boasted nominating the first (openly) homosexual or transgender justice to replace Ruth Bader Ginsburg who has been struggling with her health or the sudden and suspicious vacancy by the deceased Antonin Scalia. The Left cries about discrimination but then obsesses about giving preferences to race, sex, sexual orientation and gender.

Barack Obama and other pundits of the Diversity Movement do not want the courts to preserve the Constitution within the clear context and reasoning behind it. "Only by following that rule can our un-elected guardians (judges) save us from themselves" (Bork. p.6). Rather, they seek to re-invent the context apart from the intent of its architects. Today, the *Communist Manifesto* and Machiavelli's *The Prince* ("the ends justify the means"), appear to influence Constitutional interpretation more than the Federalist Papers. The Supreme Court has become the overseer of The New Inquisition we are suffering under.

The mainstream media do not expose the prevalence, depth, and consequences of Leftist judicial activism because they share its Marxist agenda. Those who challenge it are showcased as "bitter", "ultra-conservative", "far-right wing", and/or part of dangerous fringe groups, waving pocketsize Constitutions and hindering progress. The farther away from the "philosophy of original understanding" we move the more unassimilated, counter-culture factions will surface.

Each faction will be legitimized by the Diversity Movement and consequently, emboldened and difficult to manage. An increased frequency and scale of civil unrest will bring the United States' empire-style government to embrace a crisis management interpretation of an already compromised Constitution.

In addition to the misuse of the Supremacy Clause, the misuse of the Commerce Clause, the evolution of *The Administrative State* (an occupation government superimposed on the constitution) and the Supreme Court's power grab of judicial review — there is another cause for how the federal government's footprint grew so big in the states: The 17th Amendment. It substantively changed how U.S. Senators are selected and decreased their accountability to the states.

The argument in favor of the 17th Amendment was to curb corruption. The concerns of the time were real, but the "remedy" has given us side effects far more serious than the problem the Amendment was purported to address.

Originally, our Congress was made of The House of Representatives — a body elected by The People — and the Senate a body of "statesmen" selected by the states' legislatures, not by popular vote.

Sadly, the 17th Amendment made Congress more "democratic" — precisely what the founding fathers feared and warned against. The 17th Amendment damaged our Republic. It removed an effective safeguard and subjected us to worse (democratic) corruption than existed before by allowing the power of money to substitute statesmen with politicians. While not perfect, statesmen were more inclined to act jealously over State sovereignty, compared to the politicians that replaced them who are happy to sell your freedom.

The 17th Amendment did not prevent corruption in Illinois. It did not stop Governor Blagojevich from selling Obama's U.S. Senate seat. Furthermore, it allowed Hillary Clinton to be launched by special interest money into a U.S. Senate seat vacancy in New York — a place where she has no roots. Nonetheless, she was strategically positioned there to advance her party's national agenda and her own ambitions.

Had the 17th Amendment not been ratified, polarizing issues that have become constitutional crises like abortion or healthcare would have remained for the states to decide or ignore respectively. Candidates for U.S. Senate like Hillary could not be recruited, funded and then planted strategically like pieces on a chess board to force transformational issues to the national stage for a corrupt Congress and a stacked Supreme Court (made of members confirmed by — you guessed it: The U.S. Senate) to settle.

Restoring the process the founders gave us in Article I, Section 3 of the US Constitution would return to The People sovereign power through their states' legislatures to appoint U.S. Senators. Senators who fail to oppose federal legislation that infringe on states' powers and individual liberty could be recalled. There would be a price to pay for putting federal agendas over states' interests.

Repealing the 17th Amendment would require either a joint resolution through a two-thirds majority in both the House of Representatives and the Senate; this is highly unlikely, or a Constitutional Convention (a "con-con") voted by two-thirds of State Legislatures. A con-con is too risky given that it would open the Constitution up to be further damaged in this era of cultural anarchy. While its repeal would go a long way toward restoring the proper (intended) balance of power in our Republic (dual sovereignty) where each part — federal and state — is sometimes superior and sometimes subordinate to the other, I believe we are stuck.

So, how do we begin to challenge overreach and restore the balance of power? How do we reclaim liberty?

There is an office uniquely suited to defend individual liberty from federal and state overreach: **The County Sheriff!**

When you think of the Office of Sheriff, you may not realize how uniquely suited it is to defend individual liberty and help restore state power. The Sheriff is truly unique; one of a kind, unlike anyone else. The Sheriff is the only elected peace officer in the country.

The Sheriff does not answer to a bureaucrat in Washington DC, nor to the president, nor a judge, nor county commissioners. The Sheriff answers to his boss: The People, and has by virtue of his oath the relative autonomy to exercise some moral agency over how laws are enforced.

Sheriffs are constitutional officers in most states that have the office. By design the Sheriff is elected and close to the people, chosen to protect them from criminals of all stripes, including overreaching federal and state government. The Sheriff is: The Peoples' Guardian.

In Mack/Printz v. United States, 521 U.S. 898 (1997) the Supreme Court reaffirmed the Sheriff is the chief law enforcement officer in the county and in this country.

This begs the question: Why do we so seldom see Sheriffs assert their authority against federal overreach or challenge federal abdication of delegated duty like securing the border?

Answer: The Office of Sheriff has been compromised by ignorance and by dependence on federal money, mostly in the form of grants and gifts.

The good news: There is a movement to restore the constitutional Sheriff. Its aim is to remove the influences that compromise the office and replace it with conviction to the oath of office.

Supporting this movement is the CSPOA, (Constitutional Sheriffs and Peace Officers Association). Their mission: To equip Sheriffs, peace officers and public officials with the necessary information and public support to carry out their duties in accordance with their oaths of office.

There are about 3,100 Sheriffs in the United States. Of these, 479 are members of the CSPOA. In addition, there are county commissioners and other officials that have joined and are backing their Sheriffs. It would seem that these 479 plus elected officials have asked an important question:

Of what value is an oath when the person who takes it yields to the very forces it was intended to withstand?

So, what does it look like when Sheriffs are led by a conviction to their oath?

RED BADGE

- In Wyoming, Sheriffs require that Feds check in before making arrests, serving papers or confiscating property. This policy came about after INS (now called ICE) raided the Casteneda family's home. The problem: The Castenedas were American citizens! This Wyoming Sheriffs' policy will save lives and protect rights by providing much-needed oversight of federal actions in the states.

- Other examples of Sheriffs standing up: In New York and Colorado Sheriffs refuse to enforce state gun control laws that are unconstitutional on their face.

- The New Mexico Sheriffs' Association threatened to arrest feds who move to confiscate guns.

- Sheriff Johnny Brown of Ellis County, Texas said he would resist any effort by the federal government to confiscate firearms in his county.

- Sheriff Brad Rogers of Elkhart, Indiana told the FDA he would arrest their agents for trespass if they entered an Amish farmers land to "inspect" without a search warrant. The feds threatened to arrest the Sheriff. He did not flinch, but the feds slipped away dropping the issue.

- Sheriff Joe Baca in Serra County, California told his county commissioners he would not enforce BLM road closures in the national forest.

Sheriff Baca understands that Sheriffs cannot be pressed into service to enforce federal regulations.

- Sheriff Gil Gilbertson of Josephine, Oregon told the U.S. Forest Service and BLM he would access any closed road he deems necessary to perform his many and varied duties as the chief law enforcement officer in the county and furthermore, he would not recognize any road closures that are not coordinated through him and articulated with sound reasoning.

RED BADGE

Sheriffs are standing up! Momentum is building to defend states' powers and individual liberty.

Much of the west is deemed "federal land." How does this affect the Sheriff's authority to interpose his office between federal overreach and The Peoples' rights on public lands?

I will answer this by sharing a summary of an argument being made by Sheriff Gilbertson whose county is 68% "federal land." The entire argument is titled, "Unraveling federal jurisdiction within a state" and can be found on the Web.

Sheriff Gilbertson starts off with the fact that it is well established that the Sheriff is the chief law enforcement officer (CLEO) in the county. This he says includes on lands managed by the federal government, notwithstanding areas of exclusive control like military bases, post offices and the like mentioned in the Constitution under Article I, Section 8.

Furthermore, according to the Inventory Report on Jurisdictional Status of Federal Areas within the States (June 30, 1962), commonly referred to as the "1962 Eisenhower Report" Sheriff Gilbertson points out that there are four categories of jurisdiction over federal lands.

Josephine County, falls under Category 4: "Proprietorial Jurisdiction." This means that the state has all authority. A county is a subdivision of the state; each with its own the Chief Law Enforcement Officer (CLEO) — the elected Sheriff. The federal government has some right or title over an area, but no measure of the state's authority. The federal government operates in a governmental rather than a proprietary capacity.

In addition, Sheriff Gilbertson points out there are federal court cases that reject the empowering readings of the Commerce Clause that brought us to the point of a lording, armed, administrative state.

I will add this includes even Chief Justice Roberts' unpopular opinion on the individual mandate of the Affordable Care Act where interestingly he too rejected the Commerce Clause as the expected authoritative source that the Supreme Court would cite.

Sheriff Gilbertson and other Sheriffs and scholars like Utah's Ken Ivory are making sound, well-researched arguments that substantively rebuke federal overreach and their unconstitutional hold on "federal land." These arguments are built on organic law, the Constitution, historical documents and interestingly, even the federal court's "case law" when it is juxtaposed to their own bureaucratic regulations (I am amused by the irony of one form of pretended legislation challenging another: case law vs. regulations).

Using case law to argue what is right and what is "law" is somewhat counterproductive because it perpetuates the problem by legitimizing the unconstitutional practice of judicial review covered early in this book. However, when citing case law for the purpose of illuminating the contradictions of the federal government and how far it has veered off course it can be instructive albeit not authoritative.

One such source is a congressional report dated October 23, 2000. A land dispute between the USFS and Elko County, Nevada was resolved in part by referring to a 1907 Supreme Court case: Kansas v. Colorado, where it was ruled that the **U.S. Forest Service had no general grant of law enforcement authority within a sovereign state unless designated as such by state authority.**

Another source is Caha v. United States, 152 U.S. 211, 215 (1894) **"...within any state of this Union the preservation of peace and the protection of person and property are functions of the state government, and are not part of the primary duty, at least, of the nation."**

Following this argument, who is the Chief Law Enforcement Officer that can grant or revoke such police power to the feds? Answer: **The County Sheriff.**

This is a snapshot of a more compelling argument that Sheriff Gilbertson and others in the CSPOA are making that the feds have no constitutional basis of authority for law enforcement powers in the county.

The federal government's response has been silent for the most part, but they are behind efforts to eliminate the Office of Sheriff or diminish its power from state to state. One such effort is taking place in Sussex County, Delaware where Sheriff Jeff Christopher is fighting for his Office against efforts begun by Joe Biden's late son who was the state attorney general.

It seems the feds find themselves in the untenable position of defending its practice of overreach against sobering constitutional realities and their own corpus of historical court precedents that favor dual sovereignty over federal tyranny.

To their dismay, Constitutional Sheriffs are not going away, but are growing more numerous and bolder in standing by their oath! On January 24, 2014 I attended by invitation a private conference of the CSPOA in Las Vegas. Sheriffs and other distinguished guests drafted and signed the following powerful resolution. Since that historic day, many others have discovered it and signed it too.

Resolution Drafted by the Constitutional Sheriffs and Peace Officers Association

Pursuant to the powers and duties bestowed upon us by our citizens, the undersigned do hereby resolve that any Federal officer, agent, or employee, regardless of supposed congressional authorization, is required to obey and observe limitations consisting of the enumerated powers as detailed

within Article 1 Section 8 of the U S Constitution and the Bill Of Rights.

The people of these united States (*author's note: the small-case "u" is intentional*) are, and have a right to be, free and independent, and these rights are derived from the "Laws of Nature and Nature's God." As such, they must be free from infringements on the right to keep and bear arms, unreasonable searches and seizures, capricious detainments and infringements on every other natural right whether enumerated or not. (Ninth Amendment)

We further reaffirm that "The powers not delegated to the United States by the Constitution, nor prohibited by it to the states, are reserved to the states respectively, or to the people." (Tenth Amendment)

Furthermore, we maintain that no agency established by the U.S. Congress can develop its own policies or regulations which supersede the Bill of Rights or the Constitution, nor does the executive branch have the power to make law, overturn law or set aside law.

Therefore, in order to protect the American people, BE IT RESOLVED THAT, The following abuses will not be allowed or tolerated:

1) Registration of personal firearms under any circumstances.

2) Confiscation of firearms without probable cause, due process, and constitutionally compliant warrants issued by a local or state jurisdiction.

3) Audits or searches of a citizen's personal affairs or finances without probable cause, and due process, and constitutionally compliant warrants issued by a local or state jurisdiction.

4) Inspections of person or property without probable cause and constitutionally compliant warrants as required by the Fourth Amendment and issued by a local or state jurisdiction.

5) The detainment or search of citizens without probable cause and proper due process compliance, or the informed consent of the citizen.

6) Arrests with continued incarcerations without charges and complete due process, including, but not limited to public and speedy jury trials, in a court of state or local jurisdiction.

7) Domestic utilization of our nation's military or federal agencies operating under power granted under the laws of war against American citizens.

8) Arrest of citizens or seizure of persons or property without first notifying and obtaining the express consent of the local sheriff.

AND BE IT FURTHER RESOLVED,

That the undersigned Sheriffs, Peace Officers, Public Servants and citizens, do hereby denounce any acts or agencies which promote the aforementioned practices. All actions by the Federal Government and its agents will conform strictly and implicitly with the principles expressed within the United States Constitution, Declaration of Independence, and the Bill of Rights.

There is no greater obligation or responsibility of any government officer than to protect the rights of the people. Thus, any conduct contrary to the United States Constitution, Declaration of Independence, or the Bill of Rights will be dealt with as criminal activity.

Let me be clear. This is not talk of revolution. The revolution already took place. It occurred incrementally over the last fifty years at least, and the citizen lost! What I am sharing is an avenue toward a peaceful restoration, but there is precious little time left.

If we still live in a constitutional republic and if the rule of law still matters, there can be only one response to a legitimate challenge by a state to federal overreach: A shrinking federal footprint and citizens that stand taller.

Otherwise, we are living under some other form of centralized government hidden behind the facade of a "caring", bloated, administrative state where regulations penned by federal bureaucrats combined with presidential executive orders have replaced the Constitution as the supreme law of the land. Sheriffs with backbone can find out just where we stand.

The objective of the CSPOA is two-fold: First, encourage Sheriffs to honor their oaths to defend two constitutions, one federal and one state. Second, bring the number of elected Sheriffs high enough that they can act in unison and declare to the federal government that The People have had enough of their overreach and are reclaiming liberty.

Obviously, there are consequences to standing up to federal overreach such as loss of funding and the potential of lengthy and costly legal battles. But, for the right reason(s) at the right time and in the right measure Sheriffs are in a unique position to stand up as the guardian of The People and the Constitution.

The alternative to standing up is for states to submit to the federal government's insatiable appetite for yet more power it was not delegated, thereby turning citizens to subjects.

Whether to submit or restore: This is our decision to make now. Action cannot be left for the next generation; they have no frame of reference for the freedom stolen from them. We have a duty to posterity and precious little time remaining for the peaceful restoration I pray you will join me in working and sacrificing toward.

R.I.P. Robert "LaVoy" Finicum-American

"The duty of a true Patriot is to protect his country from its government." Thomas Paine

The sick and tragic shooting death of Arizona rancher LaVoy Finicum by the Oregon State Police on January 26, 2016 was the result of a rapid and unnecessary escalation of force directed and spun by the FBI against peaceful, pro-constitution protesters. The protesters organized a sit-in of an unoccupied, government building to draw attention to federal control and management of public lands. The federal government's swift response showed its naked zeal to crush dissent. It also illustrated its blatant double standard of tolerance, mercy and grace generously afforded to Marxist groups like Act Up, Black Lives Matter, La Raza and the New Black Panthers.

The very Administrative State that lords over us turns a deaf ear to the farmers, loggers and ranchers who have long sought to redress their grievances for the illogical, contradictory, and backward *regulations* (pretended legislation) enforced and unlawfully prosecuted (with a lower standard of proof than what is required in *legitimate* state/county courts). The weight of this consolidation of unaccountable and unconstitutional power on the citizen is tyranny. This is what LaVoy Finicum peacefully and boldly stood against.

If Al Sharpton and some Black Panthers had a sit-in at a Social Security Office demanding reparations for slavery the U.S. Gov't would not have moved in on him as they did LaVoy Finicum and the peaceful protesters 30 miles from Burns,

Oregon. The fact that some were armed was incidental. They did not threaten anyone.

A Constitutional Sheriff could have walked in the Malheur Wildlife Refuge building alone — unarmed— with a thermos of coffee in hand and brought the sit-in to a peaceful conclusion. Absent that, the government-media complex spun things up because white blood cells are dangerous to the Occupation Government. LaVoy was the nucleus of the cell. Then the Oregon Governor's posturing invited a federal escalation that resulted in the unnecessary killing of LaVoy Finicum whose "criminal" conduct measured by state law was a few innocuous misdemeanors: **trespass, unlawful entry, eluding, disorderly conduct, vandalism (cutting off a lock) and obstructing and delaying officers**.

Road blocks are deadly force! Deadly force cannot be used on a fleeing misdemeanor suspect. In contrast, "police intercepts" can be used. Intercepts allow enough room between stationary (police) cars for the fleeing vehicle to get through, but forcing it to slow down — like navigating a maze, perhaps allowing for a more effective deployment of *stop sticks* which deflate tires.

The roadblock on U.S. 395 was not the only criminal act perpetrated by government against LaVoy and his passengers. The FBI covered up that their agent(s) used deadly force by firing at the truck *prior* to it coming to a point of rest in the snow bank. We have a fleeing misdemeanor suspect with innocent, helpless passengers any of whom could have been killed by trigger happy, zealous FBI.

Before his killing, LaVoy knew his truck had already been shot. He got out of the truck and moved swiftly away from it to draw the aim of state troopers and FBI agents away from his equally innocent passengers. I understand the thought process and legal prism through which the prosecutor evaluated the shooting death of LaVoy by the Oregon trooper and deemed it "justified." It was based entirely on "furtive movement" by LaVoy when he moved his hand toward where they "reasonably believed" he wore a gun.

There is a larger matter in need of prosecution: **The conspiracy to use deadly force on a fleeing misdemeanor suspect was criminal and a violation of the civil rights of everyone in the truck. FBI agent Astarita was found not guilty of firing at LaVoy's truck, but still two of the eight shots fired at the truck or striking it remain unexplained. Who fired them and why? It was the FBI that spun emotions and steered the operation. Whoever ordered the roadblock and coordinated this deadly fiasco ought to face trial. An objective investigation could have resulted in charges of murder, conspiracy to murder and aggravated battery against FBI agents and the OSP.**

Put Sharpton and company in the truck. What would have happened? Sharpton always gets a pass (including from the tax code) because he is useful to the Left. He promotes The Big Lie that vilifies tradition. Unlike LaVoy who stood for the Constitution, Sharpton is an agent of The Marxist State. He creates division and discord needed by the Marxists in Washington D.C. to steer the country to the Left. Sharpton's grievances are legitimate in the ear of The State. The same goes for the social justice voices in favor of the violent Ferguson rioters whose arrest warrants a judge quashed in the name of social justice and tolerance.

Earlier in this book I mentioned Mecklenburg, N.C. Chief Magistrate Judge Khalif Rhodes spearheading a policy change to stop issuing arrest warrants for violent crimes. Instead, the court is issuing summonses. Local, state and federal governments are willing to look the other way, find discretion or nullify the rule of law i.e. Sanctuary Cites and federal marijuana laws – that is unless you are a heretic on the wrong side of Marxism like

LaVoy Finicum; then you will feel the full weight of The Inquisition on your throat.

In contrast to Al Sharpton INC., you don't get more "American" than the farmer and rancher, yet look at the swift and disproportionate federal response of force to their peaceful protest in Burns, Oregon. If the feds are going to play cop in local matters in violation of dual sovereignty then those kinds of personnel, intelligence gathering and para-military resources deployed as quickly in Ferguson could have saved life and property. However, such federal support and resources were absent and the local government gave "more room" for the "*protesters*" (criminal rioters) to "blow off steam."

In the spirit of the Founding Fathers Mr. LaVoy Finicum stood against tyranny. He communicated in a courteous, factual and clear way. He stood on the truth. I know his argument and he is correct, but the unconstitutional, Occupation Government would not hear him. He had no alternative. His protest was peaceful, respectful civil disobedience. He was a white blood cell that wanted to steer the country toward the restoration of constitutional government – and he was killed for it by an unnecessary escalation of force. The feds will create a dossier on anyone who holds LaVoy Finicum up as a martyr for the Constitution and file it under "Enemy of The State." Welcome to the USSA.

ACTION POINT: If you are as outraged as am I over what happened to Mr. LaVoy Finicum and the occupants of his truck I implore you to help me advance the following corrective action that will restore the proper balance of power between the states and the (rogue) federal government they gave birth to.

The problem:

Ruby Ridge, Waco, Katrina, Bundy Ranch, Bunkerville and Burns: All are examples of Federal abuse of power — without accountability. There are many more cases of federal abuse every year that do not make national news.

The remedy:

When in the opinion of the Attorney General of a respective state, reasonable suspicion exists that one or more agents of the federal government has acted criminally — as measured by state law — *it* (the federal government) shall be prohibited from investigating itself in order to eliminate a conflict of interest.

A contiguous state's Attorney General's Office shall investigate the possible crime(s).

The investigation by the neighboring state's AG shall be paid for by the federal government to ensure equally limitless resource to that of the federal government when it levels an investigation on its selective targets, like was done to the Bundy, Finicum and Hammond families.

Upon a finding of probable cause, prosecution (criminal and/or civil) will then be returned to the state where the offense(s) took place — also at the cost of the federal government.

This proposed law does not preclude the federal government from leveling federal criminal/civil rights charges against its agent(s).

CHAPTER ELEVEN

A View from the Past to See the Future

"We lie to ourselves more than to anyone else." — Dostoyevsky

Edmund Burke advised, "All that is necessary for the triumph of evil is for good men to do nothing." That famous Irish Statesman elaborated on the point by saying, "Nobody made a greater mistake than he who chose to do nothing because he could only do a little."

Plato wisely observed that "the price good men pay for indifference to public affairs is to be ruled by evil men."

In today's America, the price that otherwise good citizens pay for their apathy and indifference to their government's schemes and policies is that they are ruled by truly evil men and women.

When "We the People" fail to oppose tyrannical laws and destructive and dangerous government policies — and the evil men and women that advance them — we become accomplices to evil.

Had they been alive, there is no doubt that our Anti-Federalist Founding Fathers would have agreed with Friedrich Nietzsche when he said,

"Everything the State says is a lie, and everything it has it has stolen."

It was less than three generations ago when Henry Wallace, Vice President of the U.S. from 1941 to 1945, said of those seeking to be our domestic overlords:

"Their final objective toward which all their deceit is directed is to capture political power so that, using the power of the state and the power of the market simultaneously, they may keep the common man in eternal subjection."

The "election" (selection?) of Obama stands as a milestone in America: the triumph of the greatest con-game in history and the revelation that our electoral process is a complete sham — where "the deck is stacked" and "the fix is in" — like playing cards in a rigged casino or "voting" in a Third World dictatorship.

How can this happen?

Johann von Goethe observed that *"None are more hopelessly enslaved than those who falsely believe they are free."*

And the legendary Athenian orator Demosthenes counseled us that *"Nothing is easier than self-deceit. For what each man wishes, that he also believes to be true."*

For those who doubt just how fraudulent our electoral process is, and what a charade our political system is, let me introduce you to Georgetown University Professor Carroll Quigley.

(I encourage you to do some online research into Dr. Quigley, and check out his highly revealing 1966 book *Tragedy and Hope: A History of the World in Our Time.* See also a highly condensed version titled: *Tragedy & Hope 101* by Joseph Plummer).

Professor Carroll Quigley, a member of the "Blue-Blood" Eastern Establishment and one who was granted insider status into a powerful British secret society of the ultra-rich and powerful known to the outside world as the "Round Table Group", revealed to the citizens of the United States how truly powerless they were to change their ruling class, policies and the direction of their country.

The following is a Quigley quote from *Tragedy and Hope*:

"...it is increasingly clear that, in the twentieth century, the expert will replace the industrial tycoon in control of the economic system even as he will replace the democratic voter in control of the political system...Hopefully, the elements of choice and freedom may survive for the ordinary individual in that he may be free to make a choice between two opposing political groups and he may have the choice to switch his economic support from one large unit to another.

"But, in general, his freedom and choice will be controlled within very narrow alternative by the fact that he will be numbered from birth and followed, as a number, through his educational training, his required military or other public service, his tax contributions, his health and medical requirements, and his final retirement and death benefits."

Analyze what was forecasted 50 years ago in the paragraph above. "Numbered from birth and followed" — this alone should send chills down the spine of every freedom-loving American (Can you say "Social Security Number" or "Number of the Beast?"). Education is not supposed to be "training", unless it's indoctrination and brainwashing: Can you say Common Core? Paying obligatory taxes with the threat of prison time for non-compliance is NOT a "contribution." "Required public service" (which is service to the government, not the people): Can you say AmeriCorps, which will become obligatory if one doesn't enter the military? "Health and medical REQUIREMENTS:" Can you say Obamacare? Obamacare is government-controlled, highly regulated, socialized medicine. You SHALL enroll into Obamacare or be fined and your bank account plundered by the IRS).

Just think of the degree of control exerted over us through Common Core and Obamacare alone.

In his book *Tragedy and Hope* Professor Quigley also revealed the reality of how our electoral/political process works after having been re-engineered by the elite planners:

"The chief problem of American political life for a long time has been how to make the two Congressional parties more national and international. The argument that the two parties should represent opposed ideals and policies...is a foolish idea acceptable only to doctrinaire and academic thinkers. Instead, the two parties should be almost identical, so that the American people can 'throw the rascals out' at any election without leading to any profound or extensive shifts in policy."

Sound familiar? Has there been any meaningful change in the last 70 years at the national level? Our millionaire Congressmen and women are nothing more than high-paid prostitutes; and the U.S. Supreme Court has become just another political branch of government, which takes "international opinion" into consideration when deciding on the constitutionality of a law or case. Goodbye American sovereignty!

Just compare the 2016 establishment parties' favored presidential candidates: (D) Hillary Clinton and (R) Jeb Bush. Both were in complete agreement on four major issues: Amnesty, Unrestricted Immigration, Common Core, and Obamacare. Your choice is an illusion.

Those "invisible men" of the international central banking cartel who want to reduce the United States to Third World status, rule us with an iron fist and plunder our natural resources know that an old-fashion frontal assault — communist-style revolution by force of arms — would not work in America. The people are generally well-armed and a shock action such as this would awaken them from their slumber.

Therefore, those who seek to reduce us to a feudal state of peasant serfs realized that the best way to conquer the American people was to conquer our minds. If they could control the peoples' minds, they need not worry about their actions.

Vladimir Lenin predicted in the 1920's that eventually the American people "would fall like overripe fruit into our hands."

RED BADGE

Some of the very early high-level Soviet Communist Party secret agents who defected to the West in the 1930's and were subsequently debriefed by the U.S. Army's Military Intelligence Division used to say that the communists would not and could not take America by military force. "That's not how we're going to do it, Comrade. We will take you at the ballot box."

Fast forward to 2008. When one takes an objective and critical look at Barack Obama's past, they can't help but see that he is a radical Marxist, steeped in Communist ideology and methodology. Those prescient early warnings went unheeded!

It was Paul Volcker, the Chairman of the Federal Reserve System under the Carter and Reagan Administrations that said, "The standard of living of the average American has to decline...I don't think you can escape that." How's your "standard of living" compared to 25 years ago?

Bertrand Russell, a scientist, philosopher and member of the globalist Fabian Society (whose goal is a "One-World" totalitarian socialist oligarcy controlled by a self-anointed ruling elite), stated, "So long as the rulers are comfortable, what reasons have they to improve the lot of their serfs?"

Russell wrote a book titled *The Impact of Science on Society* in 1951. In the book Russell identified "education" as the best tool for the mass brainwashing of the population.

Russell believed education, especially government-controlled "public education", could be used to effectively gain control over the minds of the nation's youth through the application and dissemination of expertly-crafted modern propaganda.

Russell stated:

"I think the subject which will be of most importance politically is mass psychology...Its importance has been enormously increased by the growth of modern methods of propaganda. Of these the most influential is what is called 'education'. Religion plays a part, though a diminishing one; the press, the cinema, and the radio play an increasing part...It may be hoped that in time anybody will be able to persuade anybody of anything if he can catch the patient young and is provided by the State with money and equipment."

"The social psychologists of the future will have a number of classes of school children on whom they will try different methods of producing an unshakable conviction that snow is black...not much can be done unless indoctrination begins before the age of ten...verses set to music and repeatedly intoned are very effective."

Nobody reading that quote would be surprised if I told them it was said by Adolf Hitler or Joseph Goebbels. But it wasn't.

It was stated in a book written shortly after World War Two by a well-connected British scientist who was openly discussing how a totalitarian state could use "education" (quotes are in Russell's original writing) as well as the media, movies, organized religion, and the radio to mass-brainwash a nation's youth and literally get them to believe anything (i.e. that Obama is noble and virtuous).

Remember that the ideas and concepts Russell was articulating were written in 1951 before the mass ownership of televisions. He and his co-conspirators couldn't have fathomed in their wildest dreams how effectively television would mold the minds and shape the opinions of whole generations and populations.

When you consider that 99.8% of American households have at least one television, and that the average child willingly watches over six hours of television "programming" every day, it is not hard to see how America got a president like Barack Hussein Obama in 2008.

One of Obama's largest sub-groups of supporters is the nation's youth. They have been successfully brainwashed, methodically and systematically, without ever being aware of it.

"Those who are unaware are unaware of being unaware."

As an example to how effectively the mass mind-control and brainwashing works one only has to look at Obama's largest following and support group: blacks.

97% of blacks voted for Obama in 2008 and 96% of blacks voted for him again in 2012. Blacks continue to blindly support Obama even as he works them out of life, liberty, and property.

Most of the blacks I've seen interviewed could not name a single position, stance or policy of Obama's, nor could they cite one thing he had done for them (oftentimes they were astoundingly clueless!) but they nonetheless admitted to voting for him and said they continued to support him.

Voting for someone just because of their race is just as RACIST as voting against someone just because of their race.

{Watch and listen to the multiple YouTube videos posted under the headings "Howard Stern interviews Obama supporters" and "Howard Stern exposes Obama supporters" for an eye opener!}

Commenting on black voting behavior and how blacks have been completely hood-winked by black politicians and the Democrat Party, black author Erik Rush states in his book *Negrophilia* that blacks are "beyond brainwashed — they are absolutely spellbound."

Bertrand Russell knew that the concepts and methods he was outlining in his book were both sinister and highly effective, and meant only for elite consumption.

Even though this was all largely unknown to "we the people" in 1951, Russell feared that these methods and techniques for mass mind control could be discovered by the very people it was being planned for:

"Although this science will be diligently studied, it will be rigidly confined to the governing class. The populace will not be allowed to know how its convictions were generated. When the technique has been perfected, every government that has been in charge of education for a generation will be able to control its subjects securely without the need of armies or policemen."

Russell was a member of the British Fabian Society and a contemporary of George Orwell and Aldous Huxley (the authors of *1984*, *Animal Farm*, and *Brave New World*, respectively).

Both Orwell's and Huxley's nightmarish novels accurately "predicted" {foretold?} of a future dystopian world of all-powerful governments that were totalitarian in their control, absolute in their central planning, engineering and regimenting of society, and omnipresent in their surveillance of the citizenry, including constant government monitoring of individuals inside their own homes.

The totalitarian government portrayed in Orwell's *1984* maintained power and control over its citizen subjects through secret police intimidation and torture (the secret police force was called the "Ministry of Love"), non-stop propaganda (the government's propaganda agency was called the "Ministry of Truth") and various forms of mind control, including the re-writing of history, the re-defining of speech and concepts, destroying old books, and the outlawing of certain words, ideas and thoughts, called "Newspeak." "Political Correctness" is literally "Newspeak."

George Orwell wrote that "He who controls the past controls the future. He who controls the present controls the past."

Think about that quote and what Orwell is actually saying. If only the "victors" and the ruling class write the history books, why should we believe them? Aren't there at least two sides to every story?

Napoleon Bonaparte said, "History is a set of lies that people have agreed upon."

President Harry Truman said, "There is nothing new in the world except the history you do not know."

Truman is informing us that there is a great deal of factual information out there that is deliberately suppressed. I believe he is also insinuating, by omission, that most modern day historians are paid liars and deceivers like Howard Zinn as Dinesh D'Souza proved in his film, *"America – What Would The World Be Without Her."* A great deal of the published "establishment history" is nothing but propaganda and lies about the past, commonly agreed upon by those "in the know."

Orwell warned us, "Believe nothing, or next to nothing, of what you read about internal affairs on the Government side. It is all party propaganda — that is to say, lies."

The Communist Party of the Soviet Union, the one and only political party that held power in the world's first socialist dictatorship, had an official newspaper for dissemination of government and Communist Party propaganda called "Pravda", which translated means "truth." Even the name was a lie.

Orwell wrote an article for the *London Tribune* on March 22, 1946, titled "In Front of Your Nose." In it he wrote:

"The point is that we are all capable of believing things which we know to be untrue, and then, when we are finally proved wrong, impudently twisting the facts so as to show that we were right. Intellectually, it is possible to carry this process for an indefinite time: the only check on it is that sooner or later a false belief bumps up against solid reality, usually on a battlefield."

Does anybody really believe that our paratrooper, Ranger, Green Beret, SEAL, and Marine Infantry units will be more fearsome and effective fighting forces with women in their ranks? Really? Name one major military victory in U.S. history that would have been more decisive or successful with females in the ranks.

In *The Epistles*, written from 20 B.C. to 14 B.C., Horace stated, "You can drive out Nature with a pitchfork, but she keeps on coming back." I would add, "With a vengeance!"

Aldous Huxley was a famous and well-connected English intellectual, teacher, philosopher, and novelist. A contemporary of Bertrand Russell's, Huxley wrote a frightening novel in 1931 titled *Brave New World* about a future scientific dictatorship.

In 1949 Huxley wrote a letter to George Orwell (one of Huxley's former students), congratulating Orwell on his new book *1984*.

In his letter Huxley made a disturbing prediction:

"Within the next generation I believe that the world's leaders will discover that infant conditioning and narco-hypnosis are more efficient, as instruments of government, than clubs and prisons, and that the lust for power can be just as completely satisfied by suggesting people into loving their servitude as by flogging them and kicking them into obedience."

Remember that the above quote was written in 1949!

In an updated edition of his book titled *Brave New World Revisited*, which was published in 1958, Aldous Huxley made the following prediction about Western societies and governments:

RED BADGE

"Under the relentless thrust of accelerating over-population and increasing over-organization, and by means of ever more effective methods of mind-manipulation, the democracies will change their nature; the quaint old forms—elections, parliaments, Supreme Courts and all the rest—will remain. The underlying substance will be a new kind of non-violent totalitarianism.

"All the traditional names, all the hallowed slogans will remain exactly what they were in the good old days. Democracy and freedom will be the theme of every broadcast and editorial — but Democracy and freedom in a strictly Pickwickian sense. Meanwhile the ruling oligarchy and its highly trained elite of soldiers, policemen, thought-manufacturers and mind-manipulators will quietly run the show as they see fit."

Huxley continued:

"Under a dictatorship the Big Business, made possible by advancing technology and the consequent ruin of Little Business, is controlled by the State — that is to say, by a small group of party leaders and the soldiers, policemen and civil servants who carry out their orders. In a capitalist democracy such as the United States, it is controlled by what Professor C. Wright Mills has called the Power Elite. This Power Elite directly employs several millions of the country's working force in its factories, offices and stores, controls many millions more by lending them the money to buy its products, and, through its ownership of the media of mass communications, influences the thoughts, the feelings and the actions of virtually everybody."

"The impersonal forces of overpopulation and over-organization, and the social engineers, who are trying to direct these forces, are pushing us in the direction of a new medieval system. This revival will be made more acceptable...by such amenities as infant conditioning, sleep-teachings and drug-induced euphoria; but, for the majority of men and women, it will still be a kind of servitude."

Huxley compared Western societies in 1958 with ancient Rome:

"For conditions even remotely comparable to those now prevailing we must return to imperial Rome, where the populace was kept in good humor by frequent, gratuitous doses of many kinds of entertainment — from poetical dramas to gladiator fights, from recitations of Virgil to all-out boxing...military reviews and public executions. But even in Rome there was nothing like the non-stop distractions now provided by newspapers and magazines, by radio, television and the cinema."

On the mob mentality and the herd instinct, Huxley writes:

"Assembled in a crowd, people lose their powers of reasoning and their capacity for moral choice. Their suggestibility is increased to the point where they cease to have any judgment or will of their own. They become very excitable, they lose all sense of individual or collective responsibility, they are subject to sudden accesses of rage, enthusiasm and panic. In a word, man in a crowd behaves as though he had swallowed a large dose of what I have called 'herd-poisoning'."

Think how little anyone reads anymore, especially books. Reading is an individual and private affair, not a collective activity. The author communicates directly to the individual reader, who is sitting by himself in a state of focused, mindful thought.

The orator speaks to the masses: a collective, a group, a mob. As such they are already well-primed with "herd poison." They are at his mercy and, if he knows his craft, he can manipulate their emotions as well as their actions.

On propaganda Huxley writes:

"The propagandist should adopt a systematically one-sided attitude towards every problem that has to be dealt with. He must never admit that he might be wrong or that people with a different point of view might be even partially right. Opponents should not be argued with — they should be attacked, shouted down, or, if they become too much of a nuisance, liquidated." (Look at America's political discourse today. Sound familiar?)

"The effectiveness of political and religious propaganda depends upon the methods employed, not upon the doctrines taught. These doctrines may be true or false, wholesome or pernicious — it makes little or no difference...Under favorable conditions, practically everybody can be converted to practically anything."

And on chemical mind control Huxley wrote:

"That a dictator could, if he so desired, make use of these drugs for political purposes is obvious. He could ensure himself against political unrest by changing the chemistry of his subjects' brains and so making them content with their servile condition...But how, it may be asked, will the dictator get his subjects to take the pills that will make them think, feel and behave in the ways he finds desirable? In all probability it will be enough merely to make the pill available."

Remember that all the above was written in 1958!

Just three years later in 1961, Huxley was speaking at the California Medical School in San Francisco when he made an even more disturbing prediction:

"There will be in the next generation or so a pharmacological method of making people love their servitude and producing dictatorship without tears, so to speak. Producing a kind of painless concentration camp for entire societies so that people will in fact have their liberties taken away from them but will rather enjoy it, because they will be distracted from any desire to rebel by propaganda, or brainwashing, or brainwashing enhanced by pharmacological methods. And this seems to be the final revolution."

In 1962, Aldous Huxley gave a lecture at Berkeley titled: *The Ultimate Revolution — Slavery by Consent Through Psychological Manipulation and Conditioning.*

In the 1962 lecture, Huxley again discussed the advanced scientific and psychological techniques our ruling oligarchy would use to "standardize" and homogenize humanity and reduce them to slavery all while the slaves were mentally conditioned to "love their servitude."

The following is an excerpt from the 1962 Berkeley lecture:

"It seems to me that the nature of the ultimate revolution with which we are now faced is precisely this: That we are in process of developing a whole series of techniques which will enable the controlling oligarchy who have always existed and presumably will always exist to get people to love their servitude."

"This is the, it seems to me, the ultimate in malevolent revolutions shall we say, and this is a problem which has interested me many years and about which I wrote thirty years ago, a fable, *Brave New World*, which is an account of society making use of all the devices available and some of the devices which I imagined to be possible making use of them in order to, first of all, to standardize the population, to iron out inconvenient human differences, to create, to say, mass produced models of human beings arranged in some sort of scientific caste system."

"Since then, I have continued to be extremely interested in this problem and I have noticed with increasing dismay a number of the predictions which were purely fantastic when I made them thirty years ago have come true or seem in process of coming true.

"A number of techniques about which I talked seem to be here already. And there seems to be a general movement in the direction of this kind of ultimate revolution, a method of control by which a people can be made to enjoy a state of affairs by which any decent standard they ought not to enjoy."

(I urge the reader to do an internet search for the above lecture and listen to it or read the transcript)

Huxley was not fantasizing nor speculating about a possible fairytale world — as an inner-core Fabian secret society member he had high-level "Insider" knowledge of a distinct plan and was telegraphing that plan under the guise of fiction to an unsuspecting world. The accurate realization of his prophecies is not a coincidence!

Now, think of the purposeless mass of people in America today, that segment of the population addicted to television, pornography, texting, social media, illegal drugs, pharmaceutical drugs and welfare, who go through life in a mindless, directionless, zombie-state, "loving their servitude."

And then compare Orwell's *1984* and Huxley's *Brave New World* books with today's world, replete with nameless, faceless government bureaucrats who regulate, centrally-plan and autocratically control all aspects of our lives, including (now) our top-down, Soviet-style "command-controlled" health care.

Add to this government mandated "sensitivity training", "sexual harassment training", "race and social justice" classes, lectures on "bias", "racist code words" and "trigger warnings", endless seminars and mandatory employee training about "diversity", "tolerance" and "inclusiveness", court-appointed "anger management" classes, college "Speech Codes" and "Safe Spaces", and state and local "Hate Crime" laws, all of which are modern, more sophisticated forms of totalitarian thought control, Stalinist-style "re-education camps", and dictatorial abridgements of freedom of speech and freedom of expression.

And yet we find this elite desire to socially engineer and control the minds of the American people through carefully crafted propaganda is over a century old.

Walter Lippmann was an Intelligence Officer in the U.S. Army during World War One. Immediately after the war he became an adviser to President Woodrow Wilson.

Lippmann's first book *Public Opinion*, was written in 1922. In his book Lippmann said that the great mass of a nation's people functioned as a "bewildered herd" that must be governed by a "specialized class" of elite intellectuals and self-anointed experts.

Edward Bernays was a contemporary and compatriot of Lippmann's.

Bernays worked in the Woodrow Wilson administration during World War One as a propagandist for the "Committee on Public Information" (CPI), also known as the "Creel Committee."

The Creel Committee was literally the official propaganda arm of the U.S. Government: an agency whose primary mission was to influence U.S. public opinion in favor of America's participation in World War One.

Interestingly, it was just after World War One that Willi Munzenberg, the Propaganda Chief for the Communist International, stated: "All news is lies and all propaganda is disguised as news."

Bernays believed that modern society was irrational and dangerous due to the "herd instinct" and therefore propaganda was totally justified and necessary to manipulate, control and regiment the people.

Just like today's social engineers, these early 20th Century "public masters" believed they were superior to and above "the people", and knew what was best for you and me.

In his 1928 book titled *Propaganda*, Bernays said:

"As civilization becomes more complex, and as the need for invisible government has been increasingly demonstrated, the technical means have been invented and developed by which public opinion may be regimented. With printing press and newspaper, the telephone, telegraph, radio and airplanes, ideas can be spread rapidly, and even instantaneously, across the whole of America."

(Bernays could not yet see how much better and more effectively television, which had not been invented yet, would do the job).

Bernays continued:

"The conscious and intelligent manipulation of the organized habits and opinions of the masses is an important element in a democratic society. Those who manipulate this unseen mechanism of society constitute an invisible government which is the true ruling power of our country. We are governed, our minds are molded, our tastes formed, our ideas suggested, largely by men we have never heard of.

"Whatever attitude one chooses to take toward this condition, it remains a fact that in almost every act of our daily lives, whether in the sphere of politics or business, our social conduct or our ethical thinking, we are dominated by a relatively small number of persons, a trifling fraction of our population, who understand the mental processes and social patterns of the masses. It is they who pull the wires which control the public mind, and who harness old social forces and contrive new ways to bind and guide the world."

Remember, this was said in 1928! (More than 80 years ago)

Somewhat contemporaneously, British writer H.G. Wells made some revealing — and disturbing — statements on the topic.

Unknown to most, H.G. Wells — who is most famous for his *War of the Worlds* and *Time Machine* classics — was a self-proclaimed socialist and also a high-level member of the globalist Fabian Society.

Wells wrote a non-fiction book in 1939 titled *The New World Order* in which he built on his previous non-fiction book, *The Open Conspiracy: Blue Prints for a World Revolution.*

In *The New World Order* Wells wrote:

"This new and complete Revolution we contemplate can be defined in a very few words. It is outright world-socialism; scientifically planned and directed."

Wells went on to say that "Countless people will hate the new world order and will die protesting against it."

On the topic of asserting total control over a nation and gaining the submission of its citizenry to the ruling class, Wells claimed that traditional style warfare was not necessary for conquest — that any nation could be defeated by conquering the mind of its people — what Wells called, "the mental hinterlands hidden behind the persona."

Karl Marx, author of *The Communist Manifesto*, wrote that a "worker's revolution" would lead to a SOCIALIST dictatorship. Marx, who was militantly anti-Christian, further wrote that three major pillars of Western Civilization would have to be eliminated before a socialist dictatorship could be realized. Those three pillars were religion, family and private property. Therefore, Marx called for the elimination of all rights to private property, the dissolution of the family unit, and the complete destruction of religion, especially Christianity.

RED BADGE

In the Marxist vision, anyone holding religious beliefs and engaging in the worship of a supernatural God would be displaying signs of "counter-revolutionary activity" and these activities would be outlawed. There would be no "higher power" allowed than the almighty socialist State. In practical terms, the state would monopolize and centralize all power into a single ruling party which would have total control over the citizenry and there would be zero tolerance for dissenting thoughts, opinions or beliefs. If you doubt this, just look at the contemporary example of Marxist-socialist North Korea — in reality a massive concentration camp disguised as a country — a modern-day slave society where everyone is to do and think as they are told, and are forced to bow down and worship the government. All citizens must refer to their mass-murdering dictator as "Dear Leader."

In keeping with the fatal deceit inherent in socialism, the North Korean government (which is in fact a totalitarian socialist dictatorship) lists itself officially as a "democratic peoples' republic." Nothing could be further from the truth!

Now recall Georgetown Professor Carroll Quigley's revelations gained from inside knowledge and access: the secret plan of the international banking elite to establish socialist dictatorships— controlled by them from behind the scenes — which would be disguised as "worker's democracies."

And realize that Karl Marx was financed and supported by this very same banking elite to write his *Communist Manifesto*, which was published in London, England, headquarters of the House of Rothschild's international banking dynasty and home to the "City of London", the world's most influential and powerful financial and business district.

Now look at America today, and the non-stop war against Christianity, private property, and the family unit. On February 6, 2009, less than three weeks after Barack Obama took office,

Newsweek magazine's cover story proclaimed, "We Are All Socialists Now."

From the founding days of the Marxist U.S.S.R. and throughout the 45-year-long Cold War, the Communist Party of the Soviet Union and their KGB ("the Sword and Shield of the Party") made no secret of the fact that the United States was considered their "Main Adversary." America has always been the chief target of Soviet and communist spies and subversion agents due to America being the bulwark of Western Christian Civilization and the greatest obstacle to One World Socialist Dictatorship.

The Soviet KGB's primary mission during the Cold War was not espionage and counter-espionage against America and the West, but the destruction of the United States through SUBVERSION. This encompassed a wide-range of unconventional activities (Psy-Ops, agitation-propaganda, perception manipulation, opinion forming, "framing" an issue, etc.) and its focus changed over time.

A little-known fact: When a Soviet KGB officer took his oath upon commission, he swore to carry out the "World Revolution."

Subversion of the U.S. was of such primary importance to the communist world revolutionary movement that the KGB set up and operated at Lenin University in Moscow a "School of Political Warfare." A high-level subversion course taught at the School of Political Warfare was called "Psycho Politics."

In a Psycho Politics lecture in Moscow in 1933, Professor Lavrenti Beria, a future KGB director, stated:

"Psycho-politics is an important if less known division of geopolitics. It is less known because it must necessarily deal with highly educated personnel, the very top strata of "mental healing ... By psycho politics our chief goals are effectively carried forward. **To produce a maximum of chaos in the culture of the enemy is our first most important step. Our**

fruits are grown in chaos, distrust, economic depression and scientific turmoil."

In another Psycho-politics lecture at the Lenin School of Political Warfare, this time to a visiting delegation of American Marxist psychology students in 1933, Beria stated:

"Degradation and conquest are companions. By attacking the character and morals of the people...by bringing about, through contamination of youth, a general degraded feeling, command of the populace is facilitated to a very marked degree. By perverting the institutions of a nation and bringing about a general degradation ... a population can be brought psychologically to heel."

"A psycho-politician must work hard to produce the maximum chaos in the fields of 'mental healing'. You must work until every teacher of psychology unknowingly or knowingly teaches only Communist doctrine under the guise of 'psychology'. You must labor until every doctor and psychiatrist is either a psycho-politician or an unwitting assistant to our aims. You must labor until we have dominion over the minds and bodies of every important person in your nation. You must work until suicide arising from mental imbalance is common and calls forth no general investigation or remark. You must dominate as respected men the fields of psychiatry and psychology. You must dominate the hospitals and universities...You can come and take your instruction as worshippers of Freud...Psycho-politics is a solemn charge. With it you can erase our enemies as insects. You can change their loyalties by psycho-politics. Given a short time with a psycho-politician you can alter forever the loyalty of a soldier in our hands or a statesman or a leader in his own country, or you can destroy his mind…

Use the courts, use the judges, use the Constitution of the country, use its medical societies and its laws to further our ends...By psycho-politics create chaos. Leave a nation leaderless."

RED BADGE

Kenneth Goff was a dues-paying member of the Communist Party USA in the 1930's. He was also a well-trained practitioner in the dark arts of "Psycho-politics." After years of faithful service to the cause of communism, Goff finally realized that he was being duped, and that communism was a cruel hoax which used propaganda, lofty slogans, lies and brainwashing to hoodwink and manipulate the naive masses of useful idiots into helping the communists gain power and establish a highly-centralized and militarized totalitarian slave society (police state).

Goff left the Communist Party USA and became a staunch and outspoken anti-communist. He wrote a book based on the original training textbook used in the Psycho-politics course taught in the Soviet Union in which he was formally schooled. He titled his book *The Soviet Art of Brainwashing: A Synthesis of the Russian Textbook on Psycho-politics*.

In the book Goff writes: "During my training I was trained in Psycho-politics. This was the art of capturing the minds of a nation through brainwashing and fake mental health."

The Soviet government was notorious for pronouncing as "mentally ill" dissidents, non-conformists, and anyone else who in any way resisted communist indoctrination or who refused to parrot Party propaganda.

The Communist Party frequently used doctors of psychiatry to officially declare legitimate dissidents "mental cases" (paranoid, schizophrenic, delusional, etc.) that needed to be locked up indefinitely in mental institutions "for public safety." Pay attention TEA Party members, evangelicals and Second Amendment advocates.

In this way the Party exploited the fields of psychiatry and psychology and used them as effective tools to frighten the population by painting anyone who dissented from the Communist Party line or who drew attention to official corruption or communist crimes against the people as being a dangerous, anti-social psychopath and "mentally deranged." This also made "legal" the communist state's mass incarceration of the dissident population and the "disappearing" of its political opponents. (Remember, what is "legal" is often not "lawful")

More importantly, it served as a powerful tool of intimidation, coercion, and terror, forcing the masses into fearful servitude.

The Communist International (aka "The COMINTERN") was founded at a congress in Moscow, Russia in March 1919 primarily by Marxist revolutionaries Vladimir Lenin and Leon Trotsky, founding leader of the Red Army. There were delegates from communist and socialist organizations from around the world present, but ultimately the COMINTERN was run by an executive committee of five members. The COMINTERN's members advocated "World Revolution" to achieve global communism and a one-world socialist state. They openly proclaimed that their mission was to fight "by all available means, including armed force, for the overthrow of the international bourgeoisie (middle class) and for the creation of an international Soviet republic" (a One-World socialist government).

The Soviet Art of Brainwashing: Psycho-politics and the Suppression of Man and Civilization was the very revealing title of the original Communist International (COMINTERN) textbook and training manual widely used to train communist subversives operating against the West, but especially for those operating against the United States. This COMINTERN textbook was the primary instruction manual used in the Psycho-politics course taught by Communist Party psychologists and KGB operatives at the Lenin School of Political Warfare in the Soviet Union.

Remember, the communist world revolutionary movement considered America to be their "Main Adversary," their number one target.

The manual's introduction was written by Soviet Commissar and future KGB director Lavrenti Beria. The following are some very illuminating quotes from the COMINTERN training manual:

"In order to induce a high state of hypnosis in an individual, a group, or a population, an element of terror must always be present on the part of those who would govern."

"The by-word should be built into the society that 'paranoia' is a condition 'in which the individual believes he is being attacked by Communists'."

"The populace must be brought into the belief that every individual within it who rebels...against the efforts and activities to enslave the whole, must be considered to be a deranged person...and...be given electric shocks, and reduced into unimaginative docility for the remainder of his days."

"In the United States we have been able to...place the tenets of Karl Marx, Pavlov, Lamarck, and the data of Dialectic Materialism into the textbooks of psychology, to such a degree that anyone thoroughly studying psychology becomes at once a candidate to accept the reasonableness of Communism."

"As every chair of psychology in the United States is occupied by persons in our connection, the consistent employment of such texts is guaranteed...Educating broadly the educated strata of the populace into the tenets of Communism is thus rendered relatively easy."

"Mental health organizations must carefully delete from their ranks anyone actually proficient in the handling or treatment of mental health."

"The psycho political operative should also spare no expense in smashing out of existence, by whatever means, any actual healing group."

The manual boasts of communist success in taking over Freudian psychology and Freudian psychoanalysis' emphasis on sex, using it to promote human degradation and giving communist agents another tool to extort and blackmail their targets through "defamation of character."

"Recruitment into the ranks of 'mental healing' should be confined to students who are already depraved. Recruitment is effected by making the field of mental healing very attractive financially and sexually."

"The promise of unlimited sexual opportunities, the promise of complete dominion over the bodies and minds of helpless patients, the promise of having lawlessness without detection can thus attract to 'mental healing' many desirable recruits who will willingly fall in line with psycho political activities."

"You must work until 'religion' is synonymous with 'insanity'. You must work until the officials of city, county and state governments will not think twice before they pounce upon religious groups as public enemies."

"Movements to improve youth should be invaded and corrupted, as this might interrupt campaigns to produce in youth delinquency, addiction, drunkenness, and sexual promiscuity."

"Seek out the leaders in the country's future, and educate them into the belief of the animalistic nature of Man...that Man is a mechanism without individuality...an animal with a civilized veneer."

"They must be taught to frown upon ideas, upon individual endeavor. They must be taught, above all things that the salvation of man is found only by his adjusting thoroughly to this environment. Nations which have high ethical tone are difficult to conquer."

The COMINTERN manual instructed its practitioners to work their way into control of industries and institutions whereby they would be able to successfully label as "paranoid" anyone who called attention to the communist menace and who tried to warn their fellow countrymen about the ominous communist conspiracy operating against them.

Finally, the COMINTERN manual told its operatives to "produce the maximum chaos in the culture of the enemy," and to "leave a nation leaderless."

Look at so many Americans today and especially our youth: immoral, dysfunctional, corrupt, drug and alcohol addicted, sexually promiscuous, and delinquent, etc.

In keeping with Soviet and COMINTERN strategy, in Obama's "Soviet Amerika" we increasingly saw veterans, gun owners, people who home school their kids, certain Christian denominations, folks who buy or sell milk without the approval of the U.S. Department of Agriculture, and other so-called anti-government dissidents get arrested and committed into hospitals and psychiatric wards by law enforcement for "72-hour mental health evaluations." Their firearms and ammunition are seized by the police and due to Soviet-style politicized psychiatric evaluations, these innocent citizens, most often guilty of NO CRIME, are frequently declared to have some mental ailment or condition whereby they are prescribed medication and permanently stripped of their right to keep and bear arms.

Increasingly, American war veterans are being wantonly and arbitrarily misdiagnosed with Post-Traumatic Stress Disorder (PTSD) and other trivial diagnoses, such as "unable to care for self" or "unable to care for one's finances." Once PTSD or any other number of medical issues is documented by the VA or by the computerized government-controlled and regulated healthcare system, these veterans are permanently stripped of their right to keep and bear arms. This is Soviet psycho-politics in action. It is veterans and home-schoolers today; tomorrow it might be you!

Communist propaganda chief Willi Munzenberg, who helped found the "Frankfurt School", enjoined his comrades with the following instructions:

"We must organize the intellectuals and use them to make Western civilization stink. Only then, after they have corrupted all its values and made life impossible, can we impose the dictatorship of the proletariat."

This is the template of Marxist cultural and psychological warfare directed at the United States.

Although the name changed over the doorway in Russia, the new boss is the same as the old boss. Vladimir Putin, a former KGB colonel, has filled many of the top-level positions in his regime with former KGB officers. A "Robber Baron" oligarchy made up of well-connected former Soviet officials, international financiers and industrialists run the "New Russia." And Russia's intelligence agencies still consider America the "Main Adversary."

I pointed out in Chapter Nine by contrast Putin is strangely unaffected by the suicidal forces of Frankfurt School "political correctness" killing the West as he boldly reunites the Russian people and expands his borders.

In 1991, as the "Cold War" was being declared over on two continents, two highly decorated American military men made some illuminating comments on the treason, deceit, and betrayal originating at the highest levels of the U.S. government.

Retired U.S. Air Force Colonel L. Fletcher Prouty, a distinguished author and World War Two combat veteran, served as Chief of Special Operations for the Pentagon during the Cold

War. Prouty was in charge of providing military support for the world-wide clandestine operations of the CIA and the Pentagon. He said:

"We have now begun to realize that one of the greatest casualties of the Cold War has been the truth. At no time in the history of mankind has the general public been so misled and so betrayed as it has been by the work of the propaganda merchants of this century and their 'historians'."

Retired U.S. Army Special Forces Lt. Colonel James "Bo" Gritz, author, Vietnam combat veteran, and the most decorated Green Beret commander in American history, states definitively that America has been betrayed from within. Commenting on the high treason still plaguing the nation in May of 1991, Gritz wrote:

"A spider web of 'patriots for profit', operating from the highest positions of special trust and confidence, have successfully circumvented our constitutional system in pursuit of a New World Order. They have infused America with drugs in order to fund covert operations while sealing the fate of our servicemen left in Communist prisons.

"Hiding behind a mask of official righteousness, this secret combination seeks to impose its own concept of geopolitical navigation, nullifying liberty as the hard-won birthright of all Americans. At a time when the Constitution hangs by a thread, America has witnessed the prostitution of our appointed guardians for power and profit. Before a nation can act to regain its footing, the people must know what has happened, who caused it, and why."

Prior to his untimely death, Colonel Prouty elaborated further on the danger facing America saying:

"...The threat for the future continues. The fact that such enormous uncontrolled power has existed without challenge...speaks for itself. This country and perhaps the world are under the control of a High Cabal, unequaled for its magnitude and effectiveness in the history of civilization."

(Colonel Prouty is the author of two insightful books: *The Secret Team* and *JFK*. Lt. Colonel James Gritz is also the author of two books: *A Nation Betrayed* and *Called to Serve*)

"The duty of a true Patriot is to protect his country from its government." — Thomas Paine

"If we remain silent when our popularly elected government violates the laws it has sworn to uphold and steals the freedoms we elected it to protect, we will have only ourselves to blame when Big Brother is everywhere. Somehow, I doubt my father's generation fought the Nazis in World War Two only to permit a totalitarian government to flourish here."

— Judge Andrew Napolitano

"Those who make peaceful change impossible make violent revolution inevitable." — John F. Kennedy

"There's a plot in this country to enslave every man, woman, and child. Before I leave this high and noble office, I intend to expose this plot."

— John F. Kennedy, 7 days before his assassination

RED BADGE
CONCLUSION

We need less tolerance and more righteousness.

We need less acceptance and more absolutes.

We need less diversity and more nationalism.

We need fewer laws and more liberty.

If you are fifty years of age or older and believe that the America you were raised in can ever be reclaimed, you are delusional. Just as sure as soccer will replace baseball as the national pastime, America is forever gone on the scale you enjoyed. Too much damage has been done to our minds, our culture and our institutions. The enormity and complexity of the effort to transform us is beyond the comprehension of most Americans. If the evidence is put before them, most will refuse to accept it. Not until they are tangibly affected will they sober one by one and all too late to avoid what is coming.

World War Two resulted in the massive expansion of communism and the power of the Soviet Empire. Due to public education few Americans know that Germany occupied western Poland (former German territory seized after WWI) after repeated demands for protection came from ethnic Germans being terrorized there and more importantly, to thwart Stalin's ambitious plan to seize control of all of Europe through overwhelming military force and then spread the "World Revolution" around the globe. By 1940 the Soviet Union had already annexed the Baltic States and invaded Finland, Poland, Bessarabia (Moldova) and Bukovina (Romania).

Germany did not begin WWII; the Soviet Union did. Hitler knew the Soviets were staging for a massive "War of Extermination" against Germany and the West and pre-empted the Soviet attack on June 22, 1941. Tragically, Hitler broad brushed and targeted the Jews because so many of them he feared to be subversive communists (such as the Frankfurt School and the "Red Orchestra" spy ring in Europe).

This belief came from that fact that while Jews in Russia were between 2% and 5% of the population in 1917 they were the majority leaders behind the communist coup. While Vladimir Ulyanov Lenin was only one-quarter Jewish, the leaders of full Jewish ancestry were: Leon Trostsky (Lev Bronstein), Yakov Sverdlov (Solomon), Grigori Zinoviev (Radomyslsky), Karl Radek (Sobelsohn), Maxim Litvinov (Wallach), Lev Kamenev (Rosenfeld) and Moiseri Uritsy.[70] In 1918 nine of the twelve Central Committee members of the Bolshevik Party were of Jewish Ancestry and only three of Russian ancestry.

General George Patton was well aware of Stalin's stated designs for world conquest and wanted to seize the opportunity

---

[70]Read entries in: H. Shukman, ed., The Blackwell Encyclopedia of the Russian Revolution (Oxford: 1988), and in: G. Wigoder, ed., Dictionary of Jewish Biography (New York: Simon and Schuster, 1991). Also read: Stanley Rothman and S. Robert Lichter, Roots of Radicalism (New York: Oxford, 1982), pp. 92-94.

to crush the Soviets and take his army to Moscow, but was denied and relieved of command. Patton openly threatened to resign from the Army and expose the high treason of U.S. government officials and their collusion with the Soviets. This led to Patton's assassination — a joint OSS-NKVD operation. (NKVD was the wartime Soviet KGB) For proof, read the book *Target Patton: The Plot to Assassinate General George Patton* by Robert Wilcox.

Major Douglas deWitt Bazata was a highly decorated former OSS agent in Europe during WWII. While speaking at an OSS reunion at the Washington, D.C. Hilton Hotel on September 25, 1979 Bazata admitted to his 450 guests that he participated in the assassination of General George Patton under orders from General Bill Donovan, the OSS Director. Bazata gave additional details to author Robert Wilcox. After the staged vehicle collision Patton was quickly recovering in the hospital when Soviet agents poisoned him, finishing the job. Stephen Skubik was a U.S. Army Counter-Intelligence Corps (CIC) officer during WWII. Skubik revealed that Patton was high on Stalin's "death list" and that U.S. Government leaders thwarted CIC's attempts to prevent it. Skubik's book *Death: The Murder of General Patton* discusses the Soviet plot and OSS General Bill Donovan's involvement.

"Berlin gave me the blues. We have destroyed what could have been a good race (Germans), and we are about to replace them with Mongolian savages. It's said that for the first week after they took Berlin, all women who ran were shot and those who did not were raped. I could have taken it (instead of the Soviets) had I been allowed."

George Patton, 1945

On April 15, 1945 Supreme Allied Commander General Eisenhower ordered all Allied field commanders to halt their advance and forbid them from crossing the Elbe River. Eisenhower literally cut off fuel deliveries to General Patton's 3rd Army that was advancing at breakneck speed toward Berlin, ensuring the maverick Patton couldn't defy his order to not cross the Elbe River. This action by General Eisenhower allowed the Soviet Army to take Berlin and seize control over all of Eastern Europe. What ensued next in the Soviet Zone of occupation was the largest and most savage mass rape in recorded history, as Soviet troops gang raped, sodomized, mutilated and tortured to death over two million German women and girls (with victims as young as 8 years old to elderly women over 80) often gang raping and torturing them in front of their children, siblings, and fathers.

Soviet troops tortured and executed over one million German prisoners of war immediately after Germany's surrender, and over 10 million German civilians were expelled from their homes. Over two million civilians died as a result of the Soviet expulsions and their forced migration. An additional half million Germans were interned in Soviet slave labor camps, where they perished from a combination of exposure to the elements, starvation and exhaustion (being worked literally to death without food or water).

Significantly, 25,000 American prisoners of war located in the Soviet Zone upon Germany's surrender were sent to Siberian slave labor camps under Stalin's orders (the Gulag). President Harry Truman and General Eisenhower were fully aware of the forced transfer and internment of American POWs but did not protest. They aided and abetted Stalin by covering it up! The American troops were never released and never returned home. To this day, they are listed as "Missing in Action" by the Department of Defense.

Operation Keelhaul

Nikolai Tolstoy's book *The Secret Betrayal* describes the immoral and callous conspiracy between Britain and the United States to repatriate to the USSR nearly 2.5 million ethnic Russians. These ethnic Russians were either POWs or refugees who had fled the Bolshevik coup and joined the Wehrmacht to fight an evil even greater than Hitler: Communism. Britain and the U.S. diplomats knew that the forced repatriation of Russians to the USSR was a death sentence for them. Many Russians committed suicide upon learning of their pending forced repatriation. Prior to Operation Keelhaul the Red Army had already liberated British and American POWs from (eastern) Germany. What then did the Allied powers have to gain by Operation Keelhaul?

Tolstoy believed that British and American diplomats were in cahoots with the Soviet Union to build a new, post-war world order.

British officers witnessed the Soviet Secret Police (NKVD) execute repatriated Russians as they pulled away from the ports of Murmansk and Odessa. Other repatriated Russians were sent to the Gulag as slaves to fuel the communist economy.

From the end of WWII until the fall of the Berlin Wall we trusted our government to protect us during the Cold War. The Cold War was a distraction. The communists' true effort has long been to conquer the U.S. internally through subversion. Soviet-style PSYOPS — not bullets or bombs — destroyed America. They attacked our minds and our culture. We came to embrace suicide as enlightenment.

Without a fight, the enemy is inside the gate and inside our heads — funded to a large extent by tax dollars. The much maligned and finally vindicated patriot, Senator Joseph McCarthy, (elected 1946) was proven right about the communist infiltration of the United States government! Before him was democrat Congressman Martin Dies who in the latter 1930s discovered the same communist infiltration and who was also maligned for his efforts to expose it. The executions of Julius and Ethel Rosenberg in 1953 for espionage were proof of the communist infiltration of the United States and it persists.

Senator McCarthy was vindicated tenfold in 1995 by the release of the Venona papers, but the corrupt media did not give it traction. The Left has long made it common practice to use McCarthy's name as a noun to mean a groundless, crazy, conspiratorial, political witch hunt. The Left discredited McCarthy and coined his name into a noun used as a shield to slander and discredit any investigation of them that would prove (continued) communist infiltration. The forces targeting Trump are an extension of the same communist camp that have long infiltrated our state department (making foreign policy favorable to our enemies) and the DOJ (making domestic policy transforming policing strategy). Trump's accusers are in fact the ideological and even tribal descendants of those that created the Soviet Union and who Patriot Joe McCarthy correctly identified. The infiltration began in the 1930s, grew substantially after WWII (a war that EXPANDED communism). Clearly, it continues today.[71]

The evidence is our feeble minded ignorance and suicidal mental state that is our present condition. We allowed the U.S. Constitution to be discarded by the federal government. The Patriot Act eliminated the American Peoples' Fourth Amendment right and Habeas Corpus protections. As author and talk show host Mark Levin has opined, we are living in a "Post-Constitutional" Amerika.

All of the mechanisms of Marxism have been adopted in the U.S. as reflected in *The Communist Manifesto*. The American

---

[71] M. Stanton Evans, 2007, Three Rivers press, Blacklisted By History The Untold Story of Senator Joe McCarthy

patriot is now considered an enemy of the State. Remember, the government of the Soviet Union was at war with the Russian people; it was an "occupation government." It targeted the original Russian bloodline peoples (and Russian Christians in particular). Stalin killed more Russians than he did Germans in WWII. Likewise, the United States government is at war with the cultural and ideological descendants of its Founding Fathers. This is why you do not feel represented or protected by your government. You are the enemy. The government wants a violent reaction from you. If they can't provoke you to violence they will manufacture events to discredit you and make it appear as though groups you belong to are racists, bigots and terrorists to be rounded up and made an example of.

We had a self-avowed "socialist" named Bernie Sanders running for president on the Democrat ticket (perhaps as Michael Savage opined, to make Hillary Clinton look like a reasonable alternative). As many as 70 members of the U.S. Congress are affiliated with the treasonous Democratic Socialists of America (DSA), a sub-group of the Socialist International that actively and subversively works to destroy the independence and national sovereignty of the United States.

Brace for impact. Reality is gaining on us. The path we are on leads to an incredibly violent future. The old majority will continue to be the target of government persecution and horrific crimes motivated by racial hatred and class envy. Criminal malcontents will align with Islamic terrorists and attack on a scale never before seen in America. The ultimate act of recruitment for black criminals will be when a uniformed, white-male police officer is beheaded. The murder will go viral on You Tube, and be celebrated by the well-funded Black Lives Matter camp and the likes of predators that rioted in Ferguson.

The international Marxist-Islamic cabal will allow terrorists to attack America's schools, churches, daycare centers, recreation areas, malls and places of work. In some cities, martial law will be used when police will not be able to combat gangs and well equipped/trained terrorists with their rules of engagement and inadequate weaponry. Wanting protection, law-abiding citizens will cry for more government.

As the economy weakens more, the middle class will fall from the safety the suburbs once provided. The very suburbs that defined the American dream are transforming as more and more foreclosures and short sales turn to rentals — up for grabs by government-subsidized parvenu.

This transformation is being accelerated by HUD through the Fair Housing Act that holds the hands of the undeserving and forces the "diversification" of every white, middle class neighborhood without regard to the natural order of accomplishment — as if home ownership is a human right rather than the result of hard work.

Finally, out of self-preservation, the producers as a whole will sober up. Chief among them, whites will regenerate a long dormant racial consciousness and begin to think and act tribal and protective like every other faction has for two generations. <u>The difference is that whites will be reacting to *real* predatory hatred toward them not an imagined one.</u>

Following this awakening a nationalist party will emerge much like Greece's Golden Dawn Party, France's National Front and Britain's UKIP. This will bring us to the climax of the revolution. In response to the resurrection of consciousness among the dispossessed old *majority* producers (mostly white), yet more government force will be used. This time force will not be used to merely referee factions and restore order between recurring clashes of "victims" within the new majority. Rather, it will be used to permanently crush resistance from the corners of tradition that has been so long cast the villain in the Big Lie.

Some talk of revolution to win back America. Is it time for that lawful remedy given to us in the Declaration of

Independence? Whatever your answer it is unlikely. Who would show up? What is more likely than revolution is insurgency. Insurgents can be quite effective, but less so as technology out paces resistance and drones come on line that will be used by the fast-emerging police state preparing to meet the inevitable unrest.

While I realize violence may be inevitable I can only endorse it from the respective state governments, not from The People directly — at this juncture. In their proper role, I can imagine some states bloodying the nose of the federal government on the constitutional grounds of protecting state sovereignty, state powers and individual rights. If this happens at all, it is most likely to come first from states bordering Mexico should they activate their National Guard to stop the invasion of illegal aliens and then find themselves in conflict with federal troops for doing so. Another flash point could be gun seizures.

Certainly, for dual sovereignty to be restored states must assert their authority courageously. The Tenth Amendment was given to us as a barricade against tyranny.

America's Sheriffs play a key role in initiating the push back to federal overreach. To that end every Sheriff should form a posse large enough to take over all law enforcement in the county should city police power up with the federal government in any unconstitutional actions like gun seizures. Furthermore, Sheriffs should instruct the citizens of the county to call 911 when a federal agent knocks on their door without a uniformed deputy sheriff present. Following this policy would mean that **the absence of a deputy is evidence that the feds circumvented the Sheriff**. Without an elected, Constitutional Sheriff in the loop the citizens' civil rights are potentially in jeopardy.

Our Founding Fathers knew well the capacity of government to turn tyrannical. Consider excerpts in bold font below from the list of grievances written by Thomas Jefferson to King George III in the Declaration of Independence. Think about the parallels between the crown's behavior and that of our federal government today. Ask yourself which is worse.

When you read the following excerpts from the Declaration of Independence think about the NDAA, The Patriot Act, the cavalier abdication of border enforcement until Trump, Obamacare, the confiscation and transfer of wealth through a tax system that punishes success, the federal-corporate takeover of large sections of the economy, layers of abusive regulatory agencies, duplicate federal laws that empower the federal government to insert themselves into local issues and force their will on local jurisdictions, United Nations treaties, and Tenth Amendment usurpations. Think about National Security Letters being treated as if they are search warrants, but they are not signed by a judge. Furthermore, you are threatened with arrest if you reveal one was served on you:

He has erected a multitude of New Offices, and sent hither swarms of Officers to harass our people, and eat out their substance: TSA, NSA, HUD, USFS, FCC, Department of Education, DHS, EPA, DEQ, EEOC, OSHA, BLM, DEA, IRS, BATFE, FBI etc. Remember the murders at Waco, Ruby Ridge, the 2005 post hurricane Katrina gun confiscations and aggravating factors by the federal government surrounding the unnecessary escalation of the 2016 sit-in at the Malheur National Wildlife Refuge that resulted in the shooting death of LaVoy Finicum.

"There's no way to rule innocent men. The only power any government has is the power to crack down on criminals. Well, when there aren't enough criminals, one makes them. One declares so many things to be a crime that it becomes impossible for men to live without breaking laws." Ayn Rand, *Atlas Shrugged*

Consider federal crimes. In April 2012, the 700 Club TV program ran a story called, A Nation of Criminals. In the report it mentioned that between 2000 and 2010 nearly 800,000 people were sentenced for federal crimes.

He has affected to render the Military independent of and superior to the Civil power: NDAA

He has combined with others to subject us to a jurisdiction foreign to our constitution, and unacknowledged by our laws; giving his Assent to their Acts of pretended Legislation: UN treaties, and Agenda 21 that could do the following:

- Wipe out private property off of the face of the earth
- Force you and your family to live in a single-family energy efficient home
- Confiscate private farms
- Ban individual ownership of cars
- Regulate where we live and what we eat

For Quartering large bodies of armed troops among us: TSA has grown from 16,000 "agents" to 56,000 over ten years. It is now expanding from airports to subways, buses, trucks and cars using its "VIPER" teams (Visual Intermodal Prevention and Response). Working in tandem with duped local law enforcement they have to-date carried out 8,800 unannounced checkpoints. Furthermore, the DHS/TSA can arbitrarily place you on the no-fly list thereby suspending your constitutional right to buy a firearm without due process. In addition, spy drones are being flown over the American people. These acts are not being done to protect the people, but to condition them. They poke their finger in our eye to test our level of submission and then accordingly take more ground (liberty) — all in the name of "Public Safety."

RED BADGE

For protecting them, by a mock Trial, from punishment for any Murders which they should commit on the Inhabitants of these States: NDAA

For cutting off our Trade with all parts of the world: Over-regulation making our products less competitively priced in the world market. We have the highest corporate tax rate in the world.

For imposing Taxes on us without our Consent: Obamacare, Cap and Trade, and The (unratified) 16th Amendment. Irwin Schiff, tax protester/evader and author of many books including *The Federal Mafia – How it Illegally Imposes and Unlawfully Collects Income Taxes.* He paid the price for speaking the truth. He died in federal custody October 16, 2015 at age 87 of lung cancer while serving his third prison term, a 14-year sentence. This non-violent offender was cuffed to a bed and denied the grace of early release argued on medical grounds after already serving more than 10 years.

For depriving us in many cases, of the benefits of Trial by Jury: NDAA

For transporting us beyond Seas to be tried for pretended offenses: Expanding recognition of a World Court.

For taking away our Charters, abolishing our most valuable Laws, and altering fundamentally the Forms of our Governments: The misuse of Executive Orders, a gaggle of Czars that circumvent Congress, and the misuse of the Commerce Clause to step on states' powers.

For suspending our own legislatures, and declaring themselves invested with power to legislate for us in all cases whatsoever: Obamacare, the misuse of the Commerce Clause, and denying Arizona the right to protect itself from invasion. Presidential Executive Orders that circumvent Congress make it a ceremonial branch and the president a dictator. President Obama has unilaterally and unlawfully made 24 changes to the

Obamacare law by executive order and even more casually by presidential memoranda. (32 unilateral, arbitrary changes, all of which are illegal!). The Supreme Court has also made significant changes to the Obamacare law twice, which exceeds their constitutional authority and function. Furthermore, the Supreme Court and the numerous circuit and district courts throughout the country routinely usurp the power of the legislative branch by "making law" and striking down referendums, which are popular votes by the people, thus allowing one black-robed tyrant to overrule the will of the people and make a mockery of the constitutional separation of powers.

On July 6, 2012 Executive Order 13618 was signed: "Assignment of National Security and Emergency Preparedness Communications Functions." This order empowers the president to shut down all domestic communications in the event of a national emergency, which includes an internet "kill switch" and the ability to completely disable all telephone and cell phone service. Previous Executive Orders (NSPD 51 and HSPD 20) empower the president to single-handedly determine just what constitutes an "emergency." It could be anything from the Avian Flu to a legitimate terrorist attack to a fake assassination attempt that makes it look like TEA Party members were behind it. This is far too much power for any one person to hold over America.

He has abdicated Government here, by declaring us out of his Protection and waging War against us: Abdicating the Constitutional duty to police the border from repeated Mexican military incursions and armed drug traffickers. Failure to protect or even advocate on behalf of American citizens unlawfully and arbitrarily arrested overseas. A total failure to protect our diplomatic mission in Benghazi, Libya from a full-scale military assault by terrorists, resulting in the mutilation and murder of the U.S. ambassador, the deaths of three brave American military men and the destruction of our consulate. And then the repeated lies and on-going government cover up regarding this horrific crime, dereliction of duty and humiliating national disgrace.

He has plundered our seas, ravaged our Coasts, burnt our towns, and destroyed the lives of our people: Intentionally lowering America's standard of living by damaging the economy through draconian EPA and OSHA regulations that strangle and discourage domestic businesses; the highest corporate income tax in the world (sending factories, industry and companies overseas), resulting in tens of millions of permanently unemployed, many losing their homes and businesses; repeatedly granting the mass-murdering communist Chinese government "Most Favored Nation" trade status, resulting in a financially devastating trade deficit of $600 billion annually; the 2010 BP oil spill, where more than 200 million gallons of crude oil was pumped into the Gulf of Mexico for 87 days, making it the biggest oil spill and largest environmental disaster in U.S. history, killing over 8,000 species of wildlife and ruining 16,000 miles of coastline in Texas, Louisiana, Mississippi, Alabama, and Florida. Obama did nothing for 71 days while this environmental holocaust ran amok; Allowing America to be infused with narcotics from overseas which in turn promotes organized crime and gang warfare, and doing virtually nothing to combat the criminals, gangs and drug addicts turning our cities and neighborhoods into war zones and cesspools of filth, decadence, decay and rampant crime; Waco, Texas: 76 Americans killed through the heavy-handed and direct actions of the federal government; Ruby Ridge, Idaho: 14-year-old boy shot in the back and killed by federal marshals and his unarmed mother shot in the face and killed by an FBI sniper while holding her ten-month-old baby in her arms.

He is at this time transporting large Armies of foreign Mercenaries to complete the works of death, desolation and tyranny, already begun with circumstances of cruelty & perfidy scarcely paralleled in the most barbarous ages, and

totally unworthy the Head of a civilized nation: At the Waco, Texas massacre listed above, there are credible reports that indicate foreign troops and military advisors were present, including Russian, Israeli, and British foreign nationals. Open borders and reckless refugee policies that make us vulnerable to disease (Ebola, Human Enterovirus 68, Changas, MRSA etc.), violent criminals serial killers and sexual predators; sleeper agents and millions of immigrants from backgrounds that predispose them to vote for socialism and autocratic rule; Operation Fast and Furious (The Obama Justice Department covertly and illegally trafficked rifles and other handguns to the Mexican drug cartels in the hopes that the U.S.- originated guns would turn up at crime scenes and therefore could be tied to crimes in Mexico and the U.S., giving the Obama Administration the crisis it would need to pass more gun control laws and ultimately to try to ban firearms ownership in the U.S.). This anti-Second Amendment operation resulted in the murder of Border Patrol agent Brian Terry who was shot and killed by one of Attorney General Eric Holder's trafficked guns.

He has excited domestic insurrections amongst us, and has endeavored to bring on the inhabitants of our frontiers, the merciless Indian Savages, whose known rule of warfare, is an undistinguished destruction of all ages, sexes and conditions: Stoking the fires of racial tension and class envy and ignoring murders, rapes, kidnappings and beheadings (at least a dozen since 2004) on our soil by invading Mexican drug cartels.

In every stage of these Oppressions, we have petitioned for redress in the most humble terms: Our repeated petitions have been answered only by repeated injury: The total absence of accountability for scandal after scandal and high crimes involving a whole range of thuggish, Soviet-style three-letter federal government agencies. The mocking, dismissive and insulting posture taken toward the TEA Party, suggesting they are a racist, domestic terrorist group; weaponized IRS auditing and punishing Obama's political and ideological rivals. In a case reminiscent of something out of North Korea, in an audit of a private Christian church, the IRS demanded the names of every member of the church and actually wanted to know the specific content of their prayers!! The ATF has been aggressively targeting, prosecuting and imprisoning honorably discharged veterans for extremely trivial federal gun regulation violations; Obama's politically weaponized, predatory and racist "Department of Justice" (DOJ) has literally taken over 30 local police departments and sheriff's offices nationwide and strong-armed Arizona Sheriff Joe Arpaio with the threat of a take-over ("consent decree"); the authoritarian EPA that destroyed the savings of a North Idaho couple through endless legal sanctions and court actions, fined them $40 million dollars and turned their lives into a living hell over a land dispute involving an EPA-declared "wet land" on less than one acre of purchased property; and President Bush calling the Minuteman Project "vigilantes." These were Law-abiding citizens acting as an effective force multiplier for ICE using lawn chairs, binoculars, radios and yes, a few open-carry handguns.

"A Prince whose character is thus marked by every act which may define a Tyrant, is unfit to be the ruler of a free people..." – Thomas Jefferson.

After the American War for Independence the anti-federalists were passionately critical of the brevity of the Constitution, specifically the absence of a Bill of Rights "...enumerating those essential rights of mankind without which liberty cannot exist" (Richard Henry Lee).

James Madison wrote that the Bill of Rights was, "...what the people are entitled to against every government on earth." These rights are being abolished by government intimidation — the First Amendment in particular.

RED BADGE

We cannot tolerate a government that acts outside of its authority at the expense of these God-given rights.

While I readily admit, the Left has won I know that theirs is an ideology that will fail. I also know that Americans are not quitters and that it takes only a determined minority to be victorious. We still have enough freedom to push back and represent the idea that is America as an alternative, but it must be done now. We have more freedom than time left. It is possible to slow our fall and to preserve and defend pockets of America.

Congress is a sham. They would not honor their oath and remove Obama from office. But they work feverishly to find traction for cause to impeach Trump including fabricating the Russian collusion story and lying to the FISA court. We must find and elect bold, vocal, educated and articulate leaders with a healthy suspicion of government to local, state and national office. It is not enough to elect them. We must back these leaders who reject the Big Lie with all our might. We need restorative social engineering that turns momentum toward tradition by using the rudder of truth. Our mission is to peacefully restore our Republic by nullifying the illegitimate Amerika that has been stealthily and incrementally superimposed on the Constitution. But we are running out of time fast.

Many Americans pray for a miracle. Why would God save us? We've turned our back to Israel, ignored the abortion mill known as Planned Parenthood and have mainstreamed mentally ill, sexual deviants. Is this a nation worthy of His blessing?

Prior to Trump's election a military coup (d'état) was needed to save our republic, but I believe Obama's selective purge of military commanders was a calculated measure to neutralize that possibility. Our uniformed armed forces did not honor their oath to defend the Constitution. The People suffered the edicts of dictator Obama insulated by a government-media complex while their military looked away. No general or admiral dared to comment on the obvious unconstitutional actions of the "transformational" figure who sat the Oval Office.

Trump's restorative polices have postponed or eliminated for the near future: revolution, insurgency or secession. No matter the possible outcomes of the path we are on, in the interim we must be firm and courageous in whom we are and promote truth, love and courage. We must work for a peaceful restoration now if violence is to be averted. Our time is short. Be fully engaged in the first and well prepared for the latter.

"In a time of universal deceit telling the truth is a revolutionary act."

"If liberty means anything at all, it means the right to tell people what they do not want to hear." **George Orwell**

We patriots must network and survive as a nation within a hostile country. We must preserve the language, history, heroes, faith, and values ("The American View") of the culture that made our nation.

Stop waiting for someone else to save us. It's you! You have a role. President Trump cannot restore the Republic alone. In this book I have written about nullification, and interposition. I have encouraged you to run for office or at least support with your time and money constitutional candidates for every level of elected office who will bring real opposition to this phony two-party system, where there is no accountability for scandal after scandal after scandal. I have encouraged you to educate and motivate your spheres of influence to push back against the Big Lie. And all the while I urge you to prepare for the last legal remedy to restore the Republic. This is a time for action. We are already behind. You must be bold. Absence of dissent is consent to be ruled. Our children and grandchildren will suffer the consequences of your timidity and inaction.

We must be fully engaged by using the freedom we still have, in particular our First Amendment. The momentum of the Big Lie must be stopped. From fast food worker to School Board member, City Councilmen, County Commissioners, Sheriff, State Attorney General and Governor — we all have our spheres of influence and we all must lead, prepare and educate within them. **It is not enough for me to write this book or for you to read it.**

If you are retired, you have a very valuable role to play. You have free time and a frame of reference for what has been lost. You cannot be fired for being bold! Start by educating and motivating the younger members of your family. Become an activist for truth and freedom. Respectfully, but tenaciously, challenge school districts and all levels of government when you see symptoms of the infection of social justice.

Study the compelling arguments of the American Lands Council on the transfer of public land to the states. Watch the videos by Utah's state representative, Ken Ivory on the Web. Donate and become an activist on this issue no matter if you are a resident of a western state or not. This issue can be a huge victory for restoring the balance of power.

Change your city government to make the Chief of Police an elected position like it is in Santa Clara, Ca. Doing this will provide more accountability and allow citizens to recruit and elect a Constitutional Chief who understands the oath of office and will not be a puppet of a politically correct mayor.

Visit on line The Institute on the Constitution. The Institute will help you start an "American Club" on your local High School campus. There is no work for you beyond finding a student to petition the school for the club. The Institute takes it from there, including a legal staff to fight if necessary — at no cost to you.

Please commit to making a monthly donation to the CSPOA. No matter how small, your faithful donation will go a long way toward educating and defending oath-minded, Constitutional Sheriffs and peace officers.

Author Hannah Arendt, in the book *Totalitarianism*, wrote, *"It is in the moment of defeat that the inherent weakness of totalitarian propaganda becomes visible. Without the force of the movement, its members cease at once to believe in the dogma for which yesterday they still were ready to sacrifice their lives. The moment the movement, that is, the fictitious world which sheltered them, is destroyed, the masses revert to their old status of isolated individuals who either happily accept a new function in a changed world or sink back into their old desperate superfluousness."*

I challenge you to ask yourself, "What role am I playing at this very moment to defend and preserve any part of America that is left?" "What did I do **today** to help restore America, to win a mind, to prepare for trouble ahead?" There is little time remaining. Two years, four years? The consequences you will suffer for doing nothing will be more painful than the consequences for taking action. We cannot restore the entire country, but we can hold and gain significant ground.

"If you will not fight for right when you can easily win without bloodshed; if you will not fight when your victory will be sure and not too costly; you may come to the moment when you will have to fight with all the odds against you and only a precarious chance of survival. There may even be a worse case. You may have to fight when there is no hope of victory, because it is better to perish than live as slaves." Winston Churchill

RED BADGE

In the face of sobering truth revealed in this book I turn to the American people. Rather than see heroes amassing on the horizon I stare into a vacuum and the last stanza of T.S. Elliot's poem, *The Hallow Men* resonates:

This is the way the world ends

This is the way the world ends

This is the way the world ends

Not with a bang but a whimper

Do not accept that ending America. Our founders pledged their wealth, their lives and their sacred honor for this country. Does that fire burn in you? **Prove it!**

Parting Thoughts

1988 was a fairly typical election year in the United States. The Cold War was raging as intensely as ever, and the rhetoric in the ideological war between the West and the East was red hot. Yet the turnover rate for the U.S. Congress was less than that of the Soviet Union's Politburo, the Communist Party's top-level governing and policy-making body made up exclusively of unelected bureaucrats.

There is something desperately wrong in America when this is the case. Since then it has only gotten worse.

No matter how many corruption scandals our Congressmen and women are involved in, no matter how blatantly they violate the Constitution, ignore the desires of their constituents, and run roughshod over the peoples' rights — the vast majority of Congressmen and women have amassed such wealth and power that they are virtually impossible to remove from office. Congress is no longer our servants — they are our OVERLORDS.

According to John Michael Greer, author of *Decline and Fall: The End of Empire and the Future of Democracy in 21st Century America*:

"The last three decades have seen America turn into something close to a Third World kleptocracy, the sort of failed state in which a handful of politically well-connected people plunder the economy for their own benefit. When bank executives vote themselves million dollar bonuses out of government bailout funds while their banks are losing billions of dollars a year, it is impossible to discuss the situation honestly without using words like 'looting.'

"It is not just special interests that take advantage of the situation; foreign countries do it as well:

"Other countries — China and Israel come to mind — have learned to make use of the diffusion of American power for their own interests. It doesn't matter how blatantly the Chinese manipulate their currency or thumb their noses at intellectual property rights... so long as they keep their lobby in Washington well-funded and well-staffed, they're secure from any meaningful response on the part of the U.S. government."

America has become an authoritarian plutocratic oligarchy.

Recall that many of the Founders, both Federalists and Anti-Federalists, cautioned us about the dangers of domestic tyranny emanating from our own government, and especially an "Imperial Congress," regal in their attitude toward the people they are supposed to serve.

Thomas Jefferson warned: "The two enemies of the people are criminals and government, so let us tie the second down with the chains of the Constitution so the second will not become the legalized version of the first."

And Martin Luther King Jr. famously pointed out, *"Never forget that everything Hitler did in Germany was LEGAL."*

Hitler was elected by popular vote in a legal election. He did not seize power in a coup or revolution. Hitler then used the administrative and legal powers of the already existing and legitimately established German government to inflict his tyranny on all under his jurisdiction. His actions were all "legal."

Fast-forward to 21st Century America.

The "Rule of Law" has been corrupted to the point that it is consistently applied arbitrarily and with a distinct racial bias, making a mockery of the whole concept.

Look at the blatantly biased manner in which Obama's minority-run Department of Justice (DOJ) under Attorneys

General Eric Holder and Loretta Lynch uses the law as a weapon to enforce their anti-White, Marxist racial agenda on the country.

This same DOJ has sued state governments (on behalf of the Mexican government and illegal aliens) for exercising their lawful, constitutional and legitimate right to police their borders and protect their citizens from crime and foreign invasion. This same DOJ has sued county sheriff's offices, county prosecuting attorney's offices, and usurped control over more municipal police departments than all other presidential administrations combined!

"The Rule of Law" in Obama's America was nothing but the naked exercise of raw power by the ruling class. It is codified revenge.

Observe and reflect on the way Obamacare was ram-rodded down the throats of the American people by a U.S. Congress that has become little more than an American Politburo: an unaccountable group of unfathomably corrupt millionaire lawyers, regal and elitist in their outlook, and communist and tyrannical in their modes operandi.

Obamacare is only one, albeit a major one, in a long list of major pieces of legislation that have been IMPOSED on the American people without our consent and against our will.

Recall the conduct of our "representatives" in Congress on the eve of the Obamacare vote: Their arrogant display of raw power, their swaggering manner as they locked arms and elbowed their way through the crowd of peaceful TEA Party protesters, falsely accusing them of hurling racist epithets as they yelled "Kill the Bill."

And yet, in spite of the wishes and demands of the literally millions of irate citizens who peacefully marched in Washington D.C. and peacefully protested right outside the halls of the U.S.

Congress so their collective voices could be heard directly, face to face with their "representatives", Congress passed the Obamacare bill, which was promptly signed by the Traitor-in-Chief Barack Hussein Obama.

This is neither "representative government" nor governing "with the consent of the governed."

Obamacare (socialist, government-controlled healthcare) usurped control over at least one-sixth of the U.S. economy. It was passed by the most partisan vote in U.S. history: not a single member of the Republican Party voted for the bill!

Unconstitutional Obamacare will probably go down as the single largest power grab by the U.S. Congress and the president in American history. And it will also carry the dubious distinction of being the most deceitfully packaged and "sold" bill ever.

Remember Obama's false promises and outright lies: "If you like your health care plan, you can keep it." And, "If you like your doctor, you can keep your doctor, period."

Great American author Mark Twain said, "It is easier to fool people than to convince them they have been fooled."

One of the bedrock principles our Founders espoused, and one which is uniquely American, is the premise that government is only legitimate when it governs with the consent of the governed. In other words, if the people do not give their consent to a law or a governing method or style, that law or that government action is null and void.

Thomas Jefferson said, "If a law is unjust, a man is not only right to disobey it, he is obligated to do so."

And our Declaration of Independence instructs us that it is The Peoples' right (DUTY, actually) to remove or abolish any government that violates this sacred trust.

Obamacare and the vast majority of laws passed by Congress are implemented against the wishes and desires of the majority of Americans; they are inflicted upon us without our consent.

When "We the People" keep telling our government "NO!" but they continue to force themselves and their tyrannical laws upon us, this is neither representation nor legitimate rule – it is rape!

America has become a very comfortable and well-disguised tyranny.

What is one to do?

Judge Andrew Napolitano reminds us that "The Second Amendment is not the right to shoot at deer. It's the right to shoot at the government if it is taken over by tyrants, and to shoot at them effectively, with the same instruments they would use upon us."

Pray it does not come to that and prepare. Exhaust every peaceful solution, and know it is our right and duty to overthrow the tyrants and restore the Constitution.

Graduating from the San Diego Sheriff's Academy

RED BADGE

Gang Patrol near the Mexico Border 1994

RED BADGE

Deputy Sheriff Traubel, Pre-shift Shotgun Check

RED BADGE

Detective Traubel at Murder Scene

RED BADGE

South Bay
Wednesday, April 6, 1994

Officer Doug Traubel helps Xochitl Dozal, 9, ride a special hand-operated bike the Chula Vista Police Officer's Association presented to her. She has spinal bifida and is unable use her legs.

We are still friends today

RED BADGE

RED BADGE

***Medal of "Valor"**

*(Honestly, it looks nice on the wall, but in my view should have an asterisk on it. I was overpraised and deserving of the lesser medal: The Chief's Star)

RED BADGE

SWAT Training on the 300-yard Range at USMC Base; Camp Pendleton, CA.

RED BADGE
Thoughts and Questions about Multiculturalism, Diversity and Tolerance by the author's dear friend John Hartmann

Just how does one "celebrate" multiculturalism?

When I see my Syrian neighbor, should I give him a high-five and do an end-zone, touchdown dance?

How does one "embrace" diversity?

When I see the Ethiopian man on my block who is a registered sex offender, should I hug him? May I send him to your family so your children or grandchildren can hug him?

If the language which represents a concept is imprecise, naive, and childish, what might that say about the concept itself?

According to the Merriam-Webster's dictionary, to "tolerate" can be defined as "to endure" or "to suffer."

To tolerate something isn't the same as to approve of it.

If I tolerate my sex offender neighbor, must I also approve of his past, and possibly future, actions?

If I agree to tolerate your beliefs and actions, will you agree to tolerate mine? Are you sure? Are you really sure? Are you really, really sure?

If you won't agree to tolerate my beliefs and actions, why should I tolerate yours?

Furthermore, what makes you think you have any right to DEMAND I tolerate your beliefs and actions when you won't tolerate mine?

Where do you derive the moral authority to impose your beliefs on me, especially against my will, when you are intolerant of my beliefs?

What right do you have to deny me my rights?

Race isn't culture, and questioning multiculturalism isn't racism.

Multiculturalism is contrary to assimilation. If those who come to this country are encouraged to retain their original cultures, why should those whose forebears have assimilated not be encouraged to dissimilate?

Under current Irish law, I can claim Irish citizenship through my paternal grandparents. If I were to do so as an act of dissimilation, which citizenship should deserve my greater loyalty? Why should it matter?

If I reclaim my Irish heritage, should I adopt the Irish culture of today, of my grandparent's time, or of an earlier era?

If my Bronze Age Celtic forebears decorated their dwellings with the heads of their enemies, why shouldn't I?

Decapitation is, after all, making a comeback – and it gets a lot more respect than turning the other cheek.

Might there be a point at which a nation based on multiculturalism could cease to have a culture or to be a nation, and become instead only a populated area?

Would Nathan Hale have said, "I regret that I have but one life to give for the multicultural, populated area in which I live?"

Must an inclusive, open society welcome those who wish to remake it into an exclusive, closed society after their own cultural image?

Must a democratic society based on the sovereign rights of the individual and self-expression welcome those who wish to change that same society into an authoritarian one based on "group rights" and forced conformity?

What would be the proper way to "embrace" those whose culture calls upon them to kill me because of my culture?

If they succeed in killing me, should I celebrate my own murder as a multicultural experience?

Why is it that so many who promote multiculturalism, diversity, and tolerance strike me as being so INTOLERANT of those who think differently than they do?

Why are they totalitarian and even "Orwellian" in their methods?

Am I alone in having these impressions?

In 1534, the Catholics and Lutherans of the north German city of Munster opened their gates to radical Anabaptists who were being persecuted elsewhere.

When the Anabaptists grew strong enough in numbers, they took political control of the city and persecuted those same people who had given them shelter and refuge, and showed them tolerance. Some, they even executed.

The study of history is a marvelous corrective to naiveté.

Required Reading for Patriots:

Suicide of a Superpower by Pat Buchanan

The Unspoken Truth: Race, Culture and Other Taboos

by Frank Borzellieri

Don't Take It Personally by Frank Borzellieri

A Race Against Time: Racial Heresies for the 21st Century

by George McDaniel & Jared Taylor

The Freedom Answer Book by Judge Andrew Napolitano

RED BADGE

Hamilton's Curse by Thomas DiLorenzo

White Girl Bleed A Lot: The Return of Racial Violence to America and How the Media Ignore It by Colin Flaherty

Don't Make the Black Kids Angry: The Hoax of Black Victimization and Those Who Enable It by Colin Flaherty

Into the Cannibal's Pot: Lessons for America from Post-Apartheid South Africa by Ilana Mercer

Adios, America! by Ann Coulter

Suicide Pact by Judge Andrew Napolitano

The Founder's Second Amendment by Stephen Halbrook

That Every Man Be Armed by Stephen Halbrook

Death by Gun Control: The Human Cost of Victim Disarmament by Aaron Zelman

Lies the Government Told You by Judge Andrew Napolitano

It's Dangerous to be Right When the Government is Wrong by Judge Andrew Napolitano

The Constitution in Exile by Judge Andrew Napolitano

Death by Government by R.J. Rummel

The Red-Green Axis: Refugees, Immigration and the Agenda to Erase America by James Simpson

Paved With Good Intentions by Jared Taylor

March of the Titans by Arthur Kemp

HIGHLY Recommended Reading:

Blacklisted By History, The Untold Stroy of Senator Joe McCarthy

by M. Stanton Evans

RED BADGE

Dismantling America by Thomas Sowell

Nullification by Thomas Woods

Liberty versus the Tyranny of Socialism

by Dr. Walter E. Williams

Organized Crime: The Unvarnished Truth About Government

by Thomas DiLorenzo

The Five Thousand Year Leap by W. Cleon Skousen

Lincoln Unmasked and **The Real Lincoln**

by Thomas DiLorenzo

Red Republicans and Lincoln's Marxists

by Walter Kennedy and Al Benson

The Dispossessed Majority by Wilmot Robertson

Negrophilia by Erik Rush

The Tempting of America by Robert Bork

The Global War on Your Guns by Wayne LA Pierre

The Origin of the Second Amendment by David Young

The Affirmative Action Hoax by Steven Farron

A Cure Worse Than The Disease by M. Lester O'Shea

The Conscience of a Conservative by Barry Goldwater

Stalin's War of Extermination

by Joachim Hoffmann

The Chief Culprit: Stalin's Grand Design to Start WWII

Viktor Suvorov

Stalin's Other War: Soviet Grand Strategy, 1939-1941

Albert Weeks

RED BADGE

The KGB: Masters of the Soviet Union

by Peter Deriabin

Red Star Rogue by Kenneth Sewell

School of Darkness by Bella Dodd

Blacklisted by History by M. Stanton Evans

On A Field of Red by Anthony Cave Brown

Masters of Deceit by J. Edgar Hoover

Venona: Decoding Soviet Espionage in America by John Haynes

The Venona Secrets: The Definitive Expose' of Soviet Espionage in America by Herbert Romerstein

The Secret World of American Communism

by Harvey Klehr and John Earl Haynes

The Black Book of Communism

by Courtois, Werth, Panne, Paczkowski, Bartosek, and Margolin

"Stasi: The Untold Story of the East German Secret Police"

by John Koehler

Are Cops Racist? by Heather MacDonald

Thy Will Be Done by Gerard Colby

The Politics of Bad Faith; Hating Whitey; Radical Son

by David Horowitz

Please Stop Helping Us by Jason L. Riley

Carnage and Culture by Victor Davis Hanson

Atlas Shrugged by Ayn Rand

RED BADGE
"Law, Legislation and Liberty: The Mirage of Social Justice"

by Friedrich A. Hayek

*I highly encourage the reader to check out the articles and books written by Pat Buchanan, Judge Andrew Napolitano, Jared Taylor, Thomas DiLorenzo, Frank Borzellieri, Ilana Mercer, Samuel Francis, Colin Flaherty, Walter Williams, Ann Coulter, Thomas Sowell, Heather MacDonald, Thomas Woods, Friedrich A. Hayek, Arthur Kemp, Larry Elder, and Erik Rush.

Quotes to Ponder

"Facts no longer play a role in American political life...A matrix has been created, an artificial reality that channels the energies and resources of the country into secret agendas that serve the interests of the ruling private interest groups. The United States Government and the American people cannot contend with reality, because they do not know what the reality is...In effect, America is both blind and deaf. It lives in delusions. Consequently, it will destroy itself and perhaps the world."   Paul Craig Roberts, February 1, 2015

"I think the subject which will be of most importance politically is Mass Psychology...its importance has been enormously increased by the growth of modern methods of propaganda...Although this science will be diligently studied, it will be rigidly confined to the governing class. The populace will not be allowed to know how its convictions were generated."   Bertrand Russell

"We'll know our disinformation program is complete when everything the American public believes is false."

CIA Director William Casey, 1981

RED BADGE

"Treason doth never prosper, what's the reason? For if it prosper, none dare call it treason."

Sir John Harrington, 1561-1612

"History is created, manipulated and written by those who are predominantly on the victorious side of the nation which has supreme political, and especially military dominance. Any 'truth' which has the slightest potential of weakening their total hold over the masses is not tolerated. Any truth which can impact their power is squelched or cunningly hidden by them, usually in a manufactured media release to the unsuspecting public, often in a jovial manner to render the information a laughing matter and display it as harmless." Clark C. McClelland, Retired NASA astronaut

"The individual is handicapped by coming face to face with a conspiracy so monstrous he cannot believe it exists. The American mind simply has not come to a realization of the evil which has been introduced into our midst."

J. Edgar Hoover, Elks magazine, 1956

FBI Director: 1935-1972
DOJ-BOI Director, 1924-1935

"We are in the midst of a phase of history in which nations will be redefined and their futures fundamentally altered."

Media Mogul Rupert Murdoch Feb 24, 2009

"Countless people will hate the new world order and will die protesting against it." H.G. Wells

"We are on the verge of a global transformation. All we need is the right major crisis and the nations will accept the New World Order." David Rockefeller September 23, 1994

"The greatest evil...is conceived and ordered...in clean, carpeted, warmed and well-lighted offices, by quiet men with white collars and cut fingernails and smooth-shaven cheeks who do not need to raise their voice." C.S. Lewis

"The issue today is the same as it has been throughout all history, whether man shall be allowed to govern himself or be ruled by a small elite."   Thomas Jefferson

"Whenever the legislators endeavor to take away and destroy the property of the people, or to reduce them to slavery under arbitrary power, they put themselves into a state of war with the people, who are thereupon absolved from any further obedience and are left to the common refuge, which God hath provided for all men, against force and violence."

John Locke, 2nd Treatise of Government

"This new and complete Revolution we contemplate can be defined in a very few words. It is outright world-socialism; scientifically planned and directed...Countless people will hate the new world order and will die protesting against it. When we attempt to evaluate its promise, we have to bear in mind the distress of a generation or so of malcontents...The term 'Internationalism' has been popularized in recent years to cover an interlocking financial, political, and economic world force for the purpose of establishing a World Government."

Fabian Society member H.G. Wells, in his 1939 non-fiction book titled, The New World Order.

Norman Mattoon Thomas (1884 - 1968) was a leading American socialist, pacifist, and six-time presidential candidate for the Socialist Party of America. In a 1944 speech Thomas said:

"The American people will never knowingly adopt socialism. But, under the name of 'liberalism' they will adopt every fragment of the socialist program, until one day America will be a socialist nation, without knowing how it happened."

Norman Thomas went on to say: "I no longer need to run as a presidential candidate for the Socialist Party. The Democratic Party has adopted our platform."

"One of the most powerful propaganda slogans propounded by Leninism and perfected by the French Communist Party was: 'There are no enemies on the Left'."

Arnold Beichman, Hoover Institute

"One of the least understood strategies of the world revolution now moving rapidly toward its goal is the use of mind control as a major means of obtaining the consent of the people who will be subjects of the New World Order."

K.M. Heaton, The National Educator

"No one will enter the New World Order unless he or she will make a pledge to worship Lucifer. No one will enter the New Age unless he will take a Luciferian Initiation."

David Spangler Director of Planetary Initiative
(a United Nations affiliated organization)

"It will of course, be understood that directly or indirectly, soon or late, every advance in the sciences of human nature will contribute to our success in controlling human nature and changing it to the advantage of the common wheel."

Edward Thorndike, Key Psychology Theorist, member of the "Eugenics Committee of the USA"

"The reduction of intelligence is an important factor in the curative process... The fact is that some of the very best cures that one gets are in those individuals whom one reduces almost to amentia (feeble-mindedness)..."

Dr. Abraham Myerson, Harvard Psychiatrist, 1942

"Those of us who work in this field see a developing potential for nearly a total control of human emotional status, mental functioning, and will to act. These human phenomena can be started, stopped or eliminated by the use of various types of chemical substances. What we can produce with our science now will affect the entire society. A 'utopia' could be found – providing a sense of stability and certainty, whether realistic or not."

Nathan Kline, psychiatrist, 1967

"We need a program of psychosurgery for political control of our society. The purpose is physical control of the mind. Everyone who deviates from the given norm can be surgically mutilated. The individual may think that the most important reality is his own existence, but this is only his personal point of view... Man does not have the right to develop his own mind... We must electronically control the brain. Someday armies and generals will be controlled by electronic stimulation of the brain."

Dr. Jose M.R. Delgado, Director of Neuropsychiatry at Yale University Medical School, Congressional Record, No. 26, Vol. 118, Feb. 24, 1974. Dr. Delgado was a major participant in the CIA's "MK-Ultra" mind-control program during the Cold War.

"Principles of mental health cannot be successfully furthered in any society unless there is progressive acceptance of the concept of world citizenship. World citizenship can be widely extended among all peoples through applications of the principles of mental health."

> National Association for Mental Health, 1948

"To achieve world government, it is necessary to remove from the minds of men their individualism, loyalty to family traditions, national patriotism and religious dogmas..."

Dr. G. Brock Chisholm, psychiatrist and co-founder of the World Federation of Mental Health

"By simplifying the thoughts of the masses and reducing them to primitive patterns, propaganda was able to present the complex process of political and economic life in the simplest terms. We have taken matters previously available only to experts and a small number of specialists and have carried them into the street and hammered them into the brain of the little man."

> Joseph Goebbels, 1935

"Of all tyrannies a tyranny sincerely exercised for the good of its victims may be the most oppressive. It may be better to live under robber barons than under omnipotent moral busybodies. The robber baron's cruelty may sometimes sleep, his cupidity may at some point be satiated, but those who torment us for our own good will torment us without end for they do so with the approval of their own consciences. This very kindness stings with intolerable insult. To be 'cured' against one's will and cured of states which we may not regard as disease is to be put on a level of those who have not yet reached the age of reason or those who never will – to be classed with infants, imbeciles, and domestic animals."   C.S Lewis

"The frightening thing, he recounted for the ten thousandth time...was that it might all be true. If the Party could thrust its hand into the past and say of this or that event, 'it never happened' – that surely was more terrifying than mere torture and death. And if all others accepted the lie which the Party imposed – if all records told the same tale – then the lie passed into history and became truth. 'Who controls the past' ran the Party slogan, 'controls the future: who controls the present controls the past.' Day by day and almost minute by minute the past was brought up to date. In this way every prediction made by the Party could be shown by documentary evidence to have been correct; nor was any item of news, or any expression of opinion, which conflicted with the needs of the moment, ever allowed to remain on record. All history was a palimpsest, scraped clean and re-inscribed exactly as often as was necessary."

George Orwell, 1984

"Through clever and constant application of propaganda, people can be made to see paradise as hell and also the other way around, to consider the most wretched sort of life as paradise."

Adolf Hitler Mein Kampf, 1923

"Every child in America who enters school at the age of five is mentally ill, because he comes to school with an allegiance to our institutions, toward the preservation of this form of government that we have. Patriotism, nationalism, and sovereignty, all that proves that children are sick because a truly well individual is one who has rejected all of those things, and is truly the international child of the future."

Dr. Chester Pierce, Harvard psychiatrist

In a variation of the above quote, during a 1973 International Education Seminar Dr. Chester Pierce, speaking as an expert in public education, said:

"Every child in America entering school at the age of five is mentally ill because he comes to school with certain allegiances to our founding fathers, toward our elected officials, toward his parents, toward a belief in a supernatural being, and toward the sovereignty of this nation as a separate entity. It's up to you as teachers to make all these sick children well by creating the international child of the future."

"Education should aim at destroying free will so that after pupils are thus schooled they will be incapable throughout the rest of their lives of thinking or acting otherwise than as their school masters would have wished ... The social psychologist of the future will have a number of classes of school children on whom they will try different methods of producing an unshakable conviction that snow is black. Various results will soon be arrived at: first, that influences of the home are 'obstructive' and verses set to music and repeatedly intoned are very effective ... It is for the future scientist to make these maxims precise and discover exactly how much it costs per head to make children believe that snow is black.

"When the technique has been perfected, every government that has been in charge of education for more than one generation will be able to control its subjects securely without the need of armies or policemen." Bertrand Russell quoting Johann Gottlieb Fichte, the head of philosophy & psychology who influenced Hegel and others – Prussian University in Berlin, 1810.

"...through schools of the world we shall disseminate a new conception of government – one that will embrace all of the collective activities of men; one that will postulate the need for scientific control and operation of economic activities in the interests of all people."

Harold Rugg, student of psychology and a disciple of John Dewey

"There's no way to rule innocent men. The only power any government has is the power to crack down on criminals. Well, when there aren't enough criminals, one makes them. One declares so many things to be a crime that it becomes impossible for men to live without breaking laws."

Ayn Rand, "Atlas Shrugged"

"Education does not mean teaching people to know what they do not know – it means teaching them to behave as they do not behave."

National Institute of Mental Health (NIMH) sponsored report: The Role of Schools in Mental Health

The school curriculum should "...be designed to bend the student to the realities of society, especially by way of vocational education... the curriculum should be designed to promote mental health as an instrument for social progress and a means of altering culture..."

Report: Action for Mental Health, 1961

"This is the idea where we drop subject matter and we drop Carnegie Unites (grading from A-F) and we just let students find their way, keeping them in school until they manifest the politically correct attitudes. You see, one of the effects of self-esteem (Values Clarification) programs is that you are no longer obliged to tell the truth if you don't feel like it. You don't have to tell the truth because if the truth you have to tell is about your own failure then your self-esteem will go down and that is unthinkable."

Dr. William Coulson, explaining Outcome Based Education (OBE)

"Men are built, not born.... Give me the baby, and I'll make it climb and use its hands in constructing buildings of stone or wood.... I'll make it a thief, a gunman or a dope fiend. The possibilities of shaping in any direction are almost endless..." John B. Watson, psychologist, founder of "Behaviorism"

"...a student attains 'higher order thinking' when he no longer believes in right or wrong." "A large part of what we call good teaching is a teacher's ability to obtain affective objectives by challenging the student's fixed beliefs. ...a large part of what we call teaching is that the teacher should be able to use education to reorganize a child's thoughts, attitudes, and feelings."

Benjamin Bloom, psychologist and educational theorist, in "Major Categories in the Taxonomy of Educational Objectives", p. 185, 1956

"The educational system should be a sieve, through which all the children of a country are passed. It is highly desirable that no child escape inspection." Paul Popenoe, Behavioral Eugenist and co-author: "Sterilization for Human Betterment"

"We do not need any more preaching about right and wrong. The old 'thou shalt nots' simply are not relevant. Values clarification is a method for teachers to change the values of children without getting caught."

Dr. Sidney Simon, educator & lecturer

"Of course, Behaviorism 'works.' So does torture. Give me a no-nonsense, down-to-earth behaviorist, a few drugs, and simple electrical appliances, and in six months I will have him reciting the Athanasian Creed in public."

W. H. Auden

Among the Founding Fathers, Thomas Jefferson was the outspoken leader warning against the unchecked powers of judges. Jefferson felt strongly that the checks against the power and authority of the judicial branch in the U.S. Constitution were weak and would ultimately prove to be ineffective. He further warned that the vaguely and insufficiently articulated powers of the judiciary and the checks against it by the other branches of government and the citizenry were a recipe for "judicial tyranny." The truth and accuracy of any prophecy is in its manifestations.

"To consider the judges as the ultimate arbiters of all constitutional questions is a very dangerous doctrine indeed, and one which would place us under the despotism of an oligarchy. Our judges are as honest as other men and not more so. They have, with others, the same passions for party, for power, and the privilege of their corps…And their power the more dangerous as they are in office for life and not responsible, as the other functionaries are, to the elective control. The Constitution has erected no such single tribunal, knowing that to whatever hands confided, with the corruptions of time and party, its members would become despots. It has more wisely made all the departments co-equal and co-sovereign within themselves."

Thomas Jefferson, Monticello, September 28, 1820

"The Federal Judiciary - an irresponsible body (for impeachment is scarcely a scarecrow), working like gravity

by night and by day, gaining a little today and a little tomorrow, and advancing its noiseless step like a thief in the night over the field of jurisdiction, until all shall be usurped from the States, and the government of all be consolidated into one. When all government, in little as in great things, shall be drawn to Washington as the center of all power, it will render powerless the checks provided of one government on another and will become as venal and oppressive as the government from which we separated."

"The Judiciary of the United States is the subtle corps of sappers and miners constantly working under ground to undermine the foundations of our confederated fabric."

"The opinion which gives to the judges the right to decide what laws are constitutional and what not, not only for themselves in their own sphere of action, but for the legislative and executive also in their spheres, would make the judiciary a despotic branch."

"Judges should be withdrawn from the bench whose erroneous biases are leading us to dissolution. It may, indeed, injure them in fame or fortune; but it saves the Republic."

"The Constitution is a mere thing of wax in the hands of the judiciary, which they may twist and shape into any form they please."

*All of the preceding quotes on the judiciary and the judicial branch are the words of Thomas Jefferson circa 1820.

"The law itself is on trial quite as much as the cause which is to be decided."

Harlan F. Stone 12th Chief Justice U.S. Supreme Court 1941

In 1771 John Adams said of the juror, "It is not his right, but his duty to find the verdict according to his own best understanding, judgment, and conscience, though in direct opposition to the direction of the court."

"I think we have more machinery of government than is necessary, too many parasites living on the labor of the industrious."

Thomas Jefferson, letter to William Ludlow, 1824

"The essence of freedom is the proper limitation of government."   George Washington

"Any government big enough to give you everything you want is powerful enough to take everything you have."

Thomas Jefferson

"Never forget that everything Hitler did in Germany was LEGAL."

Martin Luther King, Jr.

"Freedom is never more than one generation away from extinction. We didn't pass it to our children in the bloodstream. It must be fought for, protected, and handed on for them to do the same or one day we will spend our sunset years telling our children and our grandchildren what it was once like in the United States where men were free."

Ronald Reagan

"If we lose freedom here, there is no place to escape to. This is the last stand on Earth."   Ronald Reagan

"The nine most terrifying words in the English language are: 'I'm from the government and I'm here to help'."
Ronald Reagan

"Government is not reason, it is not eloquence – it is FORCE! Like fire, it is a dangerous servant and a fearful master."   George Washington

Great Quotes on Democracy, Civilization and Society:

"Democracy is the road to socialism."

Karl Marx

"Politicians are the lowest form of life on earth. Liberal Democrats are the lowest form of politicians."

General George S. Patton

"Democracies have ever been spectacles of turbulence and contention, have ever been found incompatible with personal security or the rights of property, and have in general been as short in their lives as they have been violent in their deaths."

James Madison, "Father of the U.S. Constitution"

"Democracy never lasts long. It soon wastes, exhausts, and murders itself."   Samuel Adams

"There was never a democracy that did not commit suicide."   John Adams

"Real liberty is never found in despotism or in the extremes of democracy."   Alexander Hamilton
(Signer of the U.S. Constitution & co-author of the Federalist Papers)

"Democracy means simply the bludgeoning of the people by the people for the people."   Oscar Wilde

"Damn democracy. It is a fraudulent term used, often by ignorant persons but no less often by intellectual fakers, to describe an infamous mixture of socialism, graft, confiscation of property and denial of personal rights to individuals whose virtuous principles make them offensive."

Westbrook Pegler

"A democracy is nothing more than mob rule, where fifty-one percent of the people may take away the rights of the other forty-nine."   Thomas Jefferson

"If Congress can determine what constitutes the general welfare and can appropriate money for its advancement, where is the limitation to carrying into execution whatever can be effected by money?"

South Carolina Senator William Draden, 1828

"The State is the great fiction by which everyone seeks to live at the expense of everyone else."

Frederic Bastiat

"A democracy cannot exist as a permanent form of government. It can only exist until the voters discover that they can vote themselves largesse from the public treasury. From that moment on, the majority always votes for the candidates promising the most benefits from the public treasury, with the result that a democracy always collapses over loose fiscal policy, always followed by a dictatorship."

Alexis de Tocqueville

RED BADGE

"When men get in the habit of helping themselves to the property of others, they cannot easily be cured of it."

The New York Times, in a 1909 editorial opposing the very first income tax.

"The average age of the world's greatest civilizations from the beginning of history has been about 200 years. During those 200 years, these nations always progressed through the following sequence: From bondage to spiritual faith; From spiritual faith to great courage; from courage to liberty; From liberty to abundance; From abundance to selfishness; From selfishness to complacency; From complacency to apathy; From apathy to dependence; From dependence back into bondage."

Alexander Fraser Tytler, The Fatal Sequence

"No society that has been reorganized and restructured to provide such a perverse system of incentives deserves to survive, indeed, no such civilized society ever has survived. The collapse of American empire is precisely what will bring about the end of the current system in which the unproductive prosper on the efforts of the productive, and it is certain because it is mathematically unsustainable."

Vox Day

"Pure democracy is a chimera – all government is essentially of the nature of a monarchy. The people flatter themselves that they have the sovereign power. These are, in fact, words without meaning. It is true they elected governors – but how are these elections brought about? In every instance of election by the mass of a people – through the influence of those governors themselves, and by means the most opposite to a free and disinterested choice, by the basest corruption and bribery. But those governors once selected, where is the boasted freedom of the people?

They must submit to their rule and control, with the same abandonment of their natural liberty, the freedom of their will, and the command of their actions, as if they were under the rule of a monarch."

Alexander Fraser Tytler

"If the Tenth Amendment were still taken seriously most of the federal government's present activities would not exist. That's why no one in Washington ever mentions it."

Thomas Woods

"No modern president has picked and chosen which laws to enforce and which to ignore and which to rewrite to the extremes of President Obama. His radical rejection of the 'Rule of Law'...presents a clear and present danger to the freedom of us all."

Judge Andrew Napolitano

"It does not take a majority to prevail...but rather an irate, tireless minority, keen on setting brushfires of freedom in the minds of men."

Samuel Adams (Signer of the Declaration of Independence)

"Timid men prefer the calm of despotism to the tempestuous sea of liberty."
Thomas Jefferson

"If you will not fight for right when you can easily win without bloodshed; if you will not fight when your victory will be sure and not too costly; you may come to the moment when you will have to fight with all the odds against you and only a precarious chance of survival. There may even be a worse case. You may have to fight when there is no hope of victory, because it is better to perish than live as slaves."

Winston Churchill

"The hour is fast approaching, on which the Honor and Success of this army and the safety of our bleeding Country depend. Remember, officers and soldiers, that you are Free Men, fighting for the blessings of Liberty – that slavery will be your portion, and that of your posterity, if you do not acquit yourselves like Men."

George Washington, General Orders, August 23, 1776

"The time is now near at hand which must probably determine whether Americans are to be Freemen or Slaves; whether they are to have any property they can call their own; whether their houses and farms are to be pillaged and destroyed, and they consigned to a state of wretchedness from which no human efforts will probably deliver them. The fate of unborn millions will now depend, under God, on the courage and conduct of this army. Our cruel and unrelenting enemy leaves us only the choice of brave resistance, or the most abject submission. We have, therefore, to resolve to conquer or die."

General George Washington, Speaking to his troops before the Battle of Long Island, New York, August 27, 1776

"The strongest reason for the people to retain their right to keep and bear arms is, as a last resort, to protect themselves against tyranny in government."

Thomas Jefferson

"A free people ought not only be armed and disciplined, but they should have sufficient arms and ammunition to maintain a status of independence from any who might attempt to abuse them, which would include their own government."

"Firearms stand next in importance to the Constitution itself. They are the American peoples' liberty teeth and keystone under independence...When firearms go, all goes. We need them every hour."

George Washington

"To preserve liberty, it is essential that the whole body of the people always possess arms and be taught alike, especially when young, how to use them."

Colonel Richard Henry Lee, militia commander during the War of Independence

"To disarm the people is the best and most effectual way to enslave them."

George Mason, author of the 2nd Amendment

"When government takes away citizens' right to bear arms it becomes citizens' duty to take away government's right to govern."   George Washington

"Today, we need a nation of Minutemen, citizens who are not only prepared to take arms, but citizens who regard the preservation of freedom as the basic purpose of their daily life and who are willing to consciously work and sacrifice for that freedom."

John F. Kennedy (over 50 years ago)

"The duty of a true Patriot is to protect his country from its government."

Thomas Paine

RED BADGE

"In the long history of the world, very few generations have been granted the role of defending freedom in its maximum hour of danger. This is that moment and you are that generation! Now is the time to defend our freedoms."

Judge Andrew Napolitano

"Nothing can now be believed which is seen in a newspaper. Truth itself becomes suspicious by being put into that polluted vehicle. The real extent of this state of misinformation is known only to those who are in situations to confront facts within their knowledge with the lies of the day."

Thomas Jefferson, 1807

"If voting made any difference they wouldn't let us do it."

Mark Twain

"It is no measure of health to be well-adjusted to a profoundly sick society."

Jiddu Krishnamurti

RED BADGE

Made in United States
Troutdale, OR
11/08/2024

24523009R00271